Hero of the Angry Sky

WAR AND SOCIETY IN NORTH AMERICA

Hero of the Angry Sky: The World War I Diary and Letters of David S. Ingalls, America's First Naval Ace, edited by Geoffrey L. Rossano

HERO OF THE ANGRY SKY

The World War I Diary and Letters of David S. Ingalls,
America's First Naval Ace

Edited by Geoffrey L. Rossano

Foreword by William F. Trimble

OHIO UNIVERSITY PRESS — ATHENS

Ohio University Press, Athens, Ohio 45701
ohioswallow.com
© 2013 by Ohio University Press

Printed in the United States of America
Ohio University Press books are printed on acid-free paper ⊗ ™

23 22 21 20 19 18 17 16 15 14 13   5 4 3 2 1

Library of Congress Cataloging-in-Publication Data

Ingalls, David Sinton, 1899–1985.

Hero of the angry sky : the World War I diary and letters of David S. Ingalls,
America's first naval ace / edited by Geoffrey L. Rossano ; foreword by William
F. Trimble.

p. cm.

Includes bibliographical references and index.

ISBN 978-0-8214-2018-8 (hbk. : alk. paper) — ISBN 978-0-8214-4438-2
(electronic)

1. Ingalls, David Sinton, 1899–1985—Diaries. 2. Ingalls, David Sinton,
1899–1985—Correspondence. 3. World War, 1914–1918—Aerial operations,
American—Biography. 4. United States. Navy—Aviation—Biography.
5. Fighter pilots—United States—Biography. 6. World War, 1914–1918—
Campaigns—Germany. 7. Great Britain. Royal Air Force. Squadron, No. 213—
Biography. 8. World War, 1914–1918—Aerial operations, British—Biography.
I. Rossano, Geoffrey Louis. II. Title. III. Title: World War I diary and letters of
David S. Ingalls, America's first naval ace.

D606.I54 2013

940.4'5973092—dc23

[B]

2012035494

Contents

Contents

Illustrations

Following page 178

Hand-drawn map of Dunkirk harbor by Lt. Kenneth Whiting
Lt. Godfrey Chevalier, CO at NAS Dunkirk
George Moseley
Yale Unit veteran Samuel Walker on a visit to Dunkirk, with Di Gates
Hanriot-Dupont scout being lowered into the water by derrick at
    Dunkirk
U.S. Navy station at Dunkirk after a German raid in late April 1918
Seawall at NAS Dunkirk with Hanriot-Dupont scouts
Ingalls, Ken MacLeish, and "Shorty" Smith at the Bergues aerodrome,
    April 1918

Following page 278

Ingalls with John T. "Skinny" Lawrence and acquaintance in Paris,
    May 1918
Breguet 14B.2 at Clermont-Ferrand
Observer/machine gunner Randall R. Browne of the First Aeronautic
    Detachment
DH9 day bomber
Aerial reconnaissance photograph of the dockyards and submarine pens
    at Bruges
Capt. David Hanrahan, Northern Bombing Group commander, with
    officers
Chateau at St. Inglevert, a point of rendezvous for members of the
    Yale Unit
Ingalls in Flanders, possibly during duty with Northern Bombing
    Group, July–August 1918
Ingalls with 213 Squadron mates, August 1918

Following page 308

U.S. Navy's Flight Department at Eastleigh
Warrant Officers Einar "Dep" Boydler and William "Bill" Miller at
    Eastleigh
Warrant Officer William "Bill" Miller with Liberty motor–powered DH-
    9a day bomber
Randall Browne and crew members at Eastleigh

Foreword

Curiously, given the scale and drama of the U.S. Navy's World War I aviation effort, there are no published biographies of navy combat aviators. Now, thanks to Geoffrey Rossano, a skilled and knowledgeable historian whose recent works include a comprehensive study of the navy's air arm in Europe, we have a fine-grained, up close and personal glimpse into the wartime career of David Sinton Ingalls, as told in his own words. The navy's first and only World War I "ace," credited with six victories while attached to an RAF pursuit squadron, Ingalls was still a teenager when he dropped out of Yale and volunteered for aviation training and service as a naval reserve officer. Like many members of the famed First Yale Unit, Ingalls came from the country's privileged elite, and like his comrades in arms, he dreamed of the excitement, honor, and glory that modern air warfare seemed to herald. Of course, as Ingalls himself related, the reality was often much different. He endured days and sometimes weeks of tedium on the ground, underwent seemingly endless training, and flew innumerable fruitless patrols over "Hunland" behind the front lines. What to the public appeared to be romantic, chivalrous aerial jousting was in fact a deadly industrial age war of attrition in which men and machines were consumed as appallingly as they were by the artillery and machine guns on the ground.

Using a veritable treasure trove of Ingalls's letters and diaries, Rossano brings the air war to life with informative and unobtrusive editing skill. The result is that readers will have the rare opportunity to see World War I in the air firsthand. In Ingalls's remarkably clear voice, we hear the range of emotions that often overwhelmed young men separated from their families and exposed to the dangers of flight and combat. We share Ingalls's exhilaration in the sheer intoxicating sensation of flight and the satisfaction he experienced in successfully completing a mission. We see how he carefully worded his letters home to his mother and father to mask the dangers he faced. And we see how his nearly daily diary entries paint another, more realistic picture, vividly showing that sometimes only a combination of luck and skill kept him alive in the air and got him safely back to earth.

In this book, we meet some of the key players in early American naval aviation. Among them are Yale Unit chums F. Trubee Davison, Artemus "Di" Gates, and Robert "Bob" Lovett, all of whom went on to noteworthy careers in aviation and public service. A keen observer of the strengths and weaknesses of the navy's effort in Europe, Ingalls had great respect for Ken Whiting and Hutch Cone, who oversaw the material and organizational aspects of the great enterprise. Like everyone else, Ingalls experienced loss in the merciless skies over France and Belgium. Gates went down and was held as a prisoner of war, and Kenneth MacLeish (brother of poet Archibald MacLeish) was killed only hours after joining the squadron when Ingalls, exhausted from combat, rotated back to England. Frederick Hough, Al Sturtevant, Curtis Read, Harry Velie, and Andrew Ortmeyer, to name only a few, had their lives cut short and will forever be reminders of the human cost of aerial warfare.

I feel certain that readers will agree with me that Rossano's *Hero of the Angry Sky* provides a gripping first-person account that incorporates all of the tragedy, excitement, frustration, sacrifice, and ultimately human triumph that accompanied the navy's Great War in the air.

William F. Trimble
Auburn University

Series Editors' Preface

Wars have been the engines of North American history. They have shaped the United States and Canada, their governments, and their societies from the colonial era to the present. The volumes in our War and Society in North America book series investigate the effects of military conflict on the peoples in the United States and Canada. Other series are devoted to particular conflicts, types of conflicts, or periods of conflict; ours considers the history of North America over time through the lens of warfare and its effects on states, societies, and peoples. We conceive "war and society" broadly to include the military history of conflicts in or involving North America; responses to war, support as well as opposition opinion, peace movements, and pacifist attitudes; examinations of American citizens and Canadian citizens, colonists, settlers, and Native Americans fighting in or returning from wars; and studies of institutional, political, social, cultural, economic, or environmental factors specific to North America that affected wars. Our series explores the ties between regions and nations in times of extreme crisis. Ultimately, volumes in the War and Society in North America series should be a venue for authors of books that will appeal to a wide range of audiences in military history, social history, and national and transnational history.

In *Hero of the Angry Sky*, Geoffrey Rossano fulfills all the expectations for our series. He brings to light the experiences of one of America's first flying aces, the naval aviator David Ingalls in the First World War. Ingalls, an Ohioan from Cleveland, shot down five German aircraft and became the only ace in the U.S. Navy during that conflict. Ingalls joined the preparedness movement in 1916 as an undergraduate student at Yale University and he went on to volunteer service in the war. This book is not merely a combat narrative, however, because Rossano effectively blends Ingalls's diary entries and personal letters in a whole-life story with fascinating material on flight training, aviation technology, and even France's wartime society. His book also serves to commemorate the early years of naval aviation and the upcoming one-hundredth anniversary of the formation of the First Yale Unit of volunteers for the Great War. After the war ended, Ingalls went on to careers in law, business, Ohio politics, and national politics. As an assistant secretary of the navy in President Herbert Hoover's administration, Ingalls directed the expansion of naval aviation and the development of aircraft carrier–based air power that would bear fruit in the Second World War. There can be no doubt that Ingalls's own experiences as an aviator in the Great War left lasting impressions on him and made him a strong advocate for naval air power for the rest of this life.

We are proud to have Geoffrey Rossano's *Hero of the Angry Sky* as the inaugural volume in the series War and Society in North America. Throughout the review and editing phases, Rossano has been the consummate scholar. We could not have asked for a better author and partner in publishing. We would be remiss if we did not also thank Gillian Berchowitz, the editorial director at Ohio University Press. Gillian has been very supportive throughout the process of creating our series and in working with Geoffrey Rossano on *Hero of the Angry Sky*.

David J. Ulbrich
St. Robert, Missouri

Ingo Trauschweizer
Athens, Ohio

Acknowledgments

To edit someone's private diary and correspondence is, in a way, to become part of that person's life, family, and social circle and share his or her time and place, no matter how far removed. Working with David Ingalls's papers was just such an experience. During many months poring over his writings, deciphering his tight penmanship, "meeting" his friends and acquaintances, and listening in on his thoughts, I came to know the teenage man-boy who became naval aviation's first ace. Visiting several of the places where he trained and served, literally following in his footsteps, provided additional insight. It has been a fascinating and rewarding journey.

My greatest thanks go to members of the extended Ingalls family for making David Ingalls's papers available to me and supporting this project right from the beginning. They opened both their homes and their archives. Especially helpful have been Jane Ingalls Davison, David Ingalls's daughter; Dr. Bobbie Brown, his granddaughter; and Polly Hitchcock, his great-granddaughter. I would also like to thank the staff at the Louise H. and David S. Ingalls Foundation, particularly Jay Remec. All were enthusiastic about the project from start to finish.

A great variety of individuals, organizations, and repositories made completion of this work possible. The National Archives in Washington remains the central repository for documents relating to early things naval. The large and varied resources of the Naval History and Heritage Command located at the Washington Navy Yard proved very helpful, as did the staff in the library, the Photo Section, and especially the naval aviation unit of the archives, particularly Joe Gordon and Laura Waayers. The Naval Institute library in Annapolis provided access to many scarce books and publications, as did the Emil Buehler Library at the Naval Aviation Museum in Pensacola, Florida. Jack Fine at the Buehler Library greatly assisted in the search for photographs. Archivist David Levesque at St. Paul's School helped identify many of David Ingalls's school friends and associates, and Roger Sheely generously provided access to his own father's World War I papers and photograph albums, which contained much material relating to Ingalls's involvement with the Northern Bombing Group program. Peter Mersky also permitted reproduction of several photographs from his collection. I have also enjoyed working with Darroch Greer and Ron King, producers of the outstanding documentary film *The Millionaire's Unit: America's Pioneer Pilots of the Great War.* They provided several leads and insights into the world of the First Yale Unit.

Finally, my hearty thanks go to the editors and professionals at Ohio University Press who made the task of completing this project a pleasure rather than a burden. These include series editors Ingo Trauschweizer and David Ulbrich and Editorial Director Gillian Berchowitz.

Geoffrey L. Rossano

A Note on the Text

Principal Sources:

Diary, two volumes, September 1917–November 1918

Letters to parents and others, April 1917–November 1918

Typescript diary/memoir prepared in the early postwar period

Observations/Analysis re: training at Turnberry and Ayr

Informal logbook entries scattered through the diary

Technical notebook re: gunnery, equipment lectures at Turnberry

RAF squadron reports

This book incorporates the complete chronological text of David Ingalls's extant World War I letters and diary, technical notes from his time at Turnberry, an analysis of training at Ayr and Turnberry, random flight records, and official RAF squadron reports/flight reports, supplemented where appropriate by material drawn from his postwar (c. 1924) personal memoir. Also included is the transcript of after dinner remarks made at a 1924 reunion of the Yale fliers. Obvious misspellings have been corrected. In the few instances where Ingalls's handwriting made deciphering a word or phrase problematic or where words have been inserted to provide clarity, the editor has so indicated with brackets—[ ]—in the text.

Chapter organization reflects discrete periods in Ingalls's wartime instruction and service, beginning with chapter 1, his early training in Florida and New York. Chapter 2 covers his voyage across the Atlantic and early months in England and France. Chapter 3 includes material related to training with the Royal Flying Corps from December 1917 until March 1918. Chapter 4 documents Ingalls's service at NAS Dunkirk and with No.213 Squadron, RAF, in the period March–May 1918. Chapter 5 is devoted to his months of training for duty with the Northern Bombing Group and service with an RAF bombing squadron. Chapter 6 covers his time at the front with No.213 Squadron in August–October 1918, the months when he scored all of his aerial victories. Chapter 7 describes Ingalls's final wartime duties at the navy's assembly and repair facility at Eastleigh, England, and his trip home.

The volume incorporates both editorial comments and annotations. The editorial material is designed to place Ingalls's words and actions into historical context, while offering a succinct narrative of his life and the events of his military career. Most of this information is located at the beginning of chapters or in extended footnotes. The objective is not to retell the entire story of naval aviation in this period. Rather, every attempt has been made to give substance to Ingalls's own voice, to let one young man tell his own story, completely, for the very first time.

Finally, the annotations. Throughout his surviving letters, diary, and other documents, David Ingalls mentioned a vast cast of characters, organizations, places, and events. A few are well known to the casual reader, but most are not, even to those well versed in the history of the period. Many references, at a distance of nearly a century, are quite obscure. To address this issue and help the reader understand the flow of events but not overwhelm Ingalls's narrative, the editor has indicated the terms, characters, places, and other material to be identified with a footnote number, with the actual identification/explanation placed at the bottom of the page.

Abbreviations

AA	antiaircraft
A & R	assembly and repair
AEF	American Expeditionary Force
BM	Boatswain's Mate
CNO	Chief of Naval Operations
CO	commanding officer
C.P.S.	Carson, Pirie, Scott
DFC	Distinguished Flying Cross
DSC	Distinguished Service Cross
DSI	David Sinton Ingalls
DSM	Distinguished Service Medal
DSO	Distinguished Service Order
EA	enemy aircraft
FAD	First Aeronautic Detachment
GM	Gunner's Mate
HOP	high offensive patrol
j.g.	junior grade
MG	machine gun
MM	Machinist Mate
NA	Naval Aviator
NAS	Naval Air Station
NBG	Northern Bombing Group

NRFC	Naval Reserve Flying Corps
QM	Quartermaster
RAF	Royal Air Force
RFC	Royal Flying Corps
RNAS	Royal Naval Air Service; Royal Naval Air Station
VC	Victoria Cross

Introduction

In 1925, Rear Admiral William S. Sims, commander of U.S. naval forces operating in Europe during World War I, declared, "Lieutenant David S. Ingalls may rightly be called the 'Naval Ace' of the war."[1] Of the twenty thousand pilots, observers, ground officers, mechanics, and construction workers who served overseas in the conflict, only Ingalls earned that unofficial yet esteemed status. In contrast, by November 1918, the U.S. Army Air Service counted more than 120 aces.[2]

The Cleveland, Ohio, native's unique achievement resulted from several factors. Unlike their army peers, few naval pilots engaged in air-to-air combat. Instead, most patrolled uncontested waters in search of submarines. A bare handful served with Allied squadrons along the Western Front, the true cauldron of the air war. By contrast, David Ingalls spent much of his flying career stationed at NAS Dunkirk, the navy's embattled base situated just behind enemy lines, or carrying out missions with Royal Air Force (RAF) fighting and bombing squadrons. He did three tours with the British, all without a parachute or other safety gear, and he hungered for more. The young aviator managed to be in the right place at the right time, and as was true for nearly all surviving aces, luck smiled on him.

David Ingalls's personal attributes played a crucial role in his success. A gifted athlete, he possessed extraordinary eyesight, hand-eye

---

1. See Ralph D. Paine, *The First Yale Unit: A Story of Naval Aviation, 1916–1919*, 2 vols. (Cambridge, Mass.: Riverside Press, 1925), 1:vii.

2. Ingalls was one of a small but distinguished group of Ohio aviation heroes that included Eddie Rickenbacker, the former race car driver from Columbus who ended the war as America's "ace of aces"; William Lambert from Ironton; Charles Bissonette from Toledo; and James Knowles from Cincinnati. Prominent naval aviators Robert Ireland and John Vorys hailed from Cleveland and Cincinnati, respectively.

coordination, strength, agility, and endurance. An instinctive, confident flier, Ingalls learned quickly and loved the aerial environment. With a head for detail, he easily mastered the many technical facets of his craft. He was also an excellent shot and unforgiving hunter. Finally, Ingalls possessed the heart of a youthful daredevil, a hell-raiser who gloried in the excitement and challenge of aerial combat. He seemed fearless and quickly put one day's activities behind him even as he prepared for the next mission. He went to war a schoolboy athlete and came home a national hero. And he was still only nineteen years old when the guns fell silent.

Although Ingalls's wartime experiences are compelling at a personal level, they also illuminate the larger but still relatively unexplored realm of early U.S. naval aviation. According to military historians R. D. Layman and John Abbatiello, naval aviation carried out a wide variety of missions in World War I and exercised far greater influence on the conduct of military affairs than heretofore acknowledged. Aircraft protected convoys from attack and played an increasingly vital role in the campaign against the U-boat. Aviators aided the efforts of naval units and ground troops in military theaters extending from the North Sea and English Channel to Flanders, Italy, Greece, Turkey, and Iraq. Fleet commands, most notably in Great Britain, worked to integrate the new technology into ongoing operations and develop innovative applications.[3]

As the United States developed its own aviation priorities, missions, and doctrines during 1917 and 1918, it aspired to similar success. Despite his extreme youth, David Ingalls was repeatedly selected by the navy to play a pathbreaking role in this process. He began as one of the very first pilots dispatched to Europe for active duty "over there." Once ashore, he became one of only three aviators chosen to receive advanced training at Britain's School of Special Flying at Gosport, preparatory to assuming the role of flight commander at beleaguered NAS Dunkirk. During the terrifying German advance of March–April 1918, he and three other American pilots joined a Royal Air Force fighting squadron operating

3. See R. D. Layman, *Naval Aviation in the First World War: Its Impact and Influence* (London: Chatham Publishing, 1996), 13; see also John Abbatiello, *Anti-Submarine Warfare in World War I: British Naval Aviation and the Defeat of the U-Boats* (London: Routledge, 2006), passim. The latter is an outstanding study of the subject.

over Flanders. Later that year, he became one of the initial members of the navy's most significant offensive program of the entire war, the Northern Bombing Group (NBG), and then flew several bombing missions with the RAF. After just a few weeks' ground duty with the NBG, Ingalls returned to British service for two months, becoming the only navy pilot to fly over the front lines for such an extended period. While with the RAF, he served as acting flight commander ahead of many longtime members of his squadron. In recognition of this work, he became the first American naval aviator to receive Britain's Distinguished Flying Cross. He finished his service as chief flight officer at the navy's sprawling assembly and repair depot at Eastleigh, England.

Ingalls's wartime correspondence offers a rare personal view of the evolution of naval aviation during the war, both at home and abroad. There are no published biographies of navy combat fliers from this period, and just a handful of diaries and letters are in print, the last appearing in the early 1990s.[4] Ingalls kept a detailed record of his wartime service in several forms, and his extensive and enthusiastic letters and diaries add significantly to historians' store of available material. Shortly after enlisting in the navy in March 1917, he began corresponding with his parents in Cleveland, Ohio, a practice he continued until late November 1918. Someone in his father's offices at the New York Central Railroad transcribed the handwritten letters and pasted them into a scrapbook containing materials documenting his military career.[5]

Ingalls's letters reveal a lighthearted and affectionate relationship with his parents, and they are often filled with valuable insights into the tasks he performed, though he shielded his folks from the true dangers he faced. He limned his most hair-raising experiences with the glow of a sportswriter discussing a star athlete's exploits. Though the letters contain much information about his social life in Europe, the teenage flier did not tell his

---

4. These include George Moseley, *Extracts from the War Letters of George Clark Moseley During the Period of the Great War* (privately printed, 1923); Geoffrey Rossano, ed., *The Price of Honor: The World War One Letters of Naval Aviator Kenneth MacLeish* (Annapolis, Md.: Naval Institute Press, 1991); and Lawrence Sheely, ed., *Sailor of the Air: The 1917–1919 Letters and Diary of USN CMM/A Irving Edward Sheely* (Tuscaloosa: University of Alabama Press, 1993). See also the extensive correspondence and reminiscences reprinted in Paine, *First Yale Unit.*

5. The original handwritten letters have been lost, and typewritten copies contain a few transcription errors, corrected here.

mother about the "short arm" inspections he performed on enlisted men, searching for signs of venereal disease.

Upon sailing to Europe in September 1917, the recently commissioned junior officer commenced keeping a detailed diary, eventually filling two compact notebooks. Ingalls also compiled an informal record of his flight activities by jotting down spare notations throughout his diary, listing hours and types of aircraft flown. Surprisingly, no official logbook survives. These daily entries have a very different texture from that of his letters, being more matter-of-fact and more cryptic yet still recording the major and lesser activities that structured his days and the days of those around him. He expressed frustration with endless training, occasional boredom, dislike of army fliers, and hints of fear and nerves, an altogether less sugarcoated version of reality. While training in Scotland, the neophyte aviator transcribed lengthy notes during various lectures and from technical publications. He also produced a formal analysis of instruction at Ayr and Turnberry. Both are reproduced here.

Shortly after the war but likely no later than 1924, a more mature Ingalls prepared a hundred-page typescript memoir, incorporating much of the language of his diary and letters verbatim, interspersed with material reporting additional events, descriptions drawn from memory where no letters or diary entries survived, or editorial comments about his experiences. The memoir offers yet another interpretation of Ingalls's activities, the tone by turns analytical and dramatic, with something of the flavor of a pulp novel. Wartime terror and boredom are gone, replaced by the occasional smirk or wink. His descriptions of social life and visits to nightclubs seem wiser, more knowing, as he speaks with the voice of a grown man recounting the escapades of a teenage boy.

Despite his officer status, Ingalls provided a distinctly civilian view of military life in his writings, albeit a rather privileged version of that existence. For him, this was all a great adventure, not a career. The navy's decision to keep its regular young officers with the fleet and not train any as aviators meant volunteer reservists such as Ingalls filled the ranks of combat units.[6]

---

6. A demographic analysis of the naval aviation reserve flying corps can be found in Geoffrey Rossano, *Stalking the U-Boat: U.S. Naval Aviation in Europe in World War I* (Gainesville: University Press of Florida, 2010), 249–52. Reginald Arthur's *Contact! Careers of Naval Aviators Assigned Numbers 1–2000* (Washington, D.C.: Naval Aviation Register, 1967), contains a wealth of information, including minibiographies of the first two thousand naval aviators.

And like him, many came from affluent, socially prominent families. The young Ohioan thus had much to say about the social scene in London and Paris, and his experiences differed greatly from the hardships suffered by enlisted bluejackets at sea or doughboy infantrymen in the mud and trenches.

Ingalls's story also, in the words of author Henry Berry in *Make the Kaiser Dance,* partakes of the persistent aura of glamour attached to the young Americans who flew their fragile, dangerous machines above the Western Front. Anyone who has ever raced across the sky in an open-cockpit biplane knows something of that feeling. Of Ingalls and his peers, Berry remarked, "Their names seem to conjure up the list of the romantic aspects of war—if shooting down another plane in flames, or suffering the same fate, is glamorous." In a world of mud, horror, anonymity, and mass death, they became celebrities. The less-than-unbiased Gen. William "Billy" Mitchell proclaimed, "The only interest and romance in this war was in the air," and historian Edward Coffman observed, "No other aspect of World War I so captured the public imagination."[7]

Concerning his aviation duties, Ingalls offered insight into the lengthy, varied, sometimes contradictory, and often ad hoc instruction received by the first wave of navy fliers preparing for wartime service. He bemoaned the fact that training never seemed to end. Reassignment from flying boat–patrol training, to land-based combat instruction, to seaplane escort duty, and to cross-lines bombing raids, followed by more escort duty, then training in large bombers, and finally assignment to a British combat squadron reflected the navy's continually shifting plans and priorities. The fleet entered the war with no aviation doctrine, precious few men, and little matériel, and it took many months to get the program headed on a winning course. As Capt. Thomas Craven, commander of naval aviation in France in the final months of the conflict, noted, his bases and squadrons, like John Paul Jones, "had not yet begun to fight," even as Germany prepared to surrender.[8]

Among the first collegiate fliers to jump into the game, David Ingalls began training even before Congress declared war. In the months that

---

7. See Henry Berry, *Make the Kaiser Dance: Living Memories of a Forgotten War—The American Experience in World War I* (Garden City, N.Y.: Doubleday, 1978), 224. Both Mitchell and Coffman quotes are in Edward M. Coffman, *The War to End All Wars: The American Military Experience in World War I* (Madison: University of Wisconsin Press, 1986), 187.

8. Rossano, *Stalking the U-Boat,* 367.

followed, he mastered command of flying boats, seaplanes, pursuit aircraft, and bombers, more than a dozen machines in all. Ingalls's work took him from Florida to New York and then to England, Scotland, and France. He became a trailblazer for the many that followed, and his duties included antisubmarine patrols, bombing raids, test flights, at-sea rescues, dogfights, and low-level strafing attacks. In all his assignments, he displayed intelligence, exuberance, and technical skill. His superiors entrusted him with significant responsibility, and he more than fulfilled their expectations. Ingalls achieved great success in all his endeavors and despite his youth earned the praise, admiration, and respect of those around him. His experiences mirrored the course of the navy's first venture into the crucible of aerial combat. David Ingalls's story is naval aviation's story.

By any reckoning, David Sinton Ingalls of Cleveland, Ohio, lived an extraordinary life. Long before he flew into aviation history, he seemed destined for high achievement. It was in his blood. Born into an affluent, socially and politically prominent midwestern family, he enjoyed great success as a youthful athlete. His exploits in World War I made him a national hero. The postwar era brought further accomplishments—degrees from Yale and Harvard; marriage to an heiress and a busy family life; a high-profile career in politics, law, business, and publishing; a busy and productive stint as undersecretary of the navy for aeronautics in the Hoover administration; distinguished military service in World War II; extensive activity as a sportsman and philanthropist; and a lifelong commitment to his passion for flying as both a pilot and an aviation enthusiast. And whatever activity he pursued, he did so with energy and zest.

David Ingalls's family tree incorporated some of Ohio's most prominent citizens. On his mother's side, he descended from David Sinton (1808–1900), whose parents arrived from Ireland and settled in Pittsburgh. Described much later as a man of "irregular education," Sinton was known as "a large, strong person with strong common sense."[9] He eventually relocated to southern Ohio, made a fortune in the iron business, and was at one time perhaps the richest man in the state. His elegant, Federal-style Cincinnati home survives today as the Taft Museum of Art. Sinton's only

9. Stephen Hess, *America's Political Dynasties from Adams to Kennedy* (Garden City, N.Y.: Doubleday, 1966), 306.

daughter, Anne (1850–1931), inherited $20 million from her father. She married Charles Phelps Taft (1843–1929), son of Alphonso Taft (1810–91), a man of solid Yankee stock. Originally from West Townshend, Vermont, the elder Taft graduated from Yale (Phi Beta Kappa) and Yale Law School and by 1859 had settled in Cincinnati, where he attained legal and political prominence. He ultimately served as U.S. secretary of war and attorney general and later ambassador to Austria-Hungary and Russia.

Alphonso Taft's son Charles, the older half brother of William Howard Taft (the future judge, secretary of war, president, and Chief Justice of the United States), became a prominent lawyer in his own right, as well as a congressman and publisher of the *Cincinnati Times-Star*. According to Robert A. Taft's biographer, "Wealthy brother Charley" often provided financial assistance to his justice sibling, while emerging as one of Cincinnati's leading philanthropists. Charles and Anne Taft lived in David Sinton's mansion until the late 1920s. Their only daughter, Jane Taft (1874–1962), was David Ingalls's mother. She exhibited a lifelong interest in the arts and became a patroness of many museums and organizations. She also earned a local reputation as a talented painter and sculptress.[10]

Paternal grandfather Melville Ingalls (1842–1914), another Yankee, hailed from Maine and moved to Massachusetts, where he gained distinction as a lawyer and politician. After relocating to Cincinnati, he fashioned a remarkable career in railroads and finance. In time, he became president of several rail lines, including the Indianapolis, Cincinnati & Lafayette, later part of the Cleveland, Cincinnati, Chicago, & St. Louis, known as the Big Four Railroad. Melville Ingalls also controlled the Merchants National Bank, the city's second-largest financial institution. His "imposing estate" stood in Cincinnati's fashionable East Walnut Hills neighborhood. Melville's son, Albert S. Ingalls (1874–1943), achieved great success as well, Born in Cincinnati, he

---

10. James Patterson's *Mr. Republican: A Biography of Robert A. Taft* (Boston: Houghton Mifflin, 1972), the standard biography of the influential senator from Ohio, provides considerable information concerning the Taft family's history, as well as that of their Ingalls relatives; see especially pp. 6–14. Jane Taft Ingalls and Robert A. Taft were first cousins, and David Ingalls was Robert Taft's first cousin, once removed. As a young lawyer in Cincinnati in the pre–World War I period, Robert Taft "engaged in legal tasks for relatives, especially Uncle Charley and Aunt Annie." Charles Taft's business interests included a 157,000-acre ranch in Texas, the Taft Packing House, Taft Crystal Shortening, and "countless investments." See Patterson, *Mr. Republican,* 59–60. Also see Jane Sinton Taft Ingalls's obituary, *Cleveland Plain Dealer,* March 31, 1962.

attended St. Paul's School in New Hampshire and Harvard, then went to work for his father's railroad, starting out dressed in overalls rather than a business suit. He worked his way up through the system at the Big Four, then Lake Shore Railroad, and finally New York Central Railroad, where he became vice president and general manager of operations west of Buffalo, New York. As his career blossomed, Albert Ingalls moved to Cleveland, earning some notoriety as the second man in the city to own an automobile. He was long remembered as a hard worker and quick thinker, a master of English who could clear a desk of correspondence in record time. He exhibited a democratic spirit and genial personality and an admirable mixture of culture, quick-wittedness, broad interests, and robust energy. From an early age, Albert Ingalls enjoyed smoking a clay pipe. Many of his personal traits he passed on to his children, especially David.

Albert Ingalls and Jane Taft married in Cincinnati, linking two important Ohio clans, but soon relocated to Cleveland. The young couple lived first in the city, then in Cleveland Heights. They had three children—David, Anne, and Albert. David, the eldest, was born on January 28, 1899. In 1906, the family moved to Bratenahl, one of the city's early elite residential suburbs on the shores of Lake Erie, known for its prominent families and manicured estates. Residents included members of the region's financial and industrial elite, including the Hannas, Irelands, Chisholms, Holdens, Kings, Mc-Murrays, and Pickandses. David Ingalls's lifelong friend and fellow naval aviator, Robert Livingston "Pat" Ireland, lived nearby. Ingalls spent summers at the lakeshore or visiting his many relatives, especially his Taft cousins.

His academic training included time spent at University School in Cleveland, an independent day school founded in 1890. In 1912, Ingalls entered St. Paul's School in Concord, New Hampshire, from which he graduated in 1916, having participated in the requisite campus organizations, including the mandolin club, literary society, and scientific association. He played football and tennis and was twice schoolwide squash champion. Ingalls's most notable exploits came on the ice as a standout hockey player. Some even compared him to the nonpareil athlete Hobey Baker, who preceded him by a few years. At the time, the school was "ardently Anglophile . . . High Church," and it drew much of its student body from the New York–Philadelphia Main Line. While at St. Paul's, Ingalls came under the stern influence of Rector Samuel Drury, a former missionary to the Philippines who worked diligently to improve the school's commitment to ethical and academic standards. Drury often told his charges, "From those to whom much is given, much is expected."[11]

Ingalls's schoolboy years, whether at St. Paul's or at home in Cleveland, exposed him daily to the controversies ignited by the terrible war that broke out in Europe in 1914 and America's appropriate response to it. As the history of St. Paul's School documents, there was considerable anti-German feeling at that time, and both students and faculty quickly forged many connections to the fighting. Several masters attended summer military camps. Graduates enlisted with the French or British forces. Students marched in preparedness parades, volunteered for military drill, and carried out raids on various campus buildings.[12] Like the strong winds blowing off Lake Erie, news of the war and the fierce debate it generated also buffeted Cleveland, a flourishing city with a yeasty mix of rich and poor, native and immigrant, liberal and conservative. News of the sinking of the *Lusitania* in early May 1915 covered every inch of the front page of the *Cleveland Plain Dealer*. When the German consul in Cincinnati released a statement in January 1916 defending his country's actions in the war, the story received wide

---

11. Many remembered Drury as formidable, pious, and dour; others said he was "reserved, cheerless, and solemn." The rector seemed to regard his charges as "slovenly, dilatory, and slack." See Walter Isaacson and Evan Thomas, *The Wise Men: Six Friends and the World They Made* (New York: Simon and Schuster, 1986), 57, 59–60. The rector arrived at St. Paul's in 1910 at the age of thirty-one and almost immediately earned the sobriquet "Old Drury." His young wife, Cornelia, however, quickly inspired the warm appreciation of the students, one of whom recalled her as "lovely beyond our fondest hope and expectations." See August Heckscher, *St. Paul's: The Life of a New England School* (New York: Charles Scribner's Sons, 1980), 157, 160, 170. David Ingalls's fun-loving, mischief-making personality survived Dr. Drury's assaults intact. At one point, David congratulated his younger brother, Albert, a student at St. Paul's during the war, for living down his elder sibling's bad reputation.

12. Victor Chapman, '07, flew with the Lafayette Escadrille. Charles Merton, '03, drove an ambulance. Old boy Allen Loney, '90, died when the *Lusitania* went down. Rector Drury advised one German master, trapped in Germany by the fighting in 1914, "It seems to me that many people at St. Paul's do not regard the cause which you hold with much affectionate interest in the light which you regard it." After the master returned to the school, some faculty opposed giving him his full quota of teaching hours lest he proselytize his German cause. See Heckscher, *St. Paul's,* 180–81. Drury did not, however, endorse formal military training on campus. In a letter to the *New York Times* in August 1916, he argued that such activities, though valuable, were best carried out in the summer at military facilities equipped to provide this sort of instruction. He noted, "The spirit of patriotic obligation should be more amply urged than ever before in our schools, but the experience of military service can be adequately taught only where the routine and background are wholly military." See *New York Times,* August 20, 1916.

circulation throughout the state. That same day, notices informed Cleve-landers that new war motion pictures were playing in local theaters.

Residents read about vigorous efforts by pacifist, preparedness, and interventionist groups to sway public opinion. In 1915, Mayor Newton Baker, known for his antimilitarist stance, joined social reformer Jane Addams in praising the antiwar film *Lay Down Your Arms.* In the same year, Cleveland Women for Peace held a tea to honor delegates to the World Court Congress. Mrs. Baker, the mayor's spouse, presided at the event. The miners' union came out against military preparedness in January 1916, and members of the Cleveland Young People's Socialist League celebrated an antiwar day the following September. In November 1916, Cleveland and surrounding Cuyahoga County voted for President Woodrow Wilson ("He kept us out of war") by a 52-to-44 percent margin. This result received the approbation of the November 9 *Plain Dealer* editorial page, which praised Wilson for "his sane Americanism, opposition to war-at-any-price jingoes, and professional hyphenates."

Cleveland supporters of preparedness and the Allies, however, were also vocal and well represented throughout the prewar period. Many of the city's Yale graduates urged visiting university president Arthur Hadley to support military preparedness. In July 1915, prominent citizens orga-nized a local chapter of the National Security League and campaigned actively for the next two years. The following summer, Bascom Little, an influential local businessman and philanthropist and member of the Na-tional Defense Committee of the U.S. Chamber of Commerce, traveled to Washington, D.C., to urge Congress to pass a proposed universal military training bill. Everyone, it seems, had an opinion about the war and what the United States should do about it.[13]

In the fall of 1916, David Ingalls entered Yale University to pursue med-ical studies, and he again distinguished himself on the ice as captain of the freshman hockey team. Great-uncle William Howard Taft, former president and now member of the law school faculty, lived just a few blocks away. Somewhere along the way, likely at St. Paul's or in that first year at Yale, Ingalls acquired the nickname "Crock," derivation uncertain. (Daughter

---

13. Andrew R. L. Cayton observed that even after war was declared, "the sense of moral outrage [in Ohio] that had characterized the Civil War was largely absent." The resulting war deaths were claimed by a cause "to which few people in Ohio were deeply committed." See Cayton, *Ohio: The History of a People* (Columbus: Ohio State University Press, 2002), 234.

Jane Ingalls Davison later insisted no one in Cleveland ever called him by that name.) Ingalls soon became close friends with Henry "Harry" Pomeroy Davison Jr., son of J. P. Morgan partner Henry Pomeroy Davison and younger brother of F. Trubee Davison.[14] While Ingalls was in New Haven, his childhood fascination with flight, his innate joy in reckless physical action, his social connections to influential fellow students, and the prewar preparedness frenzy sweeping eastern colleges almost inevitably turned his attention toward an aviation unit being formed by Trubee Davison.

By late 1916, concern over events in Europe, where the Great War staggered through its third year, and the debate regarding America's role in the struggle reached a fever pitch, dominating the national conversation. When war had broken out in the summer of 1914, reaction had been mixed. President Wilson, who "resolutely opposed unjustified war,"[15] insisted the United States remain neutral in the struggle and actively resisted planning for possible military intervention. Military historian Harvey DeWeerd observed, "The war was nearly two years old before Wilson allowed government officials to act as if it might sometime involve America." Newton Baker, now secretary of war, had been a spokesman for the League to Enforce Peace. Editor George B. M. Harvey of *Harper's Weekly* responded by calling Baker "a chattering ex-pacifist." Secretary of the Navy Josephus Daniels, a man of pacifist and isolationist proclivities, proved equally critical of professional soldiers and sailors and general staffs.[16]

14. Another descendant speculated that "Crock" might have been inspired by Davy Crockett, as David Ingalls was later well known within the family for wearing a coonskin cap on special occasions. Alternatively, Ingalls may have adopted his nickname from the ferocious crocodile that inhabited J. M. Barrie's popular contemporary play, *Peter Pan*. With no one left to tell the tale, the true origins of Ingalls's nickname must remain a mystery. F. Trubee Davison and Henry P. "Harry" "Dude" Davison Jr., NA #72, were sons of prominent New York banker and J. P. Morgan partner Henry Pomeroy Davison. The senior Davison later served as head of the War Council of the Red Cross.

15. See Meirion Harries and Susie Harries, *The Last Days of Innocence: America at War, 1917–1918* (New York: Random House, 1997), 50.

16. See Harvey DeWeerd, *President Wilson Fights His War: World War I and the American Intervention* (New York: Macmillan, 1968), 10, 200. English publisher Lord Rydell referred to Baker as a "nice, little trim man of the YMCA type," quoted in Harries and Harries, *Last Days of Innocence,* 50. David M. Kennedy, in *Over Here: The First World War and American Society* (New York: Oxford University Press, 1980), cited Baker's "well known anti-militaristic views." Ironically, Baker eventually compiled a wartime record that earned him accolades as one of the nation's greatest secretaries of war. The League to Enforce Peace had been founded by, among others, William Howard Taft, who served as its first president. See Herbert S. Duffy, *William Howard Taft* (New York: Minton, Balch, 1930), 305–7.

Many citizens concurred. Irish Americans opposed any aid for Britain. German Americans, including thousands in Ohio, tended to support their homeland. Antiwar sentiment ran strongly among reformers, women's organizations, and church groups. The country's large socialist movement called the conflict a capitalist conspiracy to generate profits and consume manpower. Traditionally isolationist regions of the United States strongly opposed involvement. Henry Ford chartered a "peace ship" to bring antiwar activists to an international conference held in Stockholm, Sweden in 1916. Reflecting the horrors unfolding on the Western Front, "I Didn't Raise My Boy to Be a Soldier" reigned as one of the most popular songs of 1915–16.[17]

Such feelings were not universal, however. In fact, though most Americans supported neutrality and narrowly reelected Woodrow Wilson on the belief that "he kept us out of war," they still preferred a Franco-British victory to a German triumph. DeWeerd claimed, "The country was pro-Ally and anti-German from the start."[18] Fervent supporters of Great Britain and France saw the war as a struggle between democracy and Western civilization, on the one hand, and "Kaiserism" and the brutality of the "Huns," on the other. Submarine attacks on civilian passenger liners such as the *Lusitania* almost caused a diplomatic rupture between the United States and Germany. The British blockade, protested only mildly by the Wilson government, diverted most trade to England and Western Europe, and a growing tide of orders for war materials engendered further support for the Allies. So did the ever-increasing flow of loans from major American investment banks such as J. P. Morgan.

Whether favoring or opposing active participation in Europe's seemingly endless war, many citizens demanded their government prepare for

---

17. According to Kennedy, "Feminists had been the first to take the field"—stalwarts such as Fanny Garrison Villard, Carrie Chapman Catt, and Jane Addams, who formed the Women's Peace Party. Shortly after the presidential election of 1916, war opponents joined together to form the American Union Against Militarism (AUAM). Kennedy noted, "The roster of the AUAM's charter comprised a virtual *Who's Who* of advanced progressive leadership." In fact, to "the progressive men and women who had devoted themselves . . . to all the schemes to civilize the cities and tame capitalism . . . the war [had] seemed distant, repugnant, malicious." Kennedy offered an overview of the antipreparedness, antiwar movement in *Over Here,* 14–51. See also Harries and Harries, *Last Days of Innocence,* 49–60.

18. See DeWeerd, *President Wilson Fights His War,* 7.

possible involvement in the struggle, if only to defend national interests
and American soil in case of a German victory. As David Kennedy noted,
the outbreak of war "summoned into being . . . a sizable array of preparedness lobbies."[19] Some called for universal military training (conscription)
and expansion of both the army and the navy. Former army chief of staff
Leonard Wood, ex-president Theodore Roosevelt, and previous secretaries of war Elihu Root and Henry Stimson were only the most prominent
among thousands of citizens who campaigned for such action. Leading
bankers, industrialists, lawyers, academics, and politicians advocated a
strongly Anglophile diplomatic and military policy, and a great mosaic of
organizations took up the call.[20]

Citizen training camps conducted at Plattsburgh, New York, and
elsewhere reflected the growing clamor for preparedness. College students and faculty members, recent graduates, young businessmen, and
teaching masters from a score of eastern preparatory schools spent their
summers drilling, camping, and learning to fire weapons. Another out-
growth of the preparedness movement, the National Defense Act of 1916,
doubled the size of the army (to 240,000) and authorized a tremendous
expansion of the battle fleet, though none of its provisions would be

19. See Kennedy, *Over Here,* 31, 37–38.

20. Wood, a former Indian fighter and Rough Rider who rose to become army
chief of staff, impressed some as intelligent, brave, ill tempered, and egocentric, a
man, according to Walter Lippmann, with "an apoplectic soul." As chief of staff, he
opened voluntary training camps for college men in 1913. See Harries and Har-
ries, *Last Days of Innocence,* 52. For a detailed look at Wood's life and work, see
Jack McCallum, *Leonard Wood: Rough Rider, Surgeon, Architect of American Imperialism*
(New York: New York University Press, 2006); Jack Lane, *Armed Progressive: General
Leonard Wood* (Lincoln, Neb.: Bison Books, 2009); and the older work by Hermann
Hagedorn, *Leonard Wood: A Biography,* 2 vols. (New York: Harper and Brothers, 1931).
John W. Chambers II noted, "The civilian leaders of the major conscriptionist or-
ganizations were predominantly members of the new corporate-oriented business
and professional elite . . . [including] industrialists, financiers, railroad magnates, and
major publishers, joined by corporation lawyers, university presidents, and former
diplomats. . . . They represented the top echelons of power in the new social struc-
ture of urban, industrial, corporate America" (80). Prominent advocates included
Ralph Pulitzer, Joseph Choate, Lyman Abbott, Grenville Clark, Thomas Edison,
Bernard Baruch, and Howard Coffin. For a detailed description of this movement,
see Chambers, *To Raise an Army: The Draft Comes to Modern America* (New York: Free
Press, 1987), 73–101. It was from this exact socioeconomic group that the Yale aviation unit and its circle of supporters emerged.

fully implemented for several years and thus would have little impact on the current crisis in Europe.[21]

Whatever their individual motivations, many young Americans, both men and women, took dramatic action to support the Allies. Thousands journeyed to Europe to drive ambulances, serve with the Red Cross, or perform varied volunteer duties. Others enlisted in the French Foreign Legion and eventually transferred to the aviation forces, forming what ultimately became the Lafayette Flying Corps. Still more traveled to Canada to join the British army or the Royal Flying Corps (RFC). Students at colleges such as Harvard, Princeton, and Yale formed quasi-military units and flying clubs, preparing for the day Uncle Sam might call on them.[22]

Even before Ingalls arrived in New Haven in September 1916, talk of war and preparedness monopolized much of the academic community's attention, with the discussion by no means one-sided. Author George Pierson noted, "Yale was far from rising as one man to the support of Belgium and the Triple Entente." Even as former president Taft called for strict neutrality, scholar George Adams declaimed, "Germany must be defeated in this war." Initially, though very few students or faculty members favored the Central powers, equally small numbers advocated direct American involvement.

---

21. Although some later academic analysts claimed proponents of preparedness did little to educate Americans to the realities of the time (Robert Osgood, *Ideals and Self-Interest in American Foreign Relations* [Chicago: University of Chicago Press, 1964]), others saw a campaign motivated by an ideal of public service (John Clifford, *The Citizen Soldiers* [Lexington, Ky.: University Press of Kentucky, 1972]). Yet another interpretation viewed the preparedness movement as part of the contemporary Progressive search for modernization and an opportunity to reinvigorate the nation through discipline and martial values (John Finnegan, *Against the Specter of the Dragon: The Campaign for American Military Preparedness, 1914–1917* [Westport, Conn.: Greenwood Press, 1975]). Finally, Michael Pearlman argued, in *To Make Democracy Safe for America* (Champaign: University of Illinois Press, 1984), that preparedness efforts grew from the personal, psychological, and domestic concerns of upper-class males from the northeastern region of the country and did not generate wide-based public support until after the sinking of the *Lusitania*. Richard Weiss termed this interpretation "the patrician as patriot." Chambers, in *To Raise and Army*, 300–301, offered a quick but useful summary of the historiographical landscape. Isaacson and Thomas quoted John McCloy, later to win renown as one of the eastern establishment's "Wise Men," recalling his time at the Plattsburgh summer camps: "It seemed to me that all the right people went." See Isaacson and Thomas, *Wise Men*, 69–70.

22. By the end of 1916, for example, at least 89 Harvard men, 26 Yalies, and 8 undergraduates from Princeton had driven for the American Field Service, along with volunteers from about another fifty colleges. Many more drove for the Norton-Harjes ambulance operation. See Berry, *Make the Kaiser Dance*, 266–67. The flow of American volunteers to the Western Front was also discussed in Harries and Harries, *Last Days of Innocence*, 41–48.

Nonetheless, relief efforts to aid the Allies commenced almost immediately, and by 1915, many graduates called on the university to be more active in preparing for possible American involvement. Significantly, Yale president Arthur Hadley seemed "enthralled and excited by the preparedness movement," and he praised military training for students.[23]

As early as April 1915, Hadley called for national preparedness, and later that year, he declared military training should have a place on college campuses. Addressing Yale alumni in Cleveland, he argued that the best way to keep the peace was to prepare for war. After visiting Plattsburgh in August 1915 and speaking with General Wood, Hadley in the fall announced plans to establish a field artillery battery on campus, and more than 1,000 undergraduates rushed to volunteer for the 486 available places. The faculty eventually voted to establish a Reserve Officers' Training Corps unit, a proposal backed overwhelmingly (1,112 to 288) by the student body. The National Security League sponsored mass demonstrations, and preparedness and interventionist speakers including Henry Stimson and Adm. Bradley Fiske addressed undergraduates. In the winter of 1916–17, after years of urging neutrality, William Howard Taft admitted that war could no longer be avoided.

It was in this environment that two dozen Yale students and recent alumni coalesced in 1916–17 to create an aerial defense squadron. The First Yale Unit began as the brainchild of F. Trubee Davison. After his freshman year at college, Davison spent the summer of 1915 in war-torn Paris driving an ambulance. During those months, he met many prominent participants in the effort, including several combat fliers. He first envisioned organizing a volunteer ambulance unit at Yale but later determined to establish an aviation detachment instead. This concept dovetailed with contemporary proposals by John Hayes Hammond Jr., of the Aero Club of America, and Rear Admiral Robert Peary to create a series of aerial coastal patrol groups to protect American shores in case of war.[24]

---

23. George Pierson's *Yale College: An Educational History, 1871–1921* (New Haven, Conn.: Yale University Press, 1952), 447–65, provides a good overview of the Yale community and the coming of World War I. Brooks Kelley, in *Yale — A History* (New Haven, Conn.: Yale University Press, 1974), 348–50, observed, "Yale men were not of one mind about the great war."

24. The story of the First Yale Unit is related in exhaustive detail in Paine, *First Yale Unit*. See also Marc Wortman, *The Millionaires' Unit: The Aristocratic Flyboys Who Fought the Great War and Invented American Air Power* (New York: Public Affairs, 2006), for a modern retelling of the exploits of this group.

By the spring of 1916, Davison had enlisted the support of several young comrades, including Harry Davison, Robert Lovett, Artemus "Di" Gates, Erl Gould, and John Vorys. Riding the wave of preparedness enthusiasm, he also gained the backing of influential private benefactors. Davison approached the Navy Department concerning his scheme and received modest encouragement, though no official support. Nonetheless, in July 1916, the fledgling group commenced training at aviation enthusiast Rodman Wanamaker's Trans-Oceanic seaplane facility at Port Washington, New York, under the tutelage of pioneer flier David McCulloch.[25] Of the dozen college boys who trained that summer, three soloed. Some of them also participated in naval reserve exercises.

Encouraged by the group's successes, Davison and his mates increased their efforts to gain additional recruits after classes resumed at Yale—among them David Ingalls, just arrived in New Haven and still only seventeen— while intensifying discussions with the navy. In late winter 1917, when entry into the European war seemed inevitable, members of the group, now grown to more than two dozen volunteers, made plans to leave school and enlist. They did so with the support of President Hadley and Dean of Students Frederick Jones. On March 24, 1917, the Yale fliers traveled to New London, Connecticut, to complete the process. A few days later, they boarded a train to Palm Beach, Florida, to initiate instruction.

Commencement of unrestricted submarine warfare the previous winter had pushed the reluctant administration past the breaking point, and even as Ingalls and the rest of the Yalies begin training in Florida, President Wilson addressed Congress, asking for a declaration of war against Germany. The navy and its infant aviation arm would soon be called upon to do their part to defeat the U-boat scourge. The need was huge, the dangers

---

25. Rodman Wanamaker, son of the founder of the Philadelphia department store of that name, was an aviation enthusiast and backer of many aeronautical ventures, including the transatlantic challenge posed by London's *Daily Mail*. The Curtiss-designed flying boat *America* (1914), ancestor of most American and British flying boats in World War I, resulted from that effort. See particularly William Trimble, *Hero of the Air: Glenn Curtiss and the Birth of Naval Aviation* (Annapolis, Md.: Naval Institute Press, 2010), 158–69, and Clark Reynolds, *Admiral John Towers: The Struggle for Naval Air Supremacy* (Annapolis, Md.: Naval Institute Press, 1991), 74, 80–84. David McCulloch was an early American flier and chief pilot of Rodman Wanamaker's Trans-Oceanic Company of Port Washington, New York. He enlisted in the navy following the outbreak of war, served at NAS Hampton Roads, and was assigned as first pilot on the NC-3 in its transatlantic attempt in May 1919.

great, and the threat mortal. In the first half of 1917, shipping losses to enemy submarines surged to intolerable levels, reaching nearly nine hundred thousand tons in April. Continued losses of that magnitude would quickly bring Britain to its knees. But in the opening days of hostilities, American naval aviation could not challenge the U-boat. Total flying resources consisted of a few dozen obsolete and obsolescent training aircraft; a lone underpowered, overweight dirigible; two balloons; a single under-staffed and underfunded training facility at Pensacola, Florida; two score fliers (but none who had seen combat); and a few hundred enlisted ratings. The navy possessed neither aviation doctrine nor plans. No blueprints for wartime expansion existed, either for personnel or equipment.

Although the navy made modest technical progress in the years after the first fragile airplane took off from an anchored warship in 1910, it still lagged woefully behind the European combatants. In 1916, its three lonely assistant naval attachés posted to Berlin, Paris, and London supplied limited, circumscribed information about conditions in the war zone. A single lieutenant in the offices of the Aid for Material on the staff of the Chief of Naval Operations handled aviation affairs in Washington. A simple description of naval aviation activities in Europe reflects the degree to which the navy fell behind its future allies and enemies.[26]

By the spring of 1917, Britain's Royal Naval Air Service (RNAS) operated a growing number of coastal bases stretching from Scotland to the south coast of England and Dunkirk in France, and in April 1917, it

---

26. Several good overviews of U.S. naval aviation activities in the prewar period exist, including Archibald D. Turnbull and Clifford L. Lord, *History of United States Naval Aviation* (New Haven, Conn.: Yale University Press, 1949); Clifford Lord's typescript, multivolume administrative history of naval aviation in the period 1898–1939 prepared shortly after World War II (available in the aviation history section, NHHC); and Clark Reynolds, *Admiral John H. Towers*, which details Towers's work as assistant naval attaché in London in the period 1914–16 and his duties as the sole aviation officer on the chief of naval operations staff in 1916–17. In June 1916, Britain's Royal Naval Air Service counted nearly thirteen thousand officers and men and more than one thousand aircraft, with additional massive expansion programs under way. France and Germany also built up powerful naval aviation forces. For a crisp summary of the role of naval aviation in the 1914–18 period, as well as comparative statistics for all the naval aviation services, see Layman, *Naval Aviation in the First World War*. Development of naval aviation under wartime conditions in Europe can also be traced in Lee Kennett, *The First Air War, 1914–1918* (New York: Free Press, 1991); Abbatiello, *Anti-Submarine Warfare in World War I*; and Terry Treadwell, *The First Naval Air War* (Stroud, U.K.: Tempus Publishing, 2002).

initiated the "spider web" antisubmarine patrols over the North Sea. The
Royal Navy's air arm also employed several land-based squadrons on the
Western Front, carrying out patrol, reconnaissance, and bombing missions;
its aircraft inventory included modern Sopwith Camels and Triplanes,
Handley Page heavy bombers, and huge Curtiss-derived Felixstowe flying boats. The RNAS also possessed a large fleet of SS-type airships, along
with a well-developed network of training facilities. Kite balloons operated regularly with the fleet. Naval aviators carried out combat missions in the Aegean Sea, at the Dardanelles, and in Egypt, East Africa, and
elsewhere. The RNAS had mounted bombing raids against German air-
ship facilities at Friedrichshafen, Cologne, Dusseldorf, and Cuxhaven and
against munitions and industrial targets, as well as airborne torpedo attacks
at Gallipoli. Britain led the way in marrying aircraft to the fleet, deploying
more than a dozen balloon ships, seaplane carriers, and prototype-hybrid
aircraft carriers. One of these warships, *Engadine,* played a small role at the
battle of Jutland. More sophisticated vessels were on the way. Other in-
novations included aircraft with folding wings, designed for easy, onboard
stowage; internal air bags to keep downed machines afloat; and use of
scout planes aboard battleships and cruisers by means of turret-mounted
launching platforms.

Though the RNAS developed the biggest forces, other nations followed suit. Germany built the largest fleet of rigid airships (zeppelins),
which conducted extensive scouting/reconnaissance missions for the
High Seas Fleet and launched heavy bombing raids against London and
other British sites. Germany also constructed numerous seaplane bases on
home soil, along the Baltic coast, and in Belgium, and from these locations, it operated the world's most sophisticated floatplane fighters. In
April 1917, German naval air forces initiated a series of torpedo attacks
against Allied shipping in the Dover Straits. France constructed a string
of antisubmarine patrol stations to guard the English Channel, Bay of
Biscay, and Mediterranean Sea, and its naval forces employed kite balloons during convoying operations. Italy developed the speedy, highly
maneuverable Macchi flying boat fighters, based on an Austro-Hungarian
prototype, and conducted a back-and-forth struggle across the narrow
reaches of the Adriatic Sea. In 1916, Austro-Hungarian seaplanes sank a
British submarine moored in Venice and shortly thereafter fatally damaged a French submarine at sea. As early as 1915, Russian naval forces in

the Black Sea labored, with some success, to sever Turkish sea-lanes, utilizing up to three seaplane carriers.

It was in the shadow of these developments that the United States entered the fray in April 1917. Under forced draft, naval aviation eventually amassed forty thousand officers and enlisted men, augmented by thousands of aircraft and dozens of bases, schools, and supply facilities in Europe and the United States. By autumn 1918, navy fliers were ready to make substantial contributions to the war effort, but the armistice intervened. In the short run, however, before such a force could be assembled and deployed, the country necessarily relied on the efforts of individuals such as David Ingalls and hastily organized groups such as the First Yale Unit to carry out its evolving aeronautical campaign.

1

Training with the First Yale Unit
March–September 1917

David Ingalls spent his initial months in the navy training with the First Yale Unit in Florida and on Long Island, New York, a process directed by Lt. Edward McDonnell, a 1912 graduate of the U.S. Naval Academy (USNA), where he became a champion boxer. McDonnell served at Vera Cruz, Mexico, in 1914 and received the Medal of Honor for heroism under fire. He began flight instruction at Pensacola a few months later and earned his designation as "Naval Aviator #18" (NA #18) in September 1915. In the spring of 1917, the navy ordered him to Palm Beach to direct training of the newly enrolled Yale fliers, assisted by civilians David McCulloch and Caleb Bragg, a small crew of petty officers and mechanics, and an assortment of civilian aides and staff. At the time, the college boys occupied Rodman Wanamaker's southern Trans-Oceanic facilities on Lake Worth and boarded at the Hotel Salt Air in West Palm Beach.[1]

Work for the Yalies began immediately upon arrival, with the site and aircraft guarded by local militia. Divided into small crews, the neophytes studied signaling, Lewis machine guns, motor work, dual instruction, and finally solo flight, utilizing Curtiss F Boats—small, two-place, pusher-type, single-engine flying boats.[2] Artemus "Di" Gates, who had flown in 1916, led David Ingalls's crew, which also included Kenneth MacLeish, Kenneth

---

1. Caleb Bragg, Yale '08, gained famed as an automobile racer in the prewar era; took up flying; and kept an airplane at Palm Beach, where he spent the winters. He was an expert motor mechanic and during World War I became director of flight activities at the army's McCook Field in Dayton, Ohio. The seventy-four-room Hotel Salt Air, erected in 1913 in West Palm Beach, provided accommodations for Yale Unit members for most of their stay in Florida. The building no longer stands.

2. The Curtiss F Boat was developed in the prewar period and used as a training craft by the navy throughout the conflict.

Smith, and Robert "Pat" Ireland.[3] Ingalls made his inaugural flight in early April, accumulating two hours of dual instruction in the first week, and he soloed on May 8. By late July, the unit logbook documented Ingalls's nearly fifty hours in the air.

McDonnell's work with the Yale Unit in Florida and later in New York mirrored similar ad hoc efforts in many parts of the country. Lacking sufficient capacity at its single training station in Pensacola, the navy turned to a variety of stopgap measures until larger facilities and formal courses of instruction began functioning. A group of Harvard students and a few others trained at the Curtiss Flying School in Newport News, Virginia. A second Yale unit commenced instruction in Buffalo and a third at Mastic, New York. State naval militia units began work at Bay Shore, New York, and Squantum, Massachusetts. Several Princeton fliers gathered in Rhode Island before transferring to Royal Flying Corps schools in Canada. These soon-to-be pilots, joined by a group of enlisted personnel just beginning a course of instruction in France, provided the backbone of early naval aviation efforts. The navy's frantic actions to speed aviators to the battlefield resembled the even larger campaign by the U.S. Army to supplement its still undeveloped training system. Four aerosquadrons' worth of pilots trained in Canada in the summer and fall of 1917. In September, the first of 450 fledglings departed for England for flight training. At the same time, hundreds more began receiving instruction in France and even Italy.[4]

But for most, the shooting war was still a long way off. Instead, the Yalies found Palm Beach a pleasant spot, and when not working, they enjoyed swimming, partying, hunting, athletics, various pranks, and relaxing. The group also began planning to relocate operations to northern

3. These men were: Artemus Lamb "Di" Gates, NA #65; Kenneth MacLeish, NA #74; Kenneth Rose "Scab" Smith, NA #87; and Robert Livingston "Pat" Ireland, NA #84.

4. The experiences of the Princeton-Canada contingent of navy fliers are detailed in J. Sterling Halstead, "A Mission to the Royal Flying Corps," *Naval Institute Proceedings* (February 1965): 78–94. The story of the Second Yale Unit is recounted in Ralph D. Paine, *The First Yale Unit: A Story of Naval Aviation, 1916–1919,* 2 vols. (Cambridge, Mass.: Riverside Press, 1925), 1:289–96. The enlisted First Aeronautic Detachment, led by daredevil Lt. Kenneth Whiting, represented the navy's effort to boost French morale by dispatching 122 untrained personnel and 7 officers to Europe in May 1917, to be used as their allies saw fit. Their experiences and important role in initiating combat operations "over there" are traced in Lawrence Sheely, ed., *Sailor of the Air: The 1917–1919 Letters and Diary of USN CMM/A Irving Edward Sheely* (Tuscaloosa: University of Alabama Press, 1993). The key policymaking role exercised by Lieutenant Whiting is outlined in Geoffrey

waters and in June shifted their base from Florida to the Castledge Estate at Huntington Bay, on Long Island, New York, not far from the Davison home at Peacock Point. Facilities there included hangars, runways, and machine shops accommodating a growing assortment of aircraft, including N-9, R-6, and Burgess-Dunne-type float seaplanes. Training continued; flight tests began in late July and extended into August. Soon, newly commissioned officers received orders dispersing them to Washington, Buffalo, Virginia, Florida, and elsewhere. Many headed overseas, with the first pair departing in mid-August. Ingalls followed a month later.[5]

Hotel Salt Air, West Palm Beach, Fla., April 29, 1917

My Dear Mother and Dad,

Today we rested and slept, thank goodness. It is Sunday and luckily tomorrow our instructors are going to fly to Miami so we shall have nothing to do. They tried it last Sunday but it didn't come off for some reason. It is to tell the truth a foolish project anyhow, as it does no-one any good except the fellows that are instructing.

Rossano, *Stalking the U-Boat: U.S. Naval Aviation in Europe in World War I* (Gainesville: University Press of Florida, 2010), 13–21. The life of the army pilots in Canada is well captured in Briggs Adams, *The American Spirit: The Letters of Briggs Kilburn Adams* (Boston: Atlantic Monthly Press, 1918). Adams was a Harvard graduate who enlisted in the RFC and trained in Canada in the summer and fall of 1917. For the Americans who reached England in the fall of 1917, the liveliest source is Elliott White Springs's classic *War Birds: Diary of an Unknown Aviator* (New York: Grosset and Dunlap, 1926), esp. 9–55. Instruction with the French is covered in George Moseley, *Extracts from the War Letters of George Clark Moseley During the Period of the Great War* (privately printed, 1923), esp. 40–108. A description of Americans training in Italy can be found in Rossano, "The Apprenticeship (How the Allies Trained the American Air Service)," *American Aviation Historical Society Journal* 28, no. 1 (Spring 1983): 29–30.

5. The navy developed the N-9 biplane trainer by modifying the famous Curtiss JN-4 "Jenny." Engineers reconfigured the basic aircraft as a floatplane, with a lengthened fuselage, broader wingspan, and enlarged tail surfaces. It served as an elementary training aircraft throughout the war. The navy used the Curtiss R-6 utility floatplane for both training and operational (patrol) purposes. Burgess-Dunne aircraft were manufactured in Marblehead, Massachusetts. The model mentioned in Ingalls's letters was a staggered-wing, pusher-type floatplane. Eighteen-year-old David Ingalls recorded his initial flight experiences in a series of letters written to his parents from Florida in the spring and summer of 1917. He did not begin keeping a diary until he boarded ship heading to Europe in late September.

Last night there was some excitement at the hangars. About two o'clock one of the soldiers on guard left his post to get a drink and on returning perceived a man stealing towards one of the machines. He immediately yelled halt and called the guard. The man ran out on the pier pursued by the guard who fired continually. All of them however fell over a rope anchoring a machine and before they got up the fellow had gotten far out into the lake in a speedboat. They fired some more till he was out of sight. This morning we all gazed with awe at the holes in trees, pier, ground, etc., from those simple soldiers' guns.

We had a fine week flying as the juniors had almost all gone North for their initiation, so we got a lot of flying. I am now in a squad with Caleb Bragg as our instructor. He is an old automobile racer and one of the best and most careful men in a flying machine I've seen. Since entering this squad I have learnt considerable. Our destination has at last been decided on. We are going to a place called Huntington on Long Island about fifteen miles from Glen Cove. It is an ideal place, well sheltered and equipped, and we ought to have a wonderful time there. Almost died yesterday of surprise for I got a letter from Al. He seems to be in pretty good spirits. I also hear that a lot of fellows including Brewster Jennings have been called for training in small boats to chase submarines. Brewster, the lucky dog, is stationed at Newport. He certainly does not miss much.[6] Mother, you needn't bother about keeping those photographs. It doesn't make any difference. If I get some good ones I'll keep them. Am thinking about getting some kind of Kodak like a Brownie to take pictures in the air. Much love, Dave

———

6. The absentees were Yale students being initiated into various secret fraternities and societies, such as Skull and Bones or Scroll and Key. A discussion of these groups and the role they played in the life of the university is contained in Walter Isaacson and Evan Thomas, *The Wise Men: Six Friends and the World They Made* (New York: Simon and Schuster, 1986), 81–82, 86, and Marc Wortman, *The Millionaires' Unit: The Aristocratic Flyboys Who Fought the Great War and Invented American Air Power* (New York: Public Affairs, 2006), 97–103, 136–38. Albert Ingalls, David's younger brother, was then at St. Paul's School in New Hampshire. Brewster Jennings attended St. Paul's and Yale, served in the navy during World War I, and received the Navy Cross. After the war, he became the founder and president of Socony-Vacuum Company, later Mobil. Jennings acted as a groomsman at Ingalls's wedding.

May 13, 1917

Dear Dad,

Today I just had a swim and some tennis, as we have a pretty darn good time on Sundays. Also received some good news. It has been definitely decided to go north on the 1st June to Huntington. We had a fine week last week. The weather was pretty good and what was even better I at last am flying alone for the last week. It is much more fun, as you can do anything you want, excepting that our Lieutenant [McDonnell] has absolutely forbidden anything but straight flying— no so-called trick flying. Until last Monday I had done nothing but practice starting, landings, and turns, especially landings, which for a beginner are about the hardest things. All but about ten or twelve fellows are now alone so we are really at last progressing. As soon as I got out alone I went up high—about 3,500 feet, as I never went up before, always been practicing landings. It is certainly great up there and you own the world when you get up alone and can do what you want. Up, except on a very rough day, there is almost nothing to do, as it is perfectly calm and I just set and looked down. It's funny but you never feel sick looking straight down and you can see for miles. I saw several tremendous fish in the ocean, as you can see down very far. There were a few small, light clouds, and I went through them; you can't see a thing and have to balance by feeling, which is pretty hard. Also a rain cloud or black clouds are full of puffs [of wind] and few people go through them.

I never enjoyed anything as much as going up there and guess I'll have to do it again soon. The only trouble being it takes a lot of time and you get no experience, as it is so calm, while from about 1,200 feet down there is almost always a lot to keep you busy, as even on a pretty calm day there are loads of puffs and pockets, so you are always on edge. Till Wednesday I took along a sand bag, but didn't from then on. It was to keep the balance the same, in place of the instructor. Our boat happens to be nose heavy, however, and it is very hard to fly alone, so we are always going to use a sand bag.

Wednesday I almost got into bad trouble. Having left the sand bag behind, the machine was very tail heavy with a tendency to climb and it was work to keep pushing down the "flippers" to go

level. Then when I started to come down from about 1,000 feet for
my first landing I started off at too steep an angle and went so fast
that my goggles began leaking and my eyes watered till I couldn't
see at all, so I leveled off to what seemed about right and pulled off
the glasses, so I could see all right, but being afraid of coming down
too steeply again I went to the other extreme and pancaked down
for the last 200 feet, much too flatly, losing all speed and thus use
of my controls. Fortunately, I appreciated it after dropping 100 feet
and made a good landing, but if I hadn't and a bad puff had hit me I
would have made a bad landing. Just after, when coming down again
to land a bad puff hit me and I got into a sort of sideslip—not a bad
one, and I got out of that all right. A sideslip is when you get rocked
over sidewise at such an angle that the machine starts to slide down
edge first. You seem to come to a stop in forward motion and it is a
horrible feeling.[7] Fortunately it was not a bad one, however, and I
righted the machine before it got much speed. Also it was high up.
Height is the most important thing, as if you should ever get into a
sideslip at about 100 or 200 feet before you could get out you would
hit the water sidewise, which would bust things up. That was a bad
day for me. I don't know why, one seems to fly rather erratically and
I made a lot of routine landings, in addition to the first one, which
was really dangerous. The lack of the sand bag helped in putting
the bow up and tail down on landing, also helped in my pancaking,
as I had to push the controls as far forward as possible to get out of
the pancaking, and then barely did. That afternoon the Lieutenant
took up our machine and made a rotten landing and said that we
always had to carry the sand bag, as it was hard to run it otherwise.
That sand bag certainly made a difference and I flew pretty well
then, and Friday, till our plane's engine busted and now we have to
put in a new one, and there being no engines ready, we had no flying
Saturday and won't get any till Tuesday.

---

7. *Flippers* was an informal term referring to the interplane ailerons positioned between the upper and lower wings on earlier models of the Curtiss F Boat. A pancake
landing is one where an aircraft in its final approach drops nearly straight down toward
the ground (or water), rather than gliding gently forward. A sideslip results when an
aircraft "slides" sideways through the air in a downward direction. Too severe a bank
can result in "falling off the wing" and then a potentially fatal spin.

It is funny how much feeling there is about flying. Everybody is jealous—talks about how others go and always count the bumps if anyone makes a bad landing. A bump is when you do not slip into the water just right and sort of bump into the air. A couple of inches difference in where you level off or a touch of the controls at not the right time will sometimes bump you up 30 feet or higher. Usually though you just go up a foot or two and that is a bad landing, but most everybody bumps sometime. I was certainly put in a better humor after flying so badly Wednesday when I saw everybody almost when they came in bump, and the Lieutenant gave them the deuce. Luckily I made a good landing coming in so that was all right. But someone else who was out saw me make some rotten ones and I got the—pretty well.

Well, Dad, I've got to go to dinner. Sorry I didn't write you before about what I was doing, but I wanted to fly alone first. Lots of Love, Dave

Ingalls Memoir re: Palm Beach

The first crew I was on was in charge of "Di" Gates, with "Ken" MacLeish, "Ken" Smith, and "Pat" Ireland. The competition was keen between crews. Each wanted to have the best machines and the most flying. So we went at it hard when anything needed fixing. To work one had to have tools, and to keep a machine in good shape you tried to find the best motor cover. "Di" would tell us to get something and leave us to go and get it. As burglars we were good. We became very clever at picking up good motor covers that were lying about. When we had wangled something we wished to keep we painted a big number on it. And friends were base enough to call us crooks!

There was never a thought about how much or how little we were working. The more we did the more we flew, and that was the mark we were shooting at. But it did come as a slight shock, after we had been there almost two months and had lugged gas and oil daily to the machines, to have Lotta Lawrence come wandering along with two empty cans and ask where a guy could procure some petrol.[8]

8. Ingalls was referring to George Francklyn "Lotta" Lawrence, NA #89.

According to Harry Davison:

One day Crock [Ingalls] and I certainly slipped it over the rest of the outfit. We got up long before it was light and went down to the machines. We got old Number 3 out just as dawn was breaking. Then we had one of the prettiest flights that ever happened, for about an hour. We went up about 3,000 feet and watched the sun rise. Everybody was terribly snotty about it when we came down. They all tried to work this same stunt, but Lieutenant McDonnell forbade it after that.[9]

U.S. Naval Reserve Flying Corps Detachment[10]
Huntington, Long Island, July 1917

Dear Mother and Dad,

Sorry not to have been able to write you before but we have had a busy time taking a test on a book by a man named Loening. Isn't it just the luck, since you left we have had wonderful flying weather and have been flying a lot. For instance yesterday I had two hours and my time is very short because they are giving extra to a lot such as Ireland, etc., to make them catch up. (I had been sick.) Thursday the two N-9 machines arrived and are now in commission. They are pontoon machines and pretty handy good machines. Also Monday we received a Wright Martin pontoon machine, a wonder.[11] More machines are coming soon. In a little more than a week we are going to take our tests for Naval air pilots, which I hope will not be hard. Saturday we had quite a

---

9. Quoted in Paine, *First Yale Unit,* 1:113.

10. In June, the Yalies packed their equipment, boarded the train, and headed to New York and their new base on the North Shore of Long Island. The Davisons and many of the unit's backers lived nearby, offering numerous opportunities for socializing, athletics, and other diversions.

11. The book mentioned is undoubtedly aviator Grover Loening's *Military Aeroplanes,* published in 1917 and used by the U.S. Army and U.S. Navy, the Royal Flying Corps, and the Canadian Armed Forces. The product of a short-lived venture between the Wright Company and the Glenn Martin Company, the Wright-Martin was a re-engined N-9 outfitted with a 150 hp Hispano-Suiza motor.

time, first in the afternoon several of us including little me flew over to the Davisons,[12] circled around the polo field a bit on which thousands had aggregated, and then landed, watched a base ball game between our team and one from Mineola, our side winning, then flew back. There was a lot of trick flying by the Mineola land machines, and at one time there were at least 25 or 30 machines up. It must have been quite a sight. Saturday night I had dinner at the Davisons and then went to a dance at H. P. Whitney's. Had a great time Sunday and came back that night on the yacht with all the wireless girls to accompany us.[13] Am feeling rather sleepy now as I went out to dinner Wednesday, Thursday, and Friday after you left, also last night, so have now sworn off parties with Harry. Must stop, lots of love, Dave

According to William Rockefeller:

We [Rockefeller, Ingalls, and MacLeish] made several flights over submarines operating in the [Long Island] Sound while they tested out various devices by means of which they hoped to be able to detect the presence of aircraft. Submarine officers also took flights with us

---

12. The Henry P. Davison estate at Peacock Point on the North Shore of Long Island is occupied by the Davison family to the present day.

13. During World War I, the army maintained large airfields on the Hempstead Plain at Mineola, New York, including Hazlehurst Field and Mitchell Field. Harry Payne Whitney, one of the millionaire supporters of the Yale Unit, was a noted sportsman, particularly in the area of thoroughbred horse racing. His Long Island estate was located near Wheatley Hills. Whitney married heiress and artist Gertrude Vanderbilt. Their daughter, Flora, eventually became engaged to Quentin Roosevelt, son of former president Theodore Roosevelt. The Wireless Girls, also known as the Girls Radio Unit, consisted of several young women who were part of the same social set as members of the Yale Unit. The group was organized by Mrs. H. P. Davison in April 1917, and the girls took lessons in New York City from Harry Chadwick, chief code instructor at the Marconi School. Members of the group included Alice Davison, Adele Brown, Priscilla Murdock, and Harriet Ransom. The group relocated to Huntington in June, under the instruction of Charles "Radio" Stewart. At this time, David Ingalls was a member of the informal 12:30 Club that squired the girls to nearby Huntington for milkshakes after morning radio lessons ended. Other swains included Al Sturtevant, Di Gates, and Bob Lovett. Not coincidentally, Gates later married Alice Davison and Lovett wed Adele Brown. See Paine, *First Yale Unit*, 1:172–77.

to observe the visibility of subs while submerged under different conditions. I had my one and only trip in a submarine at this time, as the officers kindly let us go out with them when we were not otherwise occupied. I don't want another ride. All I remember is a good deal of noise, being told I was under the Sound, seeing the water go through the little glass portholes in the conning tower, or whatever it is called, and coming up again.[14]

Reginald "Red" Coombe said of flying at Huntington:

The flying got a little smoother as time went on. . . . It was not an uncommon thing to see Ingalls flying upside down or doing tailspins in the largest boat.[15]

On Board *Whileaway,*[16] July 31, 1917

My Dear Mother,

Awfully sorry not to have had a second to write you before but we've been awfully hard worked. Also we've had a couple of accidents, about which I hope you won't worry. Harry had a fall from side slipping then nose dived from about 500 feet, and two days after Truby [Trubee Davison] did the same thing from about 300 feet. Harry was absolutely unhurt, thank goodness, but Truby was not so lucky as he did something to his back. The doctors say he

14. In July, David Ingalls, Ken MacLeish, and William Rockefeller traveled to the navy base in New London on temporary assignment to practice hunting submarines. Their stay lasted about a week. William Avery Rockefeller, NA #81, was a great-nephew of Standard Oil titan John D. Rockefeller. Quoted in Paine, *First Yale Unit,* 1:155–56. New London had been a center of submarine experimentation and operations since before World War I and remains so to this day.

15. Quoted from an after dinner talk given at the Brook Club in New York City in June 1924. The transcript is located in Davison Papers, Yale University Archives.

16. Sportsman H. P. Whitney loaned his elegant 175-foot, $250,000 steam yacht *Whileaway,* launched in 1915, to the First Yale Unit during its stay at Huntington, New York.

will be alright in about three months.[17] So, as a result they have let up on us a lot, as I believe they think the fellows were a bit tired. So today we are spending this afternoon on the boat and this morning I slept all morning. Now I am feeling fine and hope to take my test for naval pilot next Monday. About eight fellows, the ones who flew last summer, passed their tests Saturday, Sunday and Monday and most of them will be going to other places to instruct.[18] In about two weeks we'll probably be separated all over the country instructing. As soon as some decent machines are made, say two months, fifteen of us are probably going abroad first to instruct there. I don't know who will go. I hope you are having a great time, as good as I had last summer, also Al. Please give my love to all the Tafts. With love, Dave

Reg Coombe recalled:

I remember one day the phone rang up in the house and it was Washington on the wire. The news soon spread around and pretty soon all the Unit that were left were around that room waiting to hear what the news was, and the chief yeoman who was on the wire would repeat the orders as they came along: Landon, France; then a big yell; Ingalls, France, and so on.[19]

---

17. At the end of July, the entire group reeled when Trubee Davison, founder of the Yale Unit, crashed his aircraft during flight trials. Lieutenant McDonnell rescued Davison by diving into water and freeing him from the sinking machine. Anxious helpers took the injured flier aboard *Shuttle,* another of the yachts placed at the Yale Unit's disposal, and he was rushed to New York City for medical care. Dave Ingalls and Bob Lovett raced ahead by automobile to locate a surgeon. They reached Manhattan in fifty-five minutes, escorted by police the last part of the way. Though the doctor they sought was out visiting patients, Ingalls and Lovett tracked him down and drove him to St. Luke's Hospital. Trubee reached the New York Yacht Club landing, was quickly transferred to a waiting ambulance, and was hurried to the hospital. His injuries were far more serious than Ingalls supposed. He spent many months recuperating, did not complete flight training, and was never able to resume full active duty. To a greater or lesser extent, he was disabled for the rest of his life.

18. Ingalls passed all of his tests and was designated a naval aviator on August 14, 1917.

19. Quoted from an after dinner talk at the Brook Club on June 1924, transcript in Davison Papers, Yale University Archives.

A formal portrait of David Ingalls likely taken after the armistice, following his promotion to lieutenant. *Courtesy Ingalls Family Archives*

The First Yale Unit enlisted as a group in the U.S. Navy in late March 1917, even before Congress declared war on Germany. They quickly entrained for Florida, where they began training. The entire unit gathered for this group photograph later that spring. Ingalls is seated in the center of the second row, smiling at the camera. *Author's collection*

F. Trubee Davison, son of one of Wall Street's most powerful financiers, was the founder and guiding spirit of the First Yale Unit. His younger brother, Harry Davison, was Ingalls's closest friend in the group. Trubee was injured severely during flight certification in July 1917 and was at least partially disabled for the rest of his long life. *Courtesy Naval History and Heritage Command*

Artemus "Di" Gates, from Clinton, Iowa, was a Yale football star and a prominent member of the Yale Unit. He is shown here fashionably attired and ready to begin a flight aboard one of the Curtiss F Boats utilized for instructional purposes. Later in the war Gates and Ingalls served together at NAS Dunkirk, searching for submarines in the cold waters of the North Sea. *Courtesy Naval History and Heritage Command*

Unlike later graduates of U.S. Navy flight training, the Yale Unit never received formal ground school instruction. Instead, they listened to occasional lectures, received hands-on guidance from various instructors, and spent a lot of time watching and listening. Here a portion of the group is shown relaxing during one of their long days. Ingalls is on the right, next to Di Gates. *Courtesy Naval History and Heritage Command*

While in Florida the Yalies divided into organized crews for training purposes, each headed by a more experienced member of the Yale Unit. Ingalls was a member of Di Gates's Number 7 crew, shown here gathered next to their F Boat. Ingalls stands second from the left. *Courtesy Naval History and Heritage Command*

Each of the Yale Unit members first learned to fly in a Curtiss F Boat, a prewar design. This early flying boat was capable of speeds of 65–70 mph and could ascend to an altitude of 4,500 feet. Here a crew readies one of the unit's training aircraft for the day's instruction routine. *Courtesy Naval History and Heritage Command*

Lt. Eddie McDonnell, awarded the Medal of Honor for valor at Vera Cruz in 1914, provided guidance, instruction, and discipline to the Yale Unit as their commanding officer in the spring and summer of 1917. He is shown here (*right*) in Florida, standing next to Col. Lewis Thompson, the unit's business manager. *Courtesy Naval History and Heritage Command*

The Yalies' approach to military detail proved rather relaxed in Florida, as is evident in this photograph of the Unit gathered for muster. Ingalls stands third from the right. *Courtesy Naval History and Heritage Command*

In June 1917 the Yale Unit relocated their base of operation to Huntington, New York, close to Long Island Sound. Their bearing seems slightly more military. Perhaps Lieutenant McDonnell was having some effect. *Courtesy Naval History and Heritage Command*

The waterfront at Huntington was busy throughout the day as the group rushed to get in their required flying hours, practice new maneuvers, and prepare for flight qualification tests. This photograph, snapped in a quiet moment, shows the calm waters of Huntington Bay and the training aircraft ready for service, three F Boats and a twin-float R-6. *Courtesy Naval History and Heritage Command*

Conditions at Huntington were simple and the work sometimes hard. Here most of the Yale Unit, Ingalls included, lends a hand hauling a Curtiss R-6 trainer/scout aircraft out of the water and up the ramp. *Courtesy Naval History and Heritage Command*

After passing his flight tests and receiving his commission, the newly minted Ensign David Ingalls spent a few weeks at home in Cleveland before heading to Europe. He posed proudly in his new uniform in early September. *Courtesy Peter B. Mersky Collection*

Ingalls sailed to Europe in late September 1917 aboard the elderly liner SS *Philadelphia,* (former *City of Paris*). He referred to it as "a little thing.... I thought it was our tender." *Courtesy Naval History and Heritage Command*

Passing through submarine-infested waters thrilled and terrified passengers aboard trans-Atlantic vessels. Navy gun crews, shown here drilling aboard *Philadelphia* in summer 1917, provided some small measure of reassurance. Ingalls recorded, "Our ship also possessed four 4.7 guns, two aft and two forward. To care for these four crews of five sailors and one lieutenant, were stationed on board." *Courtesy Naval History and Heritage Command*

2

Early Days in Europe
September–December 1917

During the summer and early fall of 1917, several members of the Yale Unit received orders to proceed overseas, where the navy had begun creating an extensive system of patrol stations, flight schools, and supply bases from scratch. With aviation officers in very short supply, the Yale gang offered nearly the only available source of additional trained personnel. In fact, the navy had not yet dispatched a single flying officer to Europe for combat duty. A small force of 122 enlisted men, the First Aeronautic Detachment, reached France in early June, their exact training and mission yet to be determined. Four commissioned fliers accompanied them—Kenneth Whiting, Godfrey Chevalier, Virgil Griffin, and Grattan Dichman—with orders to oversee training of their enlisted charges. They later assumed a variety of administrative and staff positions. A few other aviators arrived during the summer, either to investigate conditions in Europe, to gather technical information, or to fill out expanding staffs in Paris and elsewhere. Until the navy's new ground and flight schools in the United States functioned smoothly, however, pilots to conduct antisubmarine missions necessarily came from the first college groups hastily trained in the spring and summer of 1917.[1]

---

1. The First Aeronautic Detachment formed at NAS Pensacola in early May 1917 under the command of Lt. Kenneth Whiting, NA #16, and departed for Europe at the end of the month. The men of this detachment reached the Continent in early June, the first organized U.S. military force to land in France. Their story is recounted in detail in Geoffrey Rossano, *Stalking the U-Boat: U.S. Naval Aviation in Europe in World War I* (Gainesville: University Press of Florida, 2010), 5–42. See also Lawrence Sheely, ed., *Sailor of the Air: The 1917–1919 Letters and Diary of USN CMM/A Irving Edward Sheely* (Tuscaloosa: University of Alabama Press, 1993), the published diary and letters

Bob Lovett and Di Gates of the Yale Unit departed first for the war zone, sailing to England in mid-August.[2] Fellow unit members John Vorys and Al Sturtevant soon followed.[3] A larger contingent, consisting of David Ingalls, Freddy Beach, Sam Walker, Ken Smith, Reginald Coombe, Chip McIlwaine, Henry Landon, and Ken MacLeish, received orders to travel in late September aboard the old liner *Philadelphia,* now pressed into service as a transport.[4] They all looked forward to their new duties with a mixture of excitement and trepidation. David Ingalls began keeping a diary, what he called "this simple book," while aboard *Philadelphia,* and with only a few interruptions, he continued to do so until the war ended fifteen months later.

Like so many Americans crossing the submarine-infested Atlantic in the fall of 1917, Ingalls experienced the exhilaration and occasional panic of traversing the war zone. According to cabinmate Henry "Hen" Landon, they heard many wild rumors and thrilling stories while aboard, so many that they slept in their clothes, with their .45 service Colts close by. When fellow aviator Ken Smith spotted a porpoise knifing through the waves, Landon "nearly died in [his] tracks," expecting an explosion to send their ship to the bottom.[5]

---

of one of the enlisted members of the unit. The officers included Lt. Grattan Dichman, NA #30; Lt. (jg) Godfrey deC. Chevalier, NA #7; and Lt. (jg) Virgil Griffin, NA #41. A similar process occurred with early army aviators. The first detachment of 53 American cadets reached Liverpool on September 2, 1918, and by December, more than 450 had made the trip. Of this group, 216 eventually flew with RAF squadrons, 90 were posted to the Allied Expeditionary Force (AEF), 20 transferred to France for further training, and 60 returned to the United States. The story of this "Lost Battalion" is engagingly related in Elliott White Springs, *War Birds: Diary of an Unknown Aviator* (New York: Grosset and Dunlap, 1926). A more academic treatment is contained in Rossano, "The Apprenticeship (How the Allies Trained the American Air Service)," *American Aviation Historical Society Journal* 28, no. 1 (Spring 1983): 22–26.

2. Both Lovett and Gates went on to successful postwar careers in finance and much additional government service. Robert Lovett labored as assistant secretary of war for air throughout World War II, then was undersecretary of state, deputy secretary of defense, and finally secretary of defense during the Korean War. Artemus Gates spent the World War II years as assistant secretary of the navy (AIR).

3. These were John Vorys, NA #73, and Albert Sturtevant, NA #77.

4. SS *Philadelphia* began life as the transatlantic liner SS *City of Paris,* launched in 1888. It served in the Spanish-American War as USS *Yale,* became a troop transport in World War I under the name SS *Philadelphia,* and was rechristened USS *Harrisburg* in 1918. MacLeish missed the boat and sailed to Europe aboard SS *New York* a few weeks later.

5. Quoted in Ralph D. Paine, *The First Yale Unit: A Story of Naval Aviation, 1916–1919,* 2 vols. (Cambridge, Mass.: Riverside Press, 1925), 2:2.

Despite such fears, the crossing proved relatively peaceful. Ingalls and the others landed safely in Liverpool, the great entrepôt on the Irish Sea, and had their first real contact with a nation at war. One enlisted sailor on his way to NAS Dunkirk called Liverpool "a quaint looking old city," nothing like those at home, lacking skyscrapers and featuring crooked streets "that could break a snake's back."[6] Newly arrived Americans spotted women working everywhere, out in the streets and in all the stores. Then it was on to London, where Ingalls and his companions toured the metropolis and began their naval duties, sometimes with comical results. They found the wartime scene eye opening—railroad stations crowded with troops and ambulances full of casualties just back from the front. Ubiquitous wounded soldiers sported blue stripes on their sleeves that indicated they could not purchase alcohol; authorities claimed abstinence promoted convalescence. Only a few months removed from happier college days, the Americans sensed despair in the populace.[7]

Ingalls and the others quickly checked in at the Savoy Hotel and readied themselves to report to navy headquarters at 30 Grosvenor Gardens. This formal duty required being properly turned out, a task somewhat beyond the ken of recently minted ensigns. Ingalls and two friends appeared in the service's new forest green aviators' uniforms, with Sam Browne belts and swagger sticks. The others donned dress blues, yellow gloves, and swords, but they could not quite figure out how to wear the ceremonial weapons. A few sarcastic remarks from headquarters staff sent the youngsters packing with, according to Ken Smith, "our tails between our legs."[8]

6. See Alonzo Hildreth, "Over There—World War I," *All Hands,* Bureau of Naval Personnel Information (June 1962), 56–63. Hildreth later served with Ingalls at NAS Dunkirk in the spring of 1918.

7. Each visitor experienced a slightly different facet of the vast London metropolis. In late August 1917, Di Gates reported having a "slick time" but noticed American soldiers in the streets wearing the sloppiest uniforms, and he commented on the shortage of both bread ("two small rolls allowed at a meal, poor quality") and sugar ("practically no cake or pastry"). Chip McIlwaine, who had vacationed in the British capital before, observed, "Place has changed a lot, doesn't seem to have that air of intense respectability that London always impressed me with, streets a mass of brown soldiers home on leave, wounded, recruits, at night pitch dark, lights shaded to cast only below, all shades drawn." Like most well-fed Americans, he remarked on the supply situation: "Certain food restrictions as to bread and sugar only, no longer any meatless days, they've shut down the serving of liquor also, the hours being 12:30–2:30 and 6:30–9:30, during those periods an immense amount of drinking, much more than in Paris." John Vorys reported, "Not hunger pinched but living on war rations, poor bread and very little sugar." See Gates to Davison, August 26, 1917; Vorys to Davison, September 25, 1917; and McIlwaine to Davison October 26, 1917, all in Davison Papers, Yale Archives.

8. For an account of this misadventure, see Paine, *First Yale Unit,* 2:6–8.

Embarrassed but unbowed, they visited British military facilities before continuing on to Paris. On October 9, Ingalls departed London, headed for the Continent via a Channel steamer out of Southampton. The crowded vessel carried hordes of soldiers returning to the front, nurses, and civilian officials, and accommodations could not be found. Instead, the Americans made the best of it, eventually landed at Le Havre, and attempted to negotiate customs and baggage handlers with a working vocabulary of only three or four French words. After an interminable railroad journey, they reached Paris at three o'clock in the morning, piled into a small fleet of decrepit taxicabs, and eventually washed ashore at the Grand-Hôtel.

War-torn France presented an arresting and varied tableau. George Moseley, a football star at Yale and friend of many in Ingalls's unit, noted that "women customs officials and examiners were the first sign we had of the lack of men." Continental timekeeping also intrigued him, with its "22 hours 40 minutes instead of 10:40," and a visit to the barbershop proved dispiriting, "full of common French soldiers, the poilus in their blue uniforms. . . . They seemed very sad, never smiling, and lonely talking now and then." Moseley could not escape wartime realities: "I noticed a number of women who were standing back of me (they were all in mourning, nearly all the women in France are in mourning)." Bob Lovett echoed these maudlin observations. Writing home to the convalescing Trubee Davison, he reported, "The condition of France you would be heartbroken. She is staggering with the weight of the war's toll, but even more to my mind under graft, honest to goodness rotten politics, and self-interests. . . . We have heard stories about men shooting their officers from sheer desperation rather than spend another winter in the hell of the front."[9]

---

9. See George Moseley, *Extracts from the War Letters of George Clark Moseley During the Period of the Great War* (privately printed, 1923), 32–36. Many visitors chronicled the war's impact on social proprieties. Ken MacLeish learned that wherever he went in Paris, women approached him and grabbed his arm—"very persistent!" At one point, Di Gates remarked how nice it was "to see some real American girls instead of these painted French beauties whose characters are always doubtful." Evelyn Preston, a member of the Yale social set who was then in Paris, offered a woman's perspective, observing, "The boys . . . have a hell of a gay time (excuse my language but you know what I mean). Of course I've given up trying to understand it, how nice respectable boys can suddenly break loose and find their fun that way." A few months later, Bob Lovett, then on the staff at Paris headquarters and living with Lt. Eddie McDonnell, informed his friends, "[We] are living together at present and are going to take a little apartment in the Latin Quarters among the long haired men and short haired women." Quoted in Geoffrey Rossano, *The Price of Honor: The World War One Letters of Naval Aviator Kenneth MacLeish* (Annapolis, Md.: Naval Institute Press, 1991), 67, 114. Lovett's remarks about men shooting their officers referred to the mutinies that convulsed the French army in May and June 1917.

After reporting to aviation headquarters at 23 Rue de la Paix,[10] Ingalls and the recent arrivals received orders, somewhat to their surprise, to head down to the infant navy school at Moutchic, about thirty miles from Bordeaux near the Bay of Biscay, rather than the French school at Tours where earlier aviation candidates had trained. There, they would learn to pilot larger aircraft such as the Franco-British Aviation (FBA) and Donnet-Denhaut flying boats,[11] similar to the types purchased for use at American patrol stations then under construction along the coast.

Sunday, September 23, 1917. This was a bit of a gloomy day, saying goodbye to Mother and Dad at the dock.[12] Unlike the good Lord we seemed to have picked on the seventh day to start our work. But then we had no personal choice, nor did we know ahead of time, for the powers that be figured out the only way to keep the Huns from knowing when a boat was to sail was not to know themselves. But here were most of the other seven who were to go to France on the *Philadelphia* of the American Line. [Freddy] Beach, [Sam] Walker, [Reg] Coombe, [Hen] Landon, [Chip] McIlwaine, [Scab] Smith. [Ken] MacLeish was not there, nor did he come later, but missed the boat and probably took the next ship.[13] When I arrived at the dock with my mother and father and saw a boat tied up there I thought it was a tender to take us out to our own ship. And then the little thing turned out to be the

10. Lt. Kenneth Whiting originally occupied space at the elegant Hôtel Meurice and then established naval aviation headquarters at 23 Rue de la Paix. Whiting soon gave way to Cdr. Hutch Cone. In November, Cone relocated headquarters to the Hôtel d'Iéna, 4 Place d'Iéna.

11. The FBA Type A flying boat was powered by a 130 hp Clerget rotary motor. The Donnet-Denhaut flying boat, most likely the DD-8 model, was equipped with a 200 hp Hispano-Suiza motor. Both were slow, cranky, undependable machines.

12. After completing work at Huntington Bay, Ingalls received a short furlough that he spent at home in Cleveland, accompanied by neighbor, friend, and fellow Yale aviator Robert Ireland. He visited relatives, relaxed, and attended various social events. His parents later traveled to New York to wish him bon voyage. See *Cleveland Plain Dealer*, September 1, 1917.

13. Ingalls was referring to Charles Frederic Beach, NA #75; Samuel Sloan Walker, NA #86; Reginald Gordon "Red" Coombe, NA #92; Henry Hutton Landon, NA #93; Archibald Graham "Chip" McIlwaine, NA #82; and Kenneth "Scab" Smith, NA #87.

good ship *Philadelphia* and it was actually our liner. All I'd read
about the luxurious liners had given me great ideas. All that kept
me going was that I'd also read about Columbus and his skiff.

We all got on board with our luggage at about 10:00 and
then had to hang around till finally at about 12:30 we pulled
out. There were quite a few people, all feeling perhaps a bit
low, standing on the wharf as we left. Our ship was painted
camouflage—a most awful looking variety of colors probably
as much to frighten the Germans as to make the ship offer no
definite object to a man training a gun upon it. Our ship also
possessed four 4.7 guns, two aft and two forward. To care for
these four crews of five sailors and one lieutenant, were stationed
on board.[14] They were fine men, especially the Lieut. Reef-Kahl,
who offered a bit of advice at odd moments during the trip. We
got out of sight of land rapidly, passing numerous transports filled
with soldiers destined for fame in France. On board there were
34 army men, medical, ordnance, and quartermaster department,
four or five women, a few English returning diplomats and
ourselves and the crew. Also a few second class. I thought they
had the boat going the wrong way. If I'd been in charge I'd have
been shipping this crowd to America to get them out of the way.

The next few days were most monotonous—rough, cloudy and
a lot of rain, we never saw the sun. We got ourselves settled as
we sailed. Hen Landon and I roomed together as far away as we
could get from fresh air. There was nothing to do but read the
Count of Monte Cristo and play bridge. However, we seven and
two diplomats on their way to The Hague, Charles Russell and
Lieut. Downs, and Lieut. Munn for Paris service, procured a table
to ourselves and had as good a time as one could expect.[15] Except
for Freddy Beach, everyone was always on deck. Downs afforded
more amusement than any clown—for he was always giving

14. Most transatlantic vessels pressed into wartime service, a total of 384 merchant
ships, were armed with deck guns manned by navy crews. Ken MacLeish, destined to
be paired with David Ingalls in virtually all their training and duty assignments, sailed
to Europe aboard SS *New York* in late October, recording, "Today [October 29] we had
a boat drill, fire drill, and finally gun drill. Of the latter I can say very little except I'm
pleased and full of hope." See Rossano, *Price of Honor,* 33.

15. Charles Welles Russell was an American diplomat and lawyer.

advice, could answer any question, and was an authority on all matters. Found immediately that he was slated for the diplomatic service and decided that he was practicing his profession on us. He was also a bad bridge player and a rotten loser—the latter fact was proved every time we played till finally he concealed himself in the engine room or coal bin. Three days out, we entered the war zone and here Downs was a hero. He advised us, and as far as I could see everyone else on board, to get out of uniform and into civilian clothes as fast as possible, because the Germans after torpedoing our ship would come up and shell any life boat with officers in it. He himself changed into civilian clothes, but none of us did, either because we didn't particularly care or because we were too proud of our uniforms, probably the latter. Everyone gave him the "rahs" all the time, especially Chip, who is rather good at that sort of thing anyway.

About that time, too, we got acquainted with an Australian major, a great boy, who had some wonderful stories. I sometimes wondered whether he had ever heard them before himself. He had lost a leg and received the D.S.O. and was now on his way to enlist in the R.F.C. It seems as though everything in the future will be known by initials. RFC means Royal Flying Corps. DSO means Distinguished Service Cross primarily. Secondarily its meaning is—unmentionable here.

We also became distantly acquainted with a few of the soldiers who were about the crudest bunch I ever saw. Except for a few majors who had been in service they would have been a disgrace to the Devil. The few women on board may have been of a good sort, but Scab Smith was the only one who knows. But at any rate they got up a very punk concert and made $200 for a seamen's home.[16]

---

16. It was common practice during wartime transatlantic crossings to conduct im-promptu auctions, raffles, and benefits to raise money for various charities and relief programs. George Moseley, a Yale football star well known to the Yale Unit crowd, crossed to Europe aboard SS *Chicago* a few weeks before Ingalls made the journey. He described "a big day on board. . . . They gave a big benefit for the Red Cross in France. There were all kinds of games in the afternoon, a concert and an auction sale during the evening . . . which cleared over $600.00." See Moseley, *Extracts from the War Letters,* 28. Other passengers included two of ex-president Theodore Roosevelt's sons, Theodore Jr. and Archibald.

Nobody else on board got very clubby with us, but we didn't particularly care, as we certainly hoped that they and we would not go to the same place when we got abroad anyway. As soon as we entered the war zone the weather became perfect and the wonderful days and the full moon scared everyone to death lest the Germans spot us.

Of course as soon as we entered the war zone the weather became perfect and Downs was apparently right when he said that the wonderful days and nights with full moon shining down were most advantageous for the Germans. The night we entered the zone, everyone sat up, especially Downs, till about 1:30! Then Hen Landon and I had a long debate as to whether we should wear our life preservers or our automatics to bed with us. We decided to carry the guns. Then we went to bed and in about five minutes Chip burst in to announce that three destroyers had been sighted and were to convoy us. So we slept well. The weather for the next three days of the trip was great and we enjoyed it immensely. The army officers kept watch to no purpose except [to] satisfy their vanity. Although we offered our services, the lieutenant didn't need them. We sighted probably three subs, one of which came up about 50 yards off by miscalculation and because we were continually zigzagging, and so fortunately missed us. We sighted land Monday but had to lay at anchor on account of lateness of hour, just outside the bar.[17]

Tuesday [October 2, 1917]—We awakened to find ourselves at anchor in the river just opposite the landing stage [Liverpool].[18] But owing to the large number of ships we could barely land at a dock about 1:45. So we got off and easily got through the customs, found our way by a devious path to the Adelphia Hotel. Storing our luggage, we started off, Scab and I, to look the place over. Then we started to examine England. It is a Hell of a place. At the first store we came upon we purchased sticks and for the rest of the day felt like

17. After a relatively uneventful passage of nine days, *Philadelphia* reached Liverpool, England, on October 2, 1917.

18. The landing stage at Liverpool was a massive, lengthy floating dock affixed to the riverfront wharf that accommodated large vessels, especially passenger liners, by mitigating the inconvenience caused by the great rise and fall of the tide.

asses.[19] The streets were full of men in khaki, and lots of wounded and convalescent in their light blue uniforms. It looked as though the whole English army had been shot up. It made us both feel pretty low to look at these latter. After [piping?] everything in this hole we returned as arranged to the Adelphia and had tea. Here we saw the elite of Liverpool and weren't elated. Here too for the first time we suffered privation—we could have but one lump of sugar per person and very little toast. In fact the tea was no success. However we chatted a bit with a couple of U.S. Lieutenants near by and were a bit cheered up. After this we took the 5:20 to London, arriving at about 11:00. We found taxis for our luggage and put up at the Savoy as Scab said we needed gaiety.[20]

Wednesday [October 3, 1917]—We got up at 10:00 and shopped till lunch, which we had at the Savoy. I felt like the deuce but perked up about lunchtime. After lunch we met a Capt. Libby, R.F.C., who is a peach and is going to U.S. as a Major in Army flying. He doped up a big party for the next night, he, and a Scotch lieutenant in our navy, named Schoen. We slipped up to the Lieut.'s room and they all drank. Chip held up the honor as Scab and I weren't in their class. Then we had tea and a big dinner—same bunch as on ship and saw "Chu Chin Chou," which was punk. After it we all went to Murray's and danced with the worst dancers, ugliest girls I ever had the misfortune to be near.[21] Some British navy lieutenant urged us to come to Albert's rooms to a dance, first ditching the

---

19. The sticks were most likely swagger sticks, short canes carried tucked under the arm, used by British officers and noncommissioned officers (NCOs) to denote authority.

20. A London luxury hotel located on the Strand embankment, the Savoy first opened in 1889.

21. Frederick Libby, with twenty-four aerial victories in the Royal Flying Corps, eventually served in the U.S. Army Air Service but did not return to combat due to failing health. He authored a postwar memoir entitled *Horses Don't Fly. Chu Chin Chou,* a fabulously popular musical comedy by Oscar Asche and Frederic Norton, premiered in London in August 1916 and ran for five years and 2,238 performances. An American version opened in October 1917. Life could not have been so burdensome for the Americans. Bob Lovett later recalled, "I believe it was reported in Paris that from the proceeds of this crowd's contributions to Murray's dance hall in London, enough surplus remained to add another room to that building so that 'Chip' McIlwaine might have more space in which to shake himself and his partner." Quoted in Paine, *First Yale Unit,* 2:6. Murray's on Beak Street opened in 1913, largely due to the efforts of American Jack May. The London facility closed in the summer and reopened as Murray's River Club near Maidenhead on the Thames.

present low ladies. Personally I couldn't see any difference in them
and those at the latter dance. Here there was lots of champagne
and most of the crude crowd partook. I danced once with a little
kipper who was as fruity as the rest and then went home to a good
bed with Scab. Unfortunately we didn't lock the door and I woke
up to find the light on and a girl pulling Ken out of bed. It seems
they had come back from the party with the navy officer and were
finishing it up in a room near us. Ken went in there but to my
infinite relief in a few minutes came back and advised that he had
turned out the lights and slipped out, locking them in.

Thursday [October 4, 1917]—Shopped all day and wrote letters
that night as I couldn't stand the party that the rest went on.
Went to attaché.[22]

Friday [October 5, 1917]—Walked a lot and saw a couple of shows
in afternoon and night, ordered a uniform at Burberry's and some
wings. Lunch at Claridges was very good.[23] Also went to attaché
and at last got some dope. We are to go to France and go to two
schools, one first for about four hours in F.B.A. and then to the
Mediterranean for real practice. After the show at night I returned
to bed but the rest of course went on a [bat?]. Poor Devils.

---

22. This was a reference to the naval attaché at the U.S. embassy at Grosvenor
Gardens, Capt. William MacDougall, who occupied the post from November 1916
until December 1917. Ingalls's brief comment in no way captures the notoriety this
event achieved in Yale Unit lore. The young ensigns, completely unfamiliar with naval
etiquette, reported in a mishmash of uniforms and accessories, failing utterly to wear
their swords properly. Bob Lovett noted, "The standing joke on the Unit ... described
the strange manner in which Coombe, McIlwaine, and a couple of others reported
to London headquarters. . . . Captain MacDougall said that his staff spent the most
hilarious ten minutes he ever remembers when these fine looking and exceedingly
natty officers strode into the room with their swords hind part before. . . . They created
a lasting impression, and had it not been for the fact that Dave Ingalls wore the same
uniform for thirteen months, the entire Unit would have gained an enviable reputation as the Beau Brummels of the air." McIlwaine recalled that he, Ingalls, and Smith
had purchased Sam Browne belts and swagger sticks and sauntered into headquarters
(HQ) and "somehow got away with it." Concerning the sartorial travails of the others,
he claimed, "Smith, Ingalls, and I enjoyed the show immensely." See Paine, *First Yale
Unit,* 2:5–8.

23. Claridge's was and still is a luxury hotel on Brook Street in the Mayfair district
of London. The present building dates to 1894.

Saturday, October 6, 1917. Left at 11:30 and went to Felixstowe to the RNAS station there.[24] We were met by a couple of autos and officers and from then on were treated like princes. There a lot of officers took us in charge and showed us around and told us some good stories of their work. This is a big station [RNAS Felixstowe] with 24 pilots and lots of men. The hangars are in wonderful shape with dugouts around because of the Boche raids. The first thing they sprang on us was the Porte or "Baby," a boat of 136 [124]-foot spread, and three 290-hp Rolls Royces. The most gigantic machines I ever saw carrying six men—two pilots as they go out for five or six hours a day at a time. They carry fuel for eight hours and each motor uses 25 gallons per hour. They have four Lewis guns that can fire in almost every direction. They make about 80 and can fly at 45. Next we saw the regular machines— somewhat smaller with two motors, three men, four guns, but still three or four times as big as our "F" boats. Besides these, there were several pontoon machines and one Sopwith "Pup," a peach of a land machine, little and just the first fighting machine I had ever seen. They also showed us the 230- and 100-pound bombs they carry, either two of the former or four of the latter.[25]

---

24. Felixstowe was described as a "favorite seaside resort," home to fifty-eight hundred permanent inhabitants, "with golf links, at the mouth of the Orwell [River] opposite Harwich." Quoted in Karl Baedeker, *Great Britain: Handbook for Travelers* (London: T. Fisher Unwin, 1910), 499. The principal operational and experimental RNAS facility on the North Sea, Felixstowe occupied a site across the harbor from the naval base at Harwich. One of the large flying boat hangars built during the war survives to this day and is used as a warehouse for the container port now covering the site of the former air station.

25. The Porte "Baby" was a huge, three-engine flying boat developed by Cdr. John C. Porte at RNAS Felixstowe, with a wingspan of 124 feet and loaded weight of nearly 15,000 pounds. The "regular" aircraft were likely British F2As or Curtiss-designed H-12 "Large Americas," both of which conducted antisubmarine patrols over the North Sea. The Sopwith Pup, a small, single-seat fighter aircraft with a loaded weight of only 1,225 pounds, was the first British aircraft to enter combat (in 1916) with a synchronized machine gun. Christopher Shores, in *Above the Trenches: A Complete Record of the Fighter Aces and Units of the British Empire Air Forces, 1915–1920* (London: Grub Street, 1990), esp. 15–16, called it "a delightful little aircraft," supplied to both RFC and RNAS squadrons. He added, "Although armed with only one Vickers gun, this rotary-engine biplane . . . was quickly found to be the equal of the new Halberstadt and Albatross scouts and superior to the Fokker D.III, which soon disappeared from the front." By late 1917, however, it had been largely outclassed by more capable machines, such as the Sopwith Camel and the SE5A.

As this is the biggest and best station they have it is frequently subjected to Boche raids. At 5:00 the gave us tea and sent us to the town where we had supper at the Felixistowe Hotel and then we left on the 7:11 for London, arriving at about 7:45 after a light supper during which I perceived the first good-looking English girl I've seen—most of them, by the way, are in terrible shape— bad teeth, big feet and ankles, but with good complexions, and can't touch the good old U.S. girls. Then I spent an hour writing in this simple book.

Sunday, October 7, 1917. Being the day of rest none of us seven arose till 1:30. Then after exactly 12 hours sleep we were feeling pretty high. From bed we hurried over to the [Ye Olde] Cheshire Cheese for a fair but large luncheon.[26] One felt very intellectual sitting in Sam[uel] Johnson's seat and reading the visitors' books. Afterwards we saw Sam's china, watch, etc. The proprietor apparently felt that with Johnson's chair, etc., his guests would not worry about the quality of the food. From this wonderful display I went back to 108 Savoy and wrote and read till about seven when Chip, Sam, Fred, and I went to the Carlton for dinner.[27] Then home again and I read a bit more before slipping between the sheets.

Monday, October 8, 1917. We all got up feeling pretty high and went to the attaché. He gave us some orders and a lot more dope, probably all bull. We were to leave Tuesday. Sam was appointed sort of leader—a hell of a job as it meant looking out for baggage, etc. Went to Burberry's to hurry on uniform with "Scab." Also a last bit of shopping. Had lunch about 3:00 at the Savoy and then frocked about till "Scab," Chip, Sam, Fred, and I went to the Carlton for dinner and then to "Bubbly," a show

26. He was referring to a famous London public house, built around 1670 and located just off Fleet Street at 16 Wine Office Court. A number of prominent literary figures were associated with the site.

27. Located at Haymarket and Pall Mall, the Carlton Hotel opened in 1899 and was managed until 1918 by the famed hotelier César Ritz. It was a major competitor for the Savoy.

in which the leading lady was a friend of Chip's! Well, the show was darn good, unusually good, and Chip's girl Teddie Gerard was pretty good.[28] He went out to her dressing room in between acts to give her a time[?]. After the show Reg and I went to the Savoy for supper like two confirmed woman haters should and saw Sam come in with his smelt. After it closed up we started up but ran into Chip, Fred, and two girls from the show who kicked me out of our rooms so they could have a party. I slept with Reg.[29]

Tuesday, October 9, 1917. We got our orders and packed and slipped off about 4:00 for Southampton. I felt awfully low and had a headache. We got to Southampton about 6:30 and tore to the boat, which was to take us to [Le] Havre. But unfortunately it had been too rough for crossings for two days and a tremendous crowd had filled up the boat. So we were unable to get berths. People were buying and selling rights to the stationary chairs in the salon. Lots of Red Cross nurses were left in the same fix. Also the crossing promised to be cold and rough and our supper was rotten. I felt awfully sick, but about ten I managed to get a berth in a room with three other men and went to sleep. Two of the men got sick and it was rough and cold so I slept little but was somewhat better off than the poor devils who sat up in the dining saloon. In the morning I waded out recovered. It seems Sam had been taken with chills during the night. The steward thought he might die, so to warm him up he put Sam in the big bread oven. When I saw him Sam looked as if he had been raised. We docked about 7 A.M.

---

28. *Bubbly* was a West End show that opened in London on May 5, 1917. Teddie Gerard (Teresa Cabre), an Argentinean-born singer, dancer, and actress, first appeared on the stage in New York in 1909. She made her film debut in 1921 in *The Cave Girl*.

29. After several days of becoming acclimated in London, the intrepid aviators continued their journey, crossing the English Channel to France and then to Paris, headquarters of U.S. Naval Aviation Forces in Foreign Service. Ingalls's reactions to the City of Lights were mixed. He did, however, find ready companionship among the vast number of Americans living in or passing through Paris, including numerous old schoolmates or social acquaintances. Many were pretty young women. *Smelt* was a derogatory term for a female companion.

Wednesday, October 10, 1917. Getting ashore about 8:00 at Havre [put] all of us in a hell of a humor, and sick and tired we beat it for a hotel, procured rooms, and fell asleep. I slept from 9:00 to 4:00 and reckon most of the others did too. Then we had tea and caught the 5:00 for Paris, arriving at 10:30. We took a couple of horse-drawn vehicles and set off to find a hotel. Believe me, Paris was full. After trying several hotels, Hen, Sam, "Scab," and I got rooms at the Chatham,[30] a rotten place, whose bar was already famous among Americans, and the others got in the Grand,[31] a very nice place. Even Chip and Hen didn't care for a party that night. While waiting out a ride, observing naught in my innocence, a sweet-faced little girl passed but stopped and returned to say "Will sleep with me?" probably all she knew. I had learned something in London but realized I would learn more in Paris. However, with perfect *sang froid* I said, "Sorry, not tonight," which passed over her head, and I realized that she had learned only as much English as was actually necessary.

Thursday, October 11, 1918. Arose to see Paris for the first time. It wasn't worth getting out of a nice warm bed. It was raining, cold, disagreeable. Had lunch at the Café de la Paix,[32] after which we reported to naval aviation headquarters at 23 Rue de la Paix. We checked up on the regulations and Reg, always a thorough individual, read from his manual that officers reporting for duty should do so in full dress. Well, full dress included some tin swords we'd been forced to buy and had brought with us in much the same spirit as a married man carries with him on a trip his rubbers. Still, Chip, Hen, and I were loath to appear as prescribed. We got ready but delayed till the other four preceded us in full dress to report. So we were in the anteroom and heard our associates enter, garbed as they were in fitting attire. And we listened to a strange voice,

30. This is likely a reference to the Hôtel Chatham at 17–19 Rue Damon, adjacent to the Place Vendôme. Ingalls rarely, if ever, stayed at less-than-elegant hotels.

31. The Grand-Hôtel de la Paix on the Rue de la Paix, adjacent to Charles Garnier's exuberant opera house, the Palais Garnier, dated from the mid-nineteenth century.

32. This popular Parisian café and eatery was designed by Charles Garnier; it opened in 1862 and occupied space in the Grand-Hôtel, across the plaza from his opera house.

"What the hell are you? Where did you get that uniform from? Are you boys in the naval cavalry?" It seems one's sword should be carried tight against the side hooked in one's belt, not dragging and swaying full length as ours were; that a U.S. naval aviator should wear ordinary naval officers' uniform, not one with RFC wings attached; and finally the blue dress uniform was not for reporting at a foreign base. Chip, Ken, and I retreated in good order to our hotels and altered our attack, with the result, "Well, thank God, at least some of you novices have some sense." Maybe we weren't thereafter the leading spirits of us seven. Actually, two very nice Lieuts. talked to us [Virgil] Griffin and [Norman] Van der Veer.[33] They said we could stay in Paris for a few days and they would take care of our pay accounts, etc.

After leaving the naval office I left the others and walked around for awhile, then went to the Chatham and wrote a couple of letters telling mother and Harry [Davison] what a hell of a trip we had. On the same day who did I run into but Cy Clark, my old friend from St. Paul's School,[34] and Wakeham, who roomed with Red Martin at college.[35] I certainly was glad to see an old Boze and arranged to dine with him. Met Cy at 6:30 and had supper in a little restaurant nearby and then went to the *Folies Bergères*.[36] After all, London is a tame city. Here I saw life—about the rottenest life that could be lived and I certainly was disgusted with the French. Here also I ran into Charlie Blackwell, senior in Sheff[ield], St. Anthony.[37] After leaving this hole I returned home

---

33. Lt. Virgil Griffin, a member of First Aeronautic Detachment, later commanded NAS St. Trojan. Lt. Norman Van der Veer edited the 1916, 1917, and 1918 editions of *The Bluejackets' Manual*. He spent much of the war as a staff officer at naval aviation headquarters in Paris.

34. Cyrus Clark, from Great Neck, New York, was a classmate of Ingalls's at St. Paul's School. Both graduated in 1916. They were at school together for four years.

35. Ingalls probably was referring to William Paul Martin Jr., Yale '20, who served overseas in the U.S. Air Service.

36. The famed music hall at 32 Rue Richer, established in 1869, was known for its scandalous performances.

37. He was referencing Sheffield Scientific School, the science and engineering school at Yale University, founded in 1854, and St. Anthony Society, a national secret society/fraternity with chapters at various elite schools.

and read for a bit till Hen came in when we both agreed that the
Lord slipped up when he made the French.

Friday, October 12, 1917. After breakfast, Hen and I reported and
received orders to leave Paris Saturday night or Sunday morning
for Bordeaux. I also was informed in a nice way that I was an
ass for leaving my commission and pilot's license behind. I had
written for them the night before. Until they come I'll get no pay.
Pay reminds me that on Thursday I went to Morgan Harjes and
got them to cash a check for $200 and I deposited another for
$100. Mr. Harjes, an old friend of Dad's, was not to be seen.[38]
After doing my bit at the naval office I met Cy at the hotel and we
got two friends of his, Wakeham and Ted Blair, also a classmate
from school. After they had all they could stand at the Creole bar
we went to the Chinese Umbrella for lunch,[39] meeting then Alan
Winslow,[40] C.B.'s roommate. It seems this is the meeting place of
Americans, American food being the reason. Why do Americans
stick to their own kind of food in France? After lunch I wrote and
then went to the Ritz for tea.[41] Then the same bunch with Scab
went to Joseph's and had a big dinner there. Got back about 10:30.

Saturday, October 13, 1917. Reported as usual, but missed
breakfast. Scab and I had an early lunch after signing at the
Yale Club. Saw Maury Jones,[42] Win Little there. Met Charley

38. Morgan, Harjes & Co., at 14 Place Vendôme, was a Paris-based component of
the J. P. Morgan & Co. banking network. The company actively facilitated placement
of loans for the Allies. The Mr. Harjes mentioned by Ingalls was likely Henry Herman
Harjes, son of founder John H. Harjes. Henry Harjes played a major role in organizing
war relief efforts in Paris, including underwriting a volunteer ambulance service and
representing the American Red Cross. He died in a polo accident in 1926.

39. This was a popular eatery among Americans in Paris. Similarly named restau-
rants could be found in Tours and other cities.

40. Alan Winslow was a member of the Lafayette Flying Corps and later an army
aviator who flew with the 94th "Hat in the Ring" Aero Squadron. He is often identified as the first U.S. Air Service pilot to score an aerial victory, on April 14, 1918. See
James Hudson, *Hostile Skies: A Combat History of the American Air Service in World War I*
(Syracuse, N.Y.: Syracuse University Press, 1968), 1–2, 67–68.

41. The luxury Paris hotel at the Place Vendôme was opened by César Ritz in 1898.

42. Charles Maury Jones, an aviator who flew with French escadrille SPA 73, later
served with the U.S. Air Service 103rd Aero Squadron, then commanded the 28th
Aero Squadron. I interviewed him in his New York City office in 1968.

at the hotel and went to [the American] hospital at Nieully [-sur-Seine] and saw Harry Thompson, wounded by shell in transport.[43] Then packed, bought wristwatch, and went to Ritz for tea. Then returned and went to Café Paris[44] for dinner with Sam, George Haven, and Reg. Scab said he was going to bed, we left him. As we walked into the restaurant who should we see but Scab and some smelt. He had apparently discovered a rather unique cure for his malady. He got fussed and came over to us and asked how he could get rid of her. How should we know? Then he slipped outside door and left her to eat and pay for the big dinner. Went to bed early, but Hen didn't get in until 5:30.

Sunday, October 14, 1917. We got up at 6:30 and took the 8:25 for Bordeaux. We went through Tours and saw all the way down to the coast beautiful scenery. Picturesque old chateaus and ruins. Had lunch in a real dining car. Arrived at 6:30, met Bob [Lovett], one of our [Yale] Unit, who was second in command at the U.S.N.

43. Henry Burling "Harry" Thompson, of Reistertown, Maryland, was another member of the St. Paul's School class of 1916. The American expatriate community founded the American Hospital in 1906. At the outbreak of war in 1914, the government made available the unfinished Lycée Pasteur in Neuilly-sur-Seine, a nearby Paris suburb, which quickly developed into an important medical center. The hospital, supported financially by many socialites, was under the daily direction of a committee of U.S. citizens but military control of the French Service de Santé as the Hospital Bénévole No. 2 Bis. Known unofficially as the American Ambulance, the facility was staffed by volunteers—first French and American doctors resident in Paris and later entire units of medical personnel from Harvard University, Western Reserve University, Pennsylvania University, and the Pennsylvania Hospital. According to Meirion and Susie Harries, the auxiliary nursing staff included socialites, actresses, art students, and even the daughter of former president Grover Cleveland. At least one Harvard doctor claimed the young women "were terribly distracting, I am free to state." The institution also spawned the (later independent) American Ambulance Field Service, whose hundreds of drivers included volunteers from many colleges and universities. In July 1917, the American Red Cross and the American Expeditionary Force assumed control of the hospital, renamed American Red Cross Military Hospital No. 1. See Meirion Harries and Susie Harries, *Last Days of Innocence: America at War, 1917–1918* (New York: Random House, 1997), 44.

44. Possibly this was a reference to the elegant Café de Paris on the Avenue de l'Opéra. This was exactly the sort of place Ingalls and his associates frequented during their stays in Paris.

station at Moutchic,[45] and had dinner and stayed at Terminus Hôtel. Bob, with his customary gravity and sincerity, tried to discourage us with tales of how awful the place was—all mud and rain.

Monday, October 15, 1917. Arose, breakfasted, and met Bob. Then we bought blankets, boots, and raincoats, till what was left of our money ran out. According to Bob it was the weather, not the Huns we were to fight. Had lunch at Bob's hotel and then met Harry LeGore.[46] Then we jumped into a slow truck and started for Moutchic. It was a 12-mile an hour Packard truck and we didn't arrive till about 6:30. (From then on I hated a Packard.) 49 kilometers. We agreed we'd never be truck drivers, not while we could, say, stoke a liner. We didn't stop at the station long but went to Lacanau and had a great dinner and went to sleep in a hotel.[47]

Tuesday, October 16, 1917. The truck had arrived to take us to Moutchic when we arose and we hurried through, or rather it hurried through, some rotten coffee. When we arrived at Moutchic they were hard at work setting up hangars, building barracks, etc. There were two long rows of tents and two barracks, several office buildings and some store houses and the nice house in which the officers lived a luxurious life.[48] We looked the place

45. Discussions between Lt. Kenneth Whiting and French naval officials during the summer of 1917 yielded a decision to construct an American aviation school at Lac Lacanau–Moutchic, about thirty miles from Bordeaux and four miles from the Bay of Biscay. Lt. John Callan served as the first commanding officer, succeeded in late October 1917 by Lt. Grattan Dichman. The Moutchic facility stood on sandy ground recently cleared of dense pines. Most personnel lived in tents and airplane packing crates. Construction of hangers, barracks, shops, and other structures had barely begun. At this time, the infant school lacked aircraft with dual controls, and thus no instruction took place.

46. Harry LeGore, the Yale baseball and football star and later prominent Maryland politician, gained notoriety by being declared athletically ineligible for playing professional baseball in 1915. During the war, he served with the U.S. Marines.

47. Lacanau was a small town located a few miles east of Lac Lacanau.

48. A few of these buildings survive today but in derelict condition, including the lakeside villa occupied by officers. There is also a small marble monument commemorating eight Americans who died while training here, the only such memorial on the French coast.

over, saw to our orders, and then Chip, Hen, Scab, and I were
sent to Hourtin in a truck while Sam, Fred, and Reg were told to
stick around a day and then go and stay at Bordeaux until orders
were received.[49] We arrived at Hourtin about 12:00 and reported.
Also saw Al [Sturtevant] and John [Vorys] who were still there.
Then we were sent to the village to eat a rotten meal. After it we
came out four miles and saw to our luggage and tents. The camp
is practically a small village. Besides the French officers house,
where we Americans also eat, there are a lot of small houses for
the men and their wives and mistresses. Also a few barracks and
a lot more under construction. Several store houses, two large
and excellent shops, three hangars. There were about 40 or 50
U.S. [Americans] there.[50] The U.S. live in tents off to one side
between the French and the German prison camp, to act as a
buffer between maybe, though we soon found the Huns were like
unto lambs.

Immediately upon arriving we went out to the sand spit in a
boat from which all the flying is done. It is about ¾ of a mile from
the hangars or a mile around. The hangars are on a narrow inlet.
There is a swamp around the lake on several sides, the soil is

49. Di Gates described Lac Hourtin as a little larger than Lake Worth (in Palm
Beach). The school, he noted, stood "in some large pine woods on the side of a hill
beside a beautiful lake. . . . Life [was] very primitive, like camping in the Adirondacks
or Maine." Hourtin attracted a great assortment of humanity. Gates noticed a group of
French sailors playing leapfrog, while nearby, several Annamites (Vietnamese) "played
some weird tunes" and not far away American bluejackets played baseball. Close by
stood a camp holding German prisoners of war. "The Germans seem perfectly peaceful," Gates reported, "but we still sleep with revolvers beside our cots." John Vorys
dismissively described Hourtin as a "temporary sort of a place" with canvas hangars
and log huts; the lake was a puddle among sand dunes, he said, with the dunes held
in place by pine trees, wild boars, and wild Moroccans. The facility utilized cranky
FBA flying boats that exhibited quirky handling characteristics imparted by the rotary
action of their 130 hp Clerget motors. Ken MacLeish later claimed, "I'm not crazy
about them . . . they do queer little tricks due to the gyroscopic action of the rotary
motor and the controls aren't very sensitive. . . . I never flew a rottener contraption in
my life." See Gates to Davison, September 16, 1917, Davison Papers Yale University;
and Paine, First Yale Unit, 2:11–14.

50. Many enlisted members of the First Aeronautic Detachment with whom Ingalls later served at NAS Dunkirk, as well as friends from the First Yale Unit, received
some flight instruction at Lac Hourtin in the fall of 1917.

very sandy, in fact the whole place for miles inland, I forgot to say that the ocean is only three miles off, used to be nothing but sand dunes till this government planted pines all over. So now when it rains as it had done for the last two weeks the water runs right off. After hanging around till about 5:00 we all walked back. We had supper with the French officers at 7:00 and then sat around a fire between the tents and listened to heartrending by Chip, Al, John, and Hen. We hit the hay pretty early.

Wednesday, October 17, 1917. About 6:00 we woke up and believe me I never was so cold. After dressing in about two seconds and swallowing a couple of cups of the best and hottest coffee that was ever boiled and a hunk of war bread, we hurried out to the boat to go to the hangar. We sat around till 8:20 when we went to the mess hall—or officers' house and had some awfully good hot chocolate and more bread. Then we went out to the point again and sat around some more. Pretty soon there was a big smash and we looked up to see the remains of a plane that hit on the edge of the marsh. Then there was the darndest noise imaginable as all the Frenchies talked at once and everyone ran to the launches to go to the scene of the disaster. A Frenchy had tried like a fool to turn near the ground and banked so much that also slipping a bit he caught one pontoon on a bush and smashed up. He was not hurt at all.

After the excitement was over we sat around till about 11:00 when flying was stopped. We sat around our tents till 12:30 when we had a fine lunch. At about 3:00 out to the point again. During the afternoon two of these simple Frenchies at different times came crashing into machines beached there. Nothing much was broken thankfully. About 5:30 flying was called off for the afternoon and the first day had passed without a flight on our part. However Al and John both soloed—each having had about four flights in the three weeks they had been waiting. Supper at 7:00, a little bull and then sleep.

Thursday, October 18, 1917. It was pretty warm when we got up at 6:00 and hurried out to the sand spit. Sat around till 8:30 and then came in for chocolate and toast. Just when we arrived at the beach again some French fool starting out circled to clear a sand bar extending from the point and losing his head crashed a wing into the hull of Douno's boat. Douno was to be our instructor, so we were laid off. We had the customary wonderful lunch and went out to the beach. When Douno told Chip and me that we'd get no flying till next day we returned and took a bath. As our luxurious suite had no tub we stood in a tent [and] used a couple of towels and pails of hot and cold water. It was great. However, we both missed flights as Douno got another boat. That afternoon John and Al both stuck on the sand bar and were promptly razzed. After supper I wrote till about 10.

Friday, October 19, 1917. Arising a bit late, Scab and I just swallowed a cup of coffee, grabbed some bread, and made the boat. After sitting around till 8:30 I started for chocolate, but saw Douno coming out with his machine so waited. I finally got out and had a rotten ride. The machine handled very stiffly and did not respond well to the controls and the engine had only just enough power to get us off the water. These F.B.A. boats are somewhat similar to an F boat but have 130 H.P. motor instead of 100. They climb pretty fast, and with a good motor get off easily. But one can't use the rudder to speak of, especially on a left turn, one merely banks and slips around. My God, what a machine! I wondered why the crashes were so few. Soon after my ride of about five minutes Douno got a better machine and gave me a good ride. We made a lot of landings, it was hard for me to land this far enough back on the tail. They can be landed on the step, but should be landed very far back.

In the afternoon as we were going out a call was received for the bomb carriers so Douno and another took two of them out. They are called DDs [Donnet-Denhauts] and are a very nice looking machine, larger than the F.B.A., with 200 H.P. motor. The first fellow up solo came down to land near us, got scared and just as he was about to land on the step, pulled back the stick, went straight up, slipped back and to the right, caught one wing, and fell into the water just turned around. Somehow it didn't sink.

He was not hurt, nor was the machine in any way injured. One
of the monitors, without any inspection, immediately took it up
and tested it, then he turned it over to Hen who was our first to
solo. After him Scab and later Chip. I did not have a turn till
late and then the beach captain said it was too glossy.[51] Chip
got stuck on the bar and has to set up drinks for all. Al finished
up his two hours and will leave for Saint Raphael as soon as
possible.[52] The enlisted men move into barracks here today, but
we are in the cold. It is fine weather, new moon tonight. Only
one D.D. returned, the other was left out in the ocean. The one
saw a boat within three miles of the boat on water but didn't
trouble to stop and ask for help. They merely telegraphed to
Verdun to send out a boat.[53] Nice fellows. No telling where the
two poor devils will drift to.

Saturday, October 20, 1917. The water was very smooth and glassy
so I didn't solo till about 9:00 and thus missed chocolate again.
It is a long wait for one cup of coffee and a small slice of bread at
6:00 then nothing till 12:30. However, I got up finally and took
a couple of turns. About 30 minutes after I came in Chip came
in and they sent out a sailor with his boat. Just after the motor
started and fortunately before he left the water the strap on top to
lift the boat came loose, caught in the propeller, and ripped the
upper wing from the front straight apart. Also made a tremendous
hole in the lower wing and the engine fell down and forward,

---

51. *Glossy* meant the water was flat and mirror-like, making it difficult for a pilot
to judge the distance to the water as he landed his aircraft.

52. Situated on the Mediterranean shore near Cannes, St. Raphael was the site of
a large French naval aviation school established in 1915. Both enlisted and commissioned American mechanic–observer and pilot candidates received instruction there
in the summer and fall of 1917, including a few members of the Yale Unit. Everyone
enjoyed the warm weather, long beaches, and young women in bathing costumes. Life
along the Riviera is described in Sheely, *Sailor of the Air,* 36–54. See also Paine, *First
Yale Unit,* 2:21–23.

53. A French military installation at Le Verdun-sur-Mer, near the mouth of the
Gironde estuary, was briefly considered as a possible location for an American seaplane
station. It would have offered protection to vessels headed along the coast and upriver
to the port of Bordeaux.

just back of the pilot's head. If it had happened in the air, *"C'est la guerre."* Just then I got another flight, three turns, and felt right at home. No flying Saturday afternoon, so Chip, Hen, and I walked to Hourtin. Scab felt badly the night before and though he flew was still low. We had tea at Hourtin and got some chocolate. As we were leaving Al and John came through on their way to Moutchic as they were finished. Also a lot of sailors. Then we walked back and had dinner; it's about 4-1/2 miles.

Sunday, October 21, 1917. Although it is the day of rest we rise at 6:15 and the bad news—no coffee and bread. After sitting around for a while suffering from cold and famine, I slipped to camp and procured a large hunk of war bread and some chocolate and brought it out. It was welcome. Then about 9:30 I got up to take four turns. I was feeling pretty good so I did three spirals and made large [toures de pistes? (triangular cross-country flights)]. When I came in, the beach captain said I was finished. At first he intended to beach me four days, but then decided that I could just go to St. Raphael. No more flying here. As my feet were sore from walking to Hourtin, stayed in camp, read, and played bridge in the afternoon. Also had a slick bath. Scab, Hen, and Doc [Stevens] walked to the ocean and took a swim.[54] When they got back, about six o'clock, Hen, Chip, Scab, and I went to the canteen, a sort of recreation room, and treated all the visitors to champagne. There were about nine of them, and they are a fine bunch of men, all petty officers. They have most of the officers here [shamed?] a mile.

Monday, October 22, 1917. Big day, as I slept 'til 8:15, being finished here. After the chocolate and toast, Chip and I went out to the beach saw Scab and the finish. Cabot telephoned to

---

54. Albert "Doc" Stevens, Yale '05, later served as medical officer at NAS Dunkirk and was captured by the Germans in July 1918 during an attempted rescue of airmen downed off the Belgian coast. He was released after the armistice. Before the war, the six foot four Stevens taught German, English, French, and poetry at The Hotchkiss School in Lakeville, Connecticut, where his students included Archibald and Kenneth MacLeish, Kenneth and Edward Smith, and Di Gates.

Moutchic that we were done.[55] About 10 the boat brought out
Reg and Sam, who had taken Al and John's place. Fred still at
Moutchic. Due to the party last night; they got a ride and said
it was easy. All four of us thought it was darned hard the first
ride. They were sore at Bob for the way they had been treated
and advised us not to stay at Moutchic when we left here. After
lunch Cabot and I played Fearing and Chip bridge.[56] Dr. Stevens,
Scab and Hen went for a walk. Later Chip and I rode to Hourtin
on Sam and Reg's bicycle and had chocolate and bought some
postcards. Supper lasted two and a half hours. Those Frenchmen
sit and talk 'til one goes wild.

Tuesday, October 23, 1917. Cabot telephoned and Moutchic said
they would send a truck for us. Packed in the morning. Rained
most of the day. Played bridge in morning and afternoon. Tea
about 3:30, telephoned again, heard that they weren't going to
send for us. They don't seem as considerate as they might be.
So Cabot and Fearing persuaded the French to send us over in
one of their camions. We loaded up and left about six. Taking
[Montrelay?] as far as Hourtin. He, finished there, was going to
St. Raphael. We arrived at Moutchic at seven, got a lukewarm
greeting, heard there were no orders, and were sent to Lacanau-
Ocean to wait.[57] It is at the end of a little railway to Bordeaux,

55. Norman Winslow Cabot, Harvard '98, an outstanding collegiate football player,
was commissioned an ensign on April 6, 1917; he performed temporary duty at the
Squantum, Massachusetts, aviation school in July, sailed to Europe in August, and was
assigned to NAS Moutchic in the fall. In December, he assumed command at NAS Île
Tudy, a position he held until April 1918, when he transferred to aviation headquarters
in Paris and then to Admiral Sims's staff in London.

56. Ensign George R. "Tote" Fearing Jr., Harvard '93, a stockbroker in the prewar
decades, received a commission in May 1917; served at the Squantum, Massachusetts,
aviation training facility in July; sailed for France in August; was sent to Moutchic; and
then spent much of the war attached to naval aviation headquarters in Paris, where
he acted as secretary of the Executive Committee and also performed liaison duties
with the U.S. Air Service. He later transferred to Admiral Sims's staff in London as a
member of the Planning Section.

57. Lacanau-Océan, a small, beachfront vacation community on the Bay of Biscay,
lay about four miles west of Lac Lacanau. Several American officers lived there in small
hotels during their time at Moutchic and commuted to the lake by truck.

on which there is one train each way each day. We stayed at the
bathroom-less hotel (and by the way in our three weeks stay we
were unable to find even a single outhouse in the place). Had a
wonderful dinner at the café and some Madeira. Bed about ten.
Hen, Scab and I had a triple room.

Wednesday, October 24, 1917. Arose 9:30, walked around resort,
after some cool chocolate and toast with Chip. This used to be an
old resort. There are two or three hotels, a café, bathhouse, casino,
skating, dancing and tennis, and a number of private houses, very
picturesque along the oceanfront. A very pretty little place. Some
way back from the sea are the houses of the all-year inhabitants.
From the appearances there must be about 15 altogether. The
little railroad ends here, two trains a day, one at 6:30 am goes
to Bordeaux and at 5:30 pm from Bordeaux. The whole place,
like the rest of the coast here about, used to be nothing but sand
dunes 'til the government planted pines. So it is very uneven
ground, little hills all over. All the pines are slashed and cups
placed to gather the turpentine. Forgot to say Beach went back on
truck to Hourtin last night. At 12:30 we had a fine lunch. After
it we walked to Moutchic, saw Bob, Dichman, Callan, Lieuts.,
Paymaster Michel.[58] They had erected another hanger, built up the
sea wall, cleared out a lot of the ground, and put up a Y.M.C.A.
building and another building; and had about 10 machines set up.
They had flown a bit. They sent us back in truck and we had fine
dinner and played bridge. [Cabot and Fearing lunched then.][59]

Thursday, October 25, 1917. Chocolate at 10:00, rain and cold.
Played bridge all morning. Good lunch. Took walk with Chip. It

58. John Lansing Callan, NA #1442, was the first commanding officer at
Moutchic. He later performed important duties at Paris headquarters and in Italy.
Paymaster Frederick Michel was a member of the First Aeronautic Detachment.
Lieutenant Dichman served as commanding officer at NAS Moutchic from Octo-
ber 1917 to February 1918.

59. In late October, the school at Moutchic had barely commenced instruction,
and Ingalls spent most of his time sleeping, playing bridge, visiting Bordeaux, staying
out of the rain, talking long walks, catching up with Yale friends, speculating about the
future, and enjoying what he could of local dining opportunities.

is a hell of a deserted place now. More bridge, left at 5:00 got ride
part way to Moutchic on French camion. Saw Bob who said that
he would take me with him to fly Nieuports and go to Dunkirk.[60]
Ran back in 30 min. Took a cold rub, had good supper, more of
that good Madeira, more bridge. Also wrote Frank and Mother.

Friday, October 26, 1917. Cloudy, rose at 9:00. Walked to Moutchic
with Scab. Wonderful lunch there, steak and onions, spaghetti,
peas. Chip and Hen arrived after lunch. We all got a flight.
They had been giving the observers practice shooting with a
Springfield at silhouettes on water. Chip made a hell of a landing,
I was accused of pancaking and D[ichman?] gave us the razz.
Walked back, bridge, good dinner and more bridge.

Saturday, October 27, 1917. Chip and Hen left for Bordeaux on
6:30. Truck arrived 8:30 to take Scab. Orders were for him to
take a number of men and go to Le Croisic under Griffin and
Corry.[61] A good station. Certainly was sorry to see Scab go. Sat
around all morning; wrote L.H.,[62] Al, and Mother. Punk lunch.

---

60. This is a reference to taking the French flying course in Nieuport pursuit ships,
perhaps at Issoudun, and then serving at NAS Dunkirk, the coastal patrol station under
construction near Calais and the Franco-Belgian border.

61. The United States established a naval air station at Le Croisic on the Bay of Bis-
cay in the fall of 1917. It was sited to patrol the approaches to the port of St. Nazaire,
expected to be a major debarkation site for eastbound American convoys. Lt. William
Corry, NA #23, served as the first commanding officer and later commanded at NAS
Brest. Several Yale Units pilots served there, including Ken Smith, Samuel Walker, Henry
Landon, and Reginald Coombe. See Rossano, *Stalking the U-Boat,* 81–84, 93–97.

62. Likely he was writing to Louise Harkness, his future wife. Originally from
Cleveland, the Harkness family prospered through extensive investments in the Standard Oil Company and eventually (in 1896) settled in New York City, with a country
estate at Glen Cove, Long Island. Louise Harkness, daughter of William L. Harkness,
attended Westover School in Middlebury, Connecticut, with Ishbel MacLeish (sister of
Kenneth MacLeish, her future husband's wartime companion) and Priscilla Murdock,
who was later Kenneth MacLeish's fiancée. Family lore is a bit unclear about where
David and Louise first met. The families may have known each other in Cleveland, for
the Harknesses maintained a residence on Euclid Avenue even after relocating to New
York, and they participated in a variety of social events, including many in Bratenahl.
The two also might have met through the Westover-Yale connection or perhaps on
Long Island in the summer of 1917 when the Yale Unit trained at Huntington Bay.
The Harkness summer compound in Glen Cove and the Davison family mansion at
Peacock Point stood barely a mile apart.

Read a bit. The rain let up and Fearing, Cabot, and I walked to Moutchic. There were Fred, Sam, Reg, and Scab. The first was on his way to Bordeaux then Hourtin to finish. The last three were on their way to Le Croisic. Bob had word that I was to go to Issoudun, Pau, and Cazaux to fly Nieuports[63]—the first is I think land school, second aerobatic, third firing. If it happens I'll have a great time and plenty to do, ending with Dunkirk. Sat around, saw off the four with a lot of enlisted men. 13 for Le Croisic, then walked home. Good dinner eggs and toast. Read till 9:30, also three hands of bridge.

Sunday, October 28, 1917. Arose 10 A.M. Fine day now. Walked about four miles on beach. Rain. Lunch at cafe. Paymaster of Bordeaux and an English-speaking smelt lunch at our hotel. After lunch Hen, Chip, Fred arrived with chocolate and a pair of goggles for me. Said Chevalier and Bartlett were at Moutchic.[64] Played bridge till 5:00 walked seven miles on beach, cloudy. Dinner, bridge, sleep.

Monday, October 29, 1917. Hen left at seven in truck for Le Croisic. Later Cabot and Fearing walked to Moutchic. I had break at 10:30, read till 12:30, had lunch at cafe with Cabot and Fearing, and Chip. Had flight in morning. Then we walked to Moutchic and Chip and I had flights. I took up Fearing. Saw Di there, was awfully glad to see him again. He expects to be stationed there. Too bad to waste such a good flyer there. No more dope. Got letters from Mother, Dad, Louise [Harkness?]. First mail, hurrah. Dinner and lost 46 francs in game. Hell. Good weather all day, thank God.

---

63. The French army operated an extensive series of aviation facilities, including these mentioned. The U.S. Army later occupied and greatly enlarged the school at Issoudun. Many navy and AEF fliers took the aerial gunnery course at Cazaux, including the Ohio-born American ace of aces, Eddie Rickenbacker.

64. Godfrey deC. Chevalier, a member of the First Aeronautic Detachment, later commanded NAS Dunkirk and the Eastleigh assembly and repair facility. He died in an airplane accident in 1922. Harold "Cueless" Bartlett, NA #21, commanded NAS Moutchic in early 1918, succeeding Lieutenant Dichman.

Tuesday, October 30, 1917. Got up late. Cold, windy, cloudy. Played bridge till lunch, more bridge, walk. Dinner at cafe. More bridge. Chip and I had the darndest luck imaginable, have lost steadily for four days. Rain most afternoon.

Wednesday, October 31, 1917. Got up at 9:00. Hell of a day. Rain. Played bridge all morning and afternoon, short walk. Fearing got orders in morning to go to Paris. He left at 6:30 for Moutchic on his way to Paris. Certainly sorry to see him go, he's a great fellow. Left me his leather coat. Dinner and bed. Today Chip and I evened up in bridge for all we lost.

Thursday, November 1, 1917. Walked to Moutchic. Lovett would never send even a truck for us. Not much flying, there is no castor oil.[65] Seems to me they might show a little pep there and get some. Walked back for lunch at cafe. Then bridge. Di came over and we walked around, supper at cafe, walked halfway back with Di.

Friday, November 2, 1917. Up at 9:30 and shaved. Bridge, lunch, walked to Moutchic. We get a hell of a lot of walking. It's 3-1/2 miles to Moutchic. Sat around and tried to get pay from the new paymaster. He's tighter than the old one. Once spent a whole day with the new paymaster trying to get some advance pay. Ensign Jorgenson executive officer is back.[66] Got letter from B.L. [Bob Lovett]. Back for supper, bridge, having planned to go to Bordeaux in morning, necessitates getting up early.

Saturday, November 3, 1917. Left here 7:30 in truck for Moutchic then Bordeaux. Di, Chip, C[abot?] and I, also lots of sailors, 1 hr 40 min trip. Shopped. Lunch at Hôtel de France, with Harry LeGore and Capt. Fitz of Marine Corps. Got a room. We went to a

65. Castor oil, obtained from the castor bean, served as the preferred lubricant for rotary motors, such as the Gnome and Clerget models. The deadly poison ricin derives from the same castor bean.

66. Nonaviator Ensign Herman Jorgenson was the long-serving executive officer at Moutchic.

public bathhouse, and I went in and was given a little bathroom
with a tub, water, and chair. Believe me, I needed a bath and took
about two minutes to get in the tub. About as I got well soaped
I happened to look up and there by my tub was a young French
dame with an armful of towels. I told her I was used to washing
myself and to get the hell out of the bathroom. I guess I'm too
bashful and shy ever to be a good Frenchman. I got haircut also.
Bought a new bag, etc. Had some chocolate, ice cream, and
patisserie. Took 5:05. Arrived at 8:00, supper at cafe. Chip got off
at Moutchic. Had supper there and then walked back. It started
to rain then so he didn't have to. Certainly was great to get into a
tub. First time for three weeks. We left our wash at Moutchic. No
mail for any of us. Also no orders.

Sunday, November 4, 1917. Big day, lots of traffic for this place.
Sailor boy with his lass over here for couple of days. Lunch here.
Then walked to sand spit from which they expect to fly. Coming
home C. and Chip refusing to take an old crockman's (myself)
advice, lost themselves and arrived on the beach five miles from
here. Di and Dichman walked over with our mail, but we missed
them. Later Jorgenson and Paymaster came over. Dinner, bridge
and bed. Rain in morning.

Monday, November 5, 1917. Fine day. Short walk, lunch with Chip
at cafe, walked to Moutchic. No flying for us, but others did.
Dichman brought back Fred and oil from Hourtin. After dinner
Di brought over four lt(jg) docs who are to stay with us.

Tuesday, November 6, 1917. Up early walked to Moutchic. No flying
though perfect weather. Di came back for lunch. Fooled around
with a football. Walked back and had a flight. Fellow leveled off
about 20 ft. high and landing in a crosswind crushed down on
right wing. No hurt, machine well smashed.

Wednesday, November 7, 1917. Wrote mother.[67] Otherwise bored.

67. This letter has not been located.

Thursday, November 8, 1917. Mail from Mother, Dad, Bert Hadden. Never enjoyed anything more.

Friday, November 9, 1917. In afternoon walked to Moutchic. No flying. Planned trip to Bordeaux.

Saturday, November 10, 1917. Got up at 6:00. Took truck to Bordeaux. After shopping all morning we met Harry LeGore and Capt Fitz, who is Major now, for lunch. Chip, being sick, did not accompany us. At the hotel, there were a lot of high army officers, generals, etc., going back to U.S. I had my weekly bath before lunch. It was splendid. Left Bordeaux at about 4:00 in truck and arrived here at 6:15.

Sunday, November 11, 1917. Customary morning. After lunch we received some enlisted men in a camion who had orders for us to report to Moutchic at once. There were orders for Bob, Di and me to go to Paris—Ho for Dunkirk and some excitement. We leave Tuesday.[68]

Monday, November 12, 1917. Rode to Moutchic, persuaded the Paymaster to part with some money—it was an all moving job. Had lunch there and then rode back. Packed and had a big farewell dinner at the cafe.

Tuesday, November 13, 1917. Bob Lovett, Di Gates, and I received our orders to proceed to Paris, with Dunkirk on the horizon after some more training. Left Lacanau-Ocean at 6:30 for Moutchic. Took on board Di, Bob, O'Connor, Young, Hough, Velie, Parker.[69]

---

68. By November, navy plans to operate a seaplane patrol and bombing station at Dunkirk were well advanced. Several labor drafts initiated construction of hangars, barracks, and other facilities. Aircraft began arriving as well. The navy assigned Lieutenant Chevalier, one of its most experienced aviators, as commanding officer. Some personnel would operate Donnet-Denhaut flying boats to conduct reconnaissance and bombing missions, and others piloted single-place Hanriot-Dupont pontoon scouts to act as escorts for the lumbering patrol machines.

69. O'Connor, Young, Hough, Velie, and Parker were enlisted pilots from the First Aeronautic Detachment who sailed to Europe in May and June 1917 and trained at Tours, St. Raphael, and other French schools. They later received instruction at Turnberry and Ayr in Scotland (where Hough and Velie died in flying accidents) and served at NAS Dunkirk, as well as other American stations.

Were in Bordeaux about one hour to get truck, washed, and passes. We left at 11:05 for Paris. On board were lots of Y.W.C.A. fruits [derogatory term for young women]. They were an awful bunch and had the best of everything. Lunched in dining car and arrived in Paris at 8:45. Finding our baggage, etc., we got to the Chatham, had a bit of supper and Di and I went for a walk. Nothing doing.[70]

Wednesday, November 14, 1917. Reported at nine. Then wandered around with Di trying to find a dentist to replace a lost filling I missed. Met Lieut. Swazzy's wife and took her to lunch, a French girl who speaks English infinitely better than the bunch of French and English we've seen lately. Reported again at two. Dinner at hotel on Rue Damon, Olympia, which was punk. Like the *Folies Bergeres*. Saw Ehrhart at dinner. May I be permitted to say there is nothing narrow about a Parisian education. Aside from a trip to the French field at Villa Coublay [*sic*],[71] where we saw thousands of machines of every sort of make, our jobs were uninteresting, but not so our pleasures. And I saw lots of Americans I had known—Hunty Ehrhart, Elmendorf Carr, Tommy Hitchcock, Cord Meyer, Quentin Roosevelt, and a lot of others, and made an inspection tour of the Hanriot factory.[72]

---

70. Despite announced plans, Ingalls did not see Dunkirk for many months. Instead, he remained in Paris for several weeks, performing limited duty at headquarters, working at the Hanriot factory in nearby Billancourt, and keeping up a busy schedule of social obligations. He then received additional flight training in England and Scotland, only reaching Dunkirk in late March 1918.

71. Villa Coublay (or Villacoublay) was a large French military aerodrome and test site located about eight miles southwest of the center of Paris and two miles east of Versailles. A modern French air force base now occupies the site.

72. Elmendorf Carr of New York attended St. Paul's School, Oxford, and Columbia. He enlisted in the navy at the outbreak of the war and served with the French Ministry of Marine and on the staff of Adm. Henry Wilson in France. Thomas Hitchcock was a famed polo player and member of the Lafayette Flying Corps. Cord Meyer, originally slated to be a member of the Yale Unit, served instead with the 103rd Aero Squadron in the U.S. Air Service. Quentin Roosevelt, youngest son of former president Theodore Roosevelt, served with the 95th Aero Squadron and was shot down and killed on July 14, 1918. The Hanriot factory produced the HD.1 pursuit ship and a floatplane version designated HD.2. The firm also developed a heavily armed two-seater (HD.3) that elicited much interest by the U.S. Navy but was never acquired.

Thursday, November 15, 1917. Reported at 9:00. Did odd jobs.
Lunched at Café Parie, dined at Ritz with Fearing and Bob. Then
went to a very good French show. Di went out on party.

Friday, November 16, 1917. Busy all day. Di got orders to go to
Havre for six trucks and get them. 50 men came in from Havre
and Di, McKay, and I met them, picked 25 for Dunkirk and sent
them off. Dined at Maxims.[73] Di was suddenly sent to Dunkirk.
We were told we were waiting to get our training at the U.S.
Army Field at Issoudun, and Ken MacLeish was appointed to
take Di's place.

Saturday, November 17, 1917. Di left at 6 A.M. I was put in charge
of the men at office. All the new men got lost and were not
rounded up till 2 P.M. Van der Veer, a snotty mean man, raised
the devil about it. Lunched at Chinese Umbrella and dined at
Maxims, then came home and went right to bed.

Sunday, November 18, 1917. Reported at 10:00. One man answered
for another at roll call and was caught. I gave him hell and
reported it. Van called him and the man he reported for up and
was about as nasty as a slave driver. They got a deck court.[74]
Lunched with Elmendorf Carr and an English lieutenant. Then
Bob, Griffin, Hull, and Doc, and I went to Villa Coublay, the
French experimental station outside Paris. Here there are
about 15000[?] machines in a tremendous field with hundreds
of hangers. All sorts of machines and experiments were there.
We saw only one flight as it was very foggy. Inspected the
Hanriot, which is to be our machine. It looks fine and beats

---

73. The prestigious Paris eatery Maxim's was established in 1893 and located at 3 Rue Royale, near the the Hôtel Crillon.

74. According to the official Paris Headquarters Log for that day, "C. L. Shaw, seaman, second class, was tried by deck court for the following offense: answering false muster. The specification was proved by plea, and the accused was sentenced to twenty days solitary confinement on bread and water, with full ration every third day." See Paris Headquarters Log, November 19, 1917, box 131, GA file, RG 45, National Archives.

and out-climbs the SPAD and others.[75] Also saw two German
Rumpler's 260 H.P. two-seater fighters.[76] Noted clever gun
mounts. Dined at Ciro's.[77]

Monday, November 19, 1917. Frocked around the office. Shaw
reporting for Archer, said he was going to desert and hadn't
reported. Later the M.P. brought him in. Sentenced to 20 days
brig on water and bread. Poor devil. Lunch at Chinese Umbrella.
Dined at Maxims.

Tuesday, November 20, 1917. Di, Bob and I and the pilots for
Dunkirk were ordered to the Hanriot factory [at Billancourt, a
suburb of Paris] to work while waiting the three weeks till they
will be ready. It is a fine place. Turning out six or seven machines
a day. Wonderful new machine [Hanriot HD.3], 260 hp with
five guns and two men under construction.[78] A lot of Sopwith
machines are made there, two-seaters about three years old,
but still good and a single pontoon not much.[79] The machine we
are to use [the Hanriot HD.2] carries one machine gun, makes
115, stagger about 1/2 cord, 3-1/2 hours range, lands about 40
and looks fine. It has 130 [hp] Clerget [rotary motor]. These are

75. The single-seat SPAD was one of the most important pursuit aircraft of World
War I, especially its model S.VII and S. XIII versions.

76. These Rumplers possibly were the 1917 C.V version with a 260 hp Mercedes
engine. According to the Paris Headquarters Log, November 20, 1917, "An inspection
was made of the Rumpler bombing machine captured from the Germans. The most
interesting thing about it was the machine-gun mounting. It was lighter than that of
the French and made of wood."

77. The immensely popular restaurant opened in 1911 in the Hôtel Daunou and
was named after a famous establishment in Monte Carlo. Situated on Rue Daunou,
reputedly the most "American" street in Paris, the eatery hosted a stage and society
clientele drawn from French, British, and American visitors. It competed with the
Café de Paris for patronage.

78. "Private inspection made of the new Hanriot fighting plane, two-seater, with
Sampson motor with which they expect to make 135 miles an hour." See Paris Headquarters Log, November 22, 1917.

79. This was likely a reference to the two-seat model of the Sopwith 1½ Strutter
manufactured under contract in large numbers by Hanriot. It was powered by a 130
hp Clerget rotary motor.

about the best motors, though slightly heavier than the other
rotating motors. Most of the Hanriots are bound for Italy. They
out-climb and beat the SPAD over 300. Learned that 10 were
already at Dunkirk.[80] Lunch at Chatham, excellent, went to H
[headquarters] and dined at Henri's and went to Follies. Pretty
good. Letters from Dad and Mother.

Wednesday, November 21, 1917. Arrived at about 10:15 and looked
around. Talked to the Sopwith inspector. Lunched at Ciro's—the
place to lunch, dropped in at Rumplemires [Rumplemeyer's] and
went to D'Iena to get pay and mail.[81] One from Dad and Mother
and Alice. Also . . . Di wrote Bob, he's stuck at Havre no trucks
and can't get away. Dined at Maxim's. Bob's friend Sonia was
there but left early.

Thursday, November 22, 1917. Saw Dichman at breakfast and
Bartlett. There is a big conference here now all C.O.s of the
stations came to Paris.[82] Lunched at Ciro's and saw Tom
Hitchcock, Q[uentin] Roosevelt and Cord Meyer. They say that
Issoudun is in bad shape with measles and mumps. Means we'll
probably be here another month. At factory noted wings of H.D.
spar's shape I covered to seem solid. All small parts of three-ply
wood. Very strong but one wing can be lifted easily on one finger.
Entering edge one pipe, trailing three, all together eight. Also
noted new machine. The ailerons flippers are worked by hollow
tubing of steel alloy very light and strong. Sampson motor 260—4
machine guns, 130–140 mph. Dined at Maxim's. I could get food

---

80. Ken MacLeish said of the HD scouts, "They sure are wonders. They go about
120 mph and handle beautifully. The only disadvantage being that the Boche machines
go 130 and handle better." See Rossano, *Price of Honor,* 51.

81. An upscale ice cream parlor at 226 Rue de Rivoli, Rumplemeyer's was also
famous for its hot chocolate. The Hôtel d'Iéna at 4 Place d'Iéna became the headquarters of American naval aviation in early November 1917 and remained so until
September 1, 1918.

82. According to the Paris Headquarters Log for November 22, 1917, "The following officers reported in Paris for conference of Commanding Officers, U. S. Naval
Air Stations. . . . Conference of Commanding Officers and heads of departments to
determine policy on lay-out of work was held today."

and liquor all right, but otherwise my French failed to improve.
Before supper, engaged a French girl to teach us the damned
language. Some say the proper way is to live with one of them.
Maybe; I know I had enough with an hour a day.

Friday, November 23, 1917. Lunched at Ciro's, stopped at office
for mail and heard that Ken [Smith] had been lost at sea at 2
o'clock.[83] Ken was out patrolling in a flying boat with a couple
of observers and miles out the motor stopped and Ken landed
in the sea. Although it was pretty rough the ship held together
pretty well and the boys stuck up a distress signal and spent
the time when not seasick bailing out water and gradually
cutting off parts of the wings as their machine went to pieces.
They had the radiator water and a couple of sandwiches. Sixty
hours after they lit a destroyer found them and took them
off. Before they were able to get a line from the boat to the
destroyer, the damn thing sank. Finely figured, I'd say. No mail.
Dinner at Madam Bonard.

Saturday, November 24, 1917. Out to factory and then came back
here after lunch and there was Di back from Havre. He and I
went to the D'Iena [headquarters] where he got his orders to
Dunkirk immediately. Certainly am sorry he is not to fly *avion de
chasse* with us. Ken MacLeish is coming instead. Then we met
Griffin, Bartlett and Dichman and Bob, went to Villa Coublay.
Arriving late we saw some flying.[84] I had an early dinner and
[French?] lesson. Di and Bob went to the Yale dinner.

83. On November 22, 1917, Ensign Kenneth Smith of the First Yale Unit and two
enlisted flight personnel set out on an antisubmarine mission from NAS Le Croisic.
Their Tellier flying boat made a forced landing at sea due to a clogged fuel line, and
they spent sixty hours adrift until rescued, just as their aircraft was about to sink. The
episode is recounted in great detail in Paine, *First Yale Unit,* 2:31–48, which includes
Smith's narrative of the situation, as well as the logs of the mechanic and observer. See
also Marc Wortman, *The Millionaires' Unit: The Aristocratic Flyboys Who Fought the Great
War and Invented American Air Power* (New York: Public Affairs, 2006), 146–52.

84. Adm. William Benson, the Chief of Naval Operations, then in Europe for an
important series of meetings with Allied officials and military leaders, also witnessed
the flying.

Sunday, November 25, 1917. French lesson at 11:00, lunch at Ciro's with Hull, Bartlett, Bob and Di. Then Di and I went to Villa Coublay and saw the Morain [*sic*] monoplane.[85] It flew circles around a SPAD. Absolutely incredible speed—it must have been 20 mph faster than the SPAD. Light dinner and movies.

Monday, November 26, 1917. Cashed a check at Morgan Harjes and shopped. Di ordered magazines, etc. Last night Bob received a package of clothes etc., from U.S. Met Bishop and Mac Whitney at Chinese Umbrella at lunch.[86]

Tuesday, November 27, 1917. Dined with Evelyn Preston,[87] father's brother, Miss Stephens, and head of YWCA. Then saw some of Parisian life, was disgusted.

November 28, 1917. Di left and Ken MacLeish arrived to take his place.

November 29, 1917. Thanksgiving, had a fine time dining with Mrs. Bowler, daughters Jane and Alice, and Chase Davis [from Cincinnati].

Friday, November 30, 1917. Ken and I had tea with Mrs. Buswir.

Hotel Chatham, Paris, Nov. 30, 1917

My Dear Mother,

Yesterday we learned, much to our delight, that we are to go to England very soon for our land training before returning to the water machines. As conditions are not now favorable for our attending the

---

85. Possibly this was a reference to the Morane-Saulnier type AI monoplane, with a top speed of 137 mph.

86. James McVickar "Mac" Whitney was another of Ingalls's St. Paul's School friends and a member of the class of 1918.

87. Evelyn Preston, a member of the Yale Unit's social set, later married Stephen Rauschenbusch and then Roger Baldwin, founder of the American Civil Liberties Union (ACLU). She was a friend of Eleanor Roosevelt's and a well-known crusader for labor rights and civil liberties.

U.S. school here in France for quite some time, an attempt was made
to send us to England and so far it is successful, so within a week or
so I hope to be again in London. It will be a great relief to have a little
more flying. I imagine from then on we shall have all we want.

Lately I've been having a fine time, as Mrs. Bonand [Bonard?] is
awfully nice and when she informed several other old friends of yours
that I was at hand and would not, with a little care, be a disgrace
to them, one and all are very cordial. Wednesday afternoon I went
to tea at Madame Bonand's [Bonard?] and met a number of people.
Yesterday, Thanksgiving Day, Mrs. Bowler invited me to the most
wonderful American Thanksgiving dinner I ever had. She has two
daughters, one in the YWCA and the younger working at the British
embassy, who are great. A Cincinnati man, Chase Davis, and I,
were guests and we enjoyed ourselves thoroughly. I hope to see Miss
Bowler in London, as she returns Saturday and we may go any time
now. This afternoon I am going to call on Mrs. Buswir, I think it is,
and take Ken along. Ken has taken Di's place with us to fly the small
fast machines as the latter is too heavy and has gone to his station.
The rest of us will have possibly two months more training.

You probably read in the paper about Ken R. S[mith] having been
compelled to land at sea while patrolling and spent 60 hours before
he was picked up. The machines are pretty strong and sea-worthy, as
may be seen by that, as it was pretty rough. Although out that long, all
three of the men are all right and in fine shape again, though they were
exhausted slightly when picked up. I've seen a lot of fellows I know
around here, especially Terry Bob who was at S.P.S. [St. Paul's School]
and came over at the beginning of the war in Ambulance, enlisted in
French aviation, flew at the front for about two years, and is now a Capt.
in our aviation. It is very interesting to hear the stories of some of these
fellows when they will open up. Bart [Read],[88] Aut, and Harry D[avison]
are expected here soon, hurrah! All of our old unit will soon be here.

I was greatly amused last night when Mrs. Bowler said that Mrs.
Bonard had come to her in great fear of how young D.S.I. was getting
along here alone in Paris, but next day said she was feeling better,

88. Russell Bartow "Bart" Read, NA #78, a member of the First Yale Unit, was one
of four Read brothers to serve as naval aviators in World War I.

as I evidently greatly surprised her by not drinking and smoking. Well, mother, what do you think? Yesterday I got two packages from you; the first one some chocolate, etc., in fine shape. The chocolate is great and when I finally get settled the prunes will be most useful, so packages come and are very welcome. Love, Dave

Saturday, December 1, 1917. Took in and sent off 100 men from Britain to Dunkirk.[89]

Sunday, December 2, 1917. Read and wrote.[90]

December 3, 1917. Lunched at Tipperary, fine place. Wrote Dad all the Navy's troubles.[91] [See letter following.]

---

89. According to Ken MacLeish, he and Ingalls had tea with the Marchioness de Chambrun that afternoon; he noted, "She's an American woman and mighty nice." He may, however, have been referring to events of the previous day. See Rossano, *Price of Honor,* 52.

90. Perhaps Ingalls's days were not quite so tame. MacLeish recorded, "Crock is in the next room with one awful-looking Frenchwoman. Now and then I hear Crock's stock phrase, which he uses on all occasions, '*Qu'est-ce que vous avez dite.*' It's a scream." See ibid., 51–52.

91. David Ingalls was a young man with strong views but capable of keen analysis. His December 3 letter was written at a time when the navy's overseas aviation effort was just getting started and the ultimate shape of the program not yet clear. On one point he was certain, an opinion repeated more than once: he was unimpressed with the training or abilities of the enlisted pilots and observers. At least one other Yale pilot, Ken MacLeish, shared these attitudes. Enlisted pilots, in turn, perceived the Yalies' disapproval and resented it. Similar attitudes were particularly widespread in the Royal Flying Corps. According to historian John Morrow, the commander of No.8 Squadron, RNAS, once remarked of his Australian and Canadian pilots, "Wonderful chaps ... great pilots ... likely to destroy a Mess or anything in five minutes at a guest night." Morrow went on, "When the Army Council raised the question of non-commissioned pilots in August [1917] the commander-in-chief was more concerned about separate messes for them than for alleviating the shortage of aircrews." Some believed noncommissioned crews displayed inadequacy and even cowardice. The U.S. Army echoed such sentiments, with one military intelligence report claiming, "As regards discipline ... the flying corps caused the British the most trouble in view of the fact that the service, owing to its picturesque nature, is very likely to attract the wrong class of men." As Morrow noted, "It was difficult for the British to divorce criteria [for aeronautical ability] from subjective notions about class." The public school boy ethos seemed to pervade the British flying services, many of whose members regarded aerial combat as "a game ... just like rugger." Many officers believed potential aces "had the attributes of the sportsman, with a keenness for flying based on the sporting instincts." The juxtaposition of aerial combat and sport pervades the literature. See Morrow, *The Great War in the Air: Military Aviation from 1909 to 1921* (Washington, D.C.: Smithsonian Institution Press, 1993), 239–41, 273, 276, 315.

Hôtel Chatham, Paris, Dec. 3rd, 1917

Dear Dad,

I received your letters of Oct. 29 and Nov. 11, enclosing a letter
of introduction to Mr. Thomas of American Express Co. and two
papers—my oath of allegiance and my commission papers. Thank you
ever so much, also please thank Mr. Taylor, as it will be invaluable to
have some one here to fall back on in case of trouble.

Naval aviation here seems to be getting along very well now as
we have several stations underway and some doing active work, but it
seems to me they are not yet going at it in the right way. So far we of
the [Yale] Unit and a few older men are the only naval pilots trained
in flying sent from the United States. The large number of men who
have been sent over have had no previous training or practically
none. Most of them are men who, on enlisting, were immediately
shipped across regardless of their ability or adaptability for aviation.
All the flyers here, except us few, have been trained here, first on
land machines, then at several French water schools. These men,
turned out as pilots ready for active service, have had very little time
in the air and from my observation do not in any way seem to be the
picked men that a country of our size and resources should send to
the front. The observers, for most of the water machines carry more
than one man, have gone through the French water observers' school.
These men have had a very primary course in bombing and machine
gun work. The mechanics, men picked from different positions of
life, are not trained mechanics; some of them with perhaps a small
knowledge of engines, have been sent through factories rapidly,
listening to lectures mostly in French, a few translated, and they have
had to pick up what they could in, at most, three weeks. The rest are
learning from these and from trying to take care of the machines at
the stations.

Now, to take the case of the pilots. Here, it is at best a long and
inefficient course because of the great scarcity of materials, oil, gas,
training machines, etc. The pilots, except for a comparatively small
number, will be used for patrolling and convoying. They do not need
advanced training in different types of machines and machine guns.
They need merely plenty of flying in large machines with practice in

rough weather and rough landing. With everything at hand and plenty of materials these men could be more easily and cheaply trained in the U.S. than here.

The observers for these large patrol machines in the same manner could be easily trained by a great deal of experience in machine gun work and especially bombing in the best large machines at home. As a patrolling machine does not necessarily have great speed, the observers would be able, on our machines, to have the same conditions in practice that they would have later when actively engaged. Thus the pilots and observers could have plenty of practical training.

Now from the number of pilots and observers, those who showed themselves superior could be taken out of the school and placed in another small school or else sent to an army school where the pilots could take a long and careful course on fast machines and could take also a course in the school of fire and in acrobatics. The observers could also take a course in bombing and machine gun work on the faster, lighter land machines. The mechanics should be men preferably taken from the class of mechanics, thoroughly drilled on aeroplane motors and if necessary sent through a factory over here if said station does not use our American motor.

When these men arrived here, the pilots for patrol could take perhaps a few hops at the school here in their future machine and then be ready and fit for work. The bombers and mechanics would be ready and able to do their work immediately upon arriving. The small number of pilots for fast single-seaters could take the short course at the army school here, and would soon be ready for duty. If necessary, the observers for the fighting planes could likewise attend for a short term the army school here. Conditions here make a man's complete training at any one of the three divisions long, inefficient, and practically impossible, while at home there is every facility to train any required number of men quickly, cheaply, and efficiently. As yet no trained man has been sent over. Of course, I know that pilots are being trained in A[rmy], but this branch is by no means one-third of aviation. When I left, there were no schools for mechanics and a school for bombing and machine gun work was unthought of, especially in naval aviation are the two latter most important.

An example of the sort of mechanic we have now can be shown in the case of Ken S[mith]. He with an observer and mechanic landed at 2 P.M., 60 miles off shore, when the motor died. Not until night fell did the mechanic find out that the first tank being empty, the second tank was not feeding, being stopped up. The men, therefore, were unable to get off that afternoon when it was calm, and when the small trouble had finally been set aright next morning the sea was too rough to get off, in an attempt a wing was broken and as a result the men were nearly lost, spending 60 hours on the water before the boat filled and sank. For just such reasons we want the very best mechanics.

Take the importance of an expert observer—the simplest case being on a patrol boat, the Navy hopes that the aeroplane will occasionally see a submarine. If the machine does and is not noticed 'till it is near, the observer may get a good crack at it. After patrolling perhaps for weeks without getting a shot, the observer must be able to make good at every occasion when luck is with him. With one shot a month perhaps he must be sure. Therefore, every effort must be made to give the men expert training bombing.

The situation then is train the men in the States, giving them what they need most, plenty of experience on any flying machine and plenty of practice dropping bombs and shooting machine guns from any machine and plenty of experience in dealing with any aeroplane motor. This has to do only with the men themselves. About the machines, until the Liberty motor or some American motor is a success,[92] I suppose we'll use the foreign machine, but now the need is for men who can fly and shoot and bomb and fight. I hope we will soon get some encouragement by receiving some capable men and remarkable machines. The longer I stay here the more I am convinced that to conquer the Germans, we must first conquer them in the air.

I expect to leave for England to train on land machines and go through the school of fire and acrobatics in a few days now, so I'll spend Xmas in England, together with Bob and Ken, Di having dropped out on account of weight. Love, Dave

---

92. The Liberty motor was designed by American engineers in a Washington, D.C., hotel in a matter of days during May 1917. Later mass-produced by the thousands, it eventually powered all types of aircraft and other vehicles.

Tuesday, December 4, 1917. Sam [Walker] left for Le Croisic.

Wednesday, December 5, 1917. Saw a good show at the Alhambra.[93]

Thursday, December 6, 1917. Saw Chevalier. Also Winterbottom and Porterfield, English officers. We are getting darn sick of hanging around Paris.

Friday, December 7, 1917. Feeling low, slept most of morning. At 12:00 Bart [Read] and Moseley Taylor appeared. We had lunch with them, frocked around, then got package from Kirt from Alice. Curt [Read], [Edward] Shorty Smith, Phillip Page, [Ashton] Tex Hawkins also arrived then.[94] Had dinner and went to show.

Saturday, December 8, 1917. Received word to leave for England to train week from Monday. I feel ill. Day in bed.

Sunday, December 9, 1917. Encore

Monday, December 10, 1917. Had dinner with Bart, Mose [Taylor], Pete Taige, Grub Clover, Fry Spenser.[95]

---

93. The Alhambra Theater at 50 Rue de Malte was an early musical hall/theater in Paris, with performances "in the English manner." See Grieben's Guide Books, vol. 124, *Paris and Environs* (Berlin: Grieben-Verlag, 1929), 45.

94. Moseley Taylor, NA #118, was member of the Harvard group trained at Hampton Roads, Virginia, in the summer of 1917. By December 1917, the original trickle of naval aviation personnel heading to Europe had increased to a steady flow. New arrivals included regular officers, more members of the First Yale Unit, several from the Harvard and Princeton groups, and the initial contingent of the Second Yale Unit. Curtis Read, NA #83 and member of First Yale Unit, died during a training flight at Dunkirk on February 27, 1918. Edward Traver "Shorty" Smith, NA #126, was the brother of Ken Smith and a member of the Second Yale Unit. Philip Page, NA #170, was killed at RNAS Felixstowe during a training flight on December 17, 1917. Ashton "Tex" Hawkins, NA #128, a member of the Second Yale Unit, saw extensive service in England, especially in operations from NAS Killingholme over the North Sea.

95. Greayer "Grub" Clover, Yale '20, and Frederick Lionel "Fry" Spenser, Yale '22, were two of Ingalls's friends. Spenser had been a driver for the American Field Service.

Tuesday, December 11, 1917. Bob [Lovett] going to England for administration.[96] Shorty to take his place, Scab arrived from Le Croisic. Packed, bed 12:00. Left at 9:10. After a delightful trip we arrived at Boulogne. As we were late, we missed the boat. We also missed our baggage. Therefore we spent a night in a wretched hotel. The best hotel was full—the Folkstone. Found our bag in morning. Took 12:00 boat. Smooth and fair trip, arriving at Folkstone at 2:15. Made quick connections and arrived in London at 4:30. Tried the Carlton and Piccadilly [hotels] and then stopped at the Savoy. Saw the "13th Chair."[97]

Friday, December 14, 1917. Reported at 30 Grosvenor Gardens [and] found that as usual Van [der Veer] had made a mistake.[98] Gosport could take one of us a week.[99] Saw [Philip] Page there. Sent Hen [Landon] some cigarettes. Called up Alice Bowler, and then dined with her [ ]. So we had some more pleasures—in London—perhaps not the same as Paris, but O.K. for all that, and some excitement.

Saturday, December 15, 1917. Reported at 30 [Grosvenor], lunched with Alice and saw "Chu Chin Chou." Dinner at Carlton and saw "Arlette."[100]

---

96. Initial navy plans would have sent Bob Lovett, Di Gates, and David Ingalls to England and Scotland for advanced training before taking up duties piloting single-seat scouts at Dunkirk. Their scheduled itinerary included time at a special school at Gosport to prepare them for their envisioned roles at flight leaders. Instead, Lovett began staff duty in Paris, with Gates ordered directly to Dunkirk, being deemed too large for the small Hanriot scouts used at the base. Ken MacLeish and Shorty Smith took their places.

97. *The 13th Chair*, a "detective play" written by Bayard Veiller, opened in New York City in 1916 and was turned into a movie in 1919.

98. The U.S. embassy and navy headquarters were located at this Grosvenor Gardens address.

99. This is a reference to the RFC School of Special Flying at Gosport, England, near the English Channel.

100. This was the second time Ingalls saw the show *Arlette*. The musical comedy opened at the Shaftsbury Theatre in London on September 6, 1917, and was recorded later that year.

Sunday, December 16, 1917. Frocked around, rotten day. Ken saw [Laurence] Callahan,[101] our old friend.

Monday, December 17, 1917. My khaki suit was altered, left my blues too, also coat. Lunched with Alice at cute little restaurant, Au Petite Blanche. Also dined with her and saw "Brewster's Millions."[102] Saw Mrs. and Mr. Burton. On reporting learned we too were to go to Gosport.

Tuesday, December 18, 1917. Got transportation and orders. Shopped a bit, in afternoon Shorty and I went to Hendon,[103] but not having a pass we failed to get into the R.F.C. station there. At 6:30 Shorty and I started for dinner and show. A raid started and we could not get a taxi. Managed to get Al[ice] and then we had dinner at the Ritz. The raid was not very exciting, a.a. guns booming, and once an aeroplane passed straight above us. The motors could be heard but the aeroplanes were invisible. This lasted about two hours. Few people remained in the streets, taxies did not move, telephones were stopped, everything just waited. After dinner we found a taxi and got Sister [Dorothy Foster] and saw "Dear Brutus," a very good show.[104] Had a great time.

101. Laurence Callahan, a member of the Princeton contingent of U.S. Air Service pilots who trained in England in the fall of 1917, later served with No.85 Squadron, RAF, and the 148th Aero Squadron, USAS.

102. A novel written by George McCutcheon in 1902, *Brewster's Millions* was adapted as a play in 1906.

103. Hendon, a sprawling British aviation production, training, and acceptance center, was located in the northwest suburbs of London.

104. *Dear Brutus* was a play written in 1917 by J. M. Barrie, the author of *Peter Pan*. Ingalls spent so much time with Alice Bowler that Ken MacLeish carped, "Crock has a good scheme. . . . He has a girl in every port. . . . I don't know who the girl is. She's an American acting as a stenographer down at Royal Navy headquarters. I think her name is Alice Bowler. Crock was so tight with her that he wouldn't even take us around to see her." See Rossano, *Price of Honor,* 72.

3

With the RFC at Gosport, Turnberry, and Ayr
December 1917–March 1918

Of the American naval air stations established in France in 1917, only Dunkirk on the English Channel coast near the Belgian border exposed aviators to encounters with enemy aircraft. Lumbering flying boats conducting antisubmarine patrols proved easy prey for German warplanes and thus required armed escorts—fast, maneuverable, single-seat *chasse* (pursuit) machines. To obtain the trained pilots necessary to fly these aircraft, the navy made arrangements with the American army to instruct a dozen enlisted aviators at their new school at Issoudun, France.[1] Others were recruited from among American pilots then serving with French escadrilles. The RFC took three additional officer-pilots (David

---

1. Known as the Third Aviation Instruction Center, the Issoudun facility offered advanced flight instruction, including acrobatics, formation flying, and camera gun work. More than 750 American pilots trained there. See James Hudson, *Hostile Skies: A Combat History of the American Air Service in World War I* (Syracuse, N.Y.: Syracuse University Press, 1968), 35–36. Many who occupied the site in the fall and winter of 1917–18 remembered it as "about the most all-around, God-forsaken place you could imagine." Trainee Laydon Brewer opined, "Issoudun—God's mudhole, where God said, 'Let there be mud,' and there was mud. Such mud as Noah might have gazed on when the ark was stranded at the top of Ararat." Quoted in Henry Berry, *Make the Kaiser Dance: Living Memories of a Forgotten War—The American Experience in World War I* (Garden City, N.Y.: Doubleday, 1978), 434. Charles Codman agreed, describing "a sea of frozen mud. Waiting in shivering lines before dawn for a spoonful of gluey porridge slapped into outstretched mess kits, cold as ice. Wretched flying equipment. Broken necks. The flu. A hell of a place, Issoudun." Quoted in Edward M. Coffman, *The War to End All Wars: The American Military Experience in World War I* (Madison: University of Wisconsin Press, 1986), 199.

Ingalls, Ken MacLeish, and Edward "Shorty" Smith) for advanced instruction at the School of Special Flying at Gosport, near Portsmouth. Evelyn Preston, a friend and correspondent of many members of the Yale Unit's social set, reported, "Bob, Dave Ingalls, and Ken MacLeish are the ones chosen for acrobatic work. Do you realize they are the only three out of the whole naval aviation that were chosen, and all of them the outcome of Huntington?"[2]

The School of Special Flying began as something of an experiment, founded in the summer of 1917 under the direction of Lt. Col. Robert Smith-Barry. An officer of forceful personality and strong views, Smith-Barry learned to fly in 1911 at Larkhill in Wiltshire and at the Central Flying School at Uphaven. He enlisted in the Royal Navy in 1914, flew night antizeppelin patrols, and later commanded No.60 Squadron. Known as both brilliant and eccentric, he received permission to reorganize the flying school at Gosport. Sir Hugh Trenchard, one of Britain's most important military aviation pioneers, claimed that Smith-Barry taught the world how to fly. According to a detailed report later compiled by Ken MacLeish, Smith-Barry "wrote repeated letters to the War Department," arguing it was a waste of time to train men at the frontline squadrons.[3] The appropriate authorities must have agreed, for the number of training fatalities and the performance of woefully unprepared replacement pilots seriously impaired morale and operations. Lee Kennet noted in *The First Air War, 1914–1918,* that "wastage" at RFC training institutions in 1917 reached as high as 17 to 28 percent. Military historian John Morrow called Smith-Barry's reforms "sorely needed," citing the crudeness and inadequacy of even advanced training. French (and later American) flight instruction was more deliberate but much safer. In fact, American training, as measured by accidental deaths, was

2. Quoted in Geoffrey Rossano, *The Price of Honor: The World War One Letters of Naval Aviator Kenneth MacLeish* (Annapolis, Md.: Naval Institute Press, 1991), 59.

3. For a complete discussion of Smith-Barry's career and the work at Gosport, see Frank Tredrey, *Pioneer Pilot: The Great Smith Barry Who Taught the World to Fly* (London: P. Davies, 1976), and D. G. Stratham, *The Gosport Diaries* (privately published, 1981). MacLeish was cited in Geoffrey Rossano, *Stalking the U-Boat: U.S. Naval Aviation in Europe in World War I* (Gainesville: University Press of Florida, 2010), 150–51. MacLeish's original report is in the National Archives in Washington, D.C., Box 1, Entry 35, Record Group 72.

the least dangerous of all—50 percent safer than the French regimen and nearly five times safer than the British.[4]

Given a chance to establish his own school, Smith-Barry personally selected the staff. His methods emphasized dual instruction, trainee-instructor communication via a speaking tube, complex aerial maneuvers, acrobatics, and forced landings, with a focus on increasing student confidence. More than anything else, he designed the Gosport school to train instructors in new methods and attitudes. Smith-Barry mandated extensive preflight briefing and detailed explanations for students. There was little or no red tape. As long as a man did his work, no questions were asked. According to Ingalls and MacLeish, the instructors were a fine bunch of men, very good fliers who had served at the front for a year or two and who now, for the first time, were really learning how to fly. There were plenty of machines available and an excellent shop where aircraft could be completely repaired and reconditioned. Moreover, the surrounding countryside offered many good landing fields. Maintenance crews typically reported about 7:30 AM to inspect and ready aircraft, with further inspections and repairs carried out between 1:30 and 2:00 PM and again between 4:30 and 6:00 PM. Flying commenced at 9:00 AM and continued until 12:30 PM; it resumed at 2:00 and finished at 4:00. Aircraft averaged five hours aloft each day.

The initial work for the Americans lasted only a few days, however, due to the Christmas holidays, and Ingalls and his pals returned to London and a joyous reunion with a gaggle of naval aviators. They headed back south on December 27, and as the only students present, enjoyed the undivided attention of their RFC instructors. Taking advantage of whatever good weather existed, the Americans went flying on New Year's Day. They made rapid progress and within a week soloed in Sopwith Camels, among the most dangerous aircraft on the Western Front. Ingalls reported to his father, "The machine handles so lightly that anything can be done and it is so easy that you simply couldn't fly straight if you wanted to." With its tremendous torque and tricky fueling system, the Sopwith Camel was a remarkably maneuverable and deadly fighter, responsible for more Allied victories (1,294) than any other aircraft. It was also responsible for

4. See Lee Kennett, *The First Air War, 1914–1918* (New York: Free Press, 1991), 127–29, and John H. Morrow Jr., *The Great War in the Air: Military Aviation from 1909 to 1921* (Washington, D.C.: Smithsonian Institution Press, 1993), 238–39, 318.

hundreds of deaths from accidents and training mishaps. The combination of careless or inexperienced handling, aircraft size, torque-producing rotary engine, small wingspan, and weight placement led to frequent fatal spins while in flight. To counteract torque on takeoff, for example, required the use of right full rudder until enough speed had built up for the tail fin to be effective. Otherwise, the airplane might ground loop and crash on the starboard wing tip.[5]

Fair weather breaks were few and far between. Ingalls told his father, "The weather has been rotten. Wind, clouds, snow, and worst of all, fog." MacLeish echoed those thoughts, observing, "Rain and hail have lost their fascination. Snow is quite the thing to fly in."[6] In mid-January, flying conditions grew so bad that Gosport temporarily suspended operations. The Yalies returned to London for a short sojourn at the American Officers Club, attended the theater, and reported to Adm. William Sims and Capt. Hutch Cone, who urged them to finish their work quickly. In the following weeks, they resumed training in a program punctuated by dramatic flights and near disasters. On more than one occasion, they fought mock battles in the skies above southern England. At other times, they took cross-country jaunts that tested their endurance, ingenuity, and navigational skills.

Not surprisingly, the rapid pace of instruction and abominable weather led to frequent mishaps. In early January, Shorty Smith nearly died while looping at twenty-five hundred feet when a loose seat belt caught the stick and he lost control of his Avro.[7] That same day, Ingalls flew into a maze of telephone lines but managed to land his damaged plane. Two weeks later, MacLeish smashed the propeller and undercarriage of his Camel while stunting with an instructor. Nonetheless, increased confidence brought

---

5. For a discussion of this and other mechanical deficiencies of the Sopwith Camel, see Morrow, *Great War in the Air*, 243. Elliott White Springs, in *War Birds: Diary of an Unknown Aviator* (New York: Grosset and Dunlap, 1926), referred often to the Camel's tendency to kill unwary pilots. The entry for March 12, 1918, for example, recorded the accidents and deaths of several American pilots at Ayr, Scotland, "all in Camels and all doing right hand spins."

6. MacLeish's correspondence from Gosport, Turnberry, and Ayr is contained in Rossano, *Price of Honor*, 59–92.

7. The Avro type 504, a two-place biplane used extensively for training by British forces in World War I, was known for its stability and ease of handling. More than eight thousand were manufactured.

aerial high jinks. The young ensigns enjoyed "buzzing" less experienced pilots, the "Huns," or looping within a few hundred feet of the ground. They also loved "bush-bouncing," racing along mere feet above the ground and then hopping over houses, trees, and startled farmers and their animals. Nineteen-year-old Ingalls enthused, "It must have been very exciting to see [four] Camels tearing along just over the ground." When returning to the aerodrome, they sometimes landed within a few feet of the hangars.

Madcap flying did not, however, divert the Americans from their true purpose at Gosport. During his weeks at the school, MacLeish made careful notes about British flight instruction methods, hoping to use the information to improve the American system. After passing through the course, he recommended that all navy flight training begin with land machines and that instructors be chosen on the basis of their interest in the pupils, flying proficiency, ability to effectively impart knowledge, and satisfaction with their jobs, with a focus entirely on instructing. Ingalls compiled a similar report.

At the beginning of February, the three navy aviators finished work at Gosport and relocated to Turnberry, a famous golf resort overlooking the Firth of Clyde, now transformed into the RFC's No.2 (Auxiliary) School of Aerial Gunnery. The school offered concentrated instruction in the mechanics, use, and maintenance of automatic weapons. Lectures and demonstrations filled the days, with evenings devoted to copying notes and studying. Ingalls described how he spent his time "sitting on hard wooden benches in sorts of classrooms, studying twice as hard as I ever did in school." MacLeish called the pamphlets they read "really libraries" and claimed he got to bed just in time to wake up for breakfast. Very little flying occurred, as the nature of the course and perpetual fog and drizzle precluded active operations. Ingalls and the others boarded in either the grand Turnberry Hotel or one of several substantial adjacent holiday villas. When not studying or seeking shelter, the officers played bridge, what Ingalls called "England's national game."[8]

Hurrying along to complete their training, Ingalls, MacLeish, and Smith soon shifted billets again, moving to nearby Ayr, home of the No.1 School of Aerial Fighting and Gunnery. Lt. Col. Lionel Wilmot Brabazon

8. MacLeish's descriptions of the place are contained in Rossano, *Price of Honor,* 93–101.

Rees, VC, an experienced pilot and squadron commander with eight confirmed victories, served as commandant. It was said that "his experience and example were employed in the training of the offensive spirit exemplified by his actions."[9]

The presence of many non-English pilots at Turnberry and Ayr reflected dramatic changes in the composition of the RFC manpower pool. Aggressive battlefield tactics, high operational tempo, inadequate training, and obsolescent equipment generated extremely high casualty rates. Ultimately, new pilots from Ireland, Scotland, and the Dominions replaced such losses. In March 1918, nearly one-quarter of all the RFC pilots in France were Canadian, and by September 1918, according to one veteran, "the majority of the best pilots . . . hail[ed] from Canada, Australia, South Africa, and so forth." In addition, more than 300 Americans flew with British squadrons, and of that number, nearly 30 became aces, 51 were killed in combat, and 32 became prisoners of war (POWs).[10]

Following successful completion of their work at Ayr, the Americans returned to Dunkirk, with patrol operations scheduled to begin in late March. During this same period, David Ingalls took the time to prepare reports on the training regimen he experienced. His detailed and lively descriptions and analysis of the instruction program at Gosport, Turnberry, and Ayr are among the best available.

———

Wednesday, December 19, 1917. At last Shorty [Smith] and I left
dear old London at 11:35 from Waterloo [Station]. Of course
there was a thick fog, when isn't there in this beclouded country,
and train was a couple of hours late, so we arrived about 4:15.
An R.F.C. man and machine met us and took us to assistant
C.O., Wells, major, a perfect prince. We were introduced to our
instructors, shown rooms, signed up our nearest relatives,[11]

---

9. See Mike O'Connor, *Airfields and Airmen of the Channel Coast* (Barnsley, South Yorkshire, U.K.: Pen and Sword Books, 2005), 177–80.

10. See Morrow, *Great War in the Air*, 172–73, 240, 314.

11. Pilots were asked to supply the names and addresses of their relatives to be notified in case of serious injury or death.

always a pleasant reminder of the hereafter, and given tea. Then we met Ken [MacLeish]. He'd been flying a lot. We saw a bit of flying and had a fine dinner.

Thursday, December 20, 1917. Rose at 8:00. No flying on account of heavy mist. This school is really for instructors, the course is two weeks. That's advancement; teach the teachers. Could be applied in most schools for mentality improvement. Machine is A.V. Roe, called Avro. It's a two-seater, very handy and easy to fly, also a few Camels and S.E.5s. It is rather extraordinary to learn that most experienced pilots don't know how to fly perfectly. Here the finishing touches are put on, every stunt is taught, side slip landings, perfectly balanced turns, etc. The idea of the school is to train men to all instruct in one way on a fast two-seater, also, instead of the present way of starting on an old Farman and working up. There are a few beginners here to prove that the method is right and they have turned out very good flyers.[12]

The school is an experiment. Lt. Colonel [Robert] Smith-Barry is in charge—he originated the idea. Under him is Wells. There is no red tape. As long as a man does his work no questions are asked. There is great freedom, the instructors are a fair bunch of men, very good flyers, of many experiences. Many of the pupils are majors, etc., who have flown even at the front for a year or two and who are now for the first time learning how to really fly. Many have Huns to their credit, and many have decorations. In instructing, the instructor first does a thing, then you follow in loops, etc. By means of simple metal tubing with rubber ends conversation is easy. There are plenty of machines and good mechanics and an instructor to a man almost, so you learn quickly or are advised to try for the commissary department. There is also an excellent shop where machines can be completely made. The country all around is full of good landing fields.

12. The Royal Aircraft Factory SE5A was an important single-seat, biplane fighter; it was stable, fast, and maneuverable, known as an excellent gun platform. The Maurice Farman "Shorthorn" was an antiquated training aircraft, first introduced in 1914, derisively known as the "Rumpty."

The barracks, offices, mess halls, etc., are within an old fort surrounded by a moat with drawbridges.[13] It is wonderfully picturesque. The rooms are great, though cold, with fires kept up by a batman. What an institution, the Batman! My first experience with a valet. There are also reading rooms, etc. The food is O.K. and there are *no* rules or regulations, only an unwritten law to do your flying and do it well. A paradise for a flyer. The only other sort of duty is to practice on the range with shotguns, pistols, or machine guns.

The men are mostly experienced fighters and a great bunch. The hangars, etc., are just beside the fort in a large perfect field. On one corner is also a range etc., for elementary machine gun practice. The field is about two miles from Gosport. As there was no flying, we walked to Gosport where Shorty cabled his girl that he was well and lonesome. As Ken asks almost nightly for some message for Priscilla [Murdock], I, this old bachelor, am again stuck to a bunch of born lovers. I foresee a hell of a time in one respect—these two are going to waste a lot of our time writing and talking about their fiancées. Sometimes I thank God I am still unshackled. Sometimes I sort of wish I were. If I am sociable and write my family whenever they write their future families, my old man will wonder what the Hell!. After a great lunch I read and wrote till tea and dinner. More reading.[14]

Friday, December 21, 1917. Started out a good day, after breakfast at 9:00, I had a wonderful hop with my instructor. I did more stunting in fifteen minutes than I knew there was. I like something that is touchy, at least in an aeroplane. I learned how to do vertical turns and tail spins, and tried a couple of landings. Never again will I fly

13. Almost certainly Fort Grange, one of the many "Palmerston Forts" built in the 1850s and 1860s to protect the British coast against attack by French naval forces. Fort Grange was the most southerly of three virtually identical fortifications erected in Gosport between 1858 and 1863 to protect the approaches to Portsmouth harbor. Each was polygonal in shape with a circular central keep, protected by a moat and small drawbridge.

14. At the time, Gosport, lying opposite Portsmouth, counted perhaps ten thousand inhabitants. Priscilla Alden Murdock was a member of the "Radio Girls" and the unofficial fiancée of Ken MacLeish.

a water machine in preference to land. It is wonderful. It was warm
flying, as we only went up to 3,000 feet, although the thermometer
was about 20 today. The continued banks made us a bit sick, but I
soon recovered, and found Shorty all in from his flight. Afternoon
mist and no flying, so walked to Gosport.

Saturday, December 22, 1917. After my second flight in morning
    when I had a great time and learnt to land the bloody bus, and
    learned more of stunting. Then learned the place closed up for
    Christmas. Ken, Shorty, and I went to Portsmouth for lunch, took
    an afternoon train 2:35 for London. Got rooms at the Curzon near
    A.O.C. [American Officers Club] where we had dinner and saw
    "A Little Bit of Fluff." Very funny, a bit crude.[15]

Sunday, December 23, 1917. Had lunch at A.O.C. and then went for
    a walk with Alice [Bowler] and had tea at Ritz.

Monday, December 24, 1917. Saw about mail, talked to [W.
    Atlee] Edwards, where I saw [Carl] Hull. Lunched and saw Al
    [Sturtevant], John [Vorys], Bob [Lovett]. Did a lot of what you do
    in London. Had dinner with Alice at The Chinese Restaurant,
    very peculiar and very cheap. Saw movie after.[16]

Tuesday, December 25, 1917, Xmas. Hell of a note. Maybe I feel
    the way I did the first two weeks away at boarding school, maybe
    a little worse. Took Alice to Westminster Abbey, big reunion
    lunch at A.O.C., wrote a number of letters. Then Shorty and I

---

15. The Curzon Hotel in Mayfair stood a few blocks from the American embassy
and naval headquarters in Grosvenor Square. The American Officers Club occupied
an elegant town house on Curzon Street, what Ken MacLeish called "the city house
of a wealthy English nobleman [Lord Leaconfield], and it's too beautiful for words."
Quoted in Rossano, *Price of Honor*, 38. Journalist Sir Henry Brittain played a major role
in organizing the club. King George V complained that the chairs there were more
luxurious than those at Buckingham Palace. *A Little Bit of Fluff*, a farce written by
Walter Ellis, premiered in London in 1915.

16. Lt. Walter Atlee Edwards, a member of the "Old Pensacola Tribe" of naval aviators, received instruction there prior to World War I and served as Adm. William Sims's
aide for aviation for most of World War I. The first Chinese restaurant in London
opened around 1907.

had dinner at Almonds Hotel with Alice and Dorothy Foster, Joe
Foster's sister, who is in R.C. [Red Cross] here.[17] We then went
to a dead dance, then to Murray's. After a lot of trouble we found
a taxi. By the time we left Murray's, Christmas was long past.
A hell of a Xmas we all agreed. Especially as I haven't had any
mail since two days before leaving Paris over two weeks. I'm very
much afraid I was just a bit low.

Wednesday, December 26, 1917. Saw Edwards and arranged our
mail if we even get any forwarded. Took Alice to lunch at La
Petite Riche, very nice, and saw the "Saving Grace," very good
show. Had tea at the Carlton. Then the old five had a farewell
dinner at A.O.C. and Shorty, Ken and I went to see "The Boy."[18]

Thursday, December 27, 1917. We got up at 6:30 to catch a train, which
Ken said left at 8:15 A.M. On arriving at Waterloo Station about 40
minutes ahead of time, we found that it was 8:15 P.M. and our train
didn't go till 9:35. After a haircut at Savoy I couldn't get a taxi and
had to run like the Devil all the way to the station and just got on
as train was leaving. After finding Ken and Shorty in a second class
compartment, the first were all taken, we had a rotten trip, arriving
about 12:30 to find that school didn't open till Friday, so after
lunch and a rubber of bridge I walked to Portsmouth and back.

Friday, December 28, 1917. Hotter weather, long walk. After lunch,
short flight making many landings.

Saturday, December 29, 1917. Cloudy at 2,300 feet, and very rough
flying. Short flight, I then soloed. As soon as I got up to about
2,000 feet, making turns all the time, I looped six or seven times,

---

17. Dorothy Foster was one of the many American women in Britain and France
doing war relief work.

18. *Saving Grace,* a comedy in three acts written by C. Haddon Chambers, opened
at London's Garrick Theatre in October 1917 and played on Broadway in New York
in the fall of 1918. One of the actors in the London production was Noel Coward. A
musical comedy by Fred Thompson, Percy Greenback, Lionel Monkton, and Howard
Talbot, *The Boy* opened at the Adelphi Theatre on September 14, 1917, and ran for 801
performances, a phenomenal run for that period.

tried three or four tail spins, several rolls and more loops. I
couldn't seem to get on to the rolls, came out in a tail spin motor
full on several turns. Looping was easy, though I hung on to
the stick like death as I did loose loops and there was not great
centrifugal force. Then I tried a few landings and one spiral and
came in a bit sick as I had been throwing the machine around a
good bit. After about an hour, I felt fine and after lunch got up
again. First I tried a number of landings in small fields and also
tried landing in one spot, it is much easier than a water machine
as you can side slip off altitude very fast. Then I started for quite
awhile and did some fairly respectable rolls. Came down and took
a look at the R.N.A.S. station nearby and then came in after about
45 minutes. My thumb was cold and stiff from [so much] buttoning
the motor and after landing as I taxied in my thumb wouldn't
keep the button off and I got off the ground near the hanger. After
cutting the gas I made a hell of a landing and lost the propeller
dead motor. I certainly was disgusted with myself as Capt. [Dirk]
Cloete, my flight C.O., was watching me come in. However, I
felt much at home and had a very good time and think I learnt a
lot about flying. Didn't have sickness afterwards. Shorty, whose
stomach has been causing him trouble, also is feeling much better
and soloed this morning too. No mail yet and we three are pretty
sore at the mail service in Paris, they were holding it till enough
came to fill a bag, till Edwards telephoned.[19]

19. The "RNAS station nearby" is possibly a reference to either RNAS Lee-on-
Solent or RNAS Calshot, the former largely a training facility and the latter an op-
erating/patrol base, both situated only a few miles away. Many aircraft equipped with
rotary motors incorporated a "blip" button on the end of the stick, which cut the
ignition and allowed the machine to descend from height or lose speed. The device
also proved very useful when maneuvering aircraft on the ground. Capt. Dirk Cloete,
MC, a South African, served as acting major as of February 1918. Following the war,
he served with the South African Air Force and then the Southern Rhodesia Air Unit.
Despite his rapid progress as a pilot, Ingalls remained a teenager in many ways. His
bunkmates complained, "He has lost all the manners he ever had, and now he makes
the most disgusting noises you ever heard, and he's so darn nervous and fidgety that
we're gradually going crazy. . . . [He] is sitting here by the fire sucking his gum and
inhaling it with such mingled and audible disgusting noises that I can't keep my mind
on what I'm doing." Quoted in Rossano, *Price of Honor*, 72, 82.

[Gosport] December 29, 1917

Dear Dad,

After leaving London Thursday morning, we were certainly glad to get here, although late as usual. On account of the holidays everything has been a little slack here, but Monday a new bunch of people came in and things will probably take a big brace. Just now we Americans are the only pupils, so we are getting some good work in.

Yesterday I got only one flight, a short one in the afternoon, with a young Englishman who is my instructor now. He is just a kid, but a very good flyer. For some reason a young Englishman seems very much younger than an American of the same age. There were heavy clouds at 2,300 feet and it was rough as the deuce, with a strong wind of twenty-five miles per hour. After about ten minutes instructing, I at last got off alone. I've been dying to get up alone and certainly had a time. As there were a lot of machines around, I had to keep a good lookout, as it is surprising how quickly you come together. I climbed to about 2,000 feet, doing several vertical turns on the way up. Then I leveled out, got up some speed, pulled back the stick and looped for the first time.

It is customary to cut the motor at the top or a little beyond, but I cut too soon for the first two loops, but it made no difference. At the top, as I was doing some very tight loops, not knowing how much strain the machine would stand, centrifugal force did not quite hold me in, though I held myself there by a very tight grasp on the stick. Of course, I had a belt on too, as a precaution, but it is not necessary. After five or six of these, to get the hang of it, I tried rolling, which is sort of turning upside down and then right side up again while going somewhat straight ahead. It is awfully peculiar, and I couldn't seem to get the hang of it at first, but ended up in a tail-spin which is simply diving straight and revolving rapidly. This last is the most dangerous stunt, as the machine is almost entirely out of control. It is a great strain on the machine. Well, I would cut the motor and get out of this, usually not until I had dropped 600 or 700 feet, and kept trying until I got into a fairly respectable roll. These machines, being large and two-seaters, of course don't roll very well anyway.

Then I did a few tumbler air turns, getting into a tail spin the first few times. It seems everything ends up in a tail-spin, if not done correctly. Following these I just mixed up stalls, side-slides, loops, etc., for a while and wasn't flying straight a quarter of a mile. Well, as I say, I was getting cold and a bit sick, so I came down, tried a few landings, and came in. It was the best flight I ever had, Dad, and I certainly enjoyed it.

Sunday, December 30, 1917. Rather punk day but I got up with [Cloete] and found I was rotten at turns. Learnt turn and also side slips and landing cross wind. Then tried it alone and learnt a lot. Feeling a bit low so sat around all afternoon as there was no flying. Two more pupils have come here.

Monday, December 31, 1917. Hell of a day. Late getting up so missed almost all breakfast. Went to Portsmouth and bought chocolate and waffles. Then hurried back for lunch as it cleared a bit. Took up my machine at about 2:20. Very foggy, also heavy clouds at 1,500 feet. Kept getting worse, almost hit several other machines, no fun so I came in soon. Ken landing behind another machine smashed wing skid. The new bunch of pupils have arrived, so mess is full again. Also USA men have arrived, none are officers yet, none have flown. Received four French learning books from Mrs. Burton, also letter from Di. No mail or packages from home yet. Shorty not having heard from his girl is wild. Ken got a lot of mail also from Priscilla.

January 1, 1918. Rotten day—no flying in morning—cold. After lunch cleared up and flying. At 2,300 feet clouds 400 feet thick going through nice and clean—most wonderful sight imaginable. I stayed till cold— . . . and stunting. Under clouds very foggy and rough. Lately I've been practicing forced landings, shutting the motor off at about 1,000 feet and then picking a field and landing in it. I find you can land almost anywhere without trouble. Big day, first mail three months. Dad, Ma, and Kate. 35 minutes in Avro.

January 2, 1918. Avro: 85 [minutes], 35 in morning, 50 after lunch
we forced landings. Shutting off at 1,000 feet and picking fields
and landing. Received letter from Dad dated November 8.

January 3, 1918. Avro: 45 [minutes]. Another perfect day. Rose 7:00
and practiced landings an hour. You can land almost anywhere,
but this morning I found the other place. Was side slipping
down, felt something catch, feeling heavy drag and ailerons
busted. Landed, just missing deep ditch. Found had carried
away five telephone wires, all still hanging on front. Aileron wire
underneath torn away. Cloete came for me and had a laugh. The
instructors keep a good eye on their pupils. He'd brought me
a mechanic and flew me home with him. Later had flight then
walked to Portsmouth with Ken and Shorty and back. Arranged to
have gunnery any day. And so we carried on. Flying if you could
see through the fog across the field, and shooting clay pigeons or
reading and eating otherwise.

[Gosport] January 3, 1918

Dear Dad:

Yesterday I received a letter written by you on Nov. 8th just
after you had been to Fort Sherman but I don't think that temptation
there could hold a candle to what it is here.[20] However, I am taking
the best possible care of myself, not only because of the moral side
of the question, but also because of the terrible effects, which latter
has been brought home to me by the pitiful condition of several of the
men directly under me. As the main trouble with my receiving mail is
due to the absolute inefficiency of the postal department headquarters
in Paris I have decided to accept Ken's suggestion having my mail

20. Camp (Fort) Sherman was an enormous U.S. Army training installation constructed in 1917 near Chillicothe, Ohio. As many as 40,000 personnel trained there at
one time. See George W. Knepper, *Ohio and Its People* (Kent, Ohio: Kent State University Press, 1997), 346. Between September 27 and October 13, 1918, a total of 13,161
men on the post fell ill with influenza and 1,101 died, which made it the hardest-hit
camp in America. See Coffman, *War to End All Wars,* 82.

sent through a bank here of which his aunt is president or manager.
So if you will please address letters in the future and packages to
Ensign D. S. Ingalls, U.S.N.R.F., care of Carson Pirie Scott et cie, 42
Faubourgh Poissioniere, Paris, I hope to get my mail in two weeks as
Ken does.[21]

For the last three days I have been having lots of flying, and so
also lots of fun. The first day was very cloudy but after getting up to
about 3,000 feet I was above the clouds in the sunlight and, Dad, it
was by far the most beautiful sight I have ever seen. It was quite warm
and the huge billows of clouds below covered the entire horizon, and
seemed to offer a big feather bed to light on. The clouds were of course
sort of uneven, tremendous mountains with valleys in between. Every
now and then machines would sort of rise out of the clouds and the
sun would stream on the wings. Yesterday was very clear and I learned
a lot about vertical turns. These men come back from the front to
this school, where flying is taught scientifically and perfectly and are
absolutely overwhelmed by the amount they do not know. Practically
no one who has not been here can make a perfect turn.

Today I had my first smash, fortunately a minor one. I was
practicing landings, the damn foolishness of myself is awful, small
fields, cutting my motor as if it had quit on me, and picking a field and
landing, when I caught seven or eight telephone wires. I had not seen
them nor had any idea what I hit, but my ailerons failed to work so I
kept on and landed, almost in a ditch. Well, after landing on the brink
of said ditch I climbed out and found the control wire running to the
bottom of the lower wing carried away, otherwise everything OK. As I
couldn't fix it I kicked myself around the field for about ten minutes
when my flight commander, who had been told of a machine down,
landed, left a mechanic, and took me home. Since then I have been
having my leg pulled as the English say. Well, as you used to say when
I smashed up an auto, it is a good thing so long as nobody is hurt, as
you have the experience. I certainly will try to keep my eyes open.

But yesterday Shorty Smith almost ended his career and taught
us all a good lesson. He went out and upon getting to about 2,500 feet

---

21. Ken MacLeish's father (Andrew MacLeish) was founder and manager of what
later became Carson, Pirie, Scott, a Chicago retail store.

looped. The strap to hold you in the front seat had been left lying on the seat loosely fastened, and when upside down with the stick pulled way back, the strap swung around and over the stick, holding it way back. This of course held the elevators way up so the machine started on a second loop with Shorty pushing for all he was worth. As he had cut the motor the machine merely pointed straight up, stalled, tail-slipped, dove down, then started up again. Fortunately his ailerons and rudder would still work. After stalling, it would of course dive several hundred feet before gaining enough speed to pull him up again. After coming down by the above process to about one hundred feet Shorty was a bit worried, but being a plucky little devil he didn't lose his head. Just as he started to go up to stall, here he saw he would, in the ensuing dive, hit the ground head on, so he cleverly side-slipped by using the ailerons and everything just happening to work out fortunately he pulled it out of the tail-slide a few feet before crashing and landed all right with only a wing slightly damaged and the aileron wing slightly broken.

He says he thought an awful lot on the way down, as it took quite some time, but he always had the hope of leveling off just as he hit. He says he didn't think of side-slipping till he saw he'd lose out if he didn't do something when he leveled off at about 180 feet. He says his brain was in good condition then. That taught us to look out for anything that would catch the stick and proves that one has wonderful control in pretty adverse conditions. Even my being able to land trailing seven or eight telephone wires after a hard shock shows that it takes a hard bump to bust anything. Well, Dad, try this new address for awhile, will you, Aff yours, Dave

P.S. Please tell mother to send some of that chocolate. D.S.I.

———

January 4, 1918. 30 Avro, heavy mist @ 300, had gunnery @ 8:00, Lewis and Vickers, short flight, very jerky. Coming in wind caught me from behind and carried me on into another machine. Cloete advised care. Said few days and take up Camel. Friday afternoon is holiday so talked and read.

January 5, 1918. 70 Avro. Fine day, no gunnery so we later had 20 minutes. After lunch another solo. Then Cloete taught me correct rolls, loops, and fluttering leaves, last a new stunt Cloete just learnt.[22] All are trying it. Ralph Bahr, Toronto, Canada, got back from London. Canadians seem as cold-blooded as English. After bed Bahr taught us a lot of English slang.

January 6, 1918. Dud day and bad headache [after gunnery stand?].

January 10, 1918. I finally took a ride in a Camel, a scout, single-seater fighting machine. It's so touchy it just seems to jump if you shiver, and goes into a spin every time you take a turn unless you do it perfectly. I was full of pride that I got back in the same world as when I started. Then later we three went to London again for some excitement. Alice is still to be found. We learned from headquarters we were to hurry through Gosport and proceed to Turnberry, the British finishing school for machine gunnery, and then go to Ayr for a course on aerial fighting.

So on the 13th we left at 6:10 for our finale at Gosport to find dud weather for several days. More bridge than flying. Ken and Shorty got more damn mail. They gloat over me till I think I'll advertise for a girl, one who will write a lot. That's all a girl is good for if she's in the old U.S.A., at least as far as I'm concerned. Me, I like them closer at hand.[23]

[Gosport] January 14, 1918

Dear Dad:
We negotiated the battle of London safely for the three days' leave we were afforded, staying at the American Officers Club, seeing shows and talking to many interesting officers, Army and Navy, who are

---

22. In this maneuver, the pilot raised the nose of his aircraft and induced a stall. Rather than allowing the machine to fall over into a vertical spin, he maintained enough control to initiate a kind of flat (horizontal) spin, with the aircraft oscillating from side to side, resembling the descent of a fluttering leaf.

23. This entry is from Ingalls's postwar memoir.

always stopping there on their way to and from France and America.
Among others we saw Admiral Sims for a minute, and Capt. [Hutch]
Cone,[24] who, as you probably are aware, is at the head of naval aviation.
The latter expressed a desire for our finishing up quickly, from which
I derived that the men who are going to make up the flights that we
are to command have almost completed their course of training at
the U. S. Army aviation school for scout pilots in France [Issoudun].
Of these men's ability to fly and fight the machines we are to use I
have unfortunately not a very high opinion. First, because they are
not a particularly capable lot although selected as the best from the
exceedingly miscellaneous and rather inferior lot of men first sent over.
I think I have previously written you concerning the type of men who
arrived in France about the time I did. Secondly, because they have
not had a great deal of time in the air. And thirdly because from what I
have learned of the school, their training cannot have been as complete
nor as thorough as the work they are to do demands. Although I fully
appreciate the impossibility of such an act, still I am very sorry that
they too could not have had the wonderful training that the English have
so kindly given us. To be sure they have received the best instruction
that the Navy could offer and I hope it is better than I have predicted.

According to a letter from "Di," who is executive officer at our
future station [Dunkirk], it is progressing as well as could be hoped
from the disadvantage of its location—it is constantly bombed
by aircraft, which occasionally breaks up the monotony of the
construction work. Evidently the authorities here have also received
orders to hurry us through, and I expect practically to live in a Camel
this week, after which we will immediately be sent to Scotland for
I imagine at least two weeks, probably three, training in gunnery
and aerial fighting. From here we shall return to France with all the
customary naval delay, and probably spend several weeks waiting
in Paris, and then perhaps longer for our men to study up on some
technical point highly important practically, such as the use of a
compass or something like that, which has been sadly neglected.

---

24. Adm. William S. Sims commanded U.S. Navy forces in Europe, with headquarters in London. Capt. Hutch Cone commanded naval aviation forces operating in
Europe, with headquarters in Paris.

Here the weather has been rotten. Wind, clouds, snow, and worst of all, fog. Any weather seems to bring on a heavy ground mist preventing flying. Today it did not clear up until afternoon very late and by that time it was almost tea time, everyone was compelled to adjourn for that important event. However, we have all been given a private Camel, to fly our heads off, which is just what we all want.

The new allotment or class came in this afternoon—they change every two weeks. We feel like old timers now, just imagine me at tea explaining to an R.F.C. flight commander, who had spent two years at the front, how to work the type of motor used here and how to put one of these dual-machines into a tail-spin. This new bunch are a bit uneasy because this afternoon before flying became possible two of the best instructors went up and did the most wonderful flying imaginable. Even the old timers had to stand around in awe. You see if these men pass here well they do not send them back to the front immediately, but are given a much needed rest for a month instructing—so they are pretty keen to do their best. By that time they are fed up and dying to get back to the front again, and they are then in wonderful shape. A great many, almost all in fact, of this class are Canadians, who I find are a great deal like Americans and have often spent a lot of time in the States, so one feels almost as if it were an American station.

Well, Dad, here's hoping for a few weeks good weather. Please tell mother I received a perfectly great chamois vest-coat today, which is just what I've been wishing Santa Claus would send. As ever aff. Yours Dave

[Gosport] January 17, 1917

Dear Dad:

Although the weather has been rotten so far this week, yesterday was passable, and I had about an hour and a half [flying]. As we now each have a Camel to ourselves, if the weather permits we can fly as much as we want. Until yesterday afternoon I had not become accustomed to the way the Camel handled, as it is a long step from an Avro, the slow dual machines, to a scout, especially a Camel, as it is about the trickiest and hardest to fly. What helped more than anything else to make me accustomed to the machine was that late in the

afternoon as I was fooling around, looping, etc., an instructor also in
a Camel suddenly appeared diving at me, and for about ten minutes
we chased each other around. It was the most enjoyable and exciting
time I have ever had. One forgets about simply flying and does so
instinctively, keeping one's eye always on the other fellow, and also a
general lookout for other machines. It is really remarkably how close
two machines can come together without colliding.

Another funny thing, Shorty had just been up before in the same
Camel—it is painted a peculiar color, and we had fooled around
together, quite a bit apart however. Well at first I thought this must
be Shorty again, but in about a second I saw I was wrong for from
quite a distance the difference in the two men's flying ability became
quite apparent. To tell the truth whereas Shorty and I had each lots of
fear of colliding, when this fellow came around I never thought about
it. He had perfect control and I just never thought about running
in to him. It seemed to me that the danger of collision is when two
machines are just fooling around, thinking themselves alone.

Well, as I have said, from this little encounter I got lots of
confidence and for the rest of the afternoon felt perfectly at home.
The machine handles so lightly that anything can be done and it is so
easy that you simply couldn't fly straight if you wanted to. But very
foolishly I did a lot, six or seven, tail-spins just before coming in and
as the darned little machine spins at a terrible rate I felt rotten for two
or three hours afterward. Also, I have broken all speed records that
I've made before, as several times looking at the air speed indicator
in a dive it would be registering 190 or more. If the weather doesn't
improve we'll be here another week. Suits me all right.

Dad, the tobacco here is rotten. When you go to New York could
you send me some M.M. (medium strength) tobacco. At the "M.M.
Importing Co." address I think 11 E. 45th St. New York. They might
be able to send a pound every three or four weeks.[25] Did you send my
license as a naval aviator? It has not yet arrived. Of course the last

25. Ingalls was rarely without his pipe, which appears in many of his wartime photographs, and was thus always in need of additional supplies of tobacco. Some months
later, Ken MacLeish reported to his fiancée, "You should see the pipe Crock has.
It's about ten feet long and he has to rest one end on the table or his break his jaw."
Quoted in Rossano, *Price of Honor*, 225.

mail from you was dated I think Nov. 23 or so. So it may come any time now. I was just talking to an R.F.C. fellow about Dunkirk. He says it isn't bad in summer but Hell in winter so we're in no hurry to get there. Well, dinner is served so must go. Aff. Dave.

January 21, 1918. We've been doing a lot of huffing in our Camels, that is, we go up and have mock air battles.[26] It's good practice for the future, provided we get to that future. Ken generally puts it all over me. He has acquired a damn fine reputation here and is considered one of the best pupils the school has had. However, I can hold my own with Shorty and there's still time for practice before we get to the front. We flew over to Beaulieu for lunch at the school there and were well entertained.[27] We had to laugh that afternoon. Some new bird got stuck in one corner of the field and a mechanic went out and got him started, then got on the wing while they just taxied back. The fool bird got going too fast and damned if he didn't leave the ground and the mechanic's love of the earth got control over him so he let go and gravity did the rest. He only broke one leg and an arm.

January 22, 1918. Lots of huffing. Ken didn't hang it on me so much. Later a fellow named Gross crashed in a field nearby. Ken was flying near and pulled him out of the machine and then got help. Gross is still unconscious. This class is getting so good now that they land all over and in every direction till it's as much as your life is worth to get into the field without landing on somebody or him on you. Ken's instructor, Williams, lit on somebody this afternoon. The two schools, gunnery and aerial fighting, will probably not be quite so comfortable and easy going as this one. As far as I can find out now, a week at each place suffices for the course, so we'll not be there long unless the weather is dud. . . .

26. *Huffing* was a slang term for conducting mock aerial battles.

27. RFC Beaulieu was a training field located in the Hampshire countryside, a few miles west of Portsmouth.

[Gosport] January 24, 1918

Dear Dad:

I was very glad to receive some mail from you and Mother dated
Dec. 6–12. All of this has doubtless been lying around the mailroom
at 4 Place d'Iena, and I hope by now you are sending my mail to
Carson Pirie Scott and Co. You certainly must be busy now and I
don't suppose you are home very much. It's lucky that Mother is
so deeply interested in and hard at work for the Red Cross. I'll be
nineteen now, in a few days,[28] and hope to celebrate my birthday
in London, as I think we shall leave this school Saturday the 26th
and go to Scotland, passing through London. As is customary when
traveling under our good navy's orders, we shall probably be delayed
in London for several days. This will not be so bad, however, as there
is usually plenty to do there.

The two schools, gunnery and aerial fighting, will probably not
be quite so comfortable and easy going as this one. As far as I can
find out now, a week in each place suffices for the course, so we'll
not be there long unless the weather is dud. Yesterday was not very
good here. The morning, which was fine, was occupied by gunnery
practice. I had one thirty-five minute flight with my Camel and a good
scrap with "Ken." Somehow or other I unfortunately broke the rudder
bar—on which one's feet rest, and also the motor is in bad shape and
is being overhauled, my Camel has been laid up since.

The afternoon was dud. An awful fog came up very suddenly and
one fellow trying to get down landed in a tree, while another hit the
foot of a tremendous wireless mast, and another crashed into the flag
pole of one of the hangars. Fortunately no one was hurt. As it cleared
a bit I went up in one of the Avros to test the motor, a two-place
machine, but the clouds were at about 150 feet. Everyone is getting
a bit frisky lately, flying around the field and landing very close. It's
very hard to get in, about five machines are continually landing within
about fifty feet of the hangars. At the end of each class everyone

28. Concerning the man-boy's appearance, MacLeish reported, "He's not quite a
man and not quite a boy—he's just nineteen. He's got nineteen hairs on his upper lip
too—pathetic spectacle. I have that many on each side, but you can see mine. You have
to feel Crock's." Quoted in Rossano, *Price of Honor*, 87.

seems to show off a bit, at this time more than usual. But today was fine, and I flew an Avro most of the morning and afternoon, getting only one ride in a Camel borrowed from another flight. I did some so-called contour-chasing, i.e., flying very low, jumping over buildings, trees, etc. It's great fun unless the motor stops, when you are "up the creek." So ho for London and Scotland. Aff yours Dave

January 25, 1918. My Camel has been laid up for repairs for three days, putting me back. Shorty's been advised that he's through, and so is Ken. I'm the black sheep, I guess. However, we had a good dance tonight, that is, we had a dance at the fort and anything is better than nothing.[29] I concentrated on some high born dame, with apparently some success.

January 26, 1918. This afternoon we went to town and had tea at the Cadena Tea Room. Why did I go? My high born dame is a waitress there. Also called on Gross at Haslar Naval Hospital.[30] He's almost unrecognizable, but is expected to pull through. Ken played poker tonight. Thank God he did something instead of write his girl.

[Gosport] Jan. 27, 1918

Dear Mother:

In spite of everything portending otherwise, we are still here at R.F.C. Gosport and hope to remain next week. As this weekend was leave week, there was practically no flying Saturday and Sunday, but we stayed here anyway. You see Friday night there was a dance here

29. MacLeish described the dancing as "three steps, then a hop, after every seven evolutions they turn . . . for an amusing spectacle give me an English couple performing said dance." Quoted in Rossano, *Price of Honor,* 87.

30. Work began on a naval hospital at Gosport near Portsmouth in 1746 on land then known as Hesler (later Haslar) Farm, with the first patients admitted in 1753. Much expanded, it was designated Royal Naval Hospital Haslar in 1902. The 1910 edition of Baedeker, *Great Britain: Handbook for Travelers,* 59, described the facility as "a spacious building, with accommodations for 2,000 sick or wounded sailors."

which the officers gave. It was great fun, though English girls have a most unusual way of dancing. So Saturday morning we slept till lunch and so couldn't go to London.

Friday afternoon Shorty, Ken, and I each taking an Avro, and Ken and I mechanics as passengers, we set out on a cross county fly to a camp about forty miles from here. Well, it was awfully foggy and we ought not to have gone as results showed. We flew over almost all the way together, but just over a city we were flying about four hundred feet to keep below the clouds and see where we were going. Shorty, who was supposed to be leading, went up into a cloud and we never saw him again. I started to follow and lost sight of Ken, so I turned over to the coast and came down to about one hundred feet. Seeing nothing of either of them and being lost I picked out what looked like a good field beyond the city, and landed. The minute we touched down we stopped as the field turned out to be muddy and watery. We both got out and looked things over. It looked bad.

While we debated, men, women, and children collected panting around us, touching the mechanic and asking if we needed an ambulance. As the mechanic is a hunk of a fellow about six feet two inches I don't know why we looked like ambulance patients. When a suitable gallery had arrived I got in and the mechanic swung the propeller and together with the motor and about one hundred people pushing and apparently endeavoring to tear off the wings as souvenirs we got to a knoll about fifteen feet square. The mechanic got aboard and starting at one side of the knoll we managed to get started so by the time we hit the mud we were almost flying. There was then an anxious second and we were off, missing surrounding people, trees, and wires equally closely.

As the fog kept getting lower we had to fly over the city very low and even then could only see a little way, just far enough to miss by inches a couple of tremendous smokestacks that suddenly loomed up ahead. When we finally got back Shorty had not returned, but telephoned later that he had landed and would come back next day. He got in yesterday afternoon and said he had stayed with a very congenial English family and had a fine time. We were pretty suspicious and pumped him until we found out that the family

included a wonderful daughter. Everyone has been kidding him since.
I think he flew around the promising looking houses till he could see
the inhabitants who of course come out to look on and picked the
best. As he is engaged to a girl in Buffalo we haven't been suspicious
of him till now. But he missed the dance at which we had a fine time.
As we can't cash a check here, we're going to fly to London in the
morning. It's only about 70 miles in our Camels. These cross-country
flights are great fun. Be sure to make stronger packages. The last
tin of chocolate we got and rock candy was broken open and the
chocolate all gone but a bit. As we have plenty of sugar don't bother
sending any. But Barking Dog tobacco would go well. Will you please
have some phonograph records "well packed" and sent, music from
"Oh Boy," etc.[31] You might ask Adele what the good ones are. We
are going to take a phonograph to Dunkirk but can't get any decent
records. Love, Dave

January 28, 1918. Well, I'm 19 today. What I want to know is what
good it does me? The only event was the departure of the first
class and arrival of a second, a more crumby crowd by far, or else
we're more particular.

January 29, 1918. I was promoted to an instructor. It appealed to my
sense of humor to have as a pupil an old major [captain] named
Smith who has had two years of flying at the front, But he was a
good sport, though I bawled Hell out of him. I realize my chances
of shooting the Hun are improved vastly by this course here, that
is, if flying has anything to do with it. Ken and Shorty flew to
London, 70 miles, to cash a check. Can't do it here. Nobody has
that much, not even the banks.

31. *Oh Boy!* was a very successful musical play created by the team of Jerome Kern,
Guy Bolton, and P. G. Wodehouse; it opened in New York City in February 1917. This
show introduced the immensely popular song "Till the Clouds Roll By."

School of Special Flying, Gosport, Jan. 29, 1918

Dear Dad,

Well, I feel pretty doggoned old now, being 19 years old yesterday, and also learning that my little brother helped beat Princeton at hockey. I knew he'd come through with the goods. Elmendorf Carr, who is in Paris, very kindly sent me clippings reporting the game. Today I received lots of mail, a couple of letters from you and three from mother, all dated about Dec. 12–22. I'm awfully glad you were able to leave Pittsburgh and be home for Christmas. Wish I'd been there too. In one of your letters I received Mr. Herrick's letter of introduction. Thank him, please, very much for it. But I have not received my license as naval pilot. So far I have not needed it, having substituted my name in a copy of Ken's paper, and certified this to be a true copy of the original. However, I might at any time need the original itself, and shall write immediately to the postal office to endeavor to trace your letter containing said license. But am I mistaken in thinking that you said, in one letter some time ago, that you would send the document to Robertson and he would send it through the embassy mail. Perhaps, if this is so, it may have been mislaid at the embassy.

I am glad to hear from you that the bad opinion of the way men were being trained for observers and bombing in the states, is erroneous; especially as these two matters are not usually accorded sufficient attention, most money and thought being devoted to the training of pilots.

This week I have been flying only Avros—the two-place machines as my Camel is laid up for repairs. As it is now O.K., however, I hope to get in some good work before we leave Saturday for Scotland. But my time has not in anyway been wasted as I have been doing almost two hours or three every decent day on these Avros. And today darned if the C.O. didn't ask me to do a bit of instructing. So I took up a captain who has been at the front flying for two years, for a couple of hops this afternoon. And I found it to be quite true that this school is the only one at which one is taught to fly really. Shorty and Ken flew to London today 70 miles to cash a check and had lunch after. Ken has not returned, so I imagine he stayed for the night. He and Shorty were separated while shopping and Shorty came back alone about 6 P.M., landing by flares as it was practically dark when he landed here. Love Dave.

—

January 30, 1918. My Camel is O.K. again, so I'll be through soon now. I flew on my back, upside down today. Funny thing, you are strapped in and can't fall out, but believe me you hold on the stick with some grip when upside down. I don't get a hell of a kick out of it anyway, being upside down things go just opposite, which is confusing, and oil and gasoline seem to pour out on you. Most unpleasant. One of the new pupils, a Captain Smith, came over in the evening. He's been flying at the front almost since the start, and having a hobby of photographs took lots of wonderful pictures of planes of all sorts, British, French, Huns. He had some of Huns scrapping, some of planes in flames, some museum should get them really, I don't think there can be any others like them.

February 1, 1918. I almost crashed. Coming into the field the pressure tank went and the motor stopped. I switched on the little extra gravity tank but the darn thing was empty and no help.[32] I got into the field by the grace of God or something without crashing.

—

School of Special Flying (Gosport), February 1, 1918

My Dear Mother:

The last five days here have been most enjoyable. Although there has been a slight fog, we've done a great deal of flying. Yesterday I

---

32. The pressurized main fuel tank located behind the seat allowed gasoline to be fed to the motor no matter what direction, motion, or position the aircraft assumed. A hand-operated pump located within the cockpit could be used to maintain pressure in the primary tank. The small, auxiliary gravity tank located atop the primary tank and behind the pilot's head could be used under certain conditions when the pressurized fuel tank failed to work or was empty.

had two hops in an Avro, one with my C.O. Captain Cloete, in which I learned a new trick. It seems as though there is no end to the amount of different things one can learn. This was a vertical spiral. That is, with the motor off, we glided down, and banked up vertically in a spiral. Although it is really very simple, it is the first time I've done it or seen it before, and Cloete tells me he has just learned it himself.

In the afternoon I was up for a long time in my Camel, which is running wonderfully, and after a short scrap with "Shorty," in which I had a comfortable time, being always at his tail—an enviable position, owing to my motor being better than his—I tried for the first time flying upside down. Of course, the motor does not run, so one simply glides down slowly on one's back. Of all the uncomfortable positions it is the worst. In the first place, the machine tends to slip off on one wing and eventually always does, about two minutes being the extent of my flight upside down. That is, the machine is very hard to keep level; one wings tends to go down, the other up. And as all the controls are reversed it is most awkward.

Then after a perfect tea (really I intend to institute tea hereafter wherever I live), "Ken" arrived from London. As I wrote, he had been unable to get away on his Camel on account of the heavy fog, so he came out in the train, and we expect to fly in tomorrow, he and Shorty going in an Avro to bring back the Camel and also Lieutenant Edwards, who is the aide [to Admiral Sims], to stunts. Funny how everyone wants to loop, etc., isn't it? He also brought me a camera, so at least I can take some photographs, though of course I'll not be able to send you any.

This morning I had two flights in my Camel besides a lot of gunnery, and managed to stay upside down a little longer that yesterday. But I almost broke up my machine, when, as I was gliding in to land, the pressure in the gas tank leaked out and I couldn't pump it up as fast as it leaked. Well, I was trying to pump and land at the same time and came too close to the hangars, so, when I was still about ten feet off the ground, the hangars were in front, I put the switch on the gravity tank and opened the valve, thinking I would go up around and land again. But the gravity tank is a fake; anyway the gas just leaked through enough to about keep the propeller turning. So I had to do a vertical bank with the motor sort of sputtering and

turn with one wing almost dragging and lit at right angles. It was a
rotten feeling, as I could feel it begin to side-slip down on account
of the slow speed at which I was going, and I should undoubtedly
have smashed a wing if everything had not gone just right. As it was
I was well kidded. The gravity tank worked all right when I tested it
some time ago, but being little used, I suppose some dirt got in the
pipes. Anyway, I took it out on the mechanics, with the result that this
afternoon the old Camel was in fine form and old Shorty and I went
with two instructors on a beautiful cross-country flight.

They knew the country well, so at good places we could roar
down low, giving the people and animals a great scare. It must have
been very exciting to see four Camels tearing along just over the
ground. As you probably know, the density of the air low down lets
the machines go considerably faster than they do at any high altitude,
so we moved right along. It was great fun jumping over hills, houses,
etc. We have certainly had a wonderful time here, and I'm sure we
will be sorry to leave, which will be now probably in two or three
days, as we are just waiting to go to Scotland to finish up.

———

February 5, 1918. We were ordered to proceed to Turnberry and
left this morning for London en route. Thank goodness. Every
time Shorty has tried to fly he has gotten sick all over the plane.
If he don't get a good rest he'll be out of flying for good. He told
me that he thought of his girl all the way down the other day
and figured he wouldn't ever think of her again, much less see
her. Maybe I'm not so darn unlucky to be unloved. Next day we
arrived at Turnberry and were split up as to rooms. I'm with a
darn good Irishman named Radcliffe, not one of the kind that
doesn't prefer not to fight the Hun. Turnberry is a great place,
a Scotch golfing resort, the hotel turned into a barracks for the
pupils, the links into a field for gunnery practice of every sort. It
is most delightful as far as scenery goes. The food is insufficiunt
and punk, the occupation is most boring.

———

(Turnberry) February 7, 1918

My Dear Mother:
   Much to our regret we left the best school day before yesterday
and took the train to London, where we spent the night. Then, leaving
early yesterday morning, we traveled up to Scotland to this, the
second school in our course. I had a fine trip and crossed the frontier
into Scotland hungry as the deuce, where beautiful Scotch girls
rushed up to the train in the station and gave us cakes, etc. Don't
know how they knew we were coming! From then on at every small
station, and none were too small for our express to stop at, we could
get out and have the time of our lives listening to any Scotchman
whom we could prevail upon to talk. Their brogue is divine. Upon our
arrival we were shown to rooms in a hotel that made me homesick for
Palm Beach. And this morning we looked out upon a beautiful golf
links by the sea, with beautiful hills rolling away inland. A really
heavenly place, evidently a once famous golfing resort! I certainly
have fallen for Scotland; it is a great place.
   Here, instead of older men, captains, etc., as were at our previous
school, there are only young, inexperienced cadets, slews of them, as
this is practically a non-flying course. We spent all day sitting on hard
benches in sort of classrooms, studying twice as hard as I ever did in
school. This will last at least two weeks, when we will take up aerial
fighting for a couple of weeks. Then our training will be over.

——————

   February 5–15, 1918. For the last two weeks we attended lectures,
      sitting for hours on benches; shot every sort of gun, studied and
      handled machine gun stoppages. We learned all about those darn
      guns; I think I can take one down and put it up in my sleep now.
      I find that a machine gun is darn hard to shoot, not like playing a
      hose, and the gears, which synchronize the propeller and bullets,
      and the sights for deflection, etc., are pretty complicated. To
      thoroughly understand them is, to me, who has had little to do
      with guns, like putting a picture puzzle together. Also, the R.F.C.
      men have had a good deal of training in the preliminary schools,
      but we had only a little. However, we finish in about seven or

eight days and then hope to go through the course in aerial fighting, which is very short.[33]

—•—

(Turnberry) February 15, 1918

My Dear Mother:

The weather up here in Scotland has been pretty rotten since our arrival. Today it is raining and cold. As this is the first day I have not been very busy due to the fact that today we have our exams in gunnery, which don't take long, the rain prevents our taking a walk. It is the first time I have had a second off since arriving. Tomorrow we start a bit more interesting work, i.e., firing from aeroplanes, at different targets, from the air. On account of the bad weather I am going to take up the sport of bridge, as otherwise there will be nothing to do during our flying course. Of course they play a rotten game on a big pool table which they call billiards, I think it was invented some thousand years ago and compares to real billiards as a bow and arrow does to a machine gun. If anyone asked me what England's national game was I'd say bridge. They play all the darned time, but as far as I can see it is not with the result that "practice makes perfect."

In spite of our excruciating labors we are having a fine time, at mess.[34] Shorty and I are at one end of a table with a South African who has been fighting since 1913, a Canadian who has been over here in France for two years in infantry and a young Australian who, having just arrived at the age, enlisted in the R.F.C. They are a mighty good bunch. The Australian, who now looks about 17, received two white feathers before he enlisted.[35] They must have handed them around to any fellow old enough to wear trousers. The other day Shorty and I walked about three or four miles to a

33. See Ingalls's instruction notes from Turnberry, appendix 2 in this book.

34. The dining room at the Turnberry Hotel was known as Officer Mess—St. 2 Auxiliary School of Aerial Gunnery, R.F.C.

35. White feathers were sometimes given as a symbol of shame to "slackers" (or those assumed to be so) who refused to enlist. This custom was especially prevalent in Britain and some of its dominions and colonies.

beautiful little Scotch village along the coast, where we heard one might obtain matches. Believe me, matches are worth their weight in gold. Well, we were in luck and each of us obtained a box. That night after supper, everyone at our end of the table got out a cigarette and turned to Shorty, who had pulled out his box. With great pride Shorty opened the box and pulled out a match. The match comfortably rubbed against its neighbor, there was a flash and Shorty ruefully looked at about 150 burnt matches. There was clearly quite a universal sorrow. I'm surprised that no monument has been erected.

Mother, just as I was smoking the last bit of Barking Dog, I received another tin from you. I certainly was de-e-e-lighted, and hope you are sending me a lot of it as a tin lasts Ken and me a very short time. I also received a wonderful sweater and a pair of socks. Thanks awfully. I seem to wear out socks pretty quickly. There was also a pack of Spearmint, evidently you sent me a box, but the package was very weakly tied up and I consider it lucky that someone didn't take the sweater also. Please make very strong parcels, will you? Love Dave

(Turnberry) February 18, 1918

Dear Dad,

I haven't received any mail or parcels lately, these things seem to run in bursts. In fact I haven't received or done a darn thing now for about four days. After passing our gunnery exams, me at 86, we have been waiting for flying weather. It has been dud—very dud— since, and there is honestly nothing to do but play bridge, except that Saturday we spent two hours going to and fro to a town about 20 miles away [Glasgow] and spent about three hours there, most of it at a movie. Also we were not in too good spirits as the Canadian who sat at our table and who is a great fellow has gone on to the school of aerial fighting [Ayr] and the South African just received a telegram announcing his brother's death in France. Certainly is hard luck.

Just received another letter from Blake Lawrence, who, I think

I told you, has come to England and expects to get a commission very soon in the British infantry. Skinny Lawrence, Cy Clark, Lloyd Kitchell, Weir Sargent, and several other fellows have also come over in our artillery, I think, hope to see some of them before going to Dunkirk, in Paris.[36] We expect to leave here now Wednesday, then have about ten days aerial fighting. I haven't heard anything about our station from Di Gates for quite some time, but all of the enlisted men who are to make up our flights have arrived here, also to take the course.[37] And I certainly would feel happy if they could fly as good as they think they can. I'm very curious to see what the men do in a machine. They were very lucky in that they received quite a lot of flying in the Army school in France. Well, Dad, dinner has been announced so I must stop. Affec.y Dave

February 16–20, 1918. The main excitement here is the posting of the overseas list every night. The British are so hard up for pilots that they can't give all the final course at Ayr and a few are posted daily to leave for the front the next day.[38] My God, most of the boys have flown in all only about 15 or 16 hours; many of them only one or two hours on the scout type they will have to fight in. There isn't a hell of a lot of conviviality when we all line up at the bulletin board after supper to find out who is to go. It sort of makes one appreciate the feelings of those in the Bastille, or wherever they kept the poor French devils en route to the guillotine, when the jailer came in with the list of those to be honored.

---

36. Brothers Blake Lawrence and John Tharp "Skinny" Lawrence from New York were friends of Ingalls's from St. Paul's, in the classes of 1916 and 1920, respectively.

37. These were the enlisted navy pilots from the First Aeronautic Detachment who trained at Tours in the summer of 1917 and later at the new AEF school at Issoudun.

38. The climactic German assault of the war was expected within a few weeks, and the RFC moved every available pilot to the front, no matter how inexperienced, to bring its squadrons up to full strength.

(Turnberry) February 21, 1918

Dear Dad:

The last few days have been no vacation. We start at 8:45 finish at 12:00, start at 1:45 and stop for tea at about 4:45. Then there is lecture from 5:30 to 6:45. After dinner we usually have to copy notes—thousands of them, but, by writing all Saturday afternoon, when we had a half holiday, but it poured rain, I have finally finished. Although at first the course seemed very monotonous and boring, now I am enjoying it immensely as it is most interesting. There is always a certain amount of excitement, even to us, as in the lists posted of the fellows who are to go "overseas" as they call it, immediately.

As it is a sort of large finishing school, fellows are continually coming in from different preliminary schools, and going out to France, home defense, etc.[39] There are quite a few army and navy men of ours, besides of course the RFC composed of a few English, a great number of Canadians, and some S. Africans, etc.

On our arrival we were split up and I am rooming with a very funny Irishman, who has had two years in the trenches. He is a mighty good fellow and we are in the same classes and have lots of competition on the ranges shooting. I find that a machine gun is darn hard to shoot, not like playing a hose, and the gears, which synchronize the propeller and the bullets and the sights for deflection, etc. are pretty complicated. To thoroughly understand them is, to me, who have had little to do with guns, like putting a picture puzzle together. All the R.F.C. men have had a good deal of training at the preliminary schools, but we had only a little. However, we finish in about seven or eight days and then hope to go through the course in aerial fighting, which is very short.

It is quite different here from our first school where all the men were older, experienced men, while here they are just a bunch of kids. Just as at school, I often wonder how some simple, sissy, youngster ever left home. But, by George, they all come along, and do their best, just as, with no war, they would have gone to school and

---

39. RFC squadrons formed to defend the homeland against German zeppelin and long-distance bomber raids. By the end of the war, fourteen such units had been organized.

college. There is one Canadian here who used to play the violin at some hotel in New York, whom I remember having seen. He is very good and plays quite a bit here. He also plays the piano and knows most of the late pieces. It certainly is great to hear him. Bridge is a popular sport here too, most everyone seems to play when not writing up notes. The only misfortune is that the food is neither quite so good nor as abundant as at our first school. But I am all the better for less food and sugar and sweets, and am still fat as ever. Love, Dave

School of Aerial Gunnery, Turnberry

Probably the most interesting and, yet, withal the most important course in the training of an R.F.C. aviator, is that at the school of aerial gunnery at Turnberry, Scotland.[40] Although the entire course is only two weeks long, however, the fact that most of the instruction is given either in the classrooms, which in this case are small wooden huts especially erected, with small tables and uncomfortable backless benches, or the ranges, excepting for the last three or four days when a little firing is done from aeroplanes, makes the two weeks seem very long indeed. Still, the wonderful quarters and food very good for England. The officers are all quartered in the hotel once popular as a summer resort, overlooking the sea and surrounded by a golf links whose beauty is somewhat marred by the large canvas hangars and hideous little wooden huts which are of course vitally necessary to the administration of the school.

To this school go all members of the R.F.C. From here some are sent overseas, and the more fortunate to Ayr, the school of aerial fighting. The school is therefore, of necessity very large, and that added to the unfortunate fact that most of those now entering the R.F.C. are of a young and irresponsible age compels strictness and red tape on the part of the authorities. This, naturally, only makes the course more boring, and causes the foolish youths to indulge somewhat too freely

40. Despite his youth, David Ingalls observed events surrounding him closely, and following his work at Turnberry, he took the time to analyze the training he received there. Such reports were forwarded to headquarters and then disseminated to other American fliers. Ken MacLeish drafted similar reports, as did U.S. naval aviators stationed at several British patrol stations.

in alcoholic drinks. This isolated nature of the country is, however, most important, as the firing of these youth, many of whom have never previously touched a firearm, is somewhat erratic. The strictness, on the other hand, has strong advantages and causes the school to carry on regularly and efficiently. A large company of men, a great number of machines guns, and much ammunition form the basis of this school. In addition, there is an aerodrome with sufficient machines, in itself almost a complete school.

Let us divide the course therefore into the ground work and the aerial work. The ground work, on which the pupil spends ten of his fourteen days, includes a practical knowledge of the Vickers gun, the Aldis and ring sight, and the C.C. or Cowper, or SPAD interrupter gear. First each of the points is taken up in the classroom by practical demonstration with the aid of a great many valuable notes which each pupil is compelled to copy and keep.[41] Further, each evening a lecture is given on one of these three points. After becoming thoroughly acquainted with these matters, the pupil is sent onto the range, where he puts to practical use what he has been shown.

With regard to the gun—the main points are thorough knowledge of parts, care, and cleaning; faults, including stoppages, defective ammunition, etc, and general handling. With regard to the sights—the knowledge of its use for deflection, the alignment and care. With regard to the gears—the faults, knowledge of parts, and care. Capable corporals and sergeants do all the instructing, and all the instructing has to do only with aerial gunnery, no land drills, sights, and stoppages are taught.

Second the aerial work. Each pupil is taken up by an instructor, and practices first ordinary target practice by diving on a target and firing. Second, clearing stoppages with one hand while flying the machine. Third, deflection target practice when with camera guns in two machines a regular fight is carried on.

When finished at this school the men have had a great deal of both theoretical and practical work in aerial gunnery and are ready to proceed to Ayr, the school of aerial fighting.

---

41. See Ingalls's transcribed technical notes in appendix 2.

February 21, 1918. We arrived at Ayr last night. This morning we
reported to Col. Rees. We are billeted here with all the other pupils.[42]

———

(Ayr) February 23, 1918

My Dear Mother,

At the present moment I am ensconced on a very comfortable
chair before a very comfortable fire, smoking a very comforting pipe.
In fact, and to be thoroughly frank, thus far I have found life in the
flying corps a very pleasant one physically, and mentally, though
perhaps one conducive to laziness. Except for a short bit of study
in gunnery, one's mind is occupied for the great part by bridge and
reading. However, in this third school I am again rooming with
my Irish friend and he continually keeps one's wits awake. In the
flying corps nature plays a major part. For in good weather we do
everything, in bad nothing. And for the last four days the weather
has been bad. During this time there has been little but bridge and
by some chance I have managed to bring to myself three or four
pounds. Mother, I have an admirable and comforting philosophy
concerning bridge. If I lose I feel I must be lucky in love, if on the
other hand I win, I conceitedly claim that it has not been all luck
but perhaps a bit of skillful playing wherefore I am not necessarily
unlucky in love. However, if I should find that I was losing more
than winning, my philosophy would tell me that I would be satisfied
at being lucky in love, and should not tempt misfortune by playing
further, since I might thus lose the wherewithal of maintaining what
I had won. This latter case, I trust, may not occur, as I am now broke
and must somehow pay my board without cashing a check as this
would necessitate the loss of at least a pound owing to the difficulty

---

42. At the time, Ayr was a town of approximately thirty thousand inhabitants,
best known as "an ancient seaport . . . chiefly interesting as the center of 'the Burns
Country.'" See Baedecker, *Great Britain: Handbook for Travelers,* 545. Among the many
students at this RFC finishing school were aviators from throughout the empire, the
small navy contingent, and dozens of U.S. Air Service fliers, such as Elliot White
Springs, Laurence Callahan, George Vaughn, and Reed Landis.

of cashing our paychecks here in Scotland. Furthermore I would then have little with which to occupy myself. You may imagine the shock I received on hearing today from Bob Lovett, that he, being second in command at Paris headquarters, owing to the Captain's being away,[43] is temporarily in complete command over there. Some jump from instructing us at Palm Beach. However, Bob has an excellent head, and I hope is kept at headquarters with much more authority. But I fear he will soon receive a station somewhere. Shorty too just heard from one of our bunch that Al Sturtevant had been shot down while submarine patrolling.[44] Poor old Al, he was a mighty fine fellow. And last night we saw off the South African and Canadian who messed with us, who are going overseas. We have become darn good friends and miss them. I hear too that we are due for further instruction in France after we finish here; the Lord only knows when we will be finished learning. Well, mother, I am looking forward to a lot of mail, as we have received none for over a week. Also some more parcels should be arriving. With love, Dave

Middleton, Ayr, February 27, 1918

Dear Dad:

It seems like an awful long time since we have flown. What with the dud weather and the over-crowdedness of this school, the outlook is full of a distant future. Moreover, all of our men who were with us in France are here with us now and we are going to take the course

---

43. Here, Ingalls referred to either Capt. Thomas Craven or Capt. Hutch Cone. Craven directed the Operations Division at headquarters; Cone commanded all naval aviation forces.

44. Al Sturtevant of the First Yale Unit, then stationed at RNAS Felixstowe, was shot down over the North Sea during an antisubmarine patrol on February 15, 1918, the first naval aviator killed in action. This event shocked First Yale Unit members and was followed only a few days later by the death of Curtis Read at NAS Dunkirk. Sturtevant's death is recounted in Ralph D. Paine, *The First Yale Unit: A Story of Naval Aviation, 1916–1919*, 2 vols. (Cambridge, Mass.: Riverside Press, 1925), 2:89–100, and Marc Wortman, *The Millionaires' Unit: The Aristocratic Flyboys Who Fought the Great War and Invented American Air Power* (New York: Public Affairs, 2006), 160–62.

together, so it will be some time before a big bunch like us will be able to start. Yesterday an Army aviator and I went to Glasgow to see what's what. We had a darn good time, saw an excellent show last night, and some good movies in the afternoon, but we had to get up in the morning to catch a 5 A.M. train in order to get here in time.

Day before yesterday there was a lot of flying—for others. One poor nut started off with his motor missing badly because he was choking it. He kept on, however, and did a circle about the field, refusing to land while he had a chance. So just as he got over our heads the motor stopped completely and he came down on top of a hangar, the wheels caught and he stuck straight up with the bow embedded in the roof. It was the stupidest and funniest thing I ever saw. The poor nut climbed out and posed for everyone to make photos of him. As it was very cloudy I'm afraid I didn't get a good picture.

This morning I was delighted in receiving two letters from Mother, one mailed January 10 sent to 4 Place D'Iena, and the other Jan. 30 sent to Carson Pirie Scott. Therefore be sure to send all my mail to Carson Pirie Scott and Co., 42 Faubourgh Poissonniere Paris. Please tell Al [brother] I'll write Alf Ames about the motorcycle immediately.[45] Love to all, Dave.

March 1, 1918, England

My Dear Mother,

Yesterday, as the weather was dud and there seemed to be no chance of our flying for some time, Shorty and I went to Glasgow. You are probably aware that it is a good-sized city, and a fine place. We had an excellent time, walking all over the place and getting acquainted with the Scotch ways. That night we saw a couple of shows and had a tremendous dinner. This morning we stayed over and wandered around doing a bit of shopping and then took the afternoon train out. On arriving we found we were at last placed in a flight and as it was a good day had missed a lot of flying. Rotten

45. Yale Unit member Allan Wallace "Alphy" Ames, NA #67, served in the United States until July 1918 and thereafter performed staff duties in France and England.

luck. Ken had not gone and had some flying and all our men, having
arrived from the other school also had flown. You may remember
I said these men had come from training in France, and have had
quite a bit of time on Nieuports. As a result they think they are
pretty slick and have made us sick with all their bull. Well, Ken saw
the first four of them go up today in an English scout and Camel and
he and everyone else say they are about the most hopeless bunch
imaginable. They can't understand at all and blame the weather,
machines, etc. We all had to laugh when Ken reported their antics.
All of them climbed to 6,000 ft. without turning and then came
straight down and landed very badly, feeling pretty cheap. One
fellow had to make three attempts before he could land and then
just missed a hangar by the grace of God. But I found some mail
from you, dad, and Al, which was great. Also by some chance the
silk underwear arrived and a box from Aunt Louise, and a couple
of days ago I received a sweater and socks, etc., from Victoria and
Mrs. Britton. I wrote thanking them but they may not get said letter
so will you also tell them how much I appreciated it? This winter
must have been a wonder.[46] Dad must have had an awful time. I
hope everything turns out all right. My Irish room-mate left tonight
for over-seas, much to our regret as he is a most amusing chap. Well
Mother, as the fire is going out and my room-mates are in bed, good
night. With love, Dave

March 2, 1918. There was no place for us here, so we just had
to wait around for our instructions. About all we did was go to
Glasgow for a couple of days, and play bridge. . . . Yesterday
Pat Radcliffe left for the front. Once the boys get to Ayr they
are generally allowed to finish before they go to the front, but it
seems just now things are going badly. It resulted in our getting
started today. I managed to move into a room with Shorty, Ken,

46. The winter of 1917–18 was one of the coldest on record in the United States,
with enormous snows in the Northeast and Midwest. New York harbor froze over,
making it possible to walk from Staten Island to Manhattan. Equally foul weather
beset those serving in Europe.

and Lloyd Hamilton today.[47] We certainly started full out, flew all day, contour chasing in formation, stunting and huffing. Contour chasing means flying just off the ground, it's good practice, because if you don't pay attention you don't miss the trees and buildings.

March 3, 1918. One of the U.S. Navy boys, to be in our squadron, stunted today. Those boys got their training at Issoudun, and think they are the berries. His name is Hough,[48] he started and did a turn only 300 feet above the field, slipped into a spin and dove into the ground. One second it was O.K., the next it just disappeared with an explosion and then there was a little pile of debris. We pulled Hough out. His legs were badly, very badly, but no other injury. He may lose his legs though.

⎯⎯⎯⎯⎯⎯

March 4, 1918

My Dear Dad,

    I was very glad to hear that, in spite of all the weather, your railroad is O.K. It must have been some winter, wish I had been there to see a little snow, and cold weather. Rain, wind, and fog is a poor excuse for our winters. Also I wish to state that the last address—Carson-Pirie—is a good one. Mail arrives in about three weeks over here, which is excellent. We are flying at last. The last few days have

---

47. Lloyd Andrews Hamilton, DSC, DFC, with ten confirmed victories, trained with the RFC in 1917–18 and served with No. 3 Squadron, RAF, and the USAS 17th Aero Squadron. He was killed during an attack on a German kite balloon on August 24, 1918, near Lagnicourt, France. See Hudson, *Hostile Skies,* 215–16.

48. Frederick Hough, a Chicago native and member of the First Aeronautic Detachment, died on March 13, 1918, of injuries sustained at Ayr on March 3. At least thirty-four American died while training with the British. See Hudson, *Hostile Skies,* 33. Many people observed the travails of the enlisted navy pilots at Ayr. In his postwar reworking of John MacGavok Grider's diary, aviator Elliott White Springs observed, "There's a big party going on here in spite of the wholesale funerals. Six [*sic*] American naval pilots were sent over from France to take the course here. They thought that Camels were as easy to fly as the Hanriots they had been flying in France, and they wouldn't listen to any advice from the instructors here. Three of them were washed out one week." See Springs, *War Birds,* 87.

been fine, and room has been made for us here. Today we got all we
wanted, flying from 9:30 'til 12:30 almost steadily. And real flying.
This course has already been a great help to me in many ways. There
seems to be no limit to what one may learn in the game. This morning,
the first thing we did was to engage in a big bombing raid. Ken, Shorty,
and I were in a big formation of scouts convoying some of the bombers.
We managed to protect our bombers fairly well, and they dropped tons
of bombs on the hostile city [Troon], which to be sure suffered not at
all. Well, when we met the enemy defending the city, there was some
fight. I've never been mixed up with a lot of machines all diving and
split assing [performing a split-S maneuver],[49] vertical turns, etc.,
around and was continuously jumping around in my seat to steer clear
of the others. Later a peculiar thing happened. Ken, Shorty, and I were
in formation, Shorty behind Ken. Shorty lost sight of him somewhere
and foolishly started to glide down to find him. He came down on top
of Ken who was going quietly along. Fortunately neither machine
was badly damaged, and they both landed alright, but it was quite a
shock to them both. And yesterday the Navy suffered. One of our crazy
enlisted men was trying to split ass above the hangars and spun into
the ground. He was badly hurt. Well, Dad, as I said, I'm darn tired and
am turning in immediately. As ever love, Dave

March 5, 1918. We were graduated today. We wired headquarters.

March 7, 1918. Well, Hough is no more. We went over to see him
the other day and the poor devil was nearly gone. His legs were
swollen about five times their ordinary size and doctors couldn't
even amputate. It was too much finally for him. This morning
Ortmeyer spun from 50 feet and was badly hurt.[50] Later Velie

---

49. The split-S is an aerial maneuver consisting of an inverted half-roll followed
by a descending half-loop, which results in the aircraft speeding away in the opposite
direction at a lower altitude. It is occasionally referred to as a reverse Immelman turn.

50. Andrew Carl Ortmeyer, Yale '06, trained in Tennessee and Illinois, served as an
instructor at British schools including Turnberry and Ayr, and died in a training accident on March 7, 1918. Springs recorded, "Then Ortmeyer, who had three hundred
hours on Curtisses at home as an instructor, spun a Camel into the ground and killed
himself." See Springs, *War Birds,* 87.

spun from about 2,000 feet and was dead before we got him separated from the pieces.

March 9, 1918. Yesterday and part of the day before we spent in Glasgow. Today we hear that Ortmeyer has gone West [died]. They were both Americans. Later Velie, one of our future squadron, spun into the ground from 1,000 feet and joined Ortmeyer. Two B.F.'s [Bristol Fighters] crashed too. We found that several Britishers had also been killed.[51]

March 10, 1918. Well, there was a strike today. All the pupils refused to fly any more in Camels. It does look like sure destruction. There are only a few machines left anyway. So this afternoon the instructors went up in what remained and stunted all over to inspire the poor devils. I never saw such marvelous flying; it was simply superb. And was without an accident. The only marring element was that two Avros hit head on at about 100 feet. However, no one was hurt.[52]

School of Aerial Fighting

The school of Aerial Fighting at Ayr, fully equipped with machines of all types now in active service and with instructors who are picked men drawn from those actively engaged overseas, is a finishing school for

51. Harry G. Velie, a Chicago native and member of the First Aeronautic Detachment, died at Ayr on March 8, 1918. Springs noted, "Dealy [Velie] spun into the ground the next day and before they got him buried, two Englishmen killed themselves." See Springs, *War Birds,* 87. The two-seater Bristol Fighter, nicknamed the "Brisfit" in the United States, entered service on April 5, 1917, with a maximum speed of 123 mph and a ceiling of 21,500 feet. More than three thousand were built.

52. Elliott Springs witnessed the same show and came away equally impressed, writing, "Col. Rees is in charge here and he tried to put pep in the boys by giving a stunting exhibition below five hundred feet. He certainly did fight the treetops and he wouldn't come out of a spin above fifty feet. Then he made all the instructors go up in Camels and do the same thing. It was a wonderful exhibition and then he made us a little speech and told us there was nothing to worry about." See Springs, *War Birds,* 87. Despite these assurances, deadly accidents at Ayr continued.

all pilots who have already flown their future service machines.[53] Here, as far as possible, the actual conditions which will meet the men overseas are offered. There is absolutely no red tape or theory, everything is done in a practical way. Each man is placed in a flight composed of his type machine and is made acquainted with different methods of attack and defense and of formation flying and convoying. The men are under no restrictions as regards to flying. They are placed in small groups under the direct supervision of a competent officer, who personally instructs them in every method of flying and fighting. As is fitting for a finishing course, this one is very short, the pilots condensing all their instruction in two or three days of almost continuous flight. There is no overcrowding, for every man there is a service machine, besides two or three dual machines for flight in which if deemed necessary the instructor may take up a pupil. Every effort is made to give each man personal training in his service machine under actual fighting conditions.

The school is divided roughly into four flights:

> For men flying Bristol Fighters
>
> For men flying Sopwith Camels
>
> For men flying S.E. 5 machines
>
> For men who have passed through the course and are waiting to be called overseas

Men who are to fly any other type than those above-mentioned, are distributed among the first three flights to take the course on Avros. These types are those that are at present the most efficient machines and therefore are those on which the greater part of the pilots are trained. The machines are all kept in perfect condition and are almost all supplied with camera guns and sights.

Excepting in a few cases, the training for all pilots is very much the same. First, they are taken up in an Avro, the standard dual-control

---

53. For Ingalls, the training regimen in Scotland was over. Just as he had at Turnberry, he drafted a lengthy description of the program at Ayr. Ingalls complimented the scope and value of the training but also documented the extreme dangers encountered there, as well as the heavy toll on men and machines. Ken MacLeish said of his time at Ayr, "It's too depressing to stay here, as they kill off too many men to suit me." Quoted in Rossano, *Price of Honor,* 110.

training machines, by an instructor until the latter is satisfied with the pupil's ability to fly well, i.e., make forced landings, sharp turns, have rolls, and customary stunts. After one or two hops the pupil is usually passed. He then soloes on an Avro. After this he takes a short hop on his service machine. Now he is ready to learn fighting and formation flying. An instructor therefore makes up his flight of pupils and leads them on one or two short formation flights. He, then, in a scout gives each pupil, first in an Avro, then in a service machine, a fight. Afterwards giving them invaluable advice in the handling of the machine in an air duel.

Now the pupil is ready to unite formation flying and fighting. One instructor therefore leads a flight across the line patrolled by several fights and a battle takes place as soon as the patrolling flyers catch sight of those crossing. For this purpose, here, the coastline offers a splendid line of defense, and the attacking party endeavors to outwit the defenders by making use of clouds, inequalities in the land, etc., and cross the line unobserved, when, if successful, they rise and show themselves offering battle. As many as possible of these maneuvers are carried out, the two parties dividing upon a given signal, and repeating the performance. Each pilot is given at least two opportunities of engaging in this work. Some time during the latter part of the course a large bombing raid is engineered in which everyone takes part. All the men training at Ayr form two flights, each led by an instructor. These are the bombing machines. Two large flights of scouts are also led by an instructor, one to convoy each set of bombers. All the Bristol Fighter pilots, the men in the pool and the remaining instructors, form the defense. The latter, the instructors, fly all types of machines, including a German Albatross and several types of English machines, including one or two of the latest or even experimental machines.

Some town or city nearby is selected as the objective. The defenders leave the home aerodrome first and get in position. Shortly after they leave, the two attacking forces go off in a wide, roundabout way, having beforehand determined upon a certain time at which they will attack the city from different sides. As nearly as possible to the predetermined time both parties of bombers and escorts attack. The convoying scouts endeavor to keep the defenders from the bombers, which in close formation dive upon the city and fly over the points to be bombed. All the machines, about 35 or 40 in all, then engage in a tremendous battle.

After about ten minutes of this, when the bombers have flown back and forward over the city several times, a signal is given and all the machines return. Then a flight of pupils alone is sent in formation and each leads the flight in turn.

Afterwards all pilots and instructors are called together, and each flight commander reports his objective, its success or failure, and gives advice on his flight's actions. Then the C.O., who always is overseeing, all while flying among the defenders, gives a talk on the different points of the raid and raids in general.

As to the differences in training of the several types, there is little to be said. The pilots for Bristol Fighters, and those training on Avros, concentrate particularly on formation flying at altitudes above 1000[0?] feet, and in their fighting machines practice so as to give their observers an opportunity to shoot as well as themselves. The S.E. 5 pilots do their formation flying and fighting also at high altitudes, but of course considering shooting only through their prop as they carry no observer. The Camel pilots, as the Camel is now used only under 6,000 feet and mostly for trench strafing and low patrols, do almost all their formation flying only a few feet off the ground, contour-chasing as it is technically described, learning to follow the inequalities of the ground very closely. Their fighting of course is carried on somewhat higher. But as this contour-chasing requires a delicate touch and continual alertness, much time is devoted to it. Thus all training is carried on under conditions similar to those at the front, and offers the men a splendid opportunity to become acquainted with every method of aerial warfare.

The men in the pool—a flight containing one or two of each type machine—practice stunting, fighting, join in the different live patrols and raids, and generally fit themselves for active work. From the pool men are taken to fill the vacancies in flights at the front and to form new squadrons.

As may be easily seen from the above, the instructors must be picked men, expert flyers, well acquainted with every method of fighting. They are all experienced men who have fought the German aviators successfully. Every few months some of them are sent to the front to learn the latest maneuvers, and new men are continually being brought back from the front with new methods of fighting to put new life in the course.

Because the course is short, only a few men are trained at a time so the flights are comparatively small. The 1st Flight at present has three

B.Es and five or six Avros. The 2nd Flight 15 Sopwith Camels and six
Avros, the 3rd Flight four or five S.E. 5s and three or four Avros, and the
pool a few of each type, including three or four Camels, two S.E. 5s, a
German Albatross, a Bristol monoplane, a D.H. 2, and two or three Avros.

Each flight has two mechanics per machine and two flight sergeants
and an office where flight reports, files for machines and motors, etc., are
kept. Large shops for taking care of both motors and planes adjoin the
field, and new machines are always arriving to replace those smashed or
discarded. The whole establishment is under Col. Rees, himself a skillful
pilot and experienced fighter. The course is subject to frequent changes,
as the advances in aviation are made, and every effort is devoted to make
the school as complete, up to date, and efficient as possible.

The School of Aerial Fighting, therefore, with active service
machines, with expert instructors, with every method of fighting, every
sort of formation, and every style of attack, defense, and bombing, with
men in charge deeply interested in making efficiency and improving the
course, this school offers practically the most advanced, comprehensive
training, under conditions as nearly as possible like those of actual aerial
warfare. DS Ingalls

Note. On account of the ever increasing need of more pilots for the
front, the total length of the course in aviation has been made as short as
possible. Even so at present many pilots are unable to take this finishing
course, but are sent overseas direct from Turnberry, the school of aerial
gunnery. Since the course at Ayr is considered so valuable it has been
made as short as possible which causes a sacrifice of men and machines.
This, I think, may be conclusively proved by mentioning the number
of accidents. During the week previous to my arrival here, the whole
flight of seven S.E. 5 machines was written off. During the ten days I
have spent here, there have been four bad smashes resulting in three
deaths and a waste[?] probably for life, besides seven or eight lesser ones,
in most of which the machines were practically written off. If only time
were available and the course could be lengthened out, perhaps to 12 or
15 hours instead of five or six, and made more gradual, a great many of
these accidents could undoubtedly be avoided.

DSI FLIGHT RECORD
AERIAL COURSE AT SCHOOL OF AERIAL FIGHTING, AYR

Date—Time	Machine Type/No.	Duration	Passenger	Remarks
3/2/18—10:25	Camel 4424	40 min.	Solo	Short hop, followed by formation
3/2/18—9:15	Camel 7418	15 min.	Solo	Practice
3/3/18—3–5	Avro 4430	25 min.	Capt. Taylor	Instruction
3/3/18—4:25	Camel 5564	25 min.	Solo	
3/4/18—9:40	Camel 7418	55 min.	Solo	Bombing raid and fight
3/4/18—11:15	Camel 5564	105 min.	Solo	Fight with Camel and formation and line patrol
3/4/18—1:35	Camel 7469	40 min.	Solo	Line patrol

Total time: 5 hrs, 5 mins.

—

Fitness Report 21 December 1917 to 21 March 1918

A particularly bright officer, greatly interested in all work assigned him, and a good pilot.

E. R. Pollock, Comdr., U.S.N.
30 Grosvenor Gardens, London, Eng.

Shortly after landing in England Ingalls outfitted himself with a walking stick, quite the thing for a new, and very junior, officer to carry. *Courtesy Peter B. Mersky Collection*

After a few weeks in London and Paris Ingalls moved on to the Bay of Biscay to continue his training, first at the French navy school at Lac Hourtin, and then at the infant U.S. Navy facility at Moutchic. The school was still essentially a construction zone and the impatient neophyte pilot did little actual flying. *Courtesy National Archives*

Instruction at both Hourtin and Moutchic was carried out aboard FBA flying boats, cranky, underpowered machines with a frightening tendency to fall off the wing into dangerous spins, a situation caused by the torque generated by the plane's rotary engine. Ken MacLeish called it the "rottenest machine I ever flew." *Courtesy National Archives*

At Moutchic Ingalls was reunited with Robert "Bob" Lovett, the Yale Unit's acknowledged "brain," and a man destined to rise to the highest levels of the American military and civilian leadership. *Author's collection*

Overseeing the work at headquarters, and tasked with directing all naval aviation activities in Europe, was Capt. Hutch I. Cone, known to his friends as "Reddy," an officer of ability, courage, and progressive views. Ingalls was assigned to Cone's Paris headquarters in November and December 1917. *Courtesy National Archives*

Ingalls, Ken MacLeish, and Edward "Shorty" Smith were assigned to the Royal Flying Corps School of Special Flying at Gosport in December 1917. There they received instruction in land flying for the first time. Their initial mount was the Avro 504 trainer, what Ingalls called a "slow, dual machine." *Courtesy Naval History and Heritage Command*

Flying schools were dangerous places, even with aircraft as stable as the Avro. This photograph, probably taken at Ayr in the winter of 1917–18, shows two smashed Avros that likely collided while maneuvering for takeoff or landing. *Courtesy Peter B. Mersky Collection*

Ken MacLeish, son of a prominent Chicago retail executive and the brother of Archibald MacLeish, was paired with Dave Ingalls through much of their aviation careers, serving in the same crews while with the Yale Unit, attending three British flight schools, serving together with various RAF units, and attending the U.S. Army bombing school at Clermont-Ferrand. In October 1918 they traded places at No.213 Squadron, RAF. Ingalls came home a hero; MacLeish died soon after in combat. *Author's collection*

The Sopwith Camel, Ingalls's favorite mount, was tricky and temperamental to fly and highly dangerous to novice pilots, but a superb dogfighter, responsible for more Allied aerial victories than any other aircraft. *Courtesy National Archives*

This upended Camel, possibly photographed in Scotland in the winter of 1918, was one of many hundreds lost in training accidents. The unstable aircraft had a deadly tendency to spin and ground loop, leading to high casualty rates among aviation cadets. *Courtesy Peter B. Mersky Collection*

4

On Patrol—At NAS Dunkirk and with the RAF in Flanders

March–May 1918

With months of instruction behind them and a massive German attack on the Western Front about to erupt, Ingalls, MacLeish, and Smith hurried down from Scotland, crossed over to France, and made their way to NAS Dunkirk, the navy's lonely outpost on the shore of the English Channel, just a few miles behind the front. They arrived on March 21, the very day the enemy began its climactic assault. Eminent military historian John Keegan called this and the events that followed "the crisis of war in the West."[1] When German forces broke through British lines, the commanding officer (CO) at Dunkirk, Godfrey Chevalier, offered pilots, observers, and ground personnel to overtaxed RNAS/RAF squadrons, and soon, a cadre of aviators, Ingalls among them, joined nearby units for combat duty. This allowed the British to replace some of the men who were previously transferred to squadrons at the point of attack that had launched nearly suicidal ground assaults in a desperate effort to stem the German tide.[2] Meanwhile, the Americans spent much of April carrying

---

1. See John Keegan, *The First World War* (New York: Knopf, 1999), 392–406. The German spring campaign of 1918, designed to win the war by defeating the British army before U.S. troops reached the Western Front in large numbers, is known by many names, including *Kaiserschlact* (the Kaiser's Battle), the Ludendorff Offensive, and Operation Michael, the first phase of the action.

2. Official communiqués issued during the opening weeks of the enemy drive reveal the intensity of Britain's aerial response to the German attack. See, in particular, Chaz Bowyer, *Royal Flying Corps Communiqués, 1917–1918* (London: Grub Street, 1998),

out missions in the skies above Flanders, especially bombing raids against the submarine center at Zeebrugge.[3] Ingalls, MacLeish, Smith, and Willis Haviland joined No.13 Squadron, RNAS, which was redesignated No.213 Squadron, RAF, on April 1, 1918.

Despite flirting with death from antiaircraft fire, air-to-air combat, or long-range artillery bombardment and despite enduring the discomfort of high-altitude flying in subzero temperatures, the Americans enjoyed their stay with the RAF. They found the work exciting and nerve-racking, exhilarating and exhausting. For the first time, they were putting their months of training to the test. Ingalls found his RAF messmates a congenial lot; several had months of service at the front. More than one was already an ace.

In late April, with his British duty ended, Ingalls returned to Dunkirk and began patrolling over the Channel and the North Sea, hunting for U-boats. On one of these missions, flying a single-place Hanriot-Dupont pontoon scout, he got lost in the mist, made a forced landing in the Channel, and fortuitously obtained a tow by a French schooner into a nearby port, more than a hundred miles from his station. The only thing permanently damaged was his pride. No sooner did Ingalls settle into the new routine of antisubmarine missions, however, than rumors began to swirl about a great new navy program designed to bomb the Germans out of their Flanders bases. CO Chevalier asked for volunteers to be trained on land-based bombers, and Ingalls and several other station pilots and observers immediately stepped forward. They soon received orders to head for the U.S. Air Service bombing school at Clermont-Ferrand, France.

238–46. In five weeks of fighting, the RAF lost 1,302 aircraft. According to John H. Morrow Jr., in *The Great War in the Air: Military Aviation from 1909 to 1921* (Washington, D.C.: Smithsonian Institution Press, 1993), 311, "One fighter plane flew so low it ran over a German company commander." Christopher Shores, in *Above the Trenches: A Complete Record of the Fighter Aces and Units of the British Empire Forces, 1915–1920* (London: Grub Street, 1990), 23, noted, "All available British squadrons were thrown into the defense, most units flying ground attack sorties."

3. Belgian place-names represent something of a challenge. The country's two largest ethnic groups are the Walloons, who speak French, and the Flemings, who speak Dutch. The RNAS and later the American Northern Bombing Group operated over the Flemish area, but their records often utilized French place-names. This was certainly true in Ingalls's case. This manuscript incorporates the spelling from the original documents. In the case of French-derived place-names, the first mention will be followed by the Dutch spelling, in parentheses.

March 12, 1918. We had to sit up all night on our way to London, one hell of a trip. Upon reporting we learned that Curt Read had been killed flying at Dunkirk. Terrible. He was one of our 1st Yale Unit and was the absolute best. He is the first of our Unit to go West. I wonder how many will follow him.[4]

March 17, 1918. Arrived at Paris at 3:15 and went to the Chatham. We saw Lloyd Hamilton en route to an R.F.C. Squadron at the front. Found Alice [Bowler]. Damned if she isn't a handy girl, she's always in every town over here. She's planning to get up near the front somehow, having left the British Admiralty, where she was working in London. Three days in London. We met Ken's brother [Archibald MacLeish],[5] and Slim Toland and had fun.

March 21, 1918. Shorty Smith having departed [from Paris] for Dunkerque yesterday, Ken and I left alone and a phonograph though no records at 9:15. I had a headache. Too much party in Paris. Ken also was a bit low. Ken and I both like *Pol Roger* 1904 or 1906 [champagne] and make a point of having a quart between us at dinner always. It was a long trip to Boulogne, Calais, Dunkirk. There we were met by a gob and a Ford, which took us out to "A" Mess to report. I was astonished to find Dunkirk is not nearly as shot up as I had imagined, in fact there are very few signs of the war, except for the almost incessant low rumble of the heavy artillery at the front some 15 miles away. We reported to Chevalier and had dinner there with Chevy, Di, Haviland, the chief pilot, of the former Lafayette Escadrille,

4. Curtis Read and his observer, Edward Eichelberger, died after their aircraft crashed during a training flight on February 27, 1918. Read expired a short time later in a French military hospital. Eichelberger's body was not recovered for several months. See Ralph D. Paine, *The First Yale Unit: A Story of Naval Aviation, 1916–1919,* 2 vols. (Cambridge, Mass.: Riverside Press, 1925), 2:190–212, and Marc Wortman, *The Millionaires' Unit: The Aristocratic Flyboys Who Fought the Great War and Invented American Air Power* (New York: Public Affairs, 2006), 185–86. Ingalls misspoke here. Yale Unit member Al Sturtevant had been shot down February 15, 1918, during an antisubmarine patrol over the North Sea, a fact Ingalls noted in a February 23 letter to his mother.

5. Archibald MacLeish was the elder brother of Ken MacLeish and later a poet, writer, and librarian of Congress. He was then training for service in the field artillery.

paymaster Stockhausen, and Ensign [C. R.] Johnson, an old
Navy man. After dinner as Di was escorting us to our mess, the
siren blew, a barrage was put up, and we could hear machines
flying east to Boulogne-Calais. During the warning this happened
five or six times. Our quarters are awfully comfortable—an old
French mansion. There are plenty of bedrooms, a nice large
dining and living room with piano and now a phonograph. The
food is *tres bon*. Things look nice.[6]

March 22, 1918. Rose at seven and had breakfast, did ironing,
however we went to hangars. There are five Hanriots, one gun,
and seven or eight D.D.s,[7] but few in commission. In afternoon
Haviland let first Ken then me take up his machine. It is
rather a nice little machine but slow handling, I couldn't loop
it. Loses height on turns, climbs fairly, loses little height in
sideslip. During Ken's flight a Hun photographer came over
and was barraged. It was very pretty. About 5:00 we had a big
indoor baseball game outside on beach. [Hanriot-Dupont, 15
minutes]

March 22, 1918

Dear Dad,
    We left Paris early yesterday morning and arrived in Dunkirk
at about seven o'clock. It is certainly great to be here, and there is a
great bunch of fellows. The C.O. and Lieutenants live in one house
and all of us Ensigns live on the shore in a wonderful old French

---

    6. *Gob* is an ancient term for an enlisted sailor. Willis Haviland, NA #577, chief
pilot and veteran of the Lafayette Escadrille, later commanded NAS Porto Corsini in
Italy. Assistant Paymaster Thomas Stockhausen served as supply officer, and Ensign C.
R. Johnson as executive officer. A barrage was the combined antiaircraft fire—shells,
flares, machine guns—directed at attacking enemy aircraft.
    7. The Hanriot-Dupont HD.2 floatplane was the seaplane version of the HD.1
pursuit ship, powered by a 120 hp LeRhone rotary motor; the Donnet-Denhaut flying
boat, likely of the DD-8 type, was powered by a 200 hp Hispano-Suiza motor. It was
slow and mechanically unreliable.

mansion. The food is perfect—we have a piano, plenty of stoves to keep nice and warm, and a phonograph but no decent records.

It was quite exciting riding out from the station to see the wrecked buildings. The night before last there was a destroyer bombardment,[8] which I was glad to miss, although the shells from a destroyer are not nearly so dangerous as a bomb from an aeroplane; there are more of them, and more noise. Last night after dinner every now and then the siren would blow, a barrage would be put up, and we could hear the twin motors of the Boche machines going on up the coast to bomb some other city. Of course, one may always hear the bigger guns at the front firing; they are just at the right distance to lull one to sleep.

This morning, as it was misty, there was no flying, but it cleared up about ten, and so this afternoon there were a lot of machines up, although at present there are not enough scouts for all of us. I got up in the flight officer's [Haviland's] scout for a short hop. I had not flown a pontoon machine for some time, but it was very easy, and I had a great ride, stunting, etc. There is no telling when my machine may get here and so there will be little to do for a time. Just before I went up, a Boche photographic plane came over, and immediately a barrage was put up. It was very pretty to see the large puffs of smoke when the shells burst all about the machine, which beat it for home as soon as the barrage was started.

After flying was called off, we had a game of baseball on the beach. It is about the first real exercise I have had since leaving southern France, and it was certainly fun. It will be great when warmer weather comes and we can also swim. At last I can appreciate that there is some truth to that saying, "Sunny France." After gloomy, foggy England, a sight of the sun is pretty slick. The day before we left Paris, we saw Mr. H. P. Davison and had a short chat with him.[9] He was a most busy man and was on his way up to the front. Every one was crazy about him. He made several awfully good speeches in

8. On the evening of March 21, 1918, a flotilla of German destroyers operating from ports along the occupied Belgian coast sortied southward and bombarded Dunkirk.

9. Henry P. Davison, patron of the First Yale Unit and chairman of the War Council of the American Red Cross, was then in Europe on an inspection trip.

Paris, though I didn't hear any of them. From what he said, I don't
expect Harry Jr., will be over for some time, though he, Harry, I know,
wants to come very much.[10]

In Paris we also saw Mrs. Bowler and Alice, and had several
parties with them. They are awfully nice to us. I also saw Mr. Thomas
of the American Express Co., but owing to the fact that I was pretty
busy all the time there out at the office and visiting the fine dentist,
I discovered during my last stay in Paris, I didn't have time to look
up Mr. Herrick's friends. When I hear about the training the other
fellows have had, I certainly thank my stars I was trained in England.
Well, Dad, I hope mother has sent some phonograph records, they
would be most enjoyed; also some more of that block chocolate. It
is very popular. Must go to bed—Here's hoping that our sleep is not
disturbed by any bombs as a result of potting that Hun photographer.
Love, Dave.

March 23, 1918. Dead morning. We mostly worked on the ground.
In afternoon Doc Read and Haviland went on patrol with the
French but they started in such a hurry that they got away from
our fellows.[11] Ken has been made Ordnance Officer, Ken and I and
Shorty had another flight. Shorty's motor stopped and he was towed
in. He always has tough luck. We had more war though, there
seems to be a little every day. The Huns bombed this place with a
big gun. 100 seconds after it is fired the shell bursts, as warning
is telephoned ahead a siren is blown and everyone can take cover.
The boys call it Lugenboom.[12] One shell hit at the gate of our

10. After extensive service in the United States, Harry Davison Jr. sailed to Europe
in the summer of 1918 and joined up with the Northern Bombing Group. He also
flew several bombing missions with No.214 Squadron, RAF.

11. Robert Emery "Doc" Read, NA #564, served with the American Field Service
and the Lafayette Flying Corps before transferring to the U.S. Navy. He assumed command of NAS Dunkirk in October 1918 after the capture of Di Gates.

12. The Lugenboom (there are various spellings) was a large-caliber naval gun
emplaced near Leugenboom/Moere, Belgium, a few miles inland from Ostend; it
was used to bombard Dunkirk throughout 1918 until German forces withdrew from
Flanders in October.

hangars and made big hole. It busted up things a bit, but so far no one has been hurt by it. It continued all afternoon at long intervals, but did not disturb our baseball game. At 7:00, a big barrage was put up over the front and we thought Hun planes were coming but they didn't. Ken, Shorty, and I all had short flights, Shorty getting stuck and being towed in. [Hanriot-Dupont, 20 minutes]

March 24, 1918. Dud day, no flying. Huns shelled us every now and then and all night regularly . . . observer service for courts.[13]

March 24, 1918

My Dear Mother,

I am in great hopes now of getting very fat. The mess here is beyond compare, and a good baseball or football game in the afternoon gives one a tremendous appetite. Today I was assigned a duty besides flying; almost everyone has something to do, to keep us busy. Well just picture me as instructor of the cadets here who are going to take a course to fit them for officers.[14] Imagine listening to me giving a lecture on Duchêne,[15] that awful man the study of whose works caused us such trouble last summer.

Last night I hear they shelled Paris with big guns.[16] Imagine a gun shooting at a city over 60 miles away. It sounds very impossible,

---

13. The disciplinary system for enlisted men included deck courts and summary courts-martial carried out by station officers. In this instance Ingalls was pressed into service as an observer of such disciplinary proceedings. A good overview is found in Norman Van der Veer, *The Bluejackets' Manual* (Annapolis, Md.: United States Naval Institute, 1917), 35–37.

14. The navy administered a short course to newly commissioned officers, familiarizing them with their various duties and offering guidance in the art and practice of command.

15. Capt. Émile Duchêne was the author of *Flight without Formulae: Simple Discussions on the Mechanics of the Aeroplane* (London: Longmans, Green, and Co., 1916), translated into English by John Ledeboer.

16. The Paris Gun was actually an engineered, large-caliber railway cannon placed in the forest of Coucy. It delivered a 210 pound projectile at a distance of up to eighty miles. Approximately 250 Parisians died during the bombardment that lasted from March to August 1918.

doesn't it? But I know their guns carry quite some distance, as they shelled us last night regularly from 5 PM to 5 AM. Thank goodness I am a sound sleeper. Only two of them on bursting woke me up, whereas poor Ken said he failed to sleep all night.

Shell just hit, and the sirens are blowing, so they evidently intend to encore last night. They might at least rest on Sunday. This morning a memorial service was held for Curt [Read's] observer,[17] who was lost when he smashed up some time ago. These shells are, I understand, of 1900 lb. weight when they land, and make quite a hole. Imagine the ones they shoot into Paris. I hope those records are en route and also some chocolate. Must stop and hit the hay, as it is very late. Love, Dave

———

March 25, 1918. Very dud day. A few shells all day and a few that night (17).

March 26, 1918. Fine day but too windy for water machines. Am beginning to get bored doing nothing. I have been appointed Senior Officer of Watch and an Instructional Officer to Mose[ley] Taylor. All that don't mean much. Played Doc [Stevens] at his game of Racerin [?], also had tea with him.[18] Steady German advance. However report this afternoon that Huns are being held. Thank goodness. They started shelling in the afternoon and at nine P.M. sent up a barrage, evidently Huns are bombing us too, shelling stopped. Doc Read and I are writing letters upstairs and we jump up every two or three minutes to look at a barrage put up to drive the damn Huns back. They usually seem to come in

17. Observer Edward "Eich" Eichelberger, a Baltimore native and member of the First Aeronautic Detachment, died in a crash at Dunkirk in February, as noted earlier. His body washed ashore near La Panne in July.

18. Moseley Taylor, NA #118, was one of the Harvard group of aviators trained at Hampton Roads, Virginia, in the summer of 1917; he later served at Moutchic, Dunkirk, and Stonehenge and with the Northern Bombing Group, including assignment to No.214 Squadron, RAF. This is the same Dr. Albert Stevens whom Ingalls had met earlier at Moutchic.

low over the sea toward the docks. They've tried three times now but no bombs dropped I think. It's very pretty to see the shrapnel bursting allover, as a sort of general barrage is put up, also four search lights are playing around. Later they began to shell. We sit outside and watch the fireworks and listen to the noise. Better than a movie.

March 27, 1918. Dud day. I, being Officer of the Day,[19] spent the night there. Played cards with Doc, and had tea with him and Chevie. About 10 P.M. the sirens blew and I posted two men to watch, but no shells were sent. I also censored mail.

March 27, 1918

My Dear Mother,

To-day has been really the first dull day since my arrival, high wind and a bit of rain; therefore, as said wind is blowing towards Germany, the Huns are fixed and cannot annoy us with their boresome shells. Also no aeroplanes could fly to-night. This little act of nature's is particularly pleasing to me because I am officer of the day, and in the event of shelling or raids I should have not only to depart from my warm couch at every warning and tear out into the cold night air to a hot and stuffy dugout,[20] but I should also be compelled to compel the men to do the same; as the latter have had very little sleep for this reason, this compelling becomes a bit serious. Thank goodness, our palace is far removed from camp and its proximity to the docks, etc., which the Huns endeavor to destroy. The French brought down a German photographer here a day or so ago. I missed the pleasant spectacle, but all the audience said it was a beautiful sight. Indeed it is extremely difficult to find any sympathy, love, and affection in anyone toward these people.

---

19. An officer of the day, assigned on a rotating, daily basis for a twenty-four-hour stretch, assisted the executive officer in carrying out the station's routine.

20. NAS Dunkirk constructed several dugouts—excavated bunkers reinforced with sandbags, timber, and sheet metal as protection against shelling and aerial bombardment.

Last night was very interesting from the viewpoint of a peace loving man like myself. The Huns endeavored to bomb us, but were repeatedly thwarted by the most excellent barrage, which the French A.A. gunners put up. I think perhaps they did drop one or two bombs but in vain and what is far better several of them were brought down. Maybe their defeat will keep them away for a while. After we were warned of their approach we went onto the porch outside our rooms and viewed the proceedings. At times one could hear the motors exceedingly plainly. They were evidently quite low. As they came over a beautiful barrage would go up, the shrapnel bursting all over the heavens.—seemingly fruitlessly but really most effectually. Of course, it being a fine night, they afterwards did a bit of shelling too.

This German advance and British retreat is greatly disturbing everyone. It is, to be sure, a very critical point and a lucky or skillful success by the Allies would, I should think, form the last chapter. But here we know very little of what is going on. I wish I could look ahead a week or so, but I think the dog-gone Germans have bitten off a bit too much, that they are taking a last chance and it is liable to turn out pretty slim. Even a partial success won't help them much.

As I have said, I am Officer of the Day, and as such am helping the Doctor censor the men's mail, a thing I have very much wanted to do, to find out their morale and feelings. They are, I think, taking everything in the right way, and are cheerful, and never complain. During the last few days I have played cards with the Doc and had tea with him. He is a mighty fine fellow, very clever, a Rhodes scholar who has been to Oxford and Germany for quite a while and has traveled all over. He's a great talker, and I certainly like to listen to him. This afternoon he quoted poetry of all sorts for about an hour. How the deuce he can do it I don't see. On account of the Hun advance, mail has been somewhat tied up, as I haven't received any letters and I doubt if any leave here. Well mother, I must beat the Doc [at] a game of Racelie now. With Love, Dave

March 28, 1918. Dud day. Everyone is worried about British
retreat. 37 out of 50 flights had to move. Lots of guns and
provisions have been lost. What's our loss is another's gain.
Bob L[ovett] brought over four RNAS pilots for tea and Di
brought Capt. Matcland [Maitland?]. Chevie came in just
before supper and told us that Ken, Haviland, Shorty and I am
to go to RNAS Camel Squadron No. 13 tomorrow.[21] This means
action all right.[22]

March 29, 1918. Rose early and bid Doc Read and Mose Taylor
goodbye. They were to take charge of the men lent RNAS for
constructional work. I finished packing then walked to camp.
Received pay $143.00. At about 11:00 we, Ken, Shorty, Haviland
and I, and Di accompanying us, set out for No.13 Sq. RNAS. It

---

21. No.213 Squadron, RAF, began life in June 1917 as the Seaplane Defense Flight,
formed to protect patrol aircraft operating out of Dunkirk, initially flying Sopwith
Baby and Pup pontoon scouts. The group transitioned to land-based Sopwith Camels
in September. The unit reorganized as No.13 Squadron, RNAS, in January 1918 and
was based at St. Pol but soon relocated to the nearby aerodrome at Bergues. Following
consolidation of the RFC and RNAS on April 1, 1918, the squadron became No.213
Squadron, RAF, with a unit insignia of a hornet and the motto "The hornet attacks
when roused." Maj. Ronald Graham (later air vice marshal) commanded the squadron throughout its wartime service. One member of the unit reported, "The CO is a
jolly decent sport and really one wouldn't think he was a major to see him acting the
goat with us. Now you know that sort of man deserves all the loyal support he can
get and certainly does get mine." Quoted in Mike O'Connor, *Airfields and Airmen of
the Channel Coast* (Barnsley, South Yorkshire, U.K.: Pen and Sword Books, 2005), 117.
Other key squadron members included Colin Brown, George Hodson, John Greene,
George MacKay, Leonard Slatter (later air marshal), John Pinder, Maurice Lea Cooper,
and H. C. Smith. See Shores, *Above the Trenches*, 42; and Frank M. Leeson, *The Hornet
Strikes: The Story of No.213 Squadron, Royal Air Force* (Tunbridge Wells, U.K.: Air-Britain
Historians, 1998), 7–16.

22. Ingalls was exactly right. When the German assault began in March 1918, British air headquarters reassigned a substantial portion of squadron flight personnel to
formations stationed directly in the path of the advance, seriously impairing the unit's
ability to carry out its assigned missions. The same situation prevailed in other squadrons, generally bombing and observation groups, based at Bergues and elsewhere. In
one ten-day period in April when fighting in the air reached a crescendo, the RAF
lost 478 aircraft. Total losses up to April 29 exceeded 1,300, more than the entire
number of British machines available on the Western Front on March 21. The severe
manpower shortage caused NAS Dunkirk's CO, Chevalier, to offer some of his under-
utilized personnel and motivated the beleaguered British units to accept the offer with
alacrity. See Morrow, *Great War in the Air*, 311.

was about 20 minute ride inland from camp, near Bergues. There
we had lunch and walked around. I was roomed with [Maurice
Lea] Cooper, a darn nice Irishman. Inspected his machine and
whole station. 13 [Squadron] uses Bentley Camels, two Vickers
guns synchronized so as to shoot through the propeller path. Two
other squadrons of DH 4s on same field.[23] Our work is to be sea
patrols to Zeebrugge back just off the coast. One in three patrols,
however, is over the lines, but I'm afraid they will have all three
over sea now, as conditions have been quite changed by British
retreat. Chet Basset came from Paris to camp this morning and
said that near Amiens the Huns line was at 2-1/2 kilometers, the
French artillery was on the opposite side of the tracks shelling
them.[24] Looks bad. But troops, guns, etc., he saw on trains
running all night within 50–100 yards of each other. This RNAS
crowd are fine and seem a lot better sort then the corresponding
R.F.C. It's the Navy and of course the Navy is better than the
Army by a darn sight, even in the flying end. Cooper is just
two months older then me, and has been here five months. His
roommate having just returned, I am in the commander's room for
time being.

March 30, 1918. Fair morning, there was an early patrol before
breakfast of three, and one after led by Brown who ran into two

---

23. Capt. Maurice Lea Cooper, DFC, with six confirmed victories, joined No.213
Squadron on November 7, 1917, and was killed in September 1918. See Leeson, *Hornet
Strikes*, 200, and Shores, *Above the Trenches*, 121. Sopwith Camels powered by Bentley
rotary motors that incorporated aluminum pistons and cylinders, with cast-iron lin-
ers, offered greater power and reliability, at reduced cost, when compared with the
130 hp Clerget 9B rotary motors utilized in most Camels. Pilots much preferred the
Bentleys. The Airco DH4 was a two-seat, British day bomber designed by Geoffrey
DeHavilland, which became operational in March 1917. Widely used by the RAF and
RNAS, it was also utilized by the U.S. Air Service, powered with American-designed
and American-manufactured Liberty motors. It continued in use long after World War
I ended. A note on aircraft designations: British-manufactured aircraft of DH type
are designated DH4, DH9, or DH9A per RAF Museum and Imperial War Museum
nomenclature. American-manufactured aircraft of the DH series are designated DH-4,
per Air Service custom.

24. Charles Chester "Chet" Bassett Jr., NA #1316, from Washington, D.C., served in
the French Foreign Legion and Lafayette Flying Corps. He enlisted in the U.S. Navy
on January 4, 1918, and later flew with No.218 Squadron, RAF.

Rumplers and two pontoons.[25] Didn't get any. I sat around all morning, dud afternoon. Read and wrote.

⎯⎯⎯⎯⎯⎯

March 30, 1918

My Dear Dad,

For the last few days have been very dull. Therefore there have been no raids or shelling episodes, nothing actively exciting. To be sure the big attack causes unusual consideration upon the war. Before that everyone seemed to have sort of forgotten about it. Well, Dad, for several different reasons, several of us, among them Ken, Shorty, and I, were placed at the disposal of the British. As a direct result of this, yesterday, we transferred our belongings and are again flying land scouts. We're all, of course, delighted to do something. Ken and I are in the same flight, which is exceedingly satisfactory to me, and apparently to him also, as we have always flown together, more or less. Our flight commander said something to me about making our debut tomorrow if the weather should be good. The men here are a great bunch, and we have very comfortable quarters, perhaps not quite so palatial as our former mansion, but yet *tres bon*. Of course I have no idea how long we shall be here, and couldn't tell you if I knew, but I hope it's long.

I was awfully glad to get three letters from mother and two from you, also, wonder of wonders, one from Al [Ingalls]. By mistake, I suppose, you enclosed a letter from Al in which he expressed doubt as to Drury's exact meaning when he put "good in two subjects" on Al's report. To look at his customary smiling and cheerful countenance, though, would make one always expect some gently

---

25. Capt. Colin Peter Brown, DFC, Croix de Guerre, with fourteen confirmed victories, served with No.213 Squadron from August 29, 1917, until October 5, 1918. See Shores, *Above the Trenches,* 89. At the time of this reference, Brown was nineteen years old. The Rumplers identified here were probably one of the two-seat "C" variants used for observation purposes throughout the war. The pontoons were German seaplanes flying out of Ostend or Zeebrugge. Several types operated along the Flanders coast in early 1918, including the Albatross W.4, Freidrichshafen FF33, Rumpler 6B-1, and Hansa-Brandenburg KDW and W.12. German naval aviation operations along the Belgian coast are nicely summarized in Alex Imrie, *German Naval Air Service* (London: Arms and Armour Press, n.d.).

humorous remark. I am very sorry for Adele with Howard going up to the front, but especially at this time it would be wonderful for the Americans to come through. Anyway cheer her up by telling her that I am attached to the 13th Squadron, RNAS. I suppose in a war, one cannot, as the hotels, leave out the 13th floor, leave out such a vital number. But I just figured out that there are 13 letters in my name David S. Ingalls. One strong point about this new location is that we are not very near to any objective of German shells or bombs, so our sleep should be undisturbed.

Before leaving our camp, I made out an allotment for $100 in your favor, starting May 1st, 1918.[26] Up till now, I have succeeded in spending most of my pay, but now cannot. I should have made it larger, but I hear a rumor that is practically confirmed, that we are going to lose our extra 50 percent for flying. This I think is damn foolishness. The whole trouble is that our Army and Navy pay extra for mechanics also, which is absurd and I think the Army also pays extra to staff officers, etc. Then too, when they take into consideration the losses as compared to other branches, they count in the whole darn outfit, not just the pilots. Therefore, as there are, I should roughly imagine, about 15 men non-flying to each pilot, and none of these 15 ever suffer a casualty, as they are far removed from any danger, but old age, of course a flying corps seems a pretty soft job. Don't imagine I'm fishing for sympathy, nor mention it to mother, but we're all dog-gone sore about the pay question. Well, Dad, must stop. Much love, Dave

March 31, 1918. Fair day but windy. No flying. Di arrived in morning to join 17th DH4. After lunch we all went by tender to La Panne (De Panne). There were Belgians galore. It is a very pretty little village, not badly shot up. Shorty and I met Ed [DeCernea] and Chet [Bassett] there and then looked up Louise Dimming at Hospital and Miss Cray [Craig?]. Walked about. On way home stopped and saw Hun Gotha in Dunkirk's square. It

26. Soldiers, officers and enlisted men alike, typically designated a portion of their pay to be sent home to their families. Aviators received hazardous-duty "flight" pay as an increment to their regular salary, a policy subject to intense criticism from various quarters within the military hierarchy.

was not very large. Looked crude and cheap. Two tremendous motors, crew of three, seven bombs. After dinner, everyone was feeling high as it is last night of R.N.A.S. Big rough house. All went over to 2 Squadron, and raised Hell and sang.[27]

April 1, 1918. Ken went on a patrol today. Lucky bugger. Fairly dud day. Harry [Smith] went later in afternoon.[28] After dinner Ken, Harry and I went to H[andley] P[age] Squadron and saw Bob.[29] They were all more or less tight [inebriated]. I had short flight and shot a bit at target. (Clerget Camel, 50 minutes)

April 2, 1918. At first a big patrol. Later MacKay, Greene, and Cooper shot down two one-seaters and one two-seater pontoon machines.[30] Darn good.

---

27. This was No.17 Squadron, RNAS, soon to be renumbered No.217 Squadron, RAF, operating DH4 day bombers. Di Gates noted, "We all have temporary jobs with British squadrons and are enjoying it immensely," as quoted in Geoffrey Rossano, *The Price of Honor: The World War One Letters of Naval Aviator Kenneth MacLeish* (Annapolis, Md.: Naval Institute Press, 1991), 120. La Panne was a small seaside village located just inside the Belgian border in the tiny corner of that country that remained in Allied hands. Edward DeCernea, NA #132, a member of the Second Yale Unit, compiled the most flight hours of any navy pilot at NAS Dunkirk. The Gotha Ingalls mentioned likely was the G.V version of this long-range, twin-engine bomber, whose missions included bombardment of London in 1917–18. On April 1, 1918, the RFC and RNAS consolidated to form the RAF. The previous evening, pilots from several naval units about to lose their identity engaged in lighthearted mayhem, including roughhousing, heavy drinking, setting off smoke bombs, and pulling other pranks. See Ken MacLeish's description of such events in Rossano, *Price of Honor*, 130–31.

28. Lt. Harry Coleman Smith, with five confirmed victories, was declared missing in action (MIA) on September 28, 1918. See Shores, *Above the Trenches*, 342.

29. No.7 Squadron, RNAS/No.207 Squadron, RAF, operated long-range Handley Page bombers from an aerodrome at Coudekerque, a few miles outside Dunkirk. These machines carried out raids against Bruges, Zeebrugge, and numerous other sites. Bob Lovett and Eddie McDonnell served with this unit in March and April 1918. See Paine, *First Yale Unit*, 2:168–75. After several raids over the lines, Lovett exulted, "I have at last been through it. I feel a different man altogether." Quoted in Geoffrey Rossano, *Stalking the U-Boat: U.S. Naval Aviation in Europe in World War I* (Gainesville: University Press of Florida, 2010), 69.

30. Capt. George Chisholm MacKay, DFC, Légion d'Honneur, Croix de Guerre, Order of Leopold, had eighteen confirmed victories. Capt. John Edmund Greene, DFC, had fifteen confirmed victories. See Shores, *Above the Trenches*, 176, 248.

RAF Flight Records, 4-2-1918: 1000, 55 minute test flight, Sopwith Camel B.6379

———

April 3, 1918. Fair day. Shorty went on early patrol. I had a hop and stunted around on base. Ken did the same. Chevy called up and said French C.O. sent report to Admiralty.[31] Fussy bugger. Tried to teach E[nglish] to play baseball. They learn slowly. Five or six were very tight and it certainly was funny. (Clerget Camel, 30 minutes)

———

RAF Flight Records, 4-3-1918: 1150, 25 minute test flight, Sopwith Camel B.6387

———

April 4, 1918. Our day off. Lots of rain so Shorty and I went to Dunkirk and saw the fellows at camp and got pay. Trouble over stunting is smoothed over.

April 5, 1918. Hellish weather, rain, wind, and clouds. Read all day, took walk in afternoon with Di to Capelle and saw Bob [Lovett] and [C. R.?] Johnson. Mail yesterday.

April 6, 1918. Fair day. I went on first patrol at about 10:00. There were five of us and I had trouble picking up four because of low clouds. Three B.R.'s [Bentley radial motors] and two Clerget. I had an old Camel with a Clerget motor, which is bum. We went straight out, along coast just in sight of land, going up gradually. About opposite Ostend I saw boats on water, we were at 8,000. A few seconds later leader dove and I saw just then four scouts above us, but soon recognized both flights as French. Then we circled around twice between Zeebrugge and Ostend (Oostende) and got up to 12,000 feet. Not very cold. Clerget could just about keep up to BR. Then we dove down to about 4,000 feet and my

---

31. Authorities strictly and repeatedly forbade stunt flying, especially directly over military installations and populated areas. Aviators brazenly and repeatedly violated these directives.

head felt as though it would split. I felt like Hell for about five minutes till the effect passed off. We came home from Nieuport (Nieuwpoort) just over land, wind came up, but at 4 PM five seaplane Huns were reported off Boulogne and four of "C" flight sent out. Returned in 15 or 20 minutes, nothing seen. Though cloudy. (12,000 ft., Clerget Camel, 80 minutes)

RAF Flight Records, 4-6-1918: 1015, Low Fleet Patrol w/four other planes, lasted 1:20, sighted three enemy destroyers, NE of Ostend five miles at sea, two more DD sighted two miles at sea.

April 7, 1918. Dud weather. I was Officer of the Day. And I'll say I felt sorry for myself. I had to call the roll, parade the men a bit and run things. My military training is about zero grade. But for the efficient sergeant, I'd have been more than badly off.

April 8, 1918. Encore, Di to dinner, baseball.

April 9, 1918. Walked to Capelle and played baseball.[32]

April 10, 1918. Dud day. Walked over and saw 217 [Squadron] play St. Pol at rugby. Dumb game. Baseball.

April 11, 1918. Clouds about 1,100 feet. Am to go on raid. After lunch clouds at 1,500 feet, eight of us set off and flew over sea at about 500, kept getting clearer but near Zeebrugge clouded heavier. At mole we turned in then up in clouds, fishing boats were a guide to location. I came out off mark twice because I turned so fast that compass didn't keep up. But finally I came out just at east end of mole and dove down. Pretty soon I saw lots of tracers on right hand and so dodged. When I thought I had fair aim on dock and was low enough I pulled lever and beat it to

---

32. La Capelle was a small town on the outskirts of Dunkirk, surrounded by military installations at Bergues, Coudekerque, Petite-Synthe, St. Pol-sur-Mer, and other locations.

clouds out to sea. Motor started to miss so I went up to 6,000 feet above clouds and headed west. After 22 minutes I turned south and came down, arriving just in sight of Dunkirk. Shorty ahead. Came home and made bum landing. Ken missed Zeebrugge and hit Ostend.[33] All returned. (Bentley radial Camel, 6,000 ft, raid, 80 minutes)

———

RAF Flight Records, 4-11-1918: seven Camels vs. Zeebrugge mole at 1400, Ingalls in Camel B.3935, landed at 1525, seven machines bombed Zeebrugge mole, each dropping one 50-lb bomb.

———

April 11, 1918

My Dear Dad,

In order to take advantage of the prevailing dud weather, a bombing raid was brought about today. They raid has been impending for several days now, but certain conditions are requisite. And so this afternoon, with the clouds about 1,500 feet, a number of pilots were selected, and small bombs attached to the machines.[34] After the weather had been tested, we all got off shortly after lunch, everyone quite excited, due both to the fact that such a raid is unusual and also because it had been so long coming. As soon as we left the ground we headed out to sea. I happened to be second, and then ran along just below the clouds about five miles out to sea. Down so low it was very warm, and quite comfortable flying along, but I could not for the life of me clearly distinguish the shore, until finally we ran over the fishing boats which always lie outside this objective.

The leader turned in and up into the clouds, and I followed, then catching sight of the nice big target. But unfortunately turning so fast set my compass swaying, and when I thought myself in position and

33. No. 213 Squadron's target that day was the heavily fortified mole enclosing Zeebrugge harbor. Ingalls's efforts are recounted in the letter that follows. Unable to locate the objective, squadron mate MacLeish bombed an antiaircraft battery at Ostend.

34. He was referring to the 25-pound Cooper bombs carried by fighting scouts such as the Sopwith Camel.

dove down, I was nowhere near. I had in fact made a half circle. So up again into the clouds, only to repeat my failure. Each time I came down I couldn't understand why nothing was shot at me. Finally at the third attempt I came down in great position, and dove upon the innocent looking place to run into a lot of tracers, as those bullets are called which leave a sort of flash from the powder in the rear. The necessity of dropping the bomb from a low altitude gives their machine guns business. Although an approximate height is given us beforehand at which to let go, my altimeter being out of order, I went down turning from side to side, until the correct thing for me seemed to be to beat it. Therefore, pulling the releasing lever, and opening the motor, I beat a retreat. And the enveloping clouds were a most pleasant locality. Of course we were all scattered in the clouds, so I saw nothing of the rest of the flight from the time we turned in till I returned to the aerodrome. Several reasons prevented me from seeing what my bomb hit, but upon questioning the others, I found that I was not the only one in doubt.

Afterwards Shorty and I wondered at how mad we were and how much we wished we had another bomb when we reached the clouds. When we got in there was some mail awaiting us, among others the letter from Dr. Drury to Al. Mighty good for the little fellow, wasn't it? I begin to think the Rector is growing wise as well as old. I congratulate Al on living down my bad reputation. Well, Dad, must to bed so *au revoir*. Aff. yours, Dave. P.S. Dear Pop, With Mother and you I thoroughly agree in avoiding publicity. D.S.I.

April 12, 1918. [Leonard] Slatter pulled me out of bed by the leg at 4:45 a.m. and mentioned a patrol.[35] Dressing and drinking a cup of tea I hopped into a Clerget [Clerget-powered Camel] and with four others set out. We climbed rapidly above the clouds over sea to about 10,000 feet. It was most beautiful so we flew along awhile enjoying it, finally coming down below to patrol, saw nothing. At 10 A.M. after breakfast [Colin] Brown, [Harry]

35. Capt. Leonard Horatio Slatter, DFC, DSC, seven confirmed victories, served with the squadron from July 2, 1917, until July 2, 1918. See Shores, *Above the Trenches,* 340.

Smith, and I set out in B.R. Camels for a shoot over Nieuport.
We climbed to about 15,000 feet and went over lines to Ypres.
Flew about seeing nothing but balloons. Then went back to
Nieuport and flew around there receiving occasional Archie.[36]
After some time we saw five biplane Albatross attack one of
our photographers or spotters.[37] We went down and out to sea,
the Huns doing the same for a time and then beating it toward
Ostend. Saw some SPADs and Camels about, and flew back from
Nieuport contour-chasing. In afternoon baseball was the extent
of our activities. (Clerget Camel, 105 minutes, 10,000 ft., patrol;
Bentley Radial, 100 minutes, shoot, 15,000 ft.)

April 13–18, 1918. Sat around doing a bit of baseball and reading.[38]
I was shifted out to a new shed to sleep and it was Hell. Awful
draft and Whiteley and Hancock talked most foully all the time.
Dud weather nothing to do. On 18 I had a flip for a few minutes
as they sent out 10 on a raid on aerodrome south of Ostend.
Wilkinson returned late with two scratches, claimed to have been
shot on hand. No holes in machine and gloves.[39] (Bentley radial
Camel, 1,000 ft., 30 minutes)

April 19, 1918. Dud, strong wind. As we were playing baseball
in afternoon we saw Huns, evidently photographers. There was
a rush for machines. I seeing one with no pilot asked C.O. if I
could take it. Slatter was up first, Greene, and I last. We climbed
up to 16,000 feet through clouds. I saw a machine at about 8,000
feet far out to sea. Also a couple of SPADs, a D.H. 4, and four
other Camels. I had a wonderful machine—best I've ever flown.

36. *Archie* was the pilots' nickname for antiaircraft fire.

37. The Albatross was one of the Albatross D series (most likely the D.V model) pursuit ships used extensively by German forces in 1917–18.

38. Ingalls spent part of April 13 visiting Di Gates and Bob Lovett at No.207 Squadron.

39. Flight Sub-lieutenant R. I. Whiteley flew with the squadron from March 27, 1918, until he was wounded on September 5, 1918. Lieutenant S. M. N. Hancock served with the squadron from April 9, 1918, until February 20, 1919. Flight Sub-lieutenant E. G. Wilkinson flew with the unit from March 9, 1918, until May 9, 1918, when he reported to the hospital. See Leeson, *Hornet Strikes*, 200–201.

I began to get cold having thin leather coat and no tunic, one pair of gloves, light shoes. So I fired and went down, followed by Greene, to about 6,000 feet, doing half rolls and having a great time. Then my pressure went down, so I used gravity [tank] for a while. Pressure worked up and I used it again. We flew over Ypres all over lines and about seven or eight miles. Then we came home and landed safely. Paynter claimed a Hun.[40] He was himself shot thru engine with explosive bullet. A little bridge and then to bed. (16,000 feet, Bentley radial Camel, 50 minutes)

RAF Flight Records, 4-19-1918: Offensive Patrol, departed 1530, Camel B.7271. Captain Paynter landed at Moeres, shot through engine w/explosive bullet, Ingalls landed at 1640; No.5 Group communiqué says a 213 pilot engaged enemy at 15,000 near Furnes, enemy last seen in a spin.

April 20, 1918. Dud morning but no wind. I had one uninteresting flight last week and our other diversions were teaching the Limeys indoor baseball and bridge. I think bridge is their national game, only the old adage doesn't seem to apply, that practice makes perfect. Signal came in to return to our base. Ken and I went up had a slick turn stunting around. After lunch Shorty went up for a while to see if he would get sick but he didn't. We left at 2:30 and got back to the base where things are looking up. I have a new two-gun machine, motor turns up 1,325 [revolutions]. Also a good mechanic. Nice to be back home again but hate to leave the Camels. (Bentley radial Camel, 25 minutes, 1,500 feet)

RAF Flight Records, 4-20-1918: 20 minutes test flight in Camel B.3909

40. Capt. John DeCamborne Paynter, DSC, ten confirmed victories, joined the squadron on November 2, 1917, after service with No.9 Squadron, RNAS. He died in June 1918 from wounds received when the Germans bombed his aerodrome. See Shores, *Above the Trenches,* 299–300.

April 20, 1918

Dad,

As I forgot to give this letter to the truck to take to mail,
I'll add a bit. Yesterday I received through 4 Place D'Iena your
letter of 21 March. Yesterday was pretty dud, but it stopped
raining and in the afternoon one would occasionally see blue
sky and the visibility was excellent. But there was a very strong
wind so we started our regular afternoon game of baseball. After
a bit someone hit a fly and on looking up darned if we didn't
see two Huns through the clouds at about 7,000 feet, evidently
photographers right above us. Well, we just dropped ball and
bat and tore for machines and about six of us were up in four or
five minutes, though the machines were all packed up in closed
hangers, quick work, eh? All of us in the hurry, as we were playing
in just shirtsleeves, just grabbed a coat and beat it. I unfortunately
caught up my very thin leather one and a pair of gloves, no
goggles, and light shoes were all I had. And we were at 16,000
feet for about an hour. It was some painful too, believe me, and I
did not see a dog gone Hun, but one fellow [Paynter], the first up,
caught one and shot it down so we feel repaid. Love, Dave[41]

April 21, 1918. Arrived at camp to find that a bomb had been
dropped before No. 1 Hangar and wrecked all the machines in
it, also five or six others in next hangar.[42] Mine had numerous
holes in it, the side of fuselage ripped off, and two stagger wires
broken. We worked all day repairing.

41. Ingalls's total April flight time with the RAF included seven hours, thirty-two
minutes of combat missions and two hours of test flights.

42. Their time with the British at an end, the Americans returned to NAS Dunkirk on
April 21 to resume patrol duties over the English Channel. For most, it must have been
quite a letdown after the intense excitement of life and work at the RAF aerodrome.

April 21, 1918

My Dear Mother,

I just received two letters from you, and was awfully glad to get
them. It is too bad that C.P.S. and Co., can't take tobacco through
their place as I was just hoping to get some. However, *c'est la
guerre* as the Irishman says, and it will eventually arrive through 4
Place D'Iena or my new address. As the above heading may already
have indicated, we have all been recalled from the British stations
and are back at our camp. Of course it is very nice here and it is
fine to see all the fellows again, but I hate to miss the invaluable
experience we were getting. Also, as I feel sure you are ready to
surmise, I greatly prefer flying a land scout, to a pontoon one. But
as you rather imagine, the fact that my personal desires are not
fulfilled will not be of vital interest to our beloved Sec. of War [*sic*],
darling Danny [Josephus Daniels].[43] So, here I am with a brand
new machine, a flight commander, when we get going. The weather
has changed, and was fine yesterday and today. So yesterday Ken
and I had our last ride (I hope it is not the last) in a land scout. We
had a great time stunting around, and certainly felt low to think of
all we were to miss. The British had hard luck today, when two of
the pilots fresh from England to replace us, crashed and entered
upon a hospital career. The poor kids were probably a bit nervous
from their first patrol and I don't blame them much. Well, Muzzy, I

---

43. The target of much criticism, Josephus Daniels, North Carolina editor, publisher, and politician, served as secretary of the navy from 1913 to 1921. He was known
for his suspicion of military hierarchies, his pacifist tendencies, his dislike for business
monopolies, and his solicitude for the welfare of the enlisted men. Daniels's initiatives
included opening Annapolis to enlisted men and banning hazing there, admitting
women to the service as yeomen (F), increasing the number of chaplains, forbidding
the issuance of contraceptives, mandating the use of pajamas for sailors, and abolishing
admirals' cocked hats. A teetotaler and flagrant racist, he equated development of a
navy general staff with "Prussianism." Many career officers believed him to be an ill-
informed amateur who took away their mess wine and beer and disrupted the navy's
traditional social order. Wealthy, sophisticated, urbanized reserve officers such as David
Ingalls often adopted these opinions of their boss. Nonetheless, Daniels supported demands for a U.S. navy "second to none." For direct insight into the secretary's attitudes
and activities, see Josephus Daniels, *The Cabinet Diaries of Josephus Daniels, 1913–1921*
(Lincoln: University of Nebraska Press, 1963).

must get busy, as I am again Officer of the Day, although, in my new position, I hope hereafter to escape this unpleasant duty. Love, Dave.

___

April 22, 1918. I was Officer of the Day and so was busy working all day.

April 23, 1918. Placed in charge of Section 4. Worked on machine.

April 24, 1918. Nothing doing, dud weather.

April 25, 1918. Finished up machine and ready to fly.

April 26, 1918. Tested out machine in morning. About 4:00 Chet [Bassett], [Charles] Wardwell, [David] Judd and I went to Ostend,[44] as we turned out to look for seaplanes that were reported spotting for shore batteries, I saw an Albatross and turned. Hun, I think, disappeared in cloud and so I went up. Everyone was lost and Wardwell landed at Dixmude (Diksmuide).[45] Had dinner with "A" Mess. (Hanriot-Dupont, 210 minutes)

April 27, 1918. Dud weather, sat around.

April 28, 1918. Dud. Played with 217 and 213 [Squadrons].

April 29, 1918. Dud. Played 213 and won 25–1.

April 30, 1918. Dud. Slatter and Graham came to mess,[46] so Shorty and I went there too.

___

44. Charles Edmund Wardwell, NA #759, a member of First Aeronautic Detachment, trained at Tours, St. Raphael, Turnberry, and Ayr. David Edward "Dave" Judd, NA #565, ambulance driver in the American Field Service and a member of the French Foreign Legion and the Lafayette Flying Corps, transferred to the U.S. Navy on January 19, 1918.

45. Ken MacLeish reported, "Crock pulled a brilliant stunt the other day. They were after a Hun, which was reported. Just as they hove into sight Crock pulled up into the clouds and lost the rest of his flight. . . . Some flight commander." Quoted in Rossano, *Price of Honor,* 152.

46. Maj. Ronald Graham, commanding officer of No.213 Squadron, RAF, DFC, DSO, DSC, Order of the Crown (Belgium), Croix de Guerre (Belgium), scored five confirmed victories in his World War I flying career. See Shores, *Above the Trenches,* 174.

May 1, 1918. Officer of the Day. Dud day.[47]

May 2, 1918. Fair day. Patrol southwest of Dunkirk for sub sighted. Another at 2:30 south of Dunkirk. (Hanriot-Dupont, 180 minutes)

May 3, 1918. It being my day off duty, I luxuriously slept till about 9:00 then wandered down to breakfast to hear that Chuck O'Connor had a bad fall.[48] He came in with Doc Stevens and except for cuts about the face, seemed *tres bon*. I went down to camp and then over to where he fell in and watched Johnson pull out the remnants. After lunch, I tested out my motor and machine guns and heard something rattle inside. On taking off the spider we found a cartridge case therein, the cylinders were badly scored. So they took out the motor.

May 4, 1918. My machine being out of business I rose late again. A general court martial for two men deserting post was in action. I tested Young's machine.[49] My new motor fitted badly and they had a lot of trouble having to file down the shaft. At 4:30 a patrol started but didn't go as one D.D. failed to get off. On landing Ken overshot and broke a pontoon on far shore. Mournful Mary sounded at 10:30 just as I finished my bath, and we heard the motors.[50] Bombing raid. (Hanriot-Dupont, 20 minutes)

May 5, 1918. Dud day. Frocked around and did *pas de deux*.

47. Ingalls's continuous reference to "dud" weather reflected the reality of life along the approaches to the North Sea. Throughout NAS Dunkirk's operational history, bad weather frequently curtailed or canceled flight activity, often for as much as a week at a time.

48. Cornelius Joseph "Chuck" O'Connor, NA #1117, Navy Cross, was a member of the First Aeronautic Detachment.

49. Franklin "Frank" Young, NA #761, was also a member of the First Aeronautic Detachment.

50. *Mournful Mary* was the nickname given to the siren that could be heard all over Dunkirk and warned of approaching enemy shelling or aircraft. Chief Machinist Mate (A) Irving Sheely made frequent references to the shelling in his diary and letters home. See, for example, pp. 125 and 128 in Lawrence Sheely, ed., *Sailor of the Air: The 1917–1919 Letters and Diary of USN CMM/A Irving Edward Sheely* (Tuscaloosa: University of Alabama Press, 1993).

May 6, 1918. What a Hell of a time I've had![51] It seems as though
our station would never get outfitted properly, and even if it did,
the weather is so bad it wouldn't make any difference. Morning
patrol, so I rose at 4:00 and called men at 5:00. Arriving at base
at 6:05, found nothing done. No organization. Finally two boats
left about 8:00 and about 10:30 pigeon came in from one of the
boats on patrol saying one DD had crashed and one lost, help.[52]
Di set out on a boat alone, Chet left in his scout and I followed
in Young's. I flew out 355 [degrees] for 15 minutes, zigzagged a
bit and then started back at 185–190. By that time the clouds
were within 100 feet of the water, and you could see only about
½ mile around. I flew along just off the water, according to the
compass in the right direction. After flying along for about an
hour I got to wondering as to where the Hell France could have
gone? I climbed above the clouds and tried to figure from the
sun whether my compass was wrong and what direction I should
take. I thought I should go more to the east in my southerly
course, but didn't dare change much as if I went too far that way
I would land in Hun territory. So down I went and kept on, having
seen nothing and seeing nothing but water and clouds. My gas
and oil were sufficient for 2 ½ hours, so I knew I couldn't go on
forever, and after I'd been out 2 ¼ hours I began to anticipate a
sea voyage in my aeroplane. Fortunately it was calm with only
little waves. At 2 hours 20 minutes I could practically see myself
bobbing on the North Sea, and I wondered if I would get seasick.
I regretted that my motor was air cooled, and that there would be

---

51. On the morning of May 6, Ingalls set out on a search and rescue mission, at-
tempting to locate one of the station's downed flying boats. Instead, he got lost in the
mist, flew until he ran out of gas, and came down in the English Channel more than
one hundred miles from Dunkirk. Ingalls's luck held, however, and a passing vessel
rescued him and his aircraft. Nonetheless, his experiences that day underscore R. D.
Layman's assertion that over water, flight was "inherently more dangerous and difficult than over land," due to more capricious weather, the greater consequences of
mechanical failure, and the infinitely greater difficulty of navigating over the sea. See
Layman, *Naval Aviation in the First World War: Its Impact and Influence* (London: Chatham
Publishing, 1996), 22–23.

52. While performing overwater missions, aircrews carried messenger pigeons in small
boxes or wicker baskets. The birds were responsible for several life-preserving rescues.

no radiator water to drink, not that I would anticipate joyously drinking radiator water, but anyway it doesn't drive you crazy like sea water does.

At 2 hours 25 minutes I began to listen for the first pop or miss that would advise me my flight was over. At 2:28 I got set to land, watching the clock on my instrument board. After being out just 2:29 I sighted a schooner. I didn't know or particularly care if it were Hun or Belgian, no drifting on the sea for me. I turned toward it, throttled the motor and landed within 100 yards. As I lit the motor missed and gradually died.

I waved at the old schooner, at the funny looking birds looking toward me over the railing. No sign of recognition. I yelled at them, and still they sailed slowly on, on and away. I yelled and waved, got out of my seat and motioned, yelled I was busted in English and French, and finally in German. They sailed still on and I wished my machine weren't broadside so I could shoot up the dirty blighters for leaving me. I thought of my Very pistol and climbed up from the pontoon to get it and shoot even that damned ineffective thing at them.[53] I got it and looked up to shoot, and they were turning. I sat and they did turn and come back, heave to and lowered an old dinghy. Five minutes later I was on board and we were sailing on, towing my ship behind us. I told them I was American and managed to understand they were French or Belgian. It was all the same to me and always will be. There were half a dozen of them, one old woman, and when they knew I was American all was jake [OK]. It seemed they thought I was a Hun; they were scared to death. They gave me bread and something else to eat and some bum wine to drink, and said we were in the middle of the Channel, opposite Fecon [Fécamp]. They said they'd tow me there, to my great gratitude. What a terrible ride.

The Capt's name was Pope and after we got about half way in trolling in he signaled a motor boat, which finished the job. At Fecon I sent wire to Di at Dunkirk so they wouldn't worry, having loosed a [messenger] pigeon on just landing, and filled up at French base, and set out up the coast. It was certainly a long way

53. The Very was a handheld pistol capable of shooting signal flares of various colors.

off my path. On starting I flew about 40 minutes, ran into fog so turned back as it was 8:15 and getting dark. Landed at French base at Dieppe and slept there. The C.O. of the station was very nice and could speak some English, thank God! He took in me and my ship. He gave me a wonderful dinner and lots of wine and then left, apologizing for having no girls handy to sleep with me. The only English he couldn't seem to understand was my statement that I didn't want to sleep with any anyway.

In morning I found my machine had been left out in rain, but was otherwise O.K. However, I couldn't leave due to the bum weather. French C.O. took me to town and introduced me to [American] consul, Mr. Fairchild [Frederick Charles Fairbanks], from whom I borrowed money and a coat, having omitted to bring them. Believe me, hereafter I carry at all times a full complement of clothes and money. Stayed for lunch, having bought a cap, and met his wife and two daughters. They had two grand pianos and could play like no one else. Then I had dinner with two Army men, Allen and another, and returned to consul Fairchild's. He is quite a musician, as are his daughters and we sang and danced till midnight. It was a peasant ending, better than drifting in the North Sea alone, by a damn sight. (Hanriot-Dupont, 150 minutes) (Hanriot-Dupont, 50 minutes)

May 7, 1918

My Dear Mother,

Yesterday was an unlucky one for our station. One of the boats on patrol crashed landing at sea, and one of the observers is missing. A pigeon brought the message, so we went out to try and find them and help. I went in a scout, and due to the wind shifting and my compass being at fault, I got lost in the misty weather, and after flying for about two and a half hours, landed by a fishing boat on account of being nearly at the end of petrol and oil. The boat was a French schooner and they towed me into Fecon, about 100 miles down the coast from Dunkirk. It took so long to get in, about five or six hours, that I was unable to return after getting filled up and had to stop at

Dieppe, at a French sea-plane base for the night. As I had set out in
a hurry to try and give immediate assistance, I had no tunic, cap, or
money. But fortunately the French commandant is a fine fellow, and
put me up for the night, and introduced me to the American consul
where I had lunch today. The latter is very nice and supplied me with
funds, besides asking me to a dance at his house tonight. He has two
daughters, who although they have never been in America talk and
act quite naturally. And so, weather permitting, I'll return tomorrow
after a very pleasant time. But you should have seen me trying to
make the fishing men and mechanics here understand what I wanted.
My French is about as good as my Italian, i.e., *tres mal*. But the
funniest part was my great surprise and wonder of what had happened
to all of France, when after going about 20 miles straight out, I turned
around and flew for almost two hours towards what I thought was
Dunkirk. I honestly thought that perhaps the Germans had really
wiped France off the map. And you should perceive your son dressed
up in a borrowed coat, an English officer's cap, and wearing a leather
flying coat about Dieppe. Hereafter besides gas and petrol I shall
carry with me a dress suit and top hat. This morning I called up Di at
our base to let them know where I was. They thought I had become
bored with the war and flown home to U.S.A. Poor old Shorty, you
know whom I mean, has always been made sick by flying and the
other day he had a physical exam and was declared unfit for flying.
So now all he is is a ground officer in charge of repairs. Of course he
feels very badly about it, and it certainly is a shame.[54]

May 8, 1918. I left at 10:00 in awful sea, almost crashing getting
off, and passed point at 11:00, Boulogne 11:12, Calais at 11:22,
arrived Dunkirk 11:31. As I came into the dock, Di sent me out
to look for sub sighted just off Dunkirk, so I flew till 12:00 but
saw nothing. It certainly was good to get back, and I am tired
out. The pigeon I sent didn't arrive until yesterday and the boys

54. Smith's airsickness, first observed by Ingalls when they were at Gosport, finally
caught up with him. Smith lost his wings and spent the remainder of the war performing a variety of ground duties in France and England.

pretty well decided Davey was food for fishes until my wire finally arrived. Quite an experience but not by no means *Tres bon*. (Hanriot-Dupont, 120 minutes)

May 9, 1918. Tested my machine early and then spent rest of day putting on Aldis sight adjusting controls.[55] (Hanriot-Dupont, 40 minutes)

May 10, 1918. Beach Officer,[56] rose at 3:00, but it looked bad so I went to bed. Got up every half hour but it got worse. At 5:15 truck arrived saying that g.m [George Moseley?] had called out everyone. I went back to bed. No flying. At 2:30 Di, Ed, Pop [Lumers], Young, and I went northeast on a patrol, nice flight but rotten weather and visibility. My machine works very well. Two Navy men came to dinner. Chevy called us in and said that all but Di and one other was going to fly DH-4s with Army. Hurrah for the land machines.[57] (Hanriot-Dupont, 70 minutes)

May 11, 1918. Slept till 7:30. Dud morning. After lunch a patrol was sent off, and then we had a formation flight five of us. It was good fun and I had a huff with Young and also a SPAD. The H.D. did very well against the SPAD much to my surprise. I couldn't loop the doggone thing to save my neck. I played Racilie ["Raily" crossed out] with Doc, getting . . . on one of two games. Brought back a motorcycle for using on early patrol. (Hanriot-Dupont, 70 minutes)

May 12, 1918. Dud day as usual. Nothing of importance.

---

55. Telescope-like Aldis sights for machine guns were used on many fighting aircraft. Ingalls received extensive training in their use and maintenance while at Turnberry.

56. The beach officer was designated on a daily basis to direct operations around the hangars and launching area, while also ensuring aircraft and personnel were available and carrying out the day's assigned missions.

57. This is Ingalls's first reference to what would become known as the Northern Bombing Group, a projected organization composed of navy day and night bombing squadrons whose sole mission was the destruction of German submarine facilities at Bruges, Ostend, and Zeebrugge. For a full discussion of the evolution of the NBG project, see Rossano, *Stalking the U-Boat*, 314–44.

May 13, 1918. Officer of the Day today. Answered mail all morning
   as the weather was too bad for flying, and as it was "Mothers
   Day." Afternoon encore. Got to sleep at about 10:00 after writing
   Harry [Davison] and Mother.

On Board, May 13, 1918

My Dear Mother,
      As you may have become aware by the above address, I am
on duty to-night, and am inclined to be thankful that the weather
is perfectly punk, thus eliminating any chance that some Boche
monstrosity, i.e., an air raid or a big-gun shoot, would necessitate my
being awake the greater part of the night. Which little thing, when
coupled with the certainty of my having an early morning patrol
would by no means raise my spirits.
      It has rained all day, in fact if I had thought to count rainy days, I
believe that common sense would urge me to build a raft. It seems to
rain here in every month at least forty days and nights. I really can't
understand why the inhabitants are not web-footed. At any rate they
soon will be. There is a rumor to the effect that the army will soon be
compelled to give up land aeroplanes and take to pontoon machines
and boats.
      Well, Muzzy, a couple of days ago I wrote to Dad that I was in for
more training. That is almost a joke, isn't it? Honestly if my further
training in aviation should ever definitely end, I should feel quite
lost. But I wish that my last six months of training would begin soon
and would be situated in a place as pleasant as the first six. Though it
would be impossible to equal Palm Beach and Huntington.
      Day before yesterday I was delighted to receive a fine letter
from you. Mr. Painter also wrote me, and sent two books, which are
exceedingly interesting. Will you thank him for me? I shall write myself
and thank him when the opportunity offers. But tonight, as I have the
customary early patrol, it is impossible. Besides which, I have censored
at least 9,000 letters, as today is YMCA "Mother's Day," on which
everyone is supposed to write Mother, and the plan certainly turned
out well, from the general point of view, though from my point of view,

having been compelled to read all of them, I am glad "Mother's Day" occurs about as often as Xmas. As I am leaving Dunkirk shortly, at least I hope I do, please address me again at U.S.N. Aviation, 4 Place D'Iena, Paris or c/o C.P.S. and Co. With love, Dave

Officer of the Day, Dunkirk May 13, 1918

Dear Old Dude [Harry Davison],

I infer from the fact that you have not written me for sometime, that you are either dead or quite well, back to your parlor tricks, and I certainly hope the latter supposition is true. You know the old bachelors' club has certainly suffered a serious loss of numbers, i.e., you and Di have just about been kicked out by the rest of the club, i.e., Me. And I'm getting darned lonesome, and am going to propose for the next member, Frank D. [likely Frances Davison]. I know she wouldn't go back on me, the way a couple of others have. But Harry, I don't blame you very much, as I know what those doggone southern girls are like—very seductive and liable to raise hell as sentimental codgers as yourself.[58]

We have been having a pretty good time frocking around here. Excepting about a week ago I got lost due to a junk compass and a number of clouds, and was finally picked up by an old fishing tub about 25 miles out at sea just off Havre. How did I get so far off nobody knows and everyone has been kidding me about my navigational abilities ever since.

However, I'm feeling good now, as a lot of us are leaving for further training on land machines, two-seaters, rumor has it, but after flying these canal boats, anything with wheels makes me feel like Ken does when he gets a letter from Priscie [Priscilla Murdock]. Talking about girls, did you hear that Ken S[mith] got a sub the other day?[59] The

58. At this point, Harry Davison labored at the naval air station at Hampton Roads, Virginia, but anticipated assignment to duty overseas with the Northern Bombing Group.

59. While at NAS Le Croisic, Kenneth Smith, NA #87 and a member of the First Yale Unit, received credit for helping sink a German submarine on April 22, 1918, for which he and his observer were awarded the Navy Cross and the Croix de Guerre. Postwar examination of available documents casts doubt on this claim.

lucky beggar. Of course you know what I mean, we used to practice it under your room at Yale and on the lawn at Huntington, especially after lunch. If you understand, keep it quiet for the present, it would be bad for his family to learn it.

Old Sam W[alker] just arrived, having toured up from his station [Le Croisic] in an ambulance meant for work on our station, somehow I don't like to say meant for us, it doesn't sound optimistic. Di is not going with us for training, but we are sure he'll probably take charge of the bunch when we get to work. I'd give anything if you were going to be with us old bear. Can't you practice up on a JN4 and pull a few wires, because it would be great if you could.[60]

Say, were you ever Officer of the Day anywhere? Well, of all the rotten jobs I've seen it is the worst! Today is "Mothers day," that is everyone is supposed to write mother. Well everyone here did, and having got interested in pen and paper, most of them wrote also to "Mothers to be" and I've had to censor so darned many letters that I haven't a thought of my own left. Also, I have a morning patrol and expect to get up about at 2:00 or 3:00 so shall repair to bed.

Don't forget to let me know anything you hear about societies— though I'm doubtful whether I'll get a crack at any. I wrote Blake Lawrence and he said to tell you to go Psi U that he wanted to, and it would be great if we all went together if we had a chance. Write me occasionally and give my best to any of either the old unit or the wireless unit you see.[61] Affectionately yours, Dave

———

May 14, 1918. Being Beach Officer, I was called at 3 A.M. The weather looked good then, so I routed out everyone and when the pilots arrived at five, had two in water and rest ready. But wind and fog had come up rapidly, and the patrol returned after a short trip, so I went home to breakfast after writing up the log.

---

60. Samuel Walker, another of Ingalls's Yale Unit comrades, was then serving at NAS Le Croisic. The Curtiss JN-4, known as the "Jenny," was America's principal elementary training aircraft throughout the war. More than sixty-eight hundred were manufactured.

61. He was referring to the young women, part of the Yale Unit's social set, who trained in wireless telegraphy on Long Island and in New York City in 1917.

Rest of day dud, but toward 6:00 the wind went down and SPADs and Camels and DH4s flew all around us. Also a Handley Page, which made a forced landing on beach the other day, took off at suppertime. And a Dolphin, which ran out of gas.[62] Expecting to leave shortly for gay Paree, and land machines, hurrah! Sam Walker arrived last night with a Ford ambulance from Le Croisic. Said that Ken Smith had sank a sub and been awarded the Croix de Guerre. Big air raid. Beautiful.

May 15, 1918. Fine day, but I did not fly being off duty. After lunch Shorty, [C. R.] Johnson, and I went to Calais with Doc and Sam who were going back to leave and Le Croisic. We shopped a bit, and Ray, Shorty, Lieut., and Eng. Lieut had dinner and came home at night in Cadillac. As we returned a hell of a raid began and continued till 12:00. We went through Dunkirk and could hear shrapnel rattling on house roofs.

May 16, 1918. Slick day, we got up at 3:30 and left at 6:30. Went to West [Hinder] (three H. D, two D. D.).[63] Then we saw five Hun seaplanes, which ran away when we got near then. Sat around rest of day. (Hanriot-Dupont, 10,000 ft., 120 minutes)

May 17, 1918. Fine day, Di having called for an extra couple [of patrols]. George [Moseley] and I went out at 5:00 for West Hinder patrol. Just after we started the D. D.'s broke down so we didn't go. Lucky for us as the English Lieutenant reported 10 Hun land scouts out there waiting for us. As it was our off day, the rest of the time we just frocked around.

---

62. The Handley Page o/400, long-range, multiengine heavy bomber was an improved version of the earlier Handley Page o/100 bomber. The Sopwith Dolphin was a staggered-wing, single-seat biplane scout introduced in 1918, with a maximum speed of approximately 125 mph.

63. Anchored just south of the southwest end of the shallows in seventeen fathoms, the West Hinder lightship provided an important navigational reference for vessels and aircraft.

May 17, 1918

[Father?]

Lately we have, by some strange freak, had fine weather, and as a result, every night here has been most picturesque and interesting. With a beautiful new moon shining down upon the smooth sea, with countless Archie batteries barking along the coast for miles on each side, with shrapnel bursting high in the heavens, whence comes— during the lulls between salvoes—the distinct and never-to-be-forgotten hum of the Boche flown motors, with the many far-reaching searchlights, star shells, flaming onions,[64] and the occasional rattle of machine guns—the last defense against some daring Hun, who slipped through the barrage, and, coming in low over the city to drop his load of bombs, has become plainly visible to those on the ground—with all this, I say Dunkirk is a wonderful sight.

In the actions of the inhabitants, however, little of the strain in which they live is apparent. For, as I sit upon the porch overlooking the beach, I see many couples, sprung from every nation, wandering along arm in arm, watching others who bathe, in spite of the cold, or lie about on the sun-warmed sands. And in the channels just off the coast, loom majestically the Hun destroyers. While continually planes of every sort and description soar overhead, either steadily climbing towards the front, or, throttled down, half gliding back to rest—their dangerous tasks completed. Now, when the evening quiet has fallen, the low rumble of the guns on the lines becomes more audible, and often, at the explosion of one of the heavier guns, the house shakes, and the whole earth seems to tremble, as if in response to some satanic blow. Surely it is well called "Tragic Dunkirk." Fortunately, however, during bad weather there is absolutely nothing doing here. So we make up for lost sleep and quiet down a bit then. With Love, Dave P.S. Three packages of tobacco from M & M Importing Co. have come through C.P.S. and Co. As it seems to come regularly, this must be a good way to send it. D.S.I.

64. Flaming onions were 37 mm pyrotechnic shells, fired by a multibarreled weapon, designed to shred and incinerate any aircraft they hit. They were effective to a height of approximately 5,000 feet.

May 18, 1918. Another good day. Small patrol early, then at 9:30,
seven H. D. started for offensive patrol and five French H. D.
But French called it off so we went up for practice. Shortly after
starting I noticed [John] Ganster left, but we went on for a couple
of hours. On landing we found Ganster had crashed on a chimney
and [been] killed, in streets[?]. Darn bad news. I certainly feel
awfully sorry about him.[65]

May 19, 1918. Off duty again. It was fine to sleep late. On arriving
at station we found Chuck O'Connor had not returned. So a patrol
was sent out to look for him. After lunch another patrol on which
I went. It was absolutely clear and one could see England at
100 meters over Calais. We covered the whole place and he was
not to be seen. Later another patrol was sent out West of Calais.
Found nothing but I am sure Chuck is O.K., though no pigeons or
signals have come in.

May 20, 1918. Patrol at 5:00. Di came over for breakfast at 3:45,
and said word had come from Chuck at Hastings, England.
[Djalma] Marshburn,[66] Di and I set out on patrol, but as we were
leaving the harbor we lost sight of Marshburn. After circling
a while, we joined the French going to West Hinder. About 12
miles out, Di landed, so I got motorboat to come out. Then I flew
back to keep an eye on Di. It was a beautiful morning and no
Huns to be seen, so I sported around Di thumbing my nose at him
and his crew of two. Suddenly I heard a machine gun and darned
if they weren't practicing with me as the target. So I hauled out
my Very pistol and did some shooting too. They were fair enough
to give up the machine guns and use Very pistols too, and a good

65. John Ganster, a member of the First Aeronautic Detachment, was killed on
May 18, 1918, when his aircraft crashed into the roof of a building on Rue Carnot
in Dunkirk. The machine fell to the street and burst into flames. Thrown clear of the
wreckage, Ganster died shortly after reaching a French military hospital. Following the
war, the owner of the home hit by the plane submitted a claim to the navy requesting
reimbursement for damage caused to his roof.

66. Djalma Marshburn, another member of the First Aeronautic Detachment, was
killed only a few days after the death of Ganster.

time was had by all. Finally the launch arrived and towed them in. But when I came in I saw two broken pontoons lying on dock and suspected trouble. On landing I heard that Marshburn had spun from 500 meters and machine and body were lost.[67] Of all the rotten luck this is the worst. I don't understand what can be wrong and had quite an argument with Pop and Chet about it. Marshburn is the 5th of the 12 sent for scout training. The spirit here is getting pretty bad due to the ineffectiveness so far of the station. Most everyone blames the machines—which are undoubtedly bad. How anything can ever be accomplished with them is beyond me. Foggy afternoon. After supper I met George's [George Moseley's] friends next door, an awfully nice French family of two daughters and one cousin and Ma and Pa. Doc came back tonight.

David Ingalls—Fitness Report

21 March to 31 March 1918 and 1 April to 24 May 1918

Very promising, excellent pilot.

Very excellent pilot. Very bold and aggressive, most promising.

G. De Chevalier, Lt., U.S.N.
Commanding U.S.N.A.S., Dunkirk

---

67. These five included enlisted pilots Harry Velie, Frederick Hough, John Ganster, M. J. Chapin, and Djalma Marshburn, as well as observers Edward Smith and Edward Eichelberger.

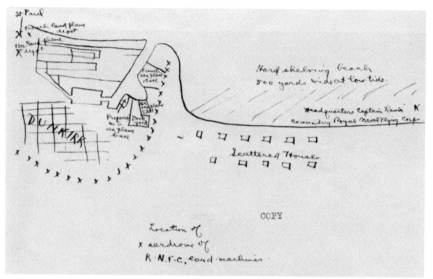

COPY

After finishing training at Turnberry and Ayr, Ingalls, MacLeish, and Smith were assigned to frontline duty at NAS Dunkirk on the northeast coast of France. This hand-drawn map of Dunkirk harbor was created by Lt. Kenneth Whiting, the naval officer responsible for committing the United States to establishing a base at this exposed site. *Courtesy National Archives*

Lt. Godfrey Chevalier served as CO at NAS Dunkirk until the summer and proved very popular among both his officers and the enlisted contingent, who admired his pep and dash. *Courtesy National Archives*

(*above*) Dunkirk proved something of a Yale reunion site. George Moseley, a Yale football star who played alongside Di Gates, had trained and flown with the French. He transferred to U.S. service and became a mainstay among the *chasse* pilots. *Courtesy Roger Sheely*

(*left*) Ingalls may have snapped this photo in May 1918 when another Yale Unit veteran, Samuel Walker, visited Dunkirk from his posting at NAS Le Croisic. He is seen here arm-in-arm with Di Gates. Ken MacLeish's personalized aircraft, *Priceless Priscilla,* is seen in the background. *Courtesy Peter B. Mersky Collection*

At Dunkirk, Ingalls flew the Hanriot-Dupont scout, a floatplane version of a land-based aircraft. Due the extreme rise and fall of tide at Dunkirk and the congested nature of the harbor, American aircraft were lowered and retrieved from the water by derricks, an inefficient and awkward process. *Courtesy National Archives*

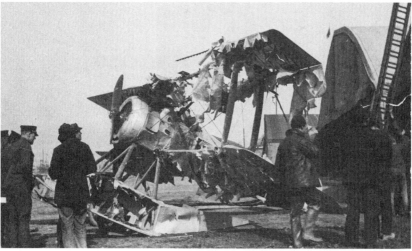

During World War I German army, navy, and air forces pummeled Dunkirk, inflicting widespread destruction. A raid in late April destroyed or severely damaged a dozen aircraft at the U.S. Navy station. Despite the large explosion, no one was seriously injured. *Courtesy National Archives*

This rare photograph shows the seawall at NAS Dunkirk with a group of Hanriot-Dupont scouts being readied for antisubmarine patrol over the North Sea. Risks included engine failure, mechanical breakdowns, and combat with faster, more maneuverable German seaplane scouts. *Courtesy Naval History and Heritage Command*

The great German spring offensive of 1918 led to enormous losses of British air crews, and CO Chevalier at NAS Dunkirk offered some of his surplus pilots and observers as temporary reinforcements. David Ingalls, Ken MacLeish, and "Shorty" Smith spent three weeks flying combat missions with No.213 Squadron, RAF. They are shown here in April 1918 standing in front of the squadron commander's hut at the Bergues aerodrome. *Courtesy Roger Sheely*

5
The Navy's Big Show—The Northern Bombing Group
May–August 1918

For many months, the navy had been analyzing the failure of its aerial patrols to intercept enemy submarines entering and exiting their lairs in Zeebrugge, Ostend, and Bruges. Patrolling was tedious, sporadic, and ineffective. Military planners had the same reservations and endured the same frustrations as Ingalls and other pilots, observers, and personnel at Dunkirk. After considerable debate on both sides of the Atlantic, the Department of the Navy decided to implement a vast new program to attack the U-boat bases through sustained heavy bombing, operating both day and night squadrons. Planners initially envisioned a force of twelve squadrons and several thousand officers and enlisted personnel. The proposed organization, known as the Northern Bombing Group, ultimately emerged as naval aviation's largest single offensive effort of the war.[1]

The First Yale Unit's Bob Lovett played a central role in the development of this organization, interviewing Allied officials and personnel, compiling reports, participating in several bombing raids across the lines, and drafting and refining policy proposals. He eventually departed Paris headquarters to be named wing commander of the Northern Bombing Group's night bombing squadrons. Lovett's support for the concept of strategic bombing only increased with time: during World War II, from his

---

1. See Geoffrey Rossano, *Stalking the U-Boat: U.S. Naval Aviation in Europe in World War I* (Gainesville: University Press of Florida, 2010), 314–44, see especially Walter Isaacson and Evan Thomas, *The Wise Men: Six Friends and the World They Made* (New York: Simon and Schuster, 1986), 202–9.

position as assistant secretary of war for air, he played a pivotal part in the nation's vast air campaign.

Bored to tears with monotonous and unproductive patrol duties, Ingalls jumped at the chance to join the new initiative. In mid-May, he and several others received orders to proceed to the Army Air Service school at Clermont-Ferrand, known as the Seventh Aviation Instruction Center and located ten miles west of Lyon in south-central France, for instruction in day bombers. Training there on Breguet 14B.2 aircraft proceeded in fits and starts, punctuated by occasional squabbles with the army and a few hair-raising incidents. The ever-opinionated Ingalls found the aircraft tiresome to fly and army instructors inexperienced and pompous. His accommodations lacked the comforts of Paris or even Dunkirk.

Ingalls and Ken MacLeish joked about leaving the program and returning to the United States to conduct flying tours to benefit the Red Cross, including sham dogfights with Sopwith Camels over New York City. Negative attitudes and poor morale were not limited to the navy contingent, however. According to aviation historian Morrow, many army trainees and instructors suffered from similar dissatisfaction and "complained that pursuit aviation received excessive publicity, and that training for observation and bomber aviation was undervalued, neglected, and used as a threat for poor fighter pilot trainees." At the command level, Col. Thomas Dewitt Milling, Chief of the Air Service, First Army, recalled, "The school was in very poor shape, discipline lax and morale poor."[2]

Day bombers such as the Breguet required a two-man crew, a pilot and an observer-gunner-bombardier who sat in the rear cockpit and operated twin machine guns. The navy paired an officer-pilot and an enlisted observer for both the training course at Clermont-Ferrand and later duty at the front. David Ingalls, for example, paired with Machinist Mate Randall R. Browne. Most of the enlisted men, from the First Aeronautic Detachment, trained first at St. Raphael, Moutchic, Cranwell, and Eastchurch/Leysdown and then carried out combat patrols at NAS Dunkirk. Unfortunately for the navy fliers, while at Clermont-Ferrand they learned Washington had assigned the day bombing role in the Northern Bombing

2. See John H. Morrow Jr., *The Great War in the Air: Military Aviation from 1909 to 1921* (Washington, D.C.: Smithsonian Institution Press, 1993), 339–40. Milling was quoted in Maurer Maurer, ed., *The U.S. Air Service in World War I*, 4 vols. (Washington, D.C.: Office of Air Force History, 1979), 4:8.

Group to the Marine Corps, leaving Ingalls and other newly qualified aviators without hope of promotion to flight or squadron leader—and even without a mission. Nonetheless, upon completion of the training program, they returned to Dunkirk and joined Nos.217 and 218 Squadrons, RAF, to carry out a series of cross-lines bombing raids.

After safely completing his allotted three missions with the British, Ingalls performed ground duties for the infant Northern Bombing Group, helping prepare aerodromes for planned operations but dreaming of returning to combat. He pestered anyone he could think of to get him reassigned to a frontline unit. Ingalls got his wish in early August with an assignment to rejoin No.213 Squadron, flying Sopwith Camels.

May 24, 1918. Left Dunkirk and took 4 P.M. to Paris. A hell of a trip, I in one compartment and about no sleep at all. Ran along France in morning, 21 hours. Went to chateau, walked around, and had supper avec A. B. [Alice Bowler] and mother. Met A. A. 1st Lieut. there.

May 26, 1918. Reported and spent day wandering around. Ran into Skinny [Lawrence]. Dined with Ken [MacLeish], A.B., and mother.

May 27, 1918. Shopped in morning, lunched with Skinny, had picture taken, ran into our observers, walked and rode around. Paris is certainly beautiful.

May 28, 1918. Took 8 a.m. train for Clermont-Ferrand and had a nice trip, arriving about 5:15. Stayed at the Hôtel Terminus, then had dinner at Café de Paris and walked around, climbed Catholic church.

May 29, 1918

My Dear Mother,
Again I am training—far from the front in an American army camp, where I expect to spend a very pleasant month. To Paris we had an absolutely wretched trip, had no sleep all night, and when

dawn broke I often stepped off and walked a bit to lighten the load on
the hills. I wish dad would come over and straighten these railroads
out a bit. However, Paris was the most beautiful city imaginable, just
like a fairy city. I really am crazy about it, and spent most of my time
walking and riding up and down the boulevards. Also had dinner
with the Bowlers a couple of times. Sunday afternoon as Ken and I
were promenading *dans* le Champs Elysee who should we run into
but Skinny Lawrence. It was great to see him again, and we had a fine
time. Then we bid fair Paree adieu and arrived here in a beautiful
village yesterday afternoon. Tomorrow being a holiday we are going
to a big dance at the camp assisted by a large number of American
nurses from a hospital nearby. It should be great fun. Our training
here I do not think will be great fun, as I'm not fond of the strictness
of the American army schools. The flying rules are very good for
beginners, but give an old experienced pilot—thank you—a pain.
You would think we were a bunch of kids. Anyway, I'm doggone sick
of training and training and never expected to do any more. There is
honestly nothing more to learn here, so far from the front, but about
half of our squadron have not flown land machines so we have to fly
around until they are finished too. Sorry to be so pessimistic, but my
patience is not too good. With love, Dave

May 29, 1918. Reported at station some way outside, a good mile
and half walk from trolley end at 11:30. We lunched and went to
town. Stopped at Hôtel Unique.

May 30, 1918. Came out after lunch and saw ball game,[3] sat around
had dinner and then went in again to Hôtel de la Porte. Our quarters
at camp are impossible now, no blankets—nothing but a small room
with 18 pieces of canvas slung between posts. The food is horrible

3. American servicemen, no matter where stationed, played baseball. Both the army
and the navy organized leagues and competed whenever time and conditions permitted. During the war, traveling teams of professional all-stars toured military bases and
played against service squads. An extensive discussion of such activities is contained in
William N. Still Jr., *Crisis at Sea: The United States Navy in European Waters in World War
I* (Gainesville: University Press of Florida, 2006), 270–74.

beyond belief. We are quartered in one big barracks. All the officers and men got sore, so the Army put a sort of partition between us. The Army men are more or less unbearable, they're so darn high hat. None of them has ever been out to the front, but Hell, you'd think they'd already won the war by themselves. They've made us take off our insignia and we have to salute even a second lieutenant. We can't get off the station and there is nothing to do.

May 31, 1918. Got out at 7:30. As truck failed to call for us. I had a fly at 8:00 and didn't like machine a bit. These Breguets are as bad as a flying boat, only maybe worse.[4] No power, clumsy, awkward, rotten. After dinner I had another hop at 6 p.m. Not much better.

June 1, 1918. Of all the rotten quarters. All of us were stiff and sore having no mattresses and but two very thin and small blankets apiece. Got up at 5:00, had a rotten breakfast, then had a lecture on Michelin sight—a damn good sight I think.[5] Had two hops later on, and was told I was all right on landings, but punk in the air, by the fat little instructor who has had probably 60 or 70 hours. But he was probably right, as I always have a great deal of trouble on a new machine. Ken at noon brought in a cable that he, Fred Beach and I were made Lieutenants (j.g.) on March 23, 1918. Pretty darn nice. I flew this evening and then George [Moseley], Eddie [Judd], Chet [Bassett], Fred [Beach], and I walked and trolleyed and taxied to Royat, a perfectly delightful little village on a sort of a hill nearby, where we spent the night at a slick hotel. We didn't have to return till Monday, so heh for a decent bed and some real food and liquor. Royat is famous for its chocolate.[6] The people are quite typical village French, the best sort the French have, I think.

---

4. The standard day bomber used by the French in 1918, the Breguet type 14 B.2, carried 660 pounds of ordnance at a top speed of approximately 110 mph. Breguets equipped several U.S. Air Service aero squadrons.

5. This bombsight was designed for use with the Breguet bomber, with settings for altitude and speed. Altitude was calculated using the aircraft's altimeter, and speed was determined with the use of a stopwatch.

6. Royat, a "thermal resort" (hot springs), had been known for its chocolate since the nineteenth century and remains so to this day, as does nearby Clermont-Ferrand.

June 1, 1918

Dear Dad,

We have settled down to routine training now, and it is a most deadly bore. After the English schools where freedom is the strongest point, the petty flying rules—for example, fly around the field turning only one way—give me an awful pain. Thank the Lord this won't last long. However, I have heard that the course is most excellent after we start the actual war formations, etc., so I'm still hoping for the best. But it certainly is trying to have the fat little shrimp who is my instructor telling me how to fly. But he is a nice fellow out of the machine and when I think that for some reason I am unusually slow in picking up a new type, I fold my hands and pray I'll get up alone soon—this afternoon probably. Anyway, I'm fine now, having receiving a cable announcing that I was commissioned a lieutenant (j.g.) on March 23, so I have a half stripe more. Ken also got a raise. It's really about time official word came through, as we've been aware of it coming a month or more. I am enclosing a picture of Skinny Lawrence—(Blake's brother)—and a fellow named Nash—who I ran into in Paris. Did you get two bunches of photos I sent you some time ago? If so, be a bit careful about who sees them, for although I sent nothing that would be useful to the Germans, someone might raise a kick. Skinny is a second lieut in the regular army in field artillery 75's I think.[7] He expects to go up to the front in a week and also expects a raise to 1st Lieutenant or Captain before going. He has been training just 30 miles from here, which is Clermont-Ferrand. We hope to be done in a month at the most, and go back to about 20 miles west of where we were. Well dad, I must go to a bombing lecture. With love to all, aff. Dave

———

June 2, 1918. Rose at about 11:00, and Chet and I had two
breakfasts. The morning was advantageously occupied writing,
then we had lunch and went to Chocolate Royat for some
wonderful chocolate ice cream, nuts, and prunes. Then we

---

7. The rapid-firing French 75 became the standard field gun used by AEF field artillery units on the Western Front. It was also the name given to a cocktail invented at Harry's New York Bar in Paris in 1915.

walked around, apparently causing the inhabitants much curiosity as to what we were. Royat is a beautiful little village filled with beautiful people wandering about.

June 3, 1918. Having arrived at camp late last night, it was hard to get up in the morning and I have an awful cold due to these rotten quarters. Had some more flying and bombing. No mail yet.

June 4, 1918. Every day so far has been fine, I went on camera flight this morning, just to let the observer drive me over a camera with a sort of harness, not much fun.

June 5, 1918. This place is certainly getting on my nerves. About one hour a day is all the time we have anything to do. My darned fat baby of an instructor finally gave me up in disgust, said I never would be able to fly decently but he couldn't waste any more time so I could go ahead and solo. I told him it was hard for me, I was so used to having something to keep my mind off the actual flying, like Archies, and he looked pop-eyed. So I added it would certainly be tough on the Huns if he ever got up to the front. Lucky for me he'd passed me, or he'd have kept me a pupil the rest of the war. I bet one thing, that he'll still be at Clermont when we have exterminated the Huns. This morning a lot of mail arrived—which was slick as hell. A couple of our boys were caught spending the night out in fair company. They are to be fired. The Army allows no Americanized repopulation of France. I wish I could get fired out of this dump.

June 5, 1918

My Dear Mother,

Today a lot of mail came, and I received two letters from you May 3 and 7. Congratulations, Muzzy, on being chairman of the Canteen and Red Cross. It is fine. And I think the canteen must be a great success. And to think of Dad and Mr. Corning, at your branch knitting socks side by side, is a happy thought. I am awfully sorry to hear about the Golf's dog going mad and causing so much danger. I hope no one suffers any ill effects from it. I hear that Pete has sailed—how are the mighty fallen—and that Jack has gone to Canada to take a look at the R.F.C. to see if he could stand joining it. Unless he uses powerful glasses I doubt if he gets within sight of it. But the best news of all is that you are doing some more modeling. Keep it up Mother. There are certainly a lot of troops over here, and I think there must be a lot at the front, and this is the time for them to bring home the bacon. As soon as I get to one of our stations I'll procure some requests for chocolate, etc., but just now I don't like to bother the army, you see they have to be typewritten too, and it's quite a job. Here it is certainly monotonous, so far we have done awfully little but sleep and walk and eat. It will be a big relief when, if it ever happens, we get definitely settled at a station of our own. Last letter I wrote I had been made a lieut., but it may not have arrived. However, I seem to receive mail very regularly from you and Dad and it is great to do so. One good thing has happened. Of course the old bunch at D[unkirk] was not big enough to fill the squadron we are to make, so a lot of newcomers have joined us, and except for a few not much. Well, three of them have already been reported to the navy by the army as unfit for flying, so we got rid of some of them. And I think we will have a better bunch join us. I hope so anyway. Well, roll call just sounded, so I have a couple of minutes to report. Love, Dave

June 6, 1918. Crosscup and Pou have been confined to camp and having spent the night out are due to get fired. They are a foul-minded pair so it's *tres bon*. Boorse will also go due to some trouble with his eyes and head.[8] I've felt low for a couple of days, sort of headache.

8. Soon separated from the Northern Bombing Group program, this unfortunate trio did not survive the war. Woldemar Crosscup, NA #332, died at Moutchic on July 6, 1918; Edwin Pou, NA #435, son of a North Carolina congressman, was ordered to NAS Ile Tudy and was killed in a seaplane crash there on October 28, 1918, when his aircraft collided with a spar buoy during landing; and Arthur Boorse, NA #333, perished in a seaplane accident at NAS Brest on August 21, 1918. See Reginald Arthur, *Contact! Careers of Naval Aviators Assigned Numbers 1–2000* (Washington, D.C.: Naval Aviation Register, 1967), 119, 144.

June 6, 1918

Dear Dad,

Three very interesting letters arrived from you yesterday—the
first mail we had for some time due to our change of location. I hope
you have long ago changed my address back to C.P.S. & Co. or 4 Place
D'Iena. It is certainly great, Dad, that you are having such success
with the N[ew] Y[ork] C[entral] and at as bad a time as this. And how
is your golf game getting along? I am getting awfully worried about
playing you again, not having had any decent exercise for 14 months. I
think croquette will be my limit. But if by some unheard of occurrence
I am actually stationed anywhere definitely, I'm going to get into
fighting trim. This morning we started the actual training here, until
now we have been merely making our acquaintance with the machine.
And I find that scientific bombing is most interesting, excellent sport,
and extremely difficult. In addition, I possess, in my own opinion, at
least, the best observer [MM Randall R. Browne] now living. He is a
great fellow, a little bit of humanity with a good homely face, scared of
nothing—not even of having me as his pilot, and a remarkable shot.
He is probably 27 or 28 years old.[9] This lengthy description is due to
the fact that I have to rely a great deal on my observer and, therefore,
take a considerable interest in him. Well, Dad, ever since being taken
from or rather never definitely assigned to a land scout, I have felt
pretty bad, but this afternoon I am particularly low, as a Nieuport
came over and stunted around these darned big machines. However,
I continually pray for another chance at a real machine. This morning
Eddie Judd, one of the Lafayette fellows, and I went into town to have
a fitting for a new uniform. I'll be pretty sporty when I appear in it.
Two of the least attractive members of our squadron from the bunch
that joined us are fired from the school today, one left from sickness

---

9. Randall Browne's Enlistment Record lists his age as thirty, height as five feet six
inches, and weight as 140 pounds. Contemporary photographs show a man with a
seamed face and big ears. He was an original member of the First Aeronautic Detachment and had been in France since early June 1917. Browne and another observer,
Irving Sheely, spent some time at Clermont-Ferrand working on an improved bombsight. Browne's papers and scrapbook are held at the Naval History and Heritage
Command, Washington, D.C.

and another goes tomorrow, so we may get a good bunch yet. Well, Dad, I must go to my work. With love, Dave.

—

> June 7, 1918. Had a crack at being observer, it was great fun. Also
> a Renault motor improves the machines a bit. Four Nieuports
> have arrived for the school, we have not used them, or hope to.[10] I
> wrote K. V. P[ainter]. Also sent some more requests for tobacco.

—

June 7, 1918

Dear Mr. Painter,

    I was awfully glad to receive your letter about three weeks ago, and since then the two very interesting books you sent. Thank you very much. I shall be sure to call on Miss Getty on the way back to the front through Paris. At present I am at an army school, exceedingly bored, somehow I had an idea that after the exceedingly thorough course, to which we were subjected in England, training was over with. However, it is a relief to be in an American school and not one of our allies, and as the course is short, we expect to finish up in at the most three weeks more. Although we were permitted only to pass through Paris on our way here, I was greatly surprised at the number and type of Americans there. They were indeed a fine looking bunch, as are the ones at all the camps I've seen. Which is quite different from the ordnance and medical officers who flooded the cafes of Paris during last fall. They were a poor lot. Of course everyone is more or less worried over the drive just now, and Paris seems pretty near the front, but we have quite a number of men up there and lots more going up, which may help stop them. Here at Clermont-Ferrand the war seems a long way off. It is a beautiful part of France, the weather is ideal, there is not much work—in fact if I were on a legitimate leave it would be fine. As it is I am any day

---

10. The Nieuport aircraft company produced a wide range of single-seat and two-seat scouts and bombers during the war. French, British, American, and Russian forces used them. It is not certain which model Ingalls was referring to in this entry.

expecting a letter from Dad kidding me about the length of time I need to become an aviator. Please give my very best to Mrs. Painter. Sincerely yours, David Ingalls.

———

June 8, 1918. Well, I've had some flying, some aerial camera shooting, which is good fun; also a crack at the camera obscura.[11] The gun has a camera set on it, and when you fire you shoot a picture and later find out how far you missed by. The observer has a sort of harness to his pilot, and looking through his sights steers you and the ship over the target, then he drops a little bomb. My observer is a fellow named Browne. He weighs about 90 pounds, but is the best darn shot I ever saw, either with the camera gun or the bombs. We'll have some fun if we ever get over the front together. Found that we can't go to Royat for the night. Damn this childish army. Kindergarten school anyway. So far all that my observer and I have done could have been done anywhere at the front in a few hours flying, and we have over two weeks more of the same rot to look forward to.[12] There is nothing to do except sit in one's bunk, read, smoke, and sleep occasionally.

June 9, 1918. Went to Royat, bath, lunch, and a pleasant concert. Dinner at Royat with Archie Mac[Leish], Tom Cornell, Nick Carter, and Ken.

June 10, 1918. Nothing all day, I have a hell of a sore throat and cold. A funny thing happened the other day. We were flying

---

11. The camera obscura is a device that uses mirrors and lenses to project an image of its exterior surroundings onto a screen, in either a box or a darkened room. The Air Service and other air forces used these devices as part of their gunnery and bombing training regimens.

12. Flight time for crews training at Clermont-Ferrand proved limited due to chronic shortages of aircraft—a total of approximately ten hours over the course of a month. Typical flights lasted twenty-five to thirty minutes, though on a few days, the pilot-observer teams might make two or three short hops. Limited flying time is documented in Chief Machinist Mate Randall Browne's daily manuscript diary entries. That the army allocated scarce training slots to navy crews in June 1918 says something about the importance accorded the Northern Bombing Group project by military authorities. Over the course of a year's activity, the school at Clermont-Ferrand graduated 212 pilots and 262 bombardiers. See James Hudson, *Hostile Skies: A Combat History of the American Air Service in World War I* (Syracuse, N.Y.: Syracuse University Press, 1968), 39–40.

in formation and having a few instructors pretend to attack us in Nieuports. One of the observers leaned over to shoot at an instructor with his camera gun, leaned too far, lost his balance, and fell out. He was up about 2,000 feet. His gun and the camera went flying and he after, but somehow his foot caught in the wires of the tail and stuck there. He clambered up, with his pilot watching pale and nervous. He got onto the fuselage and crawled along, jamming his hands and feet through the fabric, and finally got into the cockpit. When they landed he was raving gently and taken to the hospital. The devil was certainly cheated that time.[13]

June 11, 1918. My cold being worse I dropped in on the Doc, but he did nothing. I could hardly talk all day and feel low—the natural result. Received a letter from Di, it was great to hear from him, also that he hopes to be with us soon.

———

June 11, 1918

My Dear Mother,

Today my mail comprised two letters from you, as far as I could by careful mathematical calculation tell, in perfect sequence. Until today I thought that the climate here was always fine, but yesterday and today have been more like French weather. In short, it has rained and blown consistently, so there has been even less to do than usual. But dame Fortune, to relieve the monotony and keep me from becoming morbid, has given me a sore throat, so I test and keep in good form my memory, by gargling and swallowing the evil tasting pills at the regular and afore-mentioned moments. Another pleasant incident was that in addition to your fine letters I got three magazines and a couple of books, which were most desirable, from you. The three newcomers have come and they are a vast improvement over what was fired out. At least so far none of them have spoken to my knowledge, and I hear that at least two of them are good flyers. The other day I received a letter

---

13. This often-reported incident involved 1st Lt. Samuel P. Mandell, the pilot, and 1st Lt. Gardiner H. Fiske, the observer.

from a master at school, Willie Weeks,[14] enclosing a picture of my
little kid brother—he looks mighty fine, and I hope he uses his head
and sticks at school all right. Brewster Jennings wrote to me, too, he is
an ensign in charge of a small motor launch somewhere over here—I
hope to see him sometime. Bob [Lovett], who is practically the C.O. of
all of us, telephoned and said that things were getting along fine—also
that we shall probably get 10 or 14 days leave before returning to the
front. If that weather keeps bad, it may be three or four weeks before
we leave here, but we hope it won't be more than two or a little over. I
just heard that Jane Bowler is engaged. Aff. yours, Dave[15]

—————

June 11–30, 1918. I got well somehow, and was bored from then on.
    We had some formation flying dropped smoke bombs. Met Adelaide
    Sedgwick.[16] Mr. and Mrs. Knapp—Chip's mother. The last Sunday
    at Royat. Danced that afternoon with an awful bunch of fruits.
    Arrived in camp to find we were to leave, Ken Mc., Judd, and me.[17]

---

14. This is a reference to one of two similarly named masters at St. Paul's School,
either Charles Clarence Weeks from New York City, who taught from 1910 to 1948,
or Walter Samuel Weeks, who was at St. Paul's School during the period 1917 to 1921
and would have been known to Albert Ingalls Jr. but not David Ingalls.

15. Ingalls's cold worsened, grounding him for most of June. The paucity of surviving diary entries and correspondence indicates the severity of his affliction. It might
have been a touch of the flu. Other trainees succumbed as well. Ken MacLeish wound
up in the hospital after a sudden onset of the flu, what he called "an epidemic of
grippe in our [barracks] room."

16. A prominent member of the New York debutante set, Sedgwick was described
as "one of the dozen younger society who are noted for their dancing" and who appeared in a war relief benefit performance at the Century Theater in January 1917. See
New York Times, January 28, 1917.

17. Completion of work at Clermont-Ferrand meant a return to Paris and then
Dunkirk, where Ingalls and several others served temporarily with No.218 Squadron,
RAF, gaining experience by carrying out missions over the front. This arrangement,
temporarily placing navy pilots and observers with British bombing squadrons, continued until the end of the war. Similar, even larger programs existed for many of the
Army Air Service aviators now pouring into Europe. More than 860 army pilots and
observers flew with the French, British, and Italian air forces. For a detailed description of the activities, see Hudson, Hostile Skies, 33–34, 233–57. Following service with
the RAF, the naval aviators rejoined their own Northern Bombing Group but faced
an uncertain future. The day bombing mission for which they trained was assigned to
Marine Corps crews, leaving the sailors of the air all dressed up with nowhere to go.

July 1, 1918. Said goodbye to that damned rotten army school, and
departed on 9 a.m. [train] to Paris arriving at 5 p.m. Ken and I
had an excellent dinner at [ ], Nick Carter having gone to bed.

July 2, 1918. Reported and learned that the Army was as sore as
Hell about the fight [see letter of July 3, 1918] and had advised
our headquarters and would fire all the Navy out of their school.
The Navy should worry. Our C.O. spoke fiercely, but I think he
was tickled really. We discovered that we were to go to R.A.F. and
train for flight commander. Kiely, the poor half-wit, tried to [ ] and
us right out. But Child took Ken and me out to see Liberty DH-4
on 3rd so we had to wait till 4:45 on 4th.[18]

July 3, 1918. Had lunch with Fearing and dinner at Café Paris with
[Hen?] Thompson and Tom Ewing.[19] Saw and highly approved
of Liberty D H 4 and 9. Heard satisfactory report. Also that
our machines were shipped and would be sent to Eastleigh in
England for assembly.[20] Very nice.

July 3, 1918

My Dear Dad,
   Fortunately I have escaped with a whole skin from my last
abominable location, to good old Paris. And even though of course
many people have left, it is still the wonderful fairy city of old.
We left Monday and are staying here till tomorrow noon when we

18. Lt. Ralph Kiely, NA #1076, and Lt. Warren Gerald "Gerry" Child, NA #29, both
USNA graduates, held staff positions in Paris and London during much of the war.

19. Ensign George Fearing, whom Ingalls met at Moutchic in October 1917, served
on Capt. Hutch Cone's staff in Paris and as secretary of the aviation headquarters
Executive Committee. Tom Ewing was a friend from St. Paul's School, class of 1915.
The Liberty DH-4 was the American-manufactured version of the British aircraft,
powered with the new Liberty motor.

20. Eastleigh, located near Southampton in southern England, served as the assembly and repair facility for the Northern Bombing Group. Acquired from the British in
July 1918, the partially developed site expanded into an enormous operation manned
by thousands of officers and bluejackets.

return to a British squadron probably at the same field as the one we were at before, but to be sure a bombing squadron instead of a scout. Only three of us were taken from the school, the others are to finish, when we, having obtained the necessary experience, shall be the flight commanders—Ken Mac., Eddie Judd, and myself. It will be very pleasant to be with the British again, and infinitely better than lingering at that confounded school. Our last night there was a fitting conclusion—about 12 some army flyers began to sing and yell in the adjacent barracks waking everyone, and then around one darned if they didn't come into our room and try it there. As they did not leave quickly enough we yelled at them to shut up. So they had the nerve to suggest we get up and stop them. About one second later all of us concentrated in a big push, and after we put them out one of them picked a fight with about the weakest member we have, who scientifically laid him out cold. This rather dampened their enthusiasm so they carried off their pal and left us. Tomorrow is a big day here, so we'll have a great time. There is to be a big parade and some road is to be named after Pres. Wilson. I ran into a school fellow of mine, John Hamilton, who has been at the front in Nieuports, who is in fine form.[21] Ken and I are just off to some café. Love, Dave.

July 4, 1918. We saw a lot of fellows, Dick Conover, Tom Ewing among them.[22] Saw the big parade decked with American flags and had some of the pleasures of Paris. Left on 4:45, had French

21. John Adams Hamilton, St. Paul's School, '16, was another of Ingalls's many friends serving in Europe.

22. This entry is something of a mystery. Ingalls seems to have been referring to Richard Stevens Conover II, who was an outstanding football and hockey player at St. Paul's but left school in the spring of 1917 just before graduation to join a volunteer ambulance service in France. He later transferred to the transport service, enlisted in the U.S. Army in November, and was killed at Cantigny in May 1918. See August Heckscher, *St. Paul's: The Life of a New England School* (New York: Charles Scribner's Sons, 1980), 177, and St. Paul's School Archives, *The Role of Honor: St. Paul's School in the Great War, 1914–1918,* available online at http://library.sps.edu/06archives/war/wwi/wwi_index.html. However, Ingalls may have been referring instead to Richard Stevens Conover Jr., the father of the recently deceased pilot.

Captain and some cadet Americans. Had dinner at 10:30, slept a
bit perhaps. Arrived . . .

July 5, 1918. . . . Dunkirk at 9:15. Went to station. It was great to
see Di and Shorty, felt like coming home again.

July 5, 1918

My Dear Mother,

Dunkirk forever. We arrived early this morning, at least it
was about 9:30, after a horrible trip. Really, of all the abominable
things, traveling in a day coach with a curious mixture of most
sorts of the allies on a train that is moving only about 2/3 of the
time and then at a rate of speed that could not frighten one riding
through traffic in an electric auto, well it is a pretty bum way of
covering ground. In addition to which, the French Captain, who
shared our happiness, because, perhaps, of natural old age, but
more likely of over indulgence in alcoholic liquors, this man was
quite unable to withstand the evening air, and would continually
awaken from his dozing to close the windows, which we would as
continually open when he had again shut his eyes. Fortunately,
however, there was attached to the train a diner, where we enjoyed
a late supper or dinner until 12 midnight. And we arrived here in
time for an excellent breakfast with Shorty Smith and Di Gates,
who by the way is now in charge of the station. Here we expect to
rest for two or three days before joining some British squadron.
And I think that a few days of sleep, and the wonderful food here
obtainable will put us in good shape again. Somehow the place
looks a little more shot up—if possible. But still many stores are
open, and life goes quietly on. It certainly was great to see Di and
Shorty again. They are a wonderful pair and I wish we were all
together again. Well Muzzy, I must stop for dinner. As Always,
with all my love, Dave

July 6, 1918. Loafed around "A" Mess, went to 218 Squadron where
we are to go with Di and met C.O. Wemp.[23]

July 7, 1918. Still getting rested. Wonderful food here, and good
beds and nothing to do but get fat.

———

July 7, 1918

Dear Muzzy,

It is just two P.M. and I feel exactly as though I were sitting at
home on the porch after Sunday dinner. For we have just finished a
wonderful meal, really the mess at this seaplane base is better than
any place in France or England. So, I feel pretty good, I am smoking
a most enjoyable pipe and writing. The weather is ideal, and I hope it
keeps so, that we may have plenty to do when we get with the British
tomorrow. Of course we shall have to fly British machines, which I
frankly admit is by no means a hardship. Yesterday we drove over to
the squadron and they are a great bunch, we know most of them as
they were on the same field as the Camel squadron with which we
were formerly stationed. Also the British wing C.O. says that it is his
crack squadron and has done a lot of good work. You know when we
were in Paris we saw a Liberty D.H.4 and 9 and they certainly look
fine, and ought to be mighty effective machines. This new squadron
is way back from the front, so we shall not be kept awake nights
with bombs, which is a strong point in favor. By the way Mother, has
my allotment of $100 per month been arriving, if it does not come
regularly have Dad raise a howl, as it is being subtracted from my
pay over here. Shorty Smith got Skull and Bones, did I tell you? And
Eddie [Judd] made Scroll and Keys.[24] Isn't that great? At present

---

23. No.218 Squadron originated as a day bombing unit on April 24, 1918, at an
aerodrome in Dover, Kent, under the command of Canadian major Burt Stirling
Wemp, DFC. The squadron operated DH9 day bombers and soon relocated to Petite-
Synthe, near Dunkirk, under the control of the No.5 Group, RAF. Only two pilots,
Canadian flight commanders John F. Chisholm and William F. Cleghorn, chosen per-
sonally by Major Wemp, possessed any operational experience.

24. These were some of the senior secret societies at Yale University.

Eddie's motor gave out over 30 miles out to sea and a destroyer has gone after him. Well, Mother, I must take a bit of a walk. We've had a much-needed rest, having slept the last two nights over 12 hours. Guess I was pretty tired. Love, Dave

———

July 8, 1918. Set sail for 218 Squadron after picking up account, etc. Slept at our future H[andley] P[age] station [St. Inglevert].[25]

July 9, 1918. Reported and placed our beds in position. Probably nothing to do for quite some time now. Rode motorcycle around with Juddy [Eddie Judd] in afternoon.

July 10, 1918. Bobby Rock[efeller] took Juddy and me to Dunkerque, where we greatly enjoyed the food.[26] The R.A.F. grub is not for a luxury lover like myself.

July 11, 1918. Frotched around—no machines yet.

July 12 and 13, 1918. Still hanging around.

———

July 12, 1918

Dear Dad,

Well Pops, we are firmly established with our dear allies for at least two or three weeks. There being no machines for us just yet, we have been touring around on a motorcycle—to Calais and Dunkirk. The weather has been rotten, so it is uncomfortable as the British just moved and so the barracks are not fitted up with the luxury of the Biltmore. Anyway I don't think any service in the world is as good as

---

25. Under the final organization plan developed for the Northern Bombing Group, a new aerodrome constructed at St. Inglevert (Field A), a few miles southwest of Calais, would serve as the home for night bombing squadrons 1 and 2. The navy leased a small chateau there to serve as headquarters and provide officers' accommodations.

26. William Avery Rockefeller served overseas in 1918 at NAS Killingholme.

our own navy, and I certainly would hate to have to change. Yesterday we went to Dunkirk in a Cadillac, and saw Di and Shorty and had a slick time. Then on the way back through Calais, the executive officer who is stationed at the wonderful chateau of one of our future stations, picked up a couple of WAACs whom he knew—English girls who are working over here—and brought them along for dinner.[27] The fact that there were about 15 of them and a couple of Australian officers for dinner didn't faze them at all, but they just tore around saying how priceless and hopping everything was. It certainly was funny. This squadron at which we are stuck, is a mighty full out one, and we'll have plenty of experience. The Huns are getting pretty peppy and they have a fight almost every raid. The mail is going out so I must stop. Aff. Dave P.S. Here is a picture of a squadron of the same kind of machine I flew for some time. They look pretty nice, don't they?

July 14, 1918. Sunday. Although we've been with 218 Squadron for some time no machines for us, so no flying. This morning most of the squadron went a-bombing. They had quite a fight. One of our boys was shot through the shoulders, but the others got two Huns, which is a good average. There is an American here named Chamberlain.[28] He's a hard-boiled boy from the U.S.A. all right and certainly has had some experiences in his little life, or else possesses some imagination—mostly the latter, I do believe.

July 15, 1918. At last we all got a hop. The DH-9 is a slick machine that handles beautifully, easy to fly.[29]

---

27. The Women's Auxiliary Army Corps (WAAC), founded in 1917, consisted of four departments: Cookery, Mechanical, Clerical, and Miscellaneous. Approximately nine thousand WAACs served in France. After creation of the RAF in April 1918, many of the women joined the air force as WRAFs.

28. Ingalls was referring to Lt. Edmund "Ed" Gillette Chamberlain, NA #96½, MA #7.

29. The Airco DH9 day bomber was a modification of the DH4 aircraft, powered by a 230 hp BHP/Puma motor. Despite Ingalls's endorsement, it was widely considered a failure as a frontline aircraft, exhibiting dramatically inferior performance and suffering constant mechanical problems. Monthly wastage approached 70 percent, and over a five-month period in 1918, losses exceeded 175 percent of force strength. See Morrow, Great War in the Air, 321.

July 16, 1918. Loads of mail arrived *tres bon*. I got a machine of
my very own. I tested it for 10 minutes about 8:45.

July 16, 1918

Dear Pops,
    Last night an awful lot of mail, magazines, and tobacco came in.
It certainly was great to get two letters from you of June 16 and 17,
numbers 19 and 20. Also one from Mother June 16 and one from my
fat and congenial young brother. I am not surprised that he has insisted
on enlisting, and know from experience how much good it does to
argue with the little fellow. I am very glad he is going into the navy.
In it, there is no doubt, but that one receives better treatment, food,
and quarters, and also has a better, cleaner time. But it will be awfully
hard on him being an enlisted man, tell him to work like the devil for a
commission. It is probably fine spirit to be an enlisted man, but officers
of high type are needed more than any other ranks after all. The idea
of yours to give the men a swim is *tres bon*. After a long trip nothing
could possibly be better. I'd prefer nothing to swimming with all of
you in good old Lake Erie. I am glad to hear that Uncle George has
obtained so good a job. But I am surprised to hear that you let him beat
you at golf, Pops. Well, yesterday I had a flight in one of the machines
here and it was fine. Ken and Judd went on a raid about two hours ago,
and so I'll probably get a crack soon. I hope so. It's pretty gloomifying
doing nothing. Bob [Lovett] was here today and says everything is
getting along *tres bon*. So we'll get our own machines and squadron
after a few raids here for experience, as the rest of the squadron having
finished, have gone on leave till we're ready. Mail is going out so
cheerio. Aff, Dave The tobacco is most acceptable to Ken and me.

July 17, 1918. Left at 1:20 or so flying last left in Baskerville's
formation.[30] It took us an hour and a half to get to 13,000 ft. On

---

30. Capt. M. G. Baskerville, also identified by Ingalls as "Basher," scored the unit's
first aerial victory, on June 26, against Fokker defenders during a raid against Zeebrugge.

account of sultry day, we kept circling till I got sort of impatient.
Then we finally entered along coast, just five of us, Judd having
dropped out. Crossed coast between Ostend and Zeebrugge. Then
headed straight across the locks and let go the bombs. I had 4 x
50 and got a good sight on the locks, but a cloud drifted across
so we were unable to see the hits. Then we went straight across
Zeebrugge and the mole where we got a little Archie, but not
very near us. Then we headed along coast toward home, keeping
a good lookout for Huns. When we passed Nieuport, Browne
[observer] flew the machine and did very well. Then we had a
huff with some British, shot a bit, and flew in and landed behind
Basher. After supper Juddy and I went to [S. A.?] and sat around
talking awhile.[31]

July 18, 1918. Basher, Reeves, and I went to remount station on
bike and got through.[32] Good horses and rode for quite a while
stopping in at S. A. At crossroads Bas' horse slipped and fell on
Bas' foot—looks broken. A Doc came along with an ambulance
so we sent him into hospital. Pretty hard luck after evading
Archie and Huns to fall riding. The C.O. stuck up an order
prohibiting riding hereafter as too dangerous. We had lunch Jock
and I at S. A. and saw Di who says that George Moseley, Chet
[Bassett], and Fred [Beach] are coming to 218 tomorrow. Juddy
and I biked into Calais and I had a bath. Juddy is so clean, or
should I say cleanly, he didn't need one.

July 18, 1918

My Dear Mother,
    Just received another letter June 20 from you and one from my
little brother. It must be fine to have him home, and I hope you're

---

31. On July 17, the squadron shifted to a new aerodrome at Fréthun, near Calais. A series
of German aerial assaults against RAF aerodromes near Dunkirk precipitated the move.

32. Capt. Adrian William Edmund Reeves, DFC, assumed command of No.218
Squadron shortly after the armistice. He scored four confirmed victories during the war.

all having a good time. Al wrote to me that he never saw anybody
work as hard as you do Muzzy. Be careful and don't work too hard.
Just pipe your happy if homely son in enclosed photo, and cheer up.
We had a great time yesterday as it was rather cloudy and windy.
But we went on a raid just the same—my first. And believe me it
doesn't anything compare like to bombing from a scout, i.e., low
down; which does give one some thrill. Also as it was sort of cloudy
we were not Archied much. But even so mother, it is exceedingly
pleasant watching your bombs go down toward the target and blow up
whatever they hit, sadly enough not always the exact spot on which
you and yourself had previously agreed. Well, and then this morning
my flight leader and another R.A.F. bloke (which translated into
English means fellow) took me out for a ride on a real live horse. We
rode at least three hours and it was great sport. But just as we were
entering the remount station (the horses' home) I'll be doggoned if the
flight commander, who has evaded Archies and played with Huns for
three months, didn't have his horse slip and fall on his leg, breaking a
bone in his foot. Now what do you meditate about that. Three more of
our squadron arrive here at this squadron tomorrow, it will be fine to
see them again. Must stop for tea. By the way, which do you honestly
think is the worst looking, my observer or me? With lots of love, Dave

July 19, 1918. Dud day.

July 20, 1918. Saturday. Being our last day here all of us went on
raid to the mole [Zeebrugge]. Very uninteresting. No Huns and
practically no Archie. Took 2 hrs. and 40 min. Di came for us in
the afternoon and we went to S. A. Terrible raw and wind, then
left bag at Oye and went to Dunkirk.[33]

33. Between June 11 and November 11, 1918, No.218 Squadron conducted 117
raids and dropped ninety-four tons of bombs. The unit's pilots and observers were
credited with thirty-eight confirmed kills. During this same period, several Marine
Corps pilots assigned to the Northern Bombing Group also flew missions with No.218
Squadron. Following reorganization of the Northern Bombing Group, a new aerodrome
was constructed at Oye (Field D), adjacent to the highway from Calais to Gravelines,
for day bombing squadrons 7 and 8, manned by Marine Corps personnel. It was never

July 21, 1918. Feeling very low, headache. So I stayed and took medicine. Judd was to go to Oye but went to S. A. Di, Shorty, Young left for Paris to test new two-place Hanriots and fly back airplane.[34]

July 22, 1918. Ken left for Paris early. After lunch I went to Oye, and found Doc Lee and Judd ensconced. Put up my bag on spare turf and had good dinner.

July 22, 1918

Dear Dad,

Surely the naval aviator's life is a most peculiar one. Yesterday I dropped bombs on Zeebrugge and dogged Archie. Today is a day of rest at Dunkirk with Di and tomorrow Judd and I have to reap hay, board ditches, and erect hangars, huts, etc. In short, Pops, we have been taken from the British squadron to start our own field. And believe me we felt low yesterday when we arrived at a beautiful field of oats or alfalfa or some darn vegetable, and put our luggage in one of a few tents set up in a muddy corner. However, the harder we work now the sooner we'll be able to fly and bomb. The raid Saturday was not very exciting as no Huns were to be seen, and due to our clever leader we avoided practically all the Archies. It was in the early morning soon after sun-up and was an ideal trip. We were very sorry to leave the British just as we were assigned to machines, after so very few flights. I received a letter yesterday from Mother—June 27—and number 21 June 23 from you. I was awfully sorry to hear

---

used for active operations. Other NBG fields included St. Inglevert, Campagne, Alembon, Sangotte, and La Fresne. Only St. Inglevert (night bombers) and La Fresne (day bombers) were ever used for combat missions. Most were either never completed, were ceded back to the French, or did not receive aircraft. Ingalls's responsibilities at Oye included preparing the site for use by Marine Corps units flying DH-4 and DH9A bombers. He found his duties irksome and unproductive and longed for a return to active flying over the lines.

34. The two-place Hanriot HD.3 carried four machine guns and was capable of speeds of approximately 119 mph. A small quantity of these planes were produced and delivered to the French military. A prototype was fitted with pontoons and designated HD.4, but development ceased when the war ended. See J. M. Bruce, *War Planes of the First World War* (Garden City, N.Y.: Doubleday, 1969), 19.

of the death of Mr. McBain's nephew in Italy. It is unusual to have such cold weather at home now, but over in this darn place, nothing surprises me. Yesterday morning was fine, and in the afternoon while in the machine we were caught in honestly the worst rain storm I've ever seen. The auto was blown sideways to the gutter on a macadam road and it was impossible to see 20 feet ahead the rain was so thick. The Allies are certainly doing well in this Hun push, and it wouldn't surprise me to see peace in three or four months. That would be *bon*, wouldn't it? As the hour is late, I must stop so *bon nuit*, Pops, With love, Dave.

———

July 23, 1918. Frocked around. Nothing doing, rain like hell.

July 24, 1918. Judd and I went to Dunkirk saw Hanrahan and got some awfully bad news. Stayed for lunch. Saw Burnham here, unloaded tons of lumber with only nine men. Got about 20 more men in during evening and lots more lumber, last truck, left about 1 A. M., but we had knocked off during an interval, much to truck driver's disgust, as he and his footman had to finish job.[35]

July 25, 1918. Got up at 6:00 and had roll calls short arm inspection.[36] Juddy seems to consider himself C. O. and is so efficient that he does not trouble me in the least. Being first here he does not note a half stripe difference. However, as

---

35. Though without aviation experience, Capt. David C. Hanrahan, formerly a destroyer officer and commander of the Q-ship *Santee,* led the Northern Bombing Group in 1918. Following the war, he served as naval attaché to Poland and commanded the light cruiser *Omaha.* The "bad news" Ingalls received likely related to the imminent arrival of Marine Corps aviators who had been training in Florida and the end of any likelihood navy fliers would conduct daylight raids as part of the Northern Bombing Group. A son of famed American architect Daniel Burnham, Lt. Hubert Burnham, USNA '05, later resigned his commission and became an architect himself. He rejoined the navy in 1917 and directed construction work, first at Pauillac and later at Dunkirk. Following the war, he returned to the field of architecture and enjoyed considerable prominence in his home city of Chicago.

36. *Short arm inspection* was navy slang for the venereal disease examination performed by either an officer or medical personnel.

there is nothing to do but be foreman and we are leaving today
or tomorrow according to Hanrahan who arrived today and two
Marine Capt. are arriving for good—I should worry. Took a walk
alone in afternoon. Excellent dinner and early to bed. Good day,
feeling doggone low and despondent. Eddie came over.

July 25, 1918

Dear Dad,
    In want of anything else to do, I have been reading Gerard's *Four
Years in Germany*,[37] and have just decided that his and my sense
of humor are not at one. Another point rather unfavorable, is his
fondness of the 1st person singular. He must have stopped learning
the pronouns after the very first one. Perhaps you may remember his
mentioning one Charles Russell, Jr. He came over on the steamer
with us and is a darned good fellow, though a bit fruity in appearance,
voice, and manner, due perhaps to his having acquired unfortunately
a rather foreign polish. Dad, please pardon the blot on the opposite
page. Of course I might claim that the vibration of a bomb falling from
a Hun plane to within 10 feet of my tent caused the ink to fall, but I
won't. And I might detail some thrilling experiences—I've heard so
many stories of other fellows' flights and trips into Hunland and done
so little the few times I've gone over seems like a myth—but I want to
tell the truth Dad, and let you know what really desperate straights I
am in. I'll admit that I started to write some essays, or stories, always
about what other people had done, unfortunately enough, but by good
luck I recollect my exceedingly unliterary acquirements in time and,
as it were, caught myself up on the brink of a dangerous precipice.
Well, Dad, one reason for my mental despondency is that just when
100 or so men came in last night and we worked until after midnight
unloading lumber, tents, etc., and life was beginning to become of
interest, for it is interesting to start a station and handle a number

37. James Watson Gerard served as ambassador to Germany between 1913 and 1917.
His book *My Four Years in Germany* was published 1917 and soon made into an anti-
German war movie, shown in theaters throughout the United States.

of men, the commander arrived and introduced to us two satellites, meaning Juddie and myself, two old men, gray haired, Captains both of them. These men are going to take over the work and who knows what Juddie and I are going to do. Write poetry next or jokes. Which is the worst, Pops; neither are better. No, if you really wish to know what I think, we'll go to Paris. Why Paris, I don't know, but anyway that is a nice place to go. And anticipation, as I have often told you, is a great thing to an author of poems, essays, and jokes, like me. Perhaps you remember my promising to write a diary. Well, I am doing it, recording weather, food, etc., and am awfully sorry it is doggoned uninteresting. Well, Daddy, Juddie is yelling for all the letters to be mailed. Cheer'o, Dave

———

July 26, 1918. Bum day. Breakfast at 7:30, then went to sleep again till lunch. Took long walk, arriving just in time to see Rockwood, then Burnham and chief Doc. Burnham says we are to go to Campagne Sunday, then soon to get D.H. 4 at Pauillac.[38] Thank God. Marines aren't coming till Sunday.

July 27, 1918. Sat.—Eddie and I motorcycled over to Dunkirk and saw Commander Hanrahan and Di and had lunch and a bath. Commander says we are to go to Dunkirk tomorrow and wait there till machines are ready for us to get at Pauillac, which he hopes will be quite soon. We got a lot of mail. Cheers.

July 28, 1918. Being Sunday and a day of rest, according to time honored custom, Eddie and I did nothing. However we permitted that we be frocked and driven to Dunkirk, where we enjoyed a

---

38. A new aerodrome at Campagne (Field B) southeast of Boulogne would have served as home for the Northern Bombing Group's night bombing squadrons 3 and 4. The squadrons were never organized, and the site was eventually abandoned. Pauillac, situated on the Gironde River about thirty miles north of Bordeaux, became naval aviation's principal supply, assembly, and repair base. A virtual factory city, it accommodated more than four thousand officers and enlisted men; it also served as a debarkation point for sailors returning home to the United States following the armistice.

pleasant day of gossip. Towards afternoon Eddie, being desirous
of again seeing his beloved, managed to be ordered to Paris,
wherefore he left on the train from Boulogne this night.

July 29, 1918. Until something turns up I stay here in this at present
delightful place. In the afternoon Di was kind enough to permit of
my going to 17 U.S.A. [Aero Squadron] to see Lloyd [Hamilton?],
but I found him away on leave in England—for which I consider
him lucky. Would that I now could too obtain leave.

———

July 29, 1918

My Dear Mother,

I was delighted yesterday to receive your letter of July 5th. The
mail service seems to have improved vastly, and it is a wonderful
help to get one's mail regularly. Yesterday morning Juddie and I were
relieved by two Marine Captains, and Juddie has gone to Paris for a
few days leave, while I thought I would rather much stay at the old
station of Dunkirk with Di Gates and Shorty. Of course it is a matter
of great doubt when we shall be sent down south to obtain and fly
back our machines. All the plans have been changed, and I don't
know what sort of job I'll get, as we may be compelled to fly with the
Marines for at least a month or so. To be quite frank we are all terribly
disappointed not to have our squadron with the original members, for
the fellows are the best bunch in the world, besides being excellent
pilots, and full out. Harry D[avison] has I think come over now, and I
hope to see him when I go through Paris.[39] We usually have managed
to hesitate there about as long as we want, and I'd certainly like to see
the old dude.

By the way, Mother, don't worry about your little son from a
matrimonial standpoint in connection with Miss Bowler. You had
much better worry he will ever have the good luck to become engaged

---

39. After spending much of the war stateside, Harry Davison sailed for Europe in
mid-1918 and served in Italy, Flanders, and England, participating in four night bombing raids with No.214 Squadron, RAF.

in an *affair d'amour*. Just recollect your vain endeavors to find
someone before I sailed. Muzzy, I don't like to think of you working
so hard. Please don't wear yourself out so that you have to take a long
rest, because if you weren't able to be pretty busy you would worry
so awfully much. As for Allie [DSI's brother], if he joins the Navy,
he would be alright, and anyway he will have to train for ages. I hear
that Jack Newell has enlisted and will be over here soon. That is *bon,*
Mother, and I'm glad he got up enough spunk to get away. It is fine
that my motorcycle finally got home. It is an awfully good one and
Al ought to enjoy running it around. The war news is certainly most
favorable, and everyone seems to be perking up over here. Well, I
must stop for dinner. With lots of love, Dave

July 30, 1918. Much like its predecessor. How true is that saying
that History does but repeat itself. Good old Di. The more I see I
him, the finer fellow he seems. Especially now, when he has been
apparently side-tracked into a job which no one wants,[40] he utters
not a word against his luck, but only does his best—which is a
lot. I hope he may soon be in a better position.

July 31, 1918. Today is, one might almost say, a red letter day.
Ass. Sec. of Navy Franklin Roosevelt honored the station with
a brief visit. With due ceremony he was welcomed in, staying
a few hours, then hastening to St. Inglevert to spend the night.
Two Captains, Knox, Yarnell, are staying here at a mess.[41] Capt.
Cone was here during the day. Also the admirable Bob [Lovett].
On questioning the latter, I gained us news as to my further

40. With the departure of Lt. Godfrey Chevalier to command the navy's new assembly and repair facility in Eastleigh, England, Di Gates assumed command at NAS
Dunkirk, a position he held until he was shot down and captured on October 4, 1918.

41. Assistant Secretary of the Navy Franklin D. Roosevelt conducted an extended
inspection of naval facilities in Europe during July and August 1918, beginning with a
brief visit to NAS Dunkirk. Cdr. Dudley Knox and Capt. Harry Yarnell were members of the Planning Section established at naval headquarters in London in January
1918. Knox later directed the navy's history and archive programs, gathering much of
the documentation that aided preparation of this volume.

movements. But he refuses to have me sent to Paris, where I wish greatly to go in order to see old Harry, who has just arrived. This night the old Loegenboom again forwarded its shells to poor Dunkerque. And the presence of a spotting machine overhead likewise disturbed the quiet and peace of this world. This morning too, and in the afternoon several Huns were overhead.

August 1, 1918. Nothing to do but sit around and enjoy Di Gates. He is certainly one damn fine fellow, and I'm sorry he's been sidetracked into running this station at Dunkirk. It's worse now than ever, not enough machines, bombed at and shot up all the time, no respectable excitement. Rising early I accompanied Di and the four Captains to 213 and 217 [Squadrons], seeing all the boys. Graham said, kindly, that he would like to have me back. I wish to God I could do so. To fly a Camel with good comrades is the zenith of Heaven. At 213, we saw two Hun prisoners— nice looking young fellows. We also learnt that two machines had fallen yesterday to the R.A.F. and two to the French. The Captains left after lunch. Later as usual I enjoyed a fine swim. Forgot to say that yesterday Eddie [DeCernea] saved a drowning Frenchman. After supper Di and I took Charlie for a walk and met Capt. Fenow, the C.O. of French seaplanes.

August 1, 1918

Dear Dad,

Still am confined to dear old Dunkirk. For in spite of my asking to be attached to some R.A.F. squadron, or to go on leave, nothing has been granted. However this has indeed been a most fortunate time to be here. In the first place the Asst. Sec Roosevelt came and spent a few hours inspecting the station. In his honor we had quite a reception planned, and in return he smiled upon us, and shook us by the hand. He seems like a mighty good fellow. Then by some fortunate chance two Captains, Regular navy men, have been here for three days on a tour about France. And believe me, a Captain in the Navy is some man. Well, these two are about the best navy

men I ever saw and I think everyone fell for them. They sat around
and talked and made themselves quite at home. Also they went
around inspecting British squadrons under Di's leadership, and
I, luckily, having nothing to do, went along, and really had a slick
time. Every afternoon we all go in swimming and take a run on the
beach, so we get pretty good exercise. Day before yesterday a fellow
drowned before we left, and yesterday Eddie DeCernea, our chief
pilot here, saved some Frenchman who was drowning some distance
out. So you see, there is plenty of excitement. And last night the
Huns bombarded us with the long-range gun, but, thank goodness,
accomplished nothing. This morning we saw and conversed with a
couple of Hun aviators, who were shot down yesterday and taken
prisoner. They seemed like kids, fine-looking, but very thin. It is fine
that the motorcycle arrived, Al will have an exciting time. No mail
has come in for about a week, it seems like a month when nothing
arrives. With love, Dave

———

August 2, 1918. Rain—and rain. Morning was devoted to reading
and afternoon probably the same.

August 3, 4, 5, 1918. Nothing doing. Hamilton and Welsh to Paris.

August 6, 1918. After lunch I took the red motorcycle and beat it to
Calais. Saw Bob [Lovett] and asked to be sent to 213 [Squadron].
He said he'd try. Maybe I'll get some fun yet. Also went to 218
[Squadron] saw George [Moseley], Chet [Bassett], and Fred
[Beach]. They are hoping to stay with British for some time. Had
a swim.

August 7, 1918. No doggone mail for a hell of a while. I wonder
whether the Huns are improving in sub[marines]. Got a letter
from Harry. After lunch Di and I took a sick man to Calais.
We stopped at Campagne and St. Inglevert and then went to
Boulogne, but did nothing there. On our way back we picked up a
Marine. I felt like a veteran talking to a young enthusiast. Never

thought before this war had made any difference in me. There are
400 men and some 10 officers there at Oye. It's almost a regular
station by now. The chances of a Navy D.H. squadron seem zero.
Di has been trying to persuade us to come back to his station,
and darned if I don't think it's a good plan. I don't see what the
deuce is going to happen. Pretty disheartening the rotten way
the Navy is running the thing at home. Damn that Capt. Irwin
anyway.[42] I asked Bob to be placed with 213, Di is to fix it up.

---

42. Capt. Noble "Bull" Irwin, NA #1104, director of naval aviation, had his headquarters in Washington and was the object of much criticism by naval aviators in Europe.

6

Hero of the Angry Sky—Serving with No.213 Squadron

August–October 1918

Between early August and the beginning of October 1918, David Ingalls served with his old mates at No.213 Squadron, flying Sopwith Camels over Flanders. His stay coincided with the final Allied push of the war. During a fifty-six-day period, he compiled a combat record unequaled by any other American naval aviator in World War I, performing the feats that earned him the British Distinguished Flying Cross, the American Distinguished Service Medal, and the French Légion d'Honneur. By his own accounting, he flew 108 hours, 45 minutes; conducted sixty-three flights over the lines; engaged in thirteen plane-to-plane combats; and carried out two low-level attacks on aerodromes, one against the Zeebrugge mole, and ten against German soldiers, transports, supply dumps, railroads, and artillery. In the process, he downed at least six enemy aircraft and kite balloons and emerged from the war as the navy's first and only ace.

If any military organization suited Ingalls's bold temperament, it was the RAF. The British air arm fostered a culture and doctrine of seeking out and destroying enemy forces from the air. John Morrow, in *The Great War in the Air*, described the RAF as "an aggressive, offensive arm that emphasized fighting and, increasingly, bombing and carried the fight to the Germans regardless of the consequences," and it had done so for several years. Of course, such policies often entailed enormous losses. The force suffered seven thousand casualties on the Western Front in 1918, including more than thirty-seven hundred from combat, far more than the force of any other country.[1]

By the time Ingalls rejoined the RAF in August 1918, the tide of battle had turned against Germany, and Allied flyers became increasingly assertive, even reckless, in their tactics, seeking out the enemy and daring him to fight.[2] Retreating enemy forces offered a wealth of targets, but they also constituted a great danger. Wood and canvas aircraft skimming along at a hundred miles per hour, fifty or one hundred feet above the ground, were tempting and vulnerable quarry for machine gunners and even infantrymen. In one instance, a cornered German soldier damaged a plane flown by a member of Ingalls's unit by throwing a brick at it.

Such missions, whether strafing trenches, supporting assaults, or attacking columns and cantonments of enemy forces, had long been a high priority. Morrow noted, "Ground-attack aviation was well developed by mid-1917, and that year and the next saw numerous actions in which aerial assault affected the fate of ground units ranging in size from squad to division." The Germans introduced their *Sturmflieger* (storm fliers) in 1917, utilizing a variety of aircraft, including armored "infantry planes," such as the Junkers J1 "Möbelwagen" (meaning "furniture van"). The RFC employed similar tactics before the battle of Ypres in the summer and fall of the year, assigning fighter pilots to such raids. The British made extensive use of these measures during the German advance in the spring of 1918 and again during the Allied offensives from August onward. Due to the resulting heavy casualties, many of the pilots Ingalls served with in April were gone—wounded, missing, or dead. During his second tour of duty, from August to October 1918, at least fifteen squadron members were shot down and killed or captured, and many others were severely injured,

---

1. John H. Morrow Jr., *The Great War in the Air: Military Aviation from 1909 to 1921* (Washington, D.C.: Smithsonian Institution Press, 1993), 235–36, 273, 317, 346–47.

2. The British assault across the old Somme battlefield on August 8 forced the German army to retreat back to the shadow of the Hindenburg Line by the end of the month. Gen. Erich Ludendorff called it "the black day of the German army." See John Keegan, *The First World War* (New York: Knopf, 1999), 410–12, and Martin Gilbert, *The First World War: A Complete History* (New York: Henry Holt, 1994), 450–57. Although the Allies did not launch a major attack against the Ypres salient and along the Belgian coast until late September, French and British aviation forces (including Ingalls's unit) used the intervening weeks to initiate heavy raids against German aerodromes and conduct continuous patrols along the lines.

reassigned, or returned to England—an entire squadron's worth of pilots lost in just eight weeks. In all, No.213 Squadron lost 33 of the 100 to 110 pilots who flew with the unit from June 1917 until November 1918.[3]

August 9, 1918. Lucky days, I am leaving at 2:30 for 213 [Squadron]. Di managed it for me. Saw all the boys, only four or five left I know. I have been placed in [Capt. Colin] Brown's flight and like it. He is a darned nice Englishman with several Huns to his credit and a couple of decorations. I have my own machine, a Bentley-motored Camel, and a peach. It will do anything. Then went up for a fly—It was wonderful. Then went on a patrol very nice, low clouds, so five of us were at 6,000. Flew along the lines back and forth—very unexciting. Since I was here last the Huns came over one night and bombed the hell out of the place,[4] ruining the hangars, a lot of machines, and nearly blowing up the barracks and mess hall. So now the barracks are hid in a woods a mile or so away from the field, so if the Huns come again, at least they won't get all the pilots. I'm rooming with Brown, in a little room in the temporary barracks, not so pleasant as the Ritz, but O.K. Our mess hall is at the field and we spend most of our time there, so our barracks don't particularly figure.

RAF Flight Report, August 9, 1918: practice flight, seven minute test flight Camel D.9649, departed 1525; later war flight at 1825, Camel D.1871, High Offensive Patrol with six other pilots.

---

3. Morrow's *Great War in the Air* devotes considerable attention to these tactical missions; see especially pp. 14, 218–19, 235, 276, and 311–12. See also Frank M. Leeson, *The Hornet Strikes: The Story of No.213 Squadron, Royal Air Force* (Tunbridge Wells, U.K.: Air-Britain (Historians), 1998), 200–201, and Christopher Shores, *Above the Trenches: A Complete Record of the Fighter Aces and Units of the British Empire Forces, 1915–1920* (London: Grub Street, 1990), 19, 23.

4. This raid on the aerodrome at Bergues occurred on the evening of June 29, 1918, and resulted in the loss of a dozen aircraft but no personnel. A raid eleven days earlier claimed the life of Capt. DeC. Paynter. See Leeson, *Hornet Strikes*, p. 23.

August 11, 1918. Fine weather, many patrols and lots of fun. I was in first scrap. Brown got a Hun. At 11:20 our flight had a high offensive patrol. We flew up and down the lines between Nieuport and Ypres (Ieper), going on to Ostend, but saw nary a Hun. Later Brown suggested I go off with him to see what we could see. It was a great day and we climbed to 17,000 feet and coasted along the front watching for meat. Suddenly I saw Brown wag his wings up and down to attract my attention, and I turned after him and we dove down full out. Only then did I catch sight of a camouflaged Hun far below us, going due west about a mile over the lines. We gained fast, I keeping abreast of Brown and to one side. Finally I heard him start shooting and saw his tracers, so I pulled my trigger. The Hun observer fired back, and I saw a few tracers coming at us, then a cloud of smoke burst from the Hun, it broke into flames, and dove straight down. We pulled up, turned and beat it for the lines, surrounded by Archie bursts. This afternoon I flew over to St. Inglevert and called on our boys there and had an early supper with them, saw a Caproni they had for night bombing.[5] This station is to be the Navy night bombing station.

RAF Flight Report, August 11, 1918: High Offensive Patrol, departed 0855 in Camel C.73, total five in patrol, Albatross two-seater sighted, Ingalls credited with first victory, shared with C. P. Brown.

[Undated, postwar] The individual's life with the squadron was exceedingly pleasant.[6] Ten days' official leave was given once every three

---

5. The navy planned to equip its night bombardment squadron with the much-anticipated but ultimately ill-fated Caproni Ca.5 aircraft. The Caproni program turned out to be a disaster, with several of the planes lost during aerial transhipment from Italy to France. A single combat mission was undertaken, and a fire aboard one of the machines at St. Inglevert resulted in the deaths of both pilots. See Geoffrey Rossano, *Stalking the U-Boat: U.S. Naval Aviation in Europe in World War I* (Gainesville: University Press of Florida, 2010), 340–41.

6. Ingalls's description of the duties and missions carried out by No.213 Squadron seems rather idyllic, at least as recounted in his postwar memoir. The reality was anything but. Nonetheless, the material he provided is informative as to the unit's organization and procedures.

months and 48 hours' leave could be obtained from the C.O. at any time, except during a push, or any important "show," as the British term anything out of the regular line of duty. The squadron of eighteen or twenty machines was divided into three flights, each flight having ten days on duty and one day off, on which day the men were encouraged to leave the aerodrome, flying off to some neighboring squadron or visiting Dunkirk. During the summer the beach was always crowded with people, the continual bombing and shelling having little effect on the inhabitants. Those on duty, when not actually away on patrol, spent their time shooting—from the machines, or with rifle and pistol—or loafing about the mess reading and playing cards. The quarters and food were the best, and when at home one was indeed far removed from even a thought of war.

The great amount of shooting of every sort that was always being done was pretty good proof of the importance of good marksmanship in aerial fighting. To be sure the absolutely necessary requirement is good eyesight, for if one sees the Huns first one can either easily escape if outnumbered, or perhaps so far surprise the enemy as to actually shoot them down before they are aware of the presence of hostile aircraft. The third requirement of course is actual flying ability. It seems strange that this should be secondary to marksmanship, but to get Huns one must be able to hit them, and it is surprising how well some men can shoot. This was forcibly brought home to me at the very first when three of us dove at a two-seater spotting over the lines. We were all together in the dive, and before I thought we were in range, the Hun suddenly burst into flames, the flight commander having hit him from what we afterwards agreed must have been at least 400 or 500 yards.

Now in regard to the actual work. There were several sorts of patrols. First, the sea patrols which consisted in flying low, always in sight of the fleet, to guard against seaplanes during the coastal destroyer patrols up to Ostend and Zeebrugge, or during a shoot. As there were very seldom any enemy seaplanes to be seen, and as one always looked forward to a cold bath if the motor failed, this was a rather stupid job, never preferred to line patrols. Of these, in good weather, there were usually two a day—at the time when the Huns were out en masse—between ten and twelve in the mornings and five and six in the evenings. At these times always at least two flights went, one above the other for protection. Two large groups made the most confusing affair imaginable; machines of friend and foe seemed to be everywhere. Twice I remember seeing two Huns collide, with the most gratifying result. In bad weather there were small patrols, perhaps under the clouds along the lines, or up the coast to look for some daring seaplane merchant, for Hun seaplanes were fond of bad weather. Between the regular patrols anyone who wished could go out by himself, or more often persuade a couple of his pals to accompany him, on a search for lone two-seaters spotting or photographing near the lines. Besides these patrols there was considerable escort work to be done, accompanying day bombers to Bruges or some other objective. But this too, was monotonous, for the Huns would not often attack such numbers, thirty or thirty-five machines.

———

> August 12, 1918. Got up early 2:30 [AM] as we went up on a colossal
> bomb raid on Varssenaere aerodrome.[7] I felt a bit worried
> standing around waiting, everything was sort of slow, the stewards
> did not have breakfast ready, and we were too early as clouds
> prevented the flight. After standing around for a long time, it
> was called off and we went back to bed, everyone more or less
> peeved. After breakfast had a long patrol, saw a few Huns but all
> were down low and far over lines. There were a lot of Camels and
> DHs around. The rest of the day was pretty dud.

———

August 12, 1918

Dear Pops,
  Awfully sorry not to have been able to write you before, but Friday
I left Di and am now attached to the same British scout squadron

---

7. The once-postponed Varssenaere raid is described in great detail in Ingalls's diary entry for August 13, 1918 (see later text). This mission was one of a series of large RAF attacks on German aerodromes in August and September, including raids against Epinoy (August 1), Haubourdin (August 16), Lomme (August 17), Phalempin (August 19), Gondecourt (August 22), Cantin (August 23), Linselles (September 2), Estourmel (September 15), Emerchicourt (September 17), and Lieu St. Amand (September 26). Descriptions can be found in Christopher Cole, ed., *Royal Air Force Communiqués, 1918* (London: Tom Donovan, 1990), for the dates indicated.

Ken, Shorty, and I were at before. And, Dad, it is wonderful to be here
flying a single-seater again. The weather has been **bon,** and we've
done quite a bit of flying. Yesterday morning we had a sort of a scrap
when the flight commander shot down a Hun. It happened so quickly
I didn't get a shot at the poor devil before he was spinning down out
of control. It was certainly great though to see. Yesterday after lunch
the King visited the squadron for a few minutes and said "howdee" to
everyone.[8] After that two of us flew to Bob's squadron and had tea, flew
to a British squadron, had supper and then flew back here again about
dark. Pretty soft way of going out visiting, isn't it? As we got up at 2:30
A.M. this morning I'm tired and am going to bed. With love, Dave

August 13, 1918. Thirteen is a lucky number.[9] It was a perfect day
and so all of us were out at 2:30. Of course it was pitch black and
we wondered if it was to be another fizzle, some probably hoping,
but most hardly even so daring. I felt a bit nervous but very
little, somehow a bombing raid low down seems very dangerous.
Anyway we got dressed and rode over to the mess hall. Had
breakfast and went out.

    Of course we all had our particular duties mapped out. Each
knew he was to follow a certain person and bomb a certain part of

8. King George V often visited the troops in France to present decorations and
improve morale. He also made frequent visits to hospitals, factories, and dockyards.

9. On August 13, 1918, Ingalls participated in one of the largest tactical raids of the
war, a dawn attack on the German aerodrome at Varssenaere (Jabbeke to the Germans),
located about four miles southeast of Bruges, Belgium. Planning for the raid began in
July after intelligence data indicated significant reinforcements were expected soon.
The attack plan included an initial assault of fighter aircraft, to be followed by a second
wave consisting of DH9 bombers. The raiding force was composed of Nos.210 and
213 Squadrons, flying Camels, and Nos.211 and 218 Squadrons, both equipped with
DH9 bombers. No.204 Squadron flew Camels in high cover during the attack. The
U.S. 17th Aero Squadron also joined in the assault. Allied aircraft dropped more than
150 bombs, fired many thousands machine-gun rounds, and destroyed or damaged at
least forty enemy machines. No.213 Squadron's sixteen aircraft alone expended more
than seventy-five hundred rounds. No.210 Squadron expended ninety-two hundred
rounds. All Allied fliers returned safely. See Leeson, *Hornet Strikes,* 25–27, and Mike
O'Connor, *Airfields and Airmen of the Channel Coast* (Barnsley, South Yorkshire, U.K.:
Pen and Sword Books, 2005), 57–60.

the aerodrome, and then shoot up anything to be seen. Above us was to be a squadron of scouts to wait till all was over and then try to get pictures of the wreck we hoped to make of Varssenaere aerodrome. We figured there would be 74 planes involved in this raid, supposedly the biggest ever pulled off. My target was the hangars on the westerly side of the aerodrome. I was to follow Brown meanwhile. We were all to meet over Dunkirk, 10,000 feet. Each flight commander had a different Very pistol to fire so we could know our respective C.O.'s.

Well, about 4:30 I took off in the dark, the idea being anyone could take off and fly in the dark and it would be just about dawn as we hit the coast on our way into Hunland. I had four little bombs attached below. Those on the west were to use ordinary shrapnel bombs. One flight on the east a sort of phosphorous bomb guaranteed to set fire to anything. When I was sure my motor was warm, I taxied ahead, guided by a couple of mechanics to the line, and watched the sparks fly as one after another opened his motor and roared along the ground and then took to the air. I could hear them first off, circling around above gaining altitude. All were to fly in the same direction in circles to avoid collision, bearing gradually towards Dunkirk.

Our flight was last one off. I got off first. I opened the throttle, gathered speed, bumped the ground once and was off. It was sort of weird in the dark, my first time, though easy enough to rise up in a circle over the field. As I got up I could make out the hazy wings of the plane. I was coasting around when I thought I heard a knock. Thinking my nerves were a bit shaky I opened up and listened. Sure enough there was a knock, which got worse so I pulled back the throttle just as a Hell of a crash like a machine gun started and lots of vibration. I shut off motor and glided down, hoping nothing awful would happen. It was awful dark. I could just sort of see the ground and just as I was about to land saw a D.H. taking off. Just missing it I got down all right, jumped out and ran to the flight to get another machine, hurrying to catch the flight, which was disappearing rapidly from view. I yelled at the chief mechanic my plane was busted and I wanted another. There was an extra one by the hangar; it was wheeled out by three or four mechanics and somebody hung on the bombs and another turned the propeller as I buckled myself in. A few minutes to warm up and I was off again. It was growing lighter; no planes circled overhead and my patience was weak. Wide open I climbed, heading for Dunkirk, figuring to fly below the others if they had gone on and get there eventually. Soon, however, I saw the flash of the Very pistols above the meeting place and soon I could make out planes. Funny how much lighter it is as you go up high in the morning. Lighter it grew, a bloody red sunrise befitting the occasion, tinging the few clouds still higher above us. I got up all right and climbed to the rendezvous seeing all the four squadrons of 18 above and joining the first flight of our squadron. I fell in my position and we coasted along easily.

It was quite light now and we flew along the coast at 6,000 feet able easily to see Nieuport and Ostend. Just beyond Ostend, Gray (leader) fired a Very and turned in, our squadron leading.[10] We crossed the coast without any notice and started down to 150 feet toward the aerodrome, which is about seven or eight miles inland S.E. of Ostend. The leaders swerved to the left, and a couple of miles ahead was our objective. Finally I saw it and took off my gloves opened the sight, and got ready. About then there was a bit of Archie thrown up, which at last awoke. Gray dived steeper and opened with his machine guns, as did several others including me flying fourth in the right line. There were two rows of hangars and my squadron went for west and other two for east, while 204 Squadron stayed at 8,000 ft. to protect us. There was a long row of machines on the ground lined up on the east side and five on ours. Down we went towards them and I looked through my Aldis sight at the first Fokker and a man, probably a mechanic, looking up at us, who suddenly turned and ran towards the hangars.[11] My

10. Lt. William Edrington Gray, DFC, had five confirmed victories. Previously a member of No.12 Squadron, RNAS, he served with No.213 Squadron from December 16, 1917, until October 19, 1918, when he was detached for duty in England. See Shores, *Above the Trenches*, 175.

11. Most likely, he was looking at the Fokker D.VII model, with two machine guns, powered by either a 160 hp Mercedes engine or a 185 hp BMW engine. It earned a reputation as one of the very best fighters of the war.

sight looked between the wings of the plane ahead of me straight at the Fokker and I pulled my trigger. It was only after I saw a dozen tracers going between my pal's wings when I realized he was sort of in the way and stopped shooting. I was over machines and took aim and let go bombs, seeing Brown and Gray way ahead. I leaned over to look just as I hoicked up [jerked the nose of the aircraft upward] and took the right. There were a lot of bangs and the plane was tossed about a bit. Gray climbed steeply to right followed by us and I looked around to see explosions all over the field and on hangar, and near the lines of machines also a lot of smoke in the east where the incinerating bombs hit.

The Yanks Camel squadron [17th Aero Squadron] was to stay and shoot it up while we protected, but it looked too good so we all dove down. I shot at several machines, and saw tracers shooting all over the whole place, everyone was firing down and nothing was shot back. Except for three men who ran from machines toward hangar. I saw no one move. I fired and climbed up dived and fired again at machines and saw one simply demolished by the fire of a fellow ahead and to a side of me and my own. I pulled up just in time to miss a fellow diving across and climbing looked to see fires started in four or five places, one Hun far on our side with its end busted all off and a hell of an explosion when a Gotha hangar just disappeared—evidently gasoline or bomb inside. I dove once more, but didn't seem to hurt machine I shot at.

Then as most of the machines appeared to be leaving, I took a last look, trying to memorize the hits, and flew west. I followed Gray toward Dixmude. Gray led us up to 2,000. A.A. then began to break occasionally. I saw bursts to left, dove off and fired at it from some way and came back, then a minute later repeated. Then came a lot of A.A. We could see the battery ahead to left and Gray dove, followed by all seven of us. We went right for it and I passed it at about 100 ft., all of us shooting like the deuce. It shut up just after we started shooting and stayed shut. I got a jam then as once before in right gun. Gray climbed to 2,000 feet and we went along quietly for a few seconds or so. Then a battery to the right got in some damn good shots, one exploded practically on the 3rd plane. He disappeared from view for an instant and then I was surprised to see him all right. A minute or so later, we all dove on the lines with the guns firing and they shot across the swarm, at 100 ft. or so, feeling pretty doggone happy. I saw Hun on right, a single nut, shoot at two or three Belgian posts and their lines.

We beat it home and landed. I never felt so happy in all my life, it had been one picnic. I thought no machine gun had been fired at me, but found three or four holes in the plane made by them probably crossing the trenches. Several fellows were a bit shot up, but not badly. We were all just laughing with joy, it was such fun. Later 204 [Squadron] called up to say only one of their machines had escaped the Archie, but all of the allies had returned safe. Hurrah. On a patrol later Greene and MacKay each got a Hun. In afternoon six of us escorted the King on a destroyer. Arriving back I stunted over Marines at Oye.

RAF Flight Report, August 13, 1918: Attack on Varssenaere aerodrome in response to Operations Order No.4. Ingalls in Camel N.6376 took off at 0445 hours, returned ten minutes later engine trouble; took off again 0500 in Camel D.9649; other units included No.210 and 17th Aero; two DH9, Nos. 211 and 218; Camel No.204 acted as high cover. Lt. W. E. Gray of No.213 led raid; No.213 attacked at 0530, Ingalls dropped four 25-lb Cooper bombs and landed at 0610.

Official Squadron Summary, August 13, 1918: Low bomb raid on [Varssenaere] Aerodrome. Fired 650 rounds and dropped four bombs causing considerable damage to hangars and machines. [For Ingalls] "Bombs dropped between hangers and machines on west side. Shot up machines on East side. Shot up A/A batteries. Observed three fires on east side of aerodrome. Fired 650 rounds." Bombs dropped included six 40-lb phosphorus bombs, 136 25-lb bombs. Thousands of rounds, 14 112 lb bombs, one 230 lb bomb; eight Fokkers destroyed on ground, fires among buildings, two Gotha hangers destroyed along w/six of nine aircraft, later reports claimed 20 Gothas, 18–20 Fokkers, damaged or destroyed, 50 killed.

RAF Flight Report, August 13, 1918 [same day]: Escort mission for destroyer, took off 1500, landed 1620, Camel D.1871, nothing to report.

————

August 14, 1918. [From DSI postwar memoir] Still fine weather. Nothing doing much till about 6, when I had to return from patrol with dud guns, and so went out alone; ran into three Huns, got only one shot at them. I had been at 18,000 feet, and seen nothing so thought I might find someone a little lower. The beggars saw me about when I saw them and turned and dived. It was a Hell of a way over the lines.

August 14, 1918. About 9:30 my flight had a high offensive patrol and we flew about the lines, hoping, but in vain. Saw a few Huns way east but no scraps. Then after tea we went out again. Before we crossed the lines I fired my guns as per usual to test them, and one ran away and I couldn't stop it until the ammunition was gone, and so turned and went back, totally chagrined at missing a possible fight. I frotched around till the gun was O.K. and then as it was only 7:00 thought I'd see what I could see.[12]

Careful as I was, climbing to 18,000 feet before crossing the lines and then coasting along, looking on all sides and below for Huns. Nothing nowhere and finally cold and disgusted I came down to 12,000 feet for one last trip along the front before going home. I thought I was looking about and turned from left to right and back and saw—three Hun monoplanes above and behind.[13] Just as I saw them they must have caught sight of me, for they turned and dove. I realized I'd wandered three or four miles over the lines and never regretted anything more sincerely. I headed west and down wide open for a few seconds,

---

12. Though Ingalls made only passing references to his activities on August 14, his postwar memoir contained a detailed accounting of events that day. *Frotched around* (with various spellings) was a slang expression meaning killing time, wasting time, or fooling around.

13. Perhaps he encountered the Fokker E.V/D.VIII model, a parasol monoplane aircraft. A few prototypes saw limited service in late July and early August 1918. It was sometimes called the "Flying Razor." See Shores, *Above the Trenches,* 25.

when the guns began to pop. I swerved, climbed, dived, turned and everything. The Huns would dive, shooting, till close, then hoick up and to one side, then down again, taking turns—it seemed to me—all the time I heard their damned guns and could see tracers streaking by, above, below, and even between my wings.

Soon they began coming closer on their dives and the tracers came closer to me. Finally one pulled up only a few feet away and desperately I pulled up too, turning sharp and firing at him, and almost immediately turned back towards the lines. And then I could hear the guns and see the tracers, but wasn't sure where were the other two. Then I saw them behind still and practicing on me. The same for some seconds till too close a dive again stirred me and I hoicked again, got a Hun in my sight and pulled the trigger. One burst and again I turned for home. More twisting and then suddenly both Huns turned, pulled up, and then drove back towards their homeland. Around I went and down after the nearest, firing continuously, but with no apparent result. They turned out of possible range and I turned for home the last time. Nobody was shooting at me and I could see no Huns. But I couldn't believe I was O.K. I sat, twisting and turning in my seat, jumping about almost, waiting for the expected rat-tat-tat. Why didn't somebody shoot? Where were they? There must be a Hun below. There must be some trick. And then I realized I was over the lines and safe, but cold no longer.

I landed at the field, giggling to myself. I walked over to several machines, evidently belonging to my flight, and was asked where in Hell I'd gone. I explained and said I'd gone out myself and had a fight. I couldn't help laughing and they didn't believe me till my mechanic came over and reported my machine would have to be laid up or discarded due to being shot up. The C.O. took one look at it and gave me Hell. Believe me, I didn't need any fatherly advice then or ever again.

August 15, 1918. A dud patrol in the morning with Hopewell leading, don't think much of him as a leader as we missed a nice two-seater just below us because he lost sight of him when turning to dive.[14] He made such a circle and was so slow going down that when we were properly pointed damned if the two-seater hadn't simply vanished from sight. Also missed about six off to one side. We dove and dove and saw nothing and finally went home disgusted.

On the way back one of my cylinders cracked and I limped in rather like a lame duck behind the rest. Sort of peeved I got another machine before lunch and went up alone. No-one else had any pep. And this time I was certainly not going to be caught by any Huns unawares. I went up to the heavens before I got near the lines and stayed at 21,000 feet all the time. There was nothing doing. The only planes high I saw were a bunch of Camels far away—not a Hun was out. Well, my flight seemed a total loss that day so I joined Greene's flight on its afternoon patrol. Just shows how foolish it is to look for trouble, for Greene was sick and couldn't lead and his buddy, a Canadian named MacKay, was flight commander. However, as they were a man shy, I was given No. 2 place on Mac's left.

MacKay led five of us on a fleet patrol and then over the lines at about 6,000. It was a beautiful sunny afternoon, hardly a cloud in the sky. We got up to 11,000 feet and started over the lines near Ypres. We saw six Huns below us some way over and what looked like a squadron of Camels up sun on our side of lines. So Mac dove and we were just about to be executioners when the squadron of Camels changed to Fokkers coming for us. I looked around to point them out to Mac and found him some ways ahead, diving on the six. "All right," thinks I, "maybe they're Camels, but if not, well, not so hot." As we dove I kept turning in my seat. Somehow my recent experience had given me a fervent consideration for my tail and I'd rather shoot than be shot at. And sure enough, about when we had dropped to 10,000 feet and were a mile or so over the lines, I realized that that squadron had divided and were between us and the lines. No question in my

14. Flight Sub-lieutenant G. F. C. Hopewell, originally with No.12 Squadron, RNAS, joined No.13/213 Squadron on January 2, 1918, and served until August 17, 1918, when he was detached for duty in England. See Leeson, *Hornet Strikes*, 200.

mind and I turned and fired my guns again and pointed. I saw
Mac take a long look, level off, and circle towards the left wide
open. We were almost near where the lines made a practically
right angle from east to west to north and south at Ypres, and
it looked to me like a long way home. Lord how those Fokkers
could dive! A few seconds and the nearest were taking long pot
shots at us. Denny, the right rear man of our formation, turned to
the right and dove when we turned to left and has not returned.[15]
The other man opposite me and the bird behind and to my left,
realizing what had happened, trying desperately to keep up
with Mac and me, had to lose altitude and were behind us and a
little back. The left side of our formation was in luck this time,
and my engine was good. I followed Mac while the two tail men
dove under us, being well shot up. Mac and I kept along same
level, but two below continued to dive. And then I saw another
squadron coming from the west, on the right flank and then more
behind. Mac straightened out to give our right side boy a chance
to keep up and we roared along. We couldn't very well turn as
all Huns were above. I counted about 26, Mac saw about 30.
They didn't seem to come much closer, but would occasionally
fire at us from 300 yards. When tracers would begin to come
uncomfortably close, I'd go up and down and swerve a bit. And I
sat watching the nearest, flying straight till one seemed to be on
my line and then again swerving and their tracers would go by to
one side.

Soon they were all behind us in a long line, but the nearest
staying 300 yards off. It lasted a long time, just as though they
were escorting us. I watched Mac, realizing that the time was
near when they'd be so close we'd have to turn and fight, for the
two [Camels] behind us were falling gradually back and I knew
Mac wouldn't let them go alone. Finally one bunch got close and
Mac turned to the left and crossed the lines near Nieuport and
the two [Camels] miles below now beat it, while we went toward

---

15. Lt. C. H. Denny, originally from No.212 Squadron, RAF, served with No.213
Squadron from April 7, 1918, until he was reported missing on August 15, 1918. See
Leeson, *Hornet Strikes,* 200.

Ypres along lines paralleled by a flight, when suddenly they all hoicked up and away. I stuck to Mac and we climbed and circled back. The Huns sported about, across the lines, but they were too many for us. Finally Mac waved and we started for home. "What a Hell of a day," thinks I. Chased all afternoon and nary a shot fired. We landed and reported. Four of us O.K., though the two below had their planes some shot up. The fifth man was missing, no-one knew where, except that one fellow thought he had kept diving for the six Huns when Mac pulled up.

———

RAF Flight Report, August 15, 1918: Low Fleet Patrol at 1715, Camel D.6949, flew over lines between Dixmude and Ypres (Ieper), patrol dove on six E/A, were then attacked by 15 E/A. Combat indecisive, Lt. Denney failed to return MIA, Ingalls landed 1905.

———

August 16, 1918. Sort of a dud day—just two L[ow] F[leet] P[atrols]. Awfully boring. In evening I landed at 217 [Squadron] saw Chip [McIlwaine] and Pop Lumers.[16]

———

August 16, 1918

Dear Dad,
    Well, we've certainly been having a wonderful time. The last two nights while on patrol at about 7:30, I've been chased home by superior numbers. Night before last, I was out alone, it was a great time for flying and I hadn't seen a machine in the air. Then all of a sudden three appeared above me, monoplanes. They must have seen

————

16. Archibald "Chip" McIlwaine, NA #82, one of the Yale gang, trained at Hourtin, Clermont-Ferrand, and Moutchic. He joined No.217 Squadron in July 1918, made twenty-six flights with the unit, had four dogfights, and shot down (unofficially) one enemy aircraft. His wartime experiences are outlined in Ralph D. Paine, *The First Yale Unit: A Story of Naval Aviation, 1916–1919,* 2 vols. (Cambridge, Mass.: Riverside Press, 1925), 2:255–59. "Pop" Lumers, mentioned several times in Ingalls's diary, served at Dunkirk, with No.217 Squadron, and later at Eastleigh.

me at the same time, as they turned and dove. Being a long way on
the wrong side of the lines I decided 'twas no place to display valor,
so I tried to beat it. But the lines being a long way off, they soon
caught up, shooting like the deuce, with me doing peculiar things so
they wouldn't get a bulls eye. When they were about 75 yards away
I turned, and got a burst at one of them and dove down out of it. The
other two got behind again, and when I turned both of them dove
away at about 200 miles an hour. And it was a great relief not to hear
the doggone machine guns rattling behind. Then last night five of us
dove on about six across the lines and by George if about 20 or 25
didn't coming tearing down behind us. The whole darned sky seemed
full of machines coming down shooting at long range. We turned and
started towards home, but one of our fellows evidently hadn't heard
the one above and kept going on down on the lower bunch. He has
not returned. I stuck to the leader and we were escorted for about
10 miles by 15 Huns who didn't seem to dare to come really close.
Way below us we could see the other two blokes with several behind
them. Well, they chased us back and then at the lines they dove down
to their hangars. Mac and I never had a single shot, it was a mighty
bum flight. I don't know how long I'm going to be left here, because
the Marines have taken over our old job. No mail has arrived for
some time, I think the mail service is getting awfully bum. And I
haven't told you about the big, low bombing raid we went on the other
morning. A whole bunch of squadrons combined and we bombed an
aerodrome at about 500 feet and then shot it up. It certainly was slick
fun. Love, Dave

August 19, 1918. Today we teamed up with 202 Squadron and made
two patrols with them. The Huns when out seem to go around
with such numbers we've got to do somewhat similar. However,
nothing showed up at all.

RAF Flight Report, August 19, 1918: High Offensive Patrol with nine other
pilots, took off 0930, Camel D.9649, in conjunction w/202, landed at 1110.
Poor visibility, clouds from Dunkirk to Zeebrugge; flew second HOP at

1510, Camel D.9649, landed 1705, nothing to report. [Another 213 group flew w/211, engaged six EA at 17,000 over Ypres, shot down two: Greene and MacKay]

———

August 21, 1918. Yesterday was punk, clouds and wind and only one short patrol with no Huns to be seen. But today was "jake" and we had a good ride this morning, though the only excitement was when we saw a DH observer or photographer being chased home by a Fokker. We roared to the rescue, but the Hun dived for home while we were still some miles away. Most of the time we were at 19,000 feet and I was certainly surprised there were no Huns about. Then about 4 P.M. Brown, Smith, and I slipped off for a trip. Brown is a cautious and foxy old bird and led us up and up till I thought we were trying to break the altitude record. We were over 20,000 feet before we crossed the lines and stayed there for an hour or so. It was a beautiful afternoon. I could see for miles and we flew along the lines watching below and hoping for something. Remembering my last chase, I also occasionally looked behind. Never again if I could help it was I going to be caught from the rear. Finally I suddenly saw Brown wigwag his plane, making one wing go up and then the other, and I realized he'd seen something. He made a turn and dove, Smith and I following close, and as I banked and dove I saw a two-seater miles below us headed for Hunland. Down we went at a terrific rate, as fast as we could go and not have our darned rotary motors revolve so fast they would fly apart. My whole plane hummed with the rush of air, and I swallowed nothing as fast as I could to ease my eardrums. Not till we were within 500 yards did the Hun make a move, but then he pointed straight down in a dive for safety. Almost immediately we all opened up on him. At such a speed it was hard to keep the sight on him as I pressed the triggers, but we got closer most quickly. One of my guns jammed, but just then I saw a cloud of smoke from the plane, it burst into flames, and I pulled up and turned for home, as did the others, and I leaned over and watched the poor devil's last flight. The plane still burned as it hit the ground so low we had gone. We weren't far over the lines and had only a little Archie before we were on our side. "Nice," thinks I, and waved at the other two and thumbed my nose at them for luck. While we were making out the report in the office, Greene (a Canadian, one of the flight commanders) came in and was sore our flight had gained on his. He said he thought he'd go out and even up the score, so I beat it to my mechanics and got some action on refueling my plane. It was ready by the time Greene was, so I went along with him. We took off about seven, it was a wonderful time to fly. The sun was setting in a great red ball, and the few clouds were dyed a wonderful red. No caution by Greene as we crossed the lines at 5,000 feet, looking for some late two-seater winging for its perch. Once along the lines and the sun had dropped into the ocean and Greene headed back. We landed in the gray of the evening and our flight held its lead.

RAF Flight Report, August 21, 1918: HOP w/202, took off 1120, Camel D.9649, landed 1330. Enemy aircraft following DH4s down coast, Camels unable to engage enemy machine; Afternoon HOP 1515, Camel N.6376, landed 1700, two-seater shot down by Colin Brown, Lt. Smith, and Ingalls, north of Zevecote village, southwest of Ghistelles (Gistel); Remarks on Hostile aircraft: LVG two-seater, usual type. Painted w/dark brown camouflage, with exception of tail plane and elevators which were white.

Official Squadron Report, August 21, 1918: At 1650 when Camels were at 19,000 feet between Dixmude and Ostend leader observed E.A. at 7,000 feet near Zevecote village. Camels dived and attacked, chasing E.A. down to 5,000 feet. Camels then broke off combat owing to A.A. fire, which was becoming very accurate. E.A. continued diving steeply, clouds of black smoke issuing from it right into the ground just south of Zevecote village. Captain Brown fired 200 rounds at 100 yards, Lieut. Ingalls, USNR, fired 100 rounds at 150 yards and Lieut. C. Smith fired 50 rounds at 150 yards.

August 22, 1918. While we were having breakfast the C.O. said he
had received word over the phone that one of the Handley-Page
night bombers had been seen in the sea off Ostend, still afloat, and
the U.S. seaplane station was sending out a flying boat to pick up
the survivors. It seems Di Gates was going out in a DD flying boat
and we were to escort him.

Well, five of us gobbled up our food, warmed up our motors and
set off. We set straight for Dunkirk and saw Di in his boat already far
ahead. Trust him to wait for no escort. Finally we caught him when we
were out to sea four or five miles and beyond Nieuport. Then, far ahead,
off Ostend, I picked up the Handley-Page, a mere speck on the water.

We throttled back and eased along above Di, and soon I could
make out a figure on one end of the enormous plane, which was
floating half submerged. And then I saw another figure lying on the
end of the other wing. As we circled above, Di landed his flying
boat and taxied up to one wing. As he neared it I saw him cut his
motor and the propeller stopped as his boat slid up to the wing.
"My Golly," thinks I, knowing how hard it was to start those motors.
"I bet he had a sinking feeling when he cut his motor." The figure
crawled onto Di's boat, Di pulled away and drifted as he cranked
his motor. Finally it started and I felt better. So far we'd seen no
Huns, but who could tell when they'd come. When we got back
some of the fellows said that the shore guns had fired on Di, but I
was so busy watching him and the skies above I hadn't noticed it.

Well, he taxied around and I saw him come up to the other end
of the Handley and again cut his motor. Again he slid up to the
half-sunk plane, again a figure leaped from one to the other. Again
he cranked and cranked his motor. It started and he took off. We
followed back to Dunkirk, went out to our field and from there
called up to learn the details of how the plane had been crippled
by Archie the previous evening and had finally settled down out in
the ocean, only two of its crew still alive. And we all appreciated
the guts of old Di in picking the survivors up.[17]

17. For this action, Admiral Sims recommended Gates be awarded the Medal of
Honor. For his war service, Gates received the Distinguished Flying Cross (Great Britain), the Distinguished Service Medal (United States), the Croix de Guerre (France),
and the Légion d'Honneur (France).

At 10:30 there was a call for an escort for the fleet and we set off about 11:00, five of us, flew out and guarded the destroyers.[18] It's not bad fun to do now and then, but there is no excitement. A few shells from the shore batteries lit reasonably near some of the fleet, which steamed along slowly, as far as I could see as usual uselessly. And so after a morning over the seas I enjoyed lunch and loafed till after tea. Then about five of our flight had a patrol. Some clouds had risen but not many, and we coasted along the lines, occasionally Archied, at about 17,000 feet, but saw no Huns except two-seaters coming from Zeebrugge along the coast. As we headed towards them they dove down behind Ostend and we bagged no game.

RAF Flight Report, August 22, 1918: Escort of CMB's, took off 0840, Camel D.9649, landed at 1000, some naval activity noted; LFP at 1215, Camel D.9649, sighted fleet in two portions off Zeebrugge, landed 1430; HOP w/202 squadron, took off 1735, landed 1955, Camel D.9677, two EA sighted, dove behind Ostend when Camels approached.

August 23, 1918. Greene's flight had orders for an early patrol today and I offered my services and so was called up at an ungodly hour, and we started off at 5:45. However, it was apparently too early for the Huns, or else we were too many. We had joined up with a flight from 202 Squadron.

RAF Flight Report, August 23, 1918: HOP w/202 squadron, Camel D.9649, took off 0605, landed 0730, patrol returned early because of clouds along coast; attempted HOP at 1350

18. The Royal Navy operated a great flotilla of vessels along the Belgian coast— laying mines, carrying out antisubmarine patrols, conducting shore bombardment— and the RAF often provided aerial cover.

August 25, 1918. Yesterday was indeed a dud. Outside of our regular baseball game, all we did was eat and drink. Today wasn't so bad. At least after lunch we had a pleasant patrol. Again we went to 18,000 feet and then over the lines. There was a little Archie but no Huns. Later, after tea, we escorted the Belgian King on his way to England for a while and then on our way back took a look along the lines, but saw nothing.[19]

August 30, 1918. What a week. No flying at all to speak of. If it wasn't for a trip to Dunkirk occasionally and some excitement with the nurses at the hospital at Bergues we would die of boredom. Also one of the boys got a roulette wheel the other day and we've been taking turns losing our money since. Me for bridge any day. Brains may not count for much but at least more than nothing. Well, at 1:30, although it was still cloudy, 218 Squadron (the day bombers) called for an escort to Bruges and we went out. It was certainly uninteresting though, through a haze. The clouds were really a mist. I did for the first time see an allied plane shot down by Hun Archie. I had been watching the bombers. The Archie bursts all around and between them, very close due to the presence of clouds helping the gunners with range, and suddenly I saw one of our planes turn, side slip, and then dive straight down. Later that day, after tea, a report of Huns overhead came in and a number of us set out. I never saw a soul around and finally joined up with a couple of other Camels and flew along the lines looking for trouble, but, no trouble. I forgot, yesterday we did have one flight, but the weather was awful and we saw nothing. Funny how often you play around and see nary a Hun, and then all at once you see them all the time and everywhere.

August 31, 1918. In spite of the clouds 218 requested an escort for a raid, so we sailed along the coast and watched over the boys as they dropped their stuff on Ostend. Personally, I don't see what

---

19. King Albert I of Belgium commanded a mixed army group of Belgian, British, and French units holding the far left of the Allied lines.

they bomb Ostend for. It's a total wreck as far as you can see. I doubt if anybody lives there, and certainly there is nothing there of importance, no harbor, munitions, supplies, etc. Maybe it's because it's so safe and easy to bomb and the squadron wants to keep up a good record.

September 3, 1918. Plenty of rest for the weary. The trouble is I'm not weary, and also the boys don't seem to enthuse over indoor baseball any more. About the only thing to do when not flying now is to practice with an automatic. I find I'm getting pretty good. We have blown all the tin cans we can find to atoms long ago.

This morning 208 Squadron,[20] not to be outdone, requested an escort while they went a-bombing, and where should they go but to Ostend. I had to laugh when they hastily circled in, over the dilapidated village, dropping their bombs, and out again. We sat 4,000 feet above wondering why.

After lunch the day was still fair. Imagine that, "in sunny France," so we had a patrol. As we were gazing down at the ruins of Ypres what should happen but we ran into four Huns. There were three of us and the Huns had Fokkers. We met just about on a level somewhere around 19,000 feet. There was no surprise and we simply all met shooting. The planes at that height are pretty dead anyway,[21] and though I seemed to have trouble getting a bead on any of the Huns, they were apparently in the same boat. We circled around a while shooting occasionally. After a couple of circles I happened to see a Hun behind Smith, shooting into him as he turned and swerved. It looked bad, and almost immediately he dove towards the lines, the Hun behind. I left my opponent like a shot, for Smithy is a great little fellow, and dove

20. No.208 Squadron, RAF, organized at Dunkirk in October 1916 as No.8 Squadron, RNAS, flew, successively, Sopwith Pups, Sopwith 1½ Strutters, Nieuport Scouts, and Sopwith Triplanes and Camels. For a time, the unit concentrated on artillery spotting. During the German advance in April, squadron personnel destroyed sixteen of their own Camels rather than let the enemy capture them. See Shores, *Above the Trenches*, 41–42.

21. Before the introduction of the supercharger, nearly all aircraft of the period experienced significant losses of power, speed, and maneuverability at great altitude.

after the Hun. In a moment I had my sight on him, though a long way off, and pulled the triggers, hoping I could scare him away from his victim. Down we went, the Hun shooting at Smithy and me at the Hun, so fast I thought my cylinders would just naturally all fly off by themselves. I did gain, finally, however, and got near enough to scare the Hun; he pulled off and dove towards his own side, nearly straight down, leaving me hopelessly in the rear. I pulled up, saw Smith continue on home and looked around, but I was down far below the flight and had to give up for the trip. No use climbing tediously up again as the patrol was now over.

September 4, 1918. The Germans must be off on vacation. None of the patrols have seen any to speak of lately. We flew miles over the lines today, more or less as usual trying to find a target, but to no avail.

September 5, 1918

Dear Pops,

Just received two letters from you Nos. 24, 27 dated July 8–20, and one from Mother of August 14. Wherefrom it is rather evident that C.P.S. is best way of sending the mail. Especially as, at present, since headquarters are being changed from Paris to London,[22] everything is more or less upset. It is certainly too bad about G. Russell and Reed having been shot down. But I don't know which Reed you mean. Talking about dodging Archie, I saw for the first time a couple of days ago a machine hit and brought down out of control by Archie. It happened as we were escorting a number of day bombers, and it wasn't nice to see. Anyway Russell's idea of avoiding it is wrong, I think, as it entirely a matter of luck, one may turn directly into a burst as well as away from it, and besides

---

22. On September 1, 1918, U.S. naval aviation headquarters under Capt. Hutch Cone formally relocated from Paris to London, with control of operations along the French coast (excluding NBG/Dunkirk) moving to Brest, directed by Capt. Thomas Craven, now serving on the staff of Adm. Henry B. Wilson.

the first burst is always the best as you are unaware of it and have probably been going right straight along at a fixed altitude and speed for some time, so they have the range accurately after that, when you begin to turn, dive, or climb, as I say, it is all luck. I also had rather a disagreeable scrap a day or so ago, when eight of us met four Huns, some way across the lines. The disagreeable part came when, as I was diving unseen at one son of a gun, my doggone guns jammed after the first shot, and the first shot evidently missed and as, unless they have the advantage in numbers and height, they always spin down safely, one crack is all you get if you catch a few of them alone. My flight CO goes home to England on leave tomorrow or the next day, and says I am to lead his flight during his absence, which is pretty nice for me.[23] I hope I don't lead them into any trouble. Well, cheerio, Pops

September 6, 1918. Somewhat dud, but not so terrible. My roommate and flight commander, Brown, left yesterday on a two weeks leave, and I have taken over his flight as flight commander, not bad, that is, not if I can keep the boys out of trouble as well as he did. Never have I seen anyone with such an eye for Huns. He just always sees them first somehow. Anyway, today caution was the better part of valor with me and the result was our patrol was n.g. [likely "no good"]. We saw nothing.

September 7, 1918. More clouds. We had one patrol in company with 202 Squadron.[24] Don't know why everybody is so careful, but the C.O. thinks that the Huns come out in such big bunches it's foolish not to do the same thing. This afternoon I tested a new Camel with a trick upper wing with an open section for

23. Given Ingalls's youth and nationality, being named acting flight commander of a British unit over the heads of several more experienced squadron members constituted a ringing endorsement of his abilities.

24. No.202 Squadron, RAF, began as No.2 Squadron, RNAS, formed on October 17, 1914. It conducted bombing and reconnaissance missions. During 1917–18, the squadron operated both DH4 and DH9 aircraft.

better visibility. It climbed 5000 feet in five minutes, 10,000 in 13 minutes.[25] That's pretty good. Good enough, anyway, and the visibility is infinitely better.

September 8, 1918

Dear Mother,

I think I'll have to stop ever mentioning the weather. It is always the same—bad, rotten.[26] Well, my flight commander and also room-mate leaves today for home for two weeks. The lucky fellow has been talking about it for about a month now, if he has half as good a time as he expects he'll be in about seventh heaven. In his absence who but your little son is to lead the flight? Hope I don't get ignominiously kicked out of the job. Lately I've been playing quite a lot of bridge, and of course have read volumes, but it's impossible to get any decent books. Though I received one very good one "Under Two Flags" by "Ouida."[27] Di Gates just called up and is coming out to get me for lunch as Harry Davison and Reg Coombe are here today. Reg was one of the fellows who trained with us. There was quite a good concert at the hospital today, but I didn't go. You see our sleeping quarters are at least three miles from mess so I walk home every night to get some exercise. If you remember how I detest walking you can imagine how hard up I am for some form of exercise. But they have at least organized a sports committee here and start playing all these funny English games like rugby, field hockey, etc. As I'm going to lunch with Di, I'll miss church for the first time for a month. Well, Mother, I must stop, With love, Dave

25. During the Sopwith Camel's long operational history, several versions were produced, utilizing various combinations of motor, armament, armor, pilot placement, and so forth. Many incorporated a small cutout in the upper center wing section.

26. The weather in September deteriorated to such an extent that the American seaplane station at Dunkirk suspended operations for much of the month.

27. *Under Two Flags,* the novel by Maria Louisa de la Ramee (pseud. "Ouida"), was made into a play that first appeared in 1872 and opened as a drama on Broadway in 1901.

September 10, 1918

My Dear Dad,

Things are still "As you were." It rains and blows as though France were part of Hades. Nothing could be worse than to have a wonderful machine of your own sitting uselessly idle in a hangar. Gosh, I was never so impatient and restless in all my life as now. When you know there's nothing to do, 'tis not so bad, but you see this really ought to be the best weather, and we are losing a lot of flying that can't be gotten back. Isn't it a hell of a note? I've been stepping into a sister society lately. At least that is what the nurses are called over here. Well a very pretty American girl [Miss Johnson] is stationed at the hospital in town. She knew Di Gates before the war, and the other night she was there for dinner and the CO here and I went likewise. Then yesterday she took me to tea with some British nurse friends and French [friends] of hers. There has been no mail from 4 Place D'Iena for some time. Also the headquarters have been changed to London and I don't know that address, you'd better use C.P.S. entirely. I haven't yet acted but once in my new honor and capacity as temporary flight commander. Probably won't darn this weather anyhow. Well Pops, Cheerio, Aff. Dave. P.S. That story about the Kaiser and other s.o.b.s was greatly appreciated by our C.O./DSI

September 13, 1918. We couldn't get worse weather. It's the bad weather makes the aviators live so long, though, so I suppose it is blessed. But outside of occasional trips to Dunkirk, and once in a while to Calais, there isn't a damn thing to do. Also I've walked over every road, path, and field around here enough to satisfy. I never did enjoy walking at home, and it's no different in France.

September 15, 1918. For the first half of the elapsed time I was too busy to write this, and since I've been too fed up with the abominable weather. On about 9th, Brown went on leave and I was left in charge of "C" flight. One day I met a Miss Johnson, and on the 13th I went to monitor for tea with Graham and

Johnson.[28] Well, this morning or rather at 1:15 we bombed up [loaded bombs] and left for Uytkerke aerodrome.[29] It was sort of cloudy at 2,000 feet, and cloudier at 7,000 feet. We went out to sea just beyond Blankubun (Blankenberge), they came in diving, crossing at about 2,000 feet. Very little Archie. "C" flight was to bomb workshops on west side, so I crossed almost [11?] to "A" flight. The aerodrome is only two miles over and we saw it soon. Diving down to 150 I dropped bombs on further row of buildings, noting at time three crazy beggars dropping theirs about 200 ft. higher in field straight ahead. Then turned and dove shooting up hangars twice and once two motor lorries, then seeing everyone gone I flew over close noting two fires, five or six direct hits, and the fact that one damned machine gunner was still very much alive. Then I climbed up west. Suddenly the motor missed on at least five cylinders and revs dropped to about 900 feet. I looked around for a good field, expecting to have the damned thing seize up, but suddenly it roared out full again. As the Archie was thick I dodged about finally getting into clouds and crossing was at 2,000 feet badly concealed.

I could see four or five Camels far ahead. One turned back and joined me. Smith. So we tooted along easily at 7,000 feet. Just then I saw six Huns over Zeebrugge but didn't think they could see

---

28. Monitors were a special class of relatively slow, broad-beamed, shallow-draft but heavily armed warships meant for coastal use and shore bombardment. They often incorporated the guns and turrets from other vessels.

29. The great success of the Varssenaere raid inspired plans for another attack, this one against the German aerodrome at Uytkerke, near Zeebrugge. Extensive photographic reconnaissance permitted careful planning. Capt. C. R. Swanson led the assault and later received the DFC for his actions that day. The squadron divided into four flights, each targeting a different group of hangers, dropping a total of eighty bombs while expending over twenty-two hundred rounds of ammunition. Some reports indicated that more than a hundred German mechanics died in the attack. David Ingalls led the five Camels of "C" flight. He also received the DFC for his part in the raid. His actions included making successful bombing runs on the aerodrome and single-handedly attacking six enemy aircraft, driving one down out of control. When Squadron Commander Graham recommended Ingalls for the award, he offered extraordinary praise, writing, "His keenness, courage and utter disregard of danger are exceptional and are an example to all. He is one of the finest men the Squadron has ever had." See Leeson, *Hornet Strikes*, 26–27.

us. Anyway I started to climb and just then saw apparently a two-seater climbing out of Ostend, perhaps to pick off last Camel just visible. I waved at Smithy and headed in a bit, climbing. In about four minutes he saw us four and turned east toward Ostend gliding. We dived, firing at long range, but I got to about 100 yards before he hit the clouds at 2,000 feet and got in a good burst, so did Smith. He went through clouds at Ostend pier, sort of wallowing. I dived through, and came out just behind him over beach. He was diving steeply so I opened at 50 yards and saw flames and smoke come out. Then I saw a lot of tracers from shore and beat it like Hell, meeting south above clouds. He saw the Hun crash through a drift in clouds. Then we went home, Graham joining us. After tea Smith, Hodson,[30] and two new blokes and I went on high offensive patrol, but nothing doing. Day a big success.

———

Official Squadron Summary, September 15, 1918: Low bomb raid on [Uyt-kerke] Aerodrome. Dropped four bombs and fired 300 rounds and destroyed one E.A. on return journey.

———

"An Ideal Low Bombing Raid"

For almost a week the members of the squadron had been sitting around waiting, apparently in vain, for a good day when we and several other squadrons were to bomb a certain aerodrome [Uytkerke].[31] For the first few days every one rather welcomed the dud weather which had just come on, as a low bombing raid means coming down to within fifty feet or so of the earth, some twenty or thirty miles over the lines, which fact is rather disturbing to even the calmest and coolest pilots, but after a time we became restless and impatient to get the job done with.[32]

---

30. David Ingalls received credit for a victory over a Rumpler C near Ostend at 2:00 PM, while flying Camel D9649. He shared the victory with Smith. Lt. George Stacey Hodson, ten victories, DFC, Croix de Guerre (Belgian), served with No.213 Squadron from August 29, 1918, until March 17, 1919. See Shores, *Above the Trenches,* 196–97.

31. Ingalls wrote this account of the September 15 raid for his parents, probably while serving at Eastleigh, England, and mailed it home on October 24, 1918.

32. The weather in mid-September was so bad that the U.S. Navy was forced to suspend flight operations at nearby NAS Dunkirk for an entire week.

So that it was rather a relief when the C.O., who had just been conversing with two of the flight commanders that had been testing a couple of machines in spite of the low clouds, entered the mess and announced that luncheon was to be served in half an hour, eleven-thirty, and we were to bomb the aerodrome. Only one squadron, as the weather was fine for a few machines to slip over the lines, was to drop through a break in the clouds, do their dirty work and get back safely in those clouds.

Upon hearing this, a few of the pilots, just out of the school, hurried out to get over to their machines, while the rest, well aware that all a pilot could do in the hangars was to get in the mechanics' way, gathered around the maps and discussed the different routes. A few minutes later the C.O. called a meeting and bringing forth larger maps and photographs, decided upon the leader, and fixed a particular target—a hangar hut or workshop—for each pilot, likewise detailing a man to shoot up the two or three machine-gun emplacements to be seen on the photos. Previous low raids had been done in a more haphazard manner, and this time we wanted to "bring home the bacon" as Shakespeare did not say.

By the time each man knew his objective and place in the formation, lunch was served, all but a few heads acting in a hurried and nervous fashion. Luncheon over, we adjourned to our respective flight hangars, to don a helmet and gloves, and some stuffed a toothbrush or small pistol in a pocket; at the same time everyone left behind all personal papers, letters, etc., which might be of value to the enemy in case one was captured.

Then I walked out to my machine. All R.F.C. mechanics are remarkably fine and efficient men, so I had complete confidence in mine, which is a comforting thing to have, and questioned him about a few faults in the machine, which I had told him about after the last flight. Of course, he had attended to everything and was now occupied in cleaning the windscreen and brushing the seat. We got on board and the motors were started.

When their engines were warmed up and tested, the pilots took off, flight by flight, the first three falling in behind the leader's flight. The leader climbed rapidly through a clear space in the clouds out to sea, where one and all tested the two guns with which the machines are armed. He then headed up the coast some ten miles out to sea, about 4000 feet above the clouds, which were at about 3000 feet.

The trip up to a spot opposite our objective seemed unusually long, as there was nothing to do but sit and wait. Finally, however, we turned towards shore, and I, who was leading a flight, which was to bomb a number of workshops, which were slightly to one side of the aerodrome, drew up parallel to the leader. Fortunately the clouds were thick over the coast and no Archies came up. As we crossed the leader dived down, followed closely by all, through a break. As we appeared to view the Archies started and it was mighty close, as the Huns had heard us and also had the range of the clouds, at our altitude. But not even the Hun Archies can hit a squadron of machines diving almost vertically down, and in a few seconds we were too low for them, tearing along at about 200 feet toward the junction of a canal and a railroad near our aerodrome—a landmark previously noted.

As we neared the aerodrome we slowed up and came down to about 100 feet; if lower one would be injured by the exploding of one's own bombs underneath. The hangars and huts were wonderfully placed for us, all in two lines wide enough to make a miss for almost anyone an impossibility.

Getting a fine aim at my shop, I pulled the lever loosing the four twenty-five-pound bombs I carried, and looked up just in time to see one flight almost over us let go their bombs, evidently at a perfectly smooth field beyond. I hoicked around so as not to be hit by the crazy beggars, and looked back to hear a continuous "wonk, wonk, wonk,"— practically the same sound an Archie makes when it bursts near one—to see a great number of direct hits on targets, and other explosions all around, except for the bombs of the flight which dotted the afore-mentioned field with beautifully spaced little holes.

Turning back, I dove, firing at two lorries standing near the shops, and, as I again hoicked away, I became aware of the sharp "pat-pat" of several machine gun emplacements firing from the ground. Being almost over one machine-gun emplacement, I looked at it, but it was empty. Some one else was firing at the other machine-gun emplacement, while all the other machines, but two, [were] climbing rapidly into the clouds, weaving [and] diving and zooming around the aerodrome, shooting like wild men. Why no one is hit by a pal is something I cannot understand.

I looked around for something to shoot. There were no men about or any machines in the field, so I tried to puncture several huts. With these speeded up guns one can fire an incredible amount in a slight dive from say 150 to 250 feet and it is very satisfying to see the tracers going over the roofs in a long line, an occasional one ricocheting off as it hits something at an obtuse angle. This time I could notice tracers coming from at least three machine guns but couldn't see where from.

By this time most of the machines were leaving, as there was really nothing worthwhile left to shoot up, so I flew over once more, and tried to locate correctly all the hits and two fires which were burning fiercely. At the far end of the field, as I was headed on a farm house, I located two of the machine-gun emplacements which were shooting at me, their tracers coming pretty close in spite of the maneuvering I was doing to escape them. I didn't see them in time to fire and as when I left I could see no other planes, I started after them, looking at several farm houses about the doors of which the whole family, Belgians of course, were heartily enjoying the spectacle.

Reaching 1,000 feet in no time I was taken note of by some Archie batteries, and so began turning, zooming, and climbing to get to the clouds as quickly as possible. Those clouds looked mighty like home to me. But now I got a shock, my engine almost cutting out, hitting at the most on three cylinders. I started on a gentle glide, looked at the gauges and switches, and tried running on the gravity tank, but no luck, so I looked around for a smooth field from an altitude of about 500 feet, and in the midst of Archie bursts. Then cheerio, the doggone engine grew better, though not best, and I encored my journey to the clouds, reaching them just before going over the coast, and disappeared therein. When I came out again into the clear sky I saw only one machine near, the others had almost disappeared in the direction of France. But this one turned back and I recognized one of my own flight. We waved happily, and set out at an easy pace for home, till I saw six Huns overhead coming our way, but they never saw us and turned off to one side. At which point we both breathed easier.

By this time we were opposite Ostend, and again I saw a Hun, seemingly a two-seater climbing out of the clouds, probably thinking to get the last man ahead of us. S[mith] and I put the helm over and edged in behind him, hoping he would [go] further out to sea. This he did, and thinking that he'd have to turn getting back, I opened up and started after him. At last he saw us, turned and dove back for Ostend, but we gained on him and soon opened fire at 400 yards. His observer was evidently new at the game, or killed by one of our shots, for I saw no tracers coming back. We continued to dive and shoot, he finally reaching the clouds. I was only

150 yards behind now, so followed, coming out of the clouds almost over Ostend piers, luckily right behind the Hun. One good burst and he caught fire, so I hoicked off swerving, to dodge the land machine guns from the shore. A last look showed him crashing into the water by the beach and S[mith] joined me above the clouds. He had seen the Hun burst into flames and crash through a break and we went home rejoicing.

A minute later the Commanding Officer, who on seeing the Hun and scrap, had turned back, joined us and waved. A few minutes later we climbed out of our machines and hurried into the Records Office to report. Here we learned that two fellows had been wounded, one slightly, and the other had three shots in his leg, but all machines had returned. After the tension, every one was feeling in great form, kidding one another and confirming the damage done. The reports and the official photos, taken next day, proved the raid to be one of best done so far.

Distinguished Flying Cross Citation

For exceptionally meritorious service in duty of great responsibility as a chasse pilot operating with R.A.F., Squadron 213, while attached to the Northern Bombing Group, Northern France, where as a result of his brilliant and courageous work he was made an Acting Flight Commander by the British authorities over their own pilots. Alone and in conjunction with other pilots, he shot down at least four enemy aeroplanes and one or more enemy balloons.[33]

Cable 18h 101 Amair Calais

For Lieutenant Ingalls I have been informed today by the General Officer commanding Fifth Group that you have been awarded the Distinguished Flying Cross; General Officer commanding Fifth Group conveys his heartiest congratulations; I add my congratulations; 18010 fifty seven; Hanrahan

---

33. The Prince of Wales, future King Edward VIII, presented Ingalls's medal during a visit to the United States in 1919. Ingalls cut class to meet the prince and was disciplined by Yale University for his absence.

Distinguished Service Medal Citation

This officer has been awarded the Distinguished Flying Cross by the British Government. On September 15, 1918, he led a flight of five machines on a low bombing raid on Uytkerke Aerodrome, obtaining a direct hit on his target. On the homeward journey, assisted by another Camel, he shot down a two-seater enemy aircraft in flames. He has participated in two other low raids, doing good work with bombs and machine gun fire in each case. He also shot down a kite balloon in flames near Ostende. His reckless courage and utter disregard of danger are exceptional and are an example to all.

September 16, 1918. A.M. wake-up for escort. Had H.O.P. of 15 machines in morning but saw nothing. I came back with E. and T. and went out alone.[34] Saw two-seater above and tried to climb up but he was attacked by three Belgians and chased away. Right after lunch I beat it off alone and did a patrol, hoping for some photographers, flying back and forth across the lines. At one time I did see a two-seater attacked by three Hanriots, but they were a way off and before I could get there the Hun had had enough and dived away homeward, and the Hanriots had left. There must be a pact between the Huns and the Belgians. I never saw either side shoot down any of the other, though they seemed to fly around one another every now and then. And I've been told they do shoot sometimes.[35]

----

34. Possibly he was referring to Lt. W. G. Evans and either Lt. R. A. Talbot or Lt. A. H. Turner.

35. Ingalls's disparaging remarks about Belgian forces echoed comments by many soldiers stationed in Flanders. Persistent rumors claimed the Belgians actually cooperated with the Germans, refused to fight against them, and even supplied military information. Back in April, Ken MacLeish wrote home about several supposed "events" that confirmed such suspicions. In his masterful *The Great War and Modern Memory* (Toronto, Canada: Sterling Publishing, 2009), esp. 139–48, Paul Fussell chronicled the rumors and myths—uplifting, barbaric, and profane—circulating widely among Allied troops, including the "Angel of Mons" story, the supposed "contemptible little army" remark by the kaiser, and the story of the "Crucified Canadian." Fussell noted that it was widely believed "but never, so far as I know, proved that the French, Belgians, or Alsatians living just behind the lines signaled the distant German artillery by fantastically elaborate, shrewd, and accurate means." See also MacLeish's letter of April 22, 1918, in Geoffrey Rossano, ed., *The Price of Honor: The World War One Letters of Naval Aviator Kenneth MacLeish* (Annapolis, Md.: Naval Institute Press, 1991), 145–47.

Just as I finished my report and entered the mess room for tea the C.O. yells at me to get my flight for an escort patrol for 218 Squadron against Bruges (Brugge).[36] So I missed my tea and spent the time bawling out the mechanics so my machine would be ready. It was finally O.K. and we got off together, three threes, the whole squadron meeting the D.H.s just off Dunkirk. Just beyond Ostend we crossed the coast and proceeded to Bruges. Lots of Archie at Bruges and on way home six Fokkers came up at D.H.s and we all dived, or rather four of us did, the rest buggering off yellow. I got two good bursts but the beggars dived away and the other climbed up so we couldn't finish there. Finally they all got off.

It was such a great afternoon and not time for supper, so after tea had a high offensive patrol. I got some more gas and ammunition and took another tour by myself. Useless, it was. Too late probably for any Huns. At any rate I was coasting along the lines at 18,000 feet for nearly an hour and a half, till it got too dark to see much. It was very nearly too dark to land when I finally got back. Hereafter I'll finish the day before the night has arrived.

September 17, 1918. Hell of a wind, lots of clouds. My day off duty. Lo about 12:10 I flew up to St. Inglevert with Smith. It took us almost 40 minutes and on landing, just kept motor ticking over, and settled slowly, turning up on one wing, and nearly up on nose—no damage. After Johnson had got a signal and put our planes behind a shelter we went in and had lunch. I saw Eddie McDonnell, Scab [Ken Smith], Harry [Davison] and etc. Fine lunch. Hanrahan is still in England. After lunch I took off first, climbing just about straight up in wind and did a few stunts. Came back quickly and dressed and went to Terminus [Hotel] with C.O. to dance with Miss Johnson nurse. Crazy time, French, English, and American. And of all rotten dancers the French and English were worst. Then had dinner at Di's, good fun.

---

36. Accessed by two canals extending inland from Zeebrugge and Ostend, Bruges was the principal German submarine base in Flanders, with heavily constructed submarine pens and extensive antiaircraft defenses. The RAF made repeated attacks against these facilities but with little effect.

September 18, 1918. Big day. This morning we decided to get a kite
balloon, so filled up with Buckingham Tracers. Sims took three
up to escort, Smith, Hodson, and me.[37] There were clouds at
9,000 feet so we went out and crossed coast to about 8,000 feet,
west of kite balloon. And it was Hell. About the second bunch,
one exploded just under my right wing, and I, feeling something
hit my leg, felt low. But it was evidently a splinter, though
afterwards, looking at it, I don't see why I wasn't punctured. I saw
that it broke both spars in right wing. Well, we dived down, kite
balloon was about 3,000 feet going down fast, but we caught it
at about 1,000 feet. I opened up and saw two observers dive out
with parachute. I pulled up with a couple of jams just in front
of it and it was not afire. So I hoicked around and dived again
and saw a fire start in middle where tracers were entering. There
were two machine guns shooting and plenty of Archie. I could
see Smithy near me and Hodson up above. Then I dove down to
ground watching kite balloon burst into flames and fall on three
hangars setting all afire. Nice. At about 75 feet I got no Archie
or machine gun for a couple of minutes and tore along. Finally I
heard one gun open up and split assed like the devil. It seemed
to never stop, though suppose I was in range only a half a minute
or so. Then two miles south of Middlekerke I saw a lot of huts,
apparently barracks, so I opened up with tracers. One caught fire.
I then saw Smith and we crossed the lines and beat it for home.
My machine felt awfully wobbly and I just was waiting for a wing

37. Stationary kite balloons used for observation and artillery spotting flew quite
close to the ground and could not defend themselves but were ringed by accurate
and deadly machine guns and antiaircraft artillery. They also relied on nearby aircraft
eager to pounce on unsuspecting attackers, making "balloon busting" very dangerous
indeed. Frank Luke of the U.S. Air Service was the most famous of the American
practitioners of this particular type of hunting. Luke's balloon-busting exploits are recounted in James Hudson, *Hostile Skies: A Combat History of the American Air Service in
World War I* (Syracuse, N.Y.: Syracuse University Press, 1968), 279–82, and especially in
Stephen Skinner, *The Stand: The Final Flight of Lt. Frank Luke, Jr.* (Atglen, Pa.: Schiffer
Military Publishing, 2008). Buckingham tracers were a type of blunt-nosed, incendiary bullet using white phosphorus as the flammable material. They were specifically
designed to punch a large hole in balloons and then ignite the hydrogen gas within.
Lt. Charles John Sims, DFC, nine confirmed victories, joined the squadron on May
25, 1918.

to come off or a flipper. 'Twas a relief to get down O.K. Certainly
the worst time I've had, though darned good fun, and a very
pretty sight. After lunch we had a patrol to 5 miles or 10 east of
Zeebrugge. Saw nothing but some seaplanes inside mole. C.O.
seemed mighty pleased about K.B. But I'll never cross that coast
in broad daylight at 7,000 feet again. It's not worthwhile.[38]

RAF Flight Report, September 18, 1918: KB offensive, took off 1025, Camel
D.9649.

Official Squadron Report, September 18, 1918: Camels sighted K.B. at 3,500
feet over neighborhood of La Barriere crossing coast, Camels attacked diving
from W. firing about 90 tracers each following K.B. to about 500 feet when
two observers jumped with white parachutes and K.B. burst into flames. K.B.
fell burning on one of three hangars setting [it] on fire. The other two also
caught fire making blaze visible from [Nieuport]. On return Lt. Ingalls fired
at huts apparently barracks three miles south of Middlekerke, one of which
caught fire. All machines were hit by A.A. and M.G. fire.

Sept. 18, 1918

Dear Dad:

I have been a bit busy lately, so I haven't written. It has cleared
up for whiles the last few days, so we have flown a bit. Day before
yesterday we had another low bomb raid on an airdrome and it was a
great success. We blew the place to pieces literally, from about 150 ft.

Unfortunately two of our fellows were wounded but not seriously
and got back. On the way home a fellow named Smith and I got a two-
seater. I conceitedly think I got him, as I followed him down through
some clouds, and saw him burst into flames after a short burst at him.
Altogether it was a bon show.

The next day we had lots of flying, but had only one scrap, four
of us with six Huns, but they all got away by spinning down, we

38. The RAF credited Ingalls with destruction of a kite balloon at La Barrière at
10:50 AM, flying a Camel D9649, the victory being shared with Smith and Hodson.

being unable to follow them as were escorting some bombers. Then this morning I led my flight, note the nonchalant way I say my flight, over the coast and we got a kite balloon in flames, pretty nice, eh? It was very pretty; just as it caught fire the two observers jumped with beautiful white parachutes. Luckily, the burning balloon fell on three hangars underneath and there was some fire. We contour-chased home just over the ground, and I managed to set fire to some barracks some way behind the lines.

This afternoon we saw no Huns, weather becoming very dud. Much to my regret I received orders to leave here the other day, and am afraid that as soon as some regular flight commander returns I'll have to go—to what I know what. Yesterday afternoon we had a dance, given by two American nurses who are stationed here. There were some French, English, and American girls talking all sorts of languages, so you can imagine the time we had. And, my Lord, but the French and British girls do dance most strangely. Dinner is ready so I must wash up. Cheerio Pops. Aff. Dave.

———

c. September 1918

Dear Dad,

In answer to your letter wanting to hear an experience, this is a rather interesting one:

"Aeroplane versus Kite Balloon"

Yesterday while flying along the coast towards Zeebrugge, I noticed particularly the kite balloon, which in good weather is always up near Ostend for observational purposes. And it looked like such easy meat that when we returned to the aerodrome I suggested to the flight that we go get the beggar. Although only one chap in the squadron had ever tried for a kite balloon, they all fell for it immediately, so this morning three of our flight asked the C.O.'s permission and filled our guns with Buckingham (incendiary tracers). Another flight, having offered to escort us, the six started out about 10 A.M. A thick layer of clouds covered the sky at 8,000 feet, so we flew down the coast just under them, followed by our gallant escort. Opposite Ostend we turned in and nosing over slightly, to get up more speed, approached the kite balloon in a big curve. Not until we had almost reached the coast did the Archie start in, but then, as we were only at 7,000 feet and they had plenty of time to get our range, it was some Archie. One shell, in the very first burst, broke just under my right wing, and a piece of shrapnel went through the fuselage in front of my knees, a piece of the cowling striking me on the knees, and giving me quite a start. The Archie on this coast is about the best the Huns have, and the gunners certainly must have enjoyed themselves during the two or three minutes we were diving towards the kite balloon. Later I looked back again, and in time to see the blazing mass fall directly on one of the three balloon sheds, all of which broke out almost immediately into a glorious fire. "*Beaucoup Bon*" thinks I, hearing no machine guns, and seeing no Huns anywhere in the sky. A minute or so of peace and quiet, and then at one time I see a machine headed at me slightly above about three miles off, and heard the rat tat of one or more land machine guns. Fortunately they were not using tracers, being too close to the lines, for seeing the tracers is rather disagreeable. And fortunately I recognized the other machine as a Camel, it turned out to be Smith, coming over for company. Somehow it is rather comforting to have another machine nearby when low over Hunland. A lot of more turning and twisting and no more rat tat. Then I saw some barracks, and opening up on them was delighted to see them catch fire. One more machine gun and we were in sight of the marsh between the lines. A lot of rifle fire at us, zooming and turning, and we were again in peace and quiet over our own lines. On arriving at our aerodrome we counted the holes in the machine and reported a huge success. The General was quite bucked, for upon hearing the report, he called up our C.O. and seemed very pleased. A little later photos were taken confirming the destruction of the sheds. D.S.I.

September 19, 1918. Some wind. Also a bit of rain. Wrote a few letters, then after lunch went into Dunkirk with C. O. [Graham] . . . stopped at Seaplanes [NAS Dunkirk?]. Shorty [Smith] was just circumcised and is in a most unique predicament. When

C.O. called we sent him a signal signed C. Clinton, "Sorry to hear it's all off." C.O. has planned a dance at Terminus for Tuesday. It ought to be pretty *bon*. I walked home cross field. Looks dud for tomorrow. Doggone the weather, I'll have to leave here soon.

September 20, 1918. Pretty windy, but we escorted 218 [Squadron] at about 9 a.m. 218 was bombing Bruges and the whole squadron went to protect them. We set out when they telephoned that they had started, and climbed so that we all met over La Panne (De Panne) at about 15,000 feet. On such trips one flight of Camels went on each side and slightly above and to the rear of the day bombers, while the third flight flew about 4,000 feet above us to guard against any Huns who might dive from above. Saw one Hun low down over Nieuport, then just after crossing coast I saw four more coming straight at us from the right side, some distance off, a little lower than me. We flew along for some time and then as they continued to approach, I turned and headed for them, my flight following. As there were 15 Camels . . . we met firing. Smithy got hit in tank right off and left the fight. Hodson's guns jammed right away. The other two left after awhile but we had a slick scrap. I shot straight at their leader, turning and zooming just as we almost met. I could see the four Huns and two other Camels all lined up, while my two last men had turned off and were some distance above, so I headed at one of the Huns and fired. He immediately dived, but I didn't follow, always having a dread of being caught low down over German land. When I looked around now I saw only three Fokkers at a distance, some of the bombers away off, and one Camel above.

As we ought to do our duty, I turned after the bombers to keep near them and protect them. The Fokkers flew about, but didn't come near. Soon the bombers started to return. One evidently had a poor motor and was below and behind the rest. Toward the end I saw two Fokkers attack one D.H. One of them was directly behind shooting at the bomber from about 150 yards, the other somehow had got a little ahead and as far as I could see was doing nothing. I approached at right angles and, deciding that the first named Hun was the most dangerous, I fired at rear one from the right and he went down vertically and was reported out of control and smoke coming out. Then I turned on other beggar and got a beautiful aim on him. He could not have seen me, for I got within about fifteen yards and then had a perfect shot at him. He went over on his back and dove then spun. I don't know how I could have missed, for I almost ran into him. I am sure I got him somewhere, although Greene saw him level out once very low down after about a 10,000-foot dive. I watched him go until he got very near the ground, when I heard someone shooting and saw about three Fokkers coming up at me and shooting from about 300 yards' distance. I immediately dove and fired at the nearest. They all split up and dove off in different directions, so I immediately turned and started after the bomber, who was hurrying toward the coast. But as soon as I started out, the Huns pulled up and fired from beneath and behind. All the British machines had now crossed the coast and so I kept on after them, while these three buggers kept shooting from an impossible distance until I crossed the coast. The first Hun I had shot at was officially confirmed as being destroyed in flames,[39] but someone reported having seen the other pull up after spinning a long time and flatten out apparently O.K. Two of my flight had been hit in the gas tanks the first thing and had barely managed to get home.

Dud afternoon but I tested a new bus and reported it dud. Then after tea we had a patrol, but it was too bum, came back

39. Ingalls downed an enemy aircraft at 10:45 AM near Vlissingen flying Sopwith Camel D8177. His victory seems all the more impressive because his opponent was the highly touted Fokker D.VII, regarded by many as the finest fighter of the war, especially the BMW-powered version. At least one pilot from the American 148th Aero Squadron remarked, "A Camel had to shoot down every German plane in the sky in order to get himself home, as the Camel could neither out climb nor outrun a Fokker." John Morrow, in his authoritative *Great War in the Air,* 315–16, noted that even in the final months of the war, the Fokker "remained superior to all British single-seaters, including the last to appear at the front.... Even Sopwith's successor to the Camel and Dolphin, the maneuverable Snipe that appeared in October, could not match the Fokker's speed, ceiling, and climb." Shores, in *Above the Trenches,* 25, wrote, "By this time [August 1918] the Sopwith Camel had reached a stage where it was in many respects outclassed by the BMW-Fokker D.VII ... losses had begun to rise alarmingly."

early. Sent a new fellow up for a test flight, but he gets sick over 10,000 feet so isn't going to be of any use here.[40]

———

RAF Flight Report, September 20, 1918: escort of 218 squadron, Camel D.8177, took off 0835, at 0945 at 16,000 over Varssenaere attacked four Fokkers which were approaching DH9s. Ingalls shot one down out of control, emitted smoke.

———

RAF Flight Report, September 20, 1918: Observed four E.A. heading towards D.H.'s at about 15,500 feet. Camels attacked head on. Lieut. Smith's machine shot through pressure tank and he withdrew from combat. Dog fight ensued. Lieut. Ingalls attacked an E.A., which was pursuing a D.H. 9. [Ingalls] fired 100 rounds at 100 yards range and E.A. dived vertically emitting white smoke. Machine last seen out of control very low near Bruges, still smoking and descending. (Confirmed) Lieut. Ingalls then attacked another E.A. at 25 yards range and E.A. turned on its back, diving and then spun slowly. It is thought that this machine flattened out very low down. Remaining E.A. dived and spun away when Camels attacked.

———

September 20, 1918

My Dear Mother:

Yesterday was awfully dud, so there was nothing doing, we just sit around and play bridge most of the bad days. But yesterday the C.O. had to go and arrange a dance for Tuesday, so we went auto riding, as it were. To-day was fairly good. This morning, we went out and had a scrap, and I got one, confirmed, and one other, whom I'm

---

40. The extreme motion and high altitude encountered during aerial missions often proved debilitating. Many fliers suffered from airsickness (kinetosis) or altitude sickness (hypobaropothy) or both, which would disqualify a man from active duty. Such a condition caused Edward "Shorty" Smith of the Second Yale Unit to lose his hard-earned wings.

sure I hit perhaps in the engine, for he went down about 10,000 feet out of control, then, so someone else says, leveled out. But I hardly think he'd have gone down so far if not hit. That is the trouble fighting so far over the doggone lines, one can't always be sure, and you are usually too busy to see if a fellow crashes after a long dive or not.

I've got a slick flight now, and am awfully sorry I'll probably have to leave here soon. There are only three of us just now—the others are away and so we usually borrow a couple more from some other flight, but when we three are out we certainly have a great time. Coming home, if we haven't separated, we practice formation flying, till now we come along the beach and over the aerodrome practically wing to wing. We always take off in formation and to-morrow are going to try landing in formation,—tho' the field is pretty small to do that.

Of course there is lots of rivalry among flights in getting Huns, and ours is ahead now. The balloon was also a help. Did I tell you that a day or so ago I saw Ken Smith, haven't seen him for a long time, you remember he was one of seven of us who came over together. It was great to see him again. I received three letters from you and one from Anne [sister] yesterday. One was July 27 and the others August 27 and 29. Funny how the mail arrives, isn't it? With Love, Dave

September 21, 1918. Nothing doing. Went into "A" mess for dinner Sunday night. Heard that I may be able to stay on here for a bit. Cheers.

September 23, 1918. Also dud. Di came out for lunch, and I went with him, George [Moseley], and Freddie [Beach] to Boulogne and saw Adelaide Sedgewick and got her to come tomorrow to the big dance. Stopped at St. Inglevert and saw Bob Lovett and Lt. McDonnell. Arrived late at "A" mess and had dinner 9:30. Then Shorty and Doc drove me out in a Ford. I find that "A" Flight had a scrap after lunch and got one or more. I hate to have missed it. Most everyone is at 44 C.C.S. for concert. Brown came back at noon, it is great to see him again, he is a mighty good fellow. Tonight there is an air raid on.

September 24, 1918. This morning the weather was dud, and no work. I took a little trip to keep in practice and stunted around a little. After lunch we started off on a regular patrol; it had cleared up a good deal. No sooner had we got to the lines than we saw about 12 Fokkers. They weren't all together, though, so down went the five of us on the seven that were nearest. Had a slick scrap. Brown got two, Hodson one. I got several bursts at one after another and heard some shooting at me but no hits. Funny how hard it is to hit anything. I saw a Fokker diving after Smithy, so I followed trying to scare him from long range. Finally he pulled off and spun, but I don't think I got him. When I finally got out of range I was almost down to the ground and had nothing to do but contour chase home over German land and lines. Scrap just over Nieuport.

After tea, feeling sore, I went out with Hodson. Went from the office to the hangar and got aboard our machines again . . . to look for a two-seater spotting or photographing. This was the closest shave I had, wherefore it is interesting to me. Everything seemed as usual. We flew along the lines at 21,500 [15,000] feet for an hour without seeing a thing, and then I heard Hodson shoot; I looked around and he waved in disgust, turned and started for home. I turned north and dove down parallel to the lines for one last look in the growing dusk. Arriving back I saw a lot of Archie over La Panne and on going in saw a two-seater.

I shot my guns in hopes Hodson could see or hear me and dove for the bursts. I kept looking for my partner. Hodson finally woke up and started, too, but at some distance behind. The Hun was an old Rumpler, the slowest I ever saw, and he just kept on. I opened up and caught up over lines, got under him and hoicked up, but had too much speed. I tried it three times, one time being just unable to fire and seeing the observer plainly shooting away but I was just out of range. On a turn he very nearly got me, for before I could make the outside circle his observer fired probably ten shots, the tracers all going between the struts on the left side. We were only ten yards off at the time and I could see the two Huns perfectly in their black helmets, and it was rather fascinating to be so close. All the time we were getting further over the lines, and I was getting madder. So I gave up the careful, cautious tactics, got straight behind him, and kept firing for probably 100 rounds. Finally I got up nicely and had a good burst at about 25 yards. I saw a big flash and turned and dove down south of Ostend to ground, saw Hun go into spin.

Hodson confirmed later that he finally burst into flames. I got to about 50 ft. [near Ostend] and chased for home. The only danger in this low flying is from the ground machine guns. The Huns had these scattered all over their country to get aeroplanes in similar predicaments. I knew fairly well where they were thickest and went along for about five minutes without a shot. But I passed a machine gun close and heard one burst and the engine stopped and elevators wouldn't pull back. Gas poured out of the tank below the seat and clouds of white vapor rose from it. I switched to gravity [tank] being considerably disconcerted. The machine was headed down and I couldn't get it out. Finally it came out just over the ground, as my machine is tail heavy,[41] and I missed the trees by inches. I found that the wires to go down were O.K., and that the rudder worked, but the ailerons answered very weakly. I couldn't split-ass crossing the lines, and so felt damned uncomfortable every time I heard a machine gun. Evidently I had run into a bad place for I was shot at until I crossed the lines. Usually one turns, zooms, etc., when in this predicament, but I expected the rest of the controls to go at any second, so I sat still and using the rudder kept going as fast as possible in little turns towards home. Finally I got over the lines, engine hitting on about five cylinders. Felt more than a little relieved. Then I had to land. I didn't dare go up high, but flew low down experimenting with the machine and seeing just what I could do. When I reached the aerodrome I came in slowly over the trees on the side. Came down finally and landed without crashing, by using motor. Found numerous holes right under my seat. One burst of several bullets had perforated the tank under my seat, and the one upper flipper

---

41. In level flight at low altitude, the Sopwith Camel exhibited a tendency for the nose to rise and the tail to sink, thus being "tail heavy." Correcting this situation required the pilot to exert continual forward pressure on the stick, forcing the nose down.

was cut away, the other all cut but one strand. One aileron had been hit at a hinge, and of course there were a few holes in the wings. Might say—a damn close shave. Hodson had returned. He said that he had been back of and above me and had fired from there and had seen one Hun burst into flames and crash.[42] So we felt fine, and I got a new machine next day.

I began to think I had bad nerves, as I couldn't seem to think of anything else for an hour or two, but went to the dance at Terminus and was *bon* after a few minutes. We had a great time. Miss Johnson, and Adelaide Sedgewick were there. Di took Adelaide home to Boulogne with C.O., returning at 7:30 A.M.

———

Official Squadron Report, September 24, 1918: At 11:45 when over Coukelaere (Koekelare) and Thourout (Torhout) at 16,000, observed 12 Fokker Biplanes at same height. Camels attacked and dogfight ensued. Captain Brown engaged one E.A. at point blank range and after firing a few rounds E.A.'s wings folded up and machine crashed. Second E.A. then attacked and when at 200 feet, one mile S.W. of Thourout Captain Brown after firing 40 rounds, observed E.A. to dive steeply and crash into some trees. Lieut. Ingalls mean time succeeded in driving off E.A. from tail of Lieut. Smith, who was attacked at close range and shot through the petrol tank. Lieut. Hodson then engaged another E.A. at close range and drove it down, presumably out of control, but was unable to follow it down because a further E.A. attacked him. Lieut. Hodson fired about 70 rounds and E.A. then turned on its back and crashed in road about one mile west of Mitswege.

———

RAF Flight Report, September 24, 1918: HOP at 1350, Camel D.9649, twelve Fokkers engaged at 1445 between Coukelaere and Thourout. Two crashed by Brown, one crashed out of control by Hodson. Ingalls drove EA off tail of HC Smith, who had been shot in gas tank. Remarks on Hostile Aircraft:

---

42. Ingalls was credited with a victory over a Rumpler C near St. Pierre Cappele at 5:30 PM while flying Camel D9649. He shared the victory with Hodson. The word spread quickly to other members of the Yale Unit. MacLeish noted on September 27, "Dave Ingalls got another Hun. That makes three Huns and two balloons. Isn't he the luckiest stiff who ever lived?" Quoted in Rossano, *Price of Honor,* 218.

Fokker biplanes, Painted dark grey patches, and one white band 'round fuselage, with plain crosses, one had white tail.

———

Later September 24, 1918: Test flight, 1645, Camel D.9649, w/Hodson, encountered Rumpler over Nieuport at 1730, shot it down, landed 1800.

———

Official Squadron Report, September 24, 1918: At 1730 when at 13,000 feet observed EA over Nieuport steering due east. Camels pursued and engaged over St. Pierre Capelle (Sint-Pieters-Kapelle). Lt. Ingalls USNRF fired 200 rounds at 100 yards range. Lt. Hodson 100 rounds at 200 yards range. Both pilots followed EA down to 6,000 feet when machine was observed to fall in flames.

———

Official Squadron Report, September 24, 1918: Sighted one E.A. going w. at 6,000 feet from Nieuport. Two Camels turned in from Nieuport and attacked. E.A. turned and dived towards St. Pierre Capelle, Lieut. Ingalls fired about 400 rounds from 50 to 200 yards range, following E.A. down to 500 feet just east of—. E.A. went down apparently out of control and finally burst into flames and crashed just off Ostend. (Confirmed in flames.)

———

September 25, 1918. Dud day. Flew over to Wissant and dined with Slatter.[43] C.O. and Brown came. Then stopped at St. Inglevert and saw Bob [Lovett], Harry, etc. Also Loot [McDonnell]. Left after tea and stunted a bit. Flew back over Oye. Arrived here to find four fellows missing. Lots of others out lately. Spark[e]s, Iliff, Scroggie, and Sorley.[44] Damn good fellows, especially old Sparks. Hell of a note.

———

43. Wissant was situated on the Channel coast, about ten miles southwest of Calais and near the No.4 ASD (Aviation Squadron Depot—RAF pilot pool) at Audembert.

44. The four pilots mentioned included Lt. G. Iliff, who served from August 24, 1918, to September 29, 1918, before being reported as missing in action (MIA); Lt. L. C. Scroggie, who served from August 5, 1918, to September 25, 1918, MIA; Lt. C. P. Sparkes, who served from May 26, 1918, to September 25, 1918, MIA; and 2nd Lt. J. C. Sorley, who served from August 23, 1918, to September 25, 1918, MIA. See Leeson, *Hornet Strikes,* 201.

RAF Flight Report, September 25, 1918: flew Camel D.3341 to No.4 A.S.D. at 1150, landed at 1220, accompanied by Graham and Brown, departed at 1745, landed 1815.

September 26, 1918

Dear Dad:

Lots of social activity up here just now. Night before last the C.O. gave a great dance. There were three American girls here and we had a great time. Also, to be sure, there were a lot of British nurses and a French girl, but I have sworn off dancing with either of the last two nationalities. It's physically impossible. On the afternoon of that day five of us attacked seven Huns and got three crashed. I unfortunately didn't prove a thing, as at the beginning I saw a Hun diving down on one of our fellow's tail, and drove him off by long range shooting. The Hun spun away and I was by that time out of the scrap, but Smithy got away all right.

After tea, being a little sore at everyone else shooting down Huns and me not, I went out with another fellow, saw a two-seater, chased him over the lines and got him in flames. But as it was a long way over and low I had to contour-chase back, and was shot up by a land machine gun. So my dear old machine has been scrapped, and I have a brand new one. Yesterday the C.O., Brown, and I flew over to the American station about twenty miles from here, had lunch and tea, and did a few stunts for them, and returned to find that four of our fellows are missing after a Hell of a big scrap. Mighty bad luck; our lads got only three Huns out of it. Tea is ready, so Cheerio! Aff. Dave

September 27, 1918. High offensive patrol in morning and a defensive patrol in the afternoon. I am beginning to believe the Huns know when we are going out and remain at home. After lunch a report came in that there were Huns over Bergues, so we all went out hot-foot. Of course there weren't any Huns at all. I think it was just a subterfuge. Had tea with Joe. Push is on. Got a big talk by C.O. We are to do bombing and shooting up.[45]

September 28, 1918. Four bad pieces of business. I feel just like before a football game when we start. And also it is sort of like a call on the dentist before you go. After the start it is **bon**. At the most ungodly hour the batman called Brown and me. It was still pitch dark, raining, and a strong wind was blowing. So it was a quiet bunch rode over to the aerodrome in the British lorries. The only decent thing was breakfast, breakfast and the irrepressible spirits of [Flight Sub-lieutenant M. L.] Cooper,[46] the young Irishman who hated the Huns with a most exceptional vigor. Cooper got a kick out of ordinary patrols. He had several Huns to his credit, but his contentment was complete only when bombing and shooting up Huns. There was of course more execution thus. The only other one I knew that in any way approached his queer slant was the C.O., who seldom flew on patrol, but always went on any stunt connected with bombing.

By the time we had finished our breakfast it was light enough to fly and we adjourned to the hangars. The ordnance officer was roaring around seeing that the bombs were all O.K. Cooper insisted on carrying Buckingham tracers for his guns. They were forbidden by an unwritten law, as they were an incendiary bullet and could set fire to anything they hit. Of course we all accused the Huns of using them, but I don't think anyone made a practice

45. On four successive days at the end of September, the combined Allied armies launched assaults against German forces along much of the Western Front, from the Meuse-Argonne to the English Channel. In Ingalls's sector, the Army Group of Flanders—commanded by King Albert of Belgium and consisting of twelve Belgian, ten British, and six French divisions—attacked German defenses around Ypres on September 28, quickly breaking through the enemy lines. In four days, the troops advanced eight miles. The action continued throughout October, as the Allies cleared the coast and liberated much of western Belgium. As many as five hundred Allied aircraft participated in the opening phases of the battle. See Gilbert, *First World War,* 466, 468, 480. Ingalls's diary entries and letters for the period September 28–October 4, 1918, document his activities during this phase of the Allied assault.

46. Capt. M. L. Cooper joined the squadron on November 7, 1917, from No.9 Squadron, RNAS, and served until he was killed in action in early October. See Leeson, *Hornet Strikes,* 200.

of it, and anyone caught by the enemy with his ammunition belt might as well say his prayers quickly. Of course they were used for balloon strafing and might be excused for much work as we were to do. But none followed Cooper's example.

We took off in three flights and climbed rapidly to 4,000 feet, straight for the lines in the general direction of Thourout. As we approached the lines we dove gently, leveling off at 500 feet just beyond the trenches, having been shot at only a little from the ground. Then some Archie exploded near us and we dropped to about 100 feet. The Huns seldom Archied us that low, as it was likely to do as much damage to their own side as to us. As we tore along every few seconds a machine gun opening upon us from the ground made us zigzag and zoom along, but the weather was so bad it helped us. We bombed roads to Thourout and Dixmude mostly. In morning it was cloudy and we caught an artillery squadron, bombed and shot it up a lot. Over the road went our leader and I straightened out my plane on the line with the wide road stretching between rows of trees. A few seconds and I grabbed my bomb pull, having slowed down as much as possible. Figuring as I had when throwing a stone from the train, I took aim and pulled my lever rapidly four times. Wonk, wonk, wonk, wonk, and I hoicked off to the right, circled, and dove firing at the mess of men, guns, horses, and caissons. Two teams of four horses each ran terrified along the road for several hundred feet, finally catching their caissons and piling up together. The captain of the battery, on a white horse, his coat tails and sword flying out, galloped back down the road, pursued by our C.O. shooting continuously. Finally the horse was hit, and the Captain took a head in the ditch. The C.O. banked around the tree to see what he could see and as he did so the Captain picked up a rock and hurled it up. It caught the end of the C.O.'s wing and tore an enormous hole. Imagine stoning an aeroplane. Back to the stone age versus an aeroplane.

Four or five times I dove firing, hoicked back and repeated. The place was a mass of confusion. It seemed as though the battery was totally destroyed with the exception of one plucky devil who had guts. He had somehow unhitched a team of horses

and led them to one side of the road in the field, where he stood
at their heads quieting them, a perfect target for anyone. He was
not shot at. That fellow was on the wrong side in this war.

And then I noticed some Very lights, which were fired by the
C.O. to designate the time to return. I turned for home, observing
Camels scattered about, all heading the same way. It was hard
to see much due to the rain and mist. The clouds were near the
ground. Suddenly I saw a Fokker dive down from the mist on one
of my buddies to the right. I opened up wide and headed for the
Hun, hoping to save the Camel and get a Hun. The Camel soon
saw the Hun and began to zigzag and I caught up, got behind
the Hun only a few yards off and pushed the trigger. Nothing
happened. Cursing, I reloaded, got my sight on him again, and
pushed the trigger. Again nothing. "Hell," thinks I, "out of
ammunition, of all the terrible luck." And then the Hun happened
to notice me behind him. Down he went to one side, probably
scared to death, and I had to laugh. But it was not so nice. The
Camel ahead disappeared in the mist and I had no means of
fighting and was a long way over the lines. So I went up into the
clouds, figuring on flying there by compass out of sight till beyond
the lines. So I proceeded for some 10 minutes at about 80 miles an
hour, then, not knowing where I was, I came down to take a look.
Damned if I wasn't over the same old place, and I realized I was
bucking a head wind almost as strong as my plane and I wondered
how I'd get back. If I stayed in the clouds I'd lose ground because
I couldn't fly straight enough by compass to gain on the wind.
So I stayed just under the clouds, seemingly creeping towards
the lines. That was, to me, the longest flight in my experience.
It seemed as though I'd never reach the lines. But all things end
and I dove down over the lines to gain speed and avoid the ground
shooting and then made for home just above the ground where the
wind was not so strong and the plane goes the fastest.

Upon our return we reported and then found another and
larger breakfast to which we applied ourselves with considerable
enthusiasm and agreed one with another that it hadn't been
half bad. As soon as we were through the C.O. ordered out all
whose machines were O.K. Several had been shot up and needed

repairs. Later we bombed the railroad station at Thourout. It was much the same as earlier, only the Huns were all awake and they had prepared more machine gun posts all over the ground to guard against us, so we were shot at a lot more. I dropped my bombs on the yards outside the town, shot some at different trains and returned.

We had lunch and set off again, fewer in number, for Wercken (Werken).[47] There were supposed to be a lot of Huns quartered there, and we aimed for the barracks, busting them up, and then shooting the place up generally. About the only difference on this trip was the obnoxious presence of more of those damned machine guns.

Back for tea and then off again. Only about seven or eight of 18 made this trip. We had lost one or two men; the other planes were shot up beyond use. This time we found a transport train east of Wercken, of which we made some mess. Although we were but few, we were becoming more proficient with our bombs and they were indeed deadly. When we left horses and crew were piled up three or four deep. And trucks, etc., were all overturned and busted. But this is a Hell of a business. I was pretty badly shot up again. The last time by machine gun. Wonder how long it will last. They seem to be pushing on in the lines.

Supper was one Hell of a meal. One day of this sort of work was enough even for Cooper and most of the men felt, "My God, how long will this last; about one more day and our squadron will be a thing of the past."[48]

—•—

47. Wercken, a village located a few miles behind the German lines, stands midway between Dixmude and Kortmarke.

48. During the September–October offensive in Belgium, the Allies made extensive use of aircraft carrying out ground support missions. Everywhere along the front, aviation units assailed withdrawing German troops and supply columns, usually at very low altitudes, exposing the pilots and their fragile machines to intense ground and antiaircraft fire. According to both contemporary accounts and later analysis, many pilots "reviled" such missions. Even the normally ebullient Ingalls found himself worn down by these dangerous, low-level assaults. Despite mounting casualties, these attacks continued without letup until the end of the war.

RAF Flight Report, September 28, 1918: launched ground attack raid at 0530 in support of Belgian army attack towards Dixmude, Ingalls flew four sorties, all in Camel F. 3239:

First sortie: 0815–0930, four Cooper bombs; Bombs dropped on camouflaged camp at Pralt Bosch, which was damaged. Three ammunition wagons destroyed. Direct hits on two field guns. About thirty horses stampeded on Cortemarck (Kortemark)-Thourout Road and many men and horses killed. Bombed and shot up large battery around a chateau at Cortemarck. Two machines chased back by two Fokker biplanes, but could not attack, having no ammunition left. Camel hit by M.G. fire, but not badly damaged;

Second sortie: 1130–1300, Dropped bombs on billet at Wercken. Two direct hits on lorries, five direct hits on Thourout railway station. M.G. emplacements and A.A. guns, shot up Pralt Bosch. Considerable transport activity between Wercken and Zaaren (Zarren). Machines slightly damaged by M.G. fire;

Third sortie: 1430–1525, Bombed from 100 to 400 feet. Large fire observed burning at Cortemarck. Bombed and shot up ammunition hut which caught fire north of Wercken. Direct hit on M.G. emplacement. Bombed and shot up four wagons loading up, one bolted. Camels shot up and damaged slightly;

Fourth sortie, 1720–1815, No troops visible on Gits-Hooglede Road. Bombed ten wagons on side road 3 miles NW of Gits. Obtained direct hit on barn with troops inside. Bombed and shot up 12 horse transport and killed about 25 men and 35 horses. Nothing left standing; Total squadron 185 bombs, 6,000 rounds.

Official Squadron Summary, September 28, 1918: 4 Low Bomb Raids. (1) Dropped 4 bombs on ammunition wagons at Pralt Bosch causing considerable damage. (2) Dropped 4 bombs on Thourout railway station. Two direct hits. (3) Dropped 4 bombs on and shot up ammunition hut at Wercken causing fire to break out. (4) Dropped 4 bombs and shot up horse transport 3 miles N.W. of Gits. In conjunction with four others succeeded in killing about 25 men and 35 horses.

⎯⎯

September 29, 1918. To our surprise we were not called early, and to our delight at breakfast we were ordered to get ready for an escort job—day bombers beyond Dixmude. Thank goodness for something besides these damned low bombing trips. They sort of get on one's nerves. What a pleasure it was to be high above all the damned machine guns. Nothing dangerous to do, simply fly along and see 202 Squadron wasn't shot down. And the Archie's gentle "wonk wonk" near by didn't even remotely resemble the spiteful sharp crackle of ground machine guns with their tracers flashing first on one side, then the other.

After lunch it rained, but we went on low bombing. About 12 of us slid across the trenches and dove on Gits, dropping our bombs on the outskirts and shooting up a bit. I last, due to motor trouble. Went alone to St. Michel (Sint Michiels)—south of Bruges.[49] Archie was bad, came down to only 4,000 feet, clouds from 6—8. Came back above to Ostend. Very pretty. When I landed I found the chief mechanic on an inspection tour of my dear "Norma," the old girl was a ragged wreck, holes through almost every part of her, and the chief says: "Sir, I don't see quite 'ow it can be patched sufficiently." So I reported another machine washed out. Rather tired tonight. Lots of rain too.

⎯⎯

RAF Flight Report, September 29, 1918: HOP w/202 Squadron at 1015, Camel F.3239, landed 1220, Brown left patrol w/engine trouble; evening low bomb raid on Gits, took off 1700, Camel F. 3239, w/17 other Camels, landed 1835, 30 minutes after others. Could not find formation, dropped bombs on camp at St. Michel. All planes dropped 61 bombs and 3,200 rounds.

⎯⎯

49. Though Ingalls mentioned the rain only occasionally, wet weather delayed the Allied advance in Flanders by turning the already poor road system into rivers of mud. Gits, a small Belgian town north of Roeselare and south of Thourout, stood astride a principal railway line. St. Michel lay just southwest of Bruges, also on the railway line.

Official Squadron Summary, September 29, 1918: Low Bomb Raid. Dropped
4 bombs and obtained direct hits on large camp at St. Michel.

⸺

September 30, 1918. Vacation time for me, along with the others
whose machines were washed out. The losses had been so heavy
the first two days that the depots couldn't fill up the squadrons
with either machines or pilots. Played bridge, and dined at
seaplanes [NAS Dunkirk?] with Greene and Brown. Eddie
DeCernea left for States. Several of us were sent off finally to
the nearest depot, as there were no ferry pilots at all to bring the
machines to the front. We were lucky enough to be outfitted and
flew home and turned the new ships over to the mechanics. The
poor devils are probably still putting on the finishing touches,
calibrating the compasses, synchronizing the guns, etc.[50]

October 1, 1918. No rest for the wicked. Before daybreak we
were called, had some coffee and bread, set off again to strafe.
Everyone expects each trip to be the final one for him. Funny
what different fellows take along in case they aren't killed,
only shot down and taken prisoner. One folds his girl's photo in
his breast pocket, another has gold pieces sewn in his clothes,
another a razor, another a toothbrush. I figured to Hell with the
stuff, you couldn't fool the Devil's habitat for any appreciable
length of time by taking along a few lumps of ice, so I just stuck a
box of cartridges in my pocket for the little .32 caliber automatic
I have always carried. The gun is to me my rabbit's foot. I've
gotten so I'd come back from a trip if I didn't have it along. Ever
since I realized how helpless an aviator is when his plane lands,

---

50. Edward DeCernea, a member of the Second Yale Unit, conducted an early
evening test flight of a DD flying boat near Dunkirk on August 14, 1918. The aircraft
crashed, and DeCernea suffered serious injuries, including a broken back. He later
returned to the United States to recuperate. His observer, Harry Laven, died in the
hospital from injuries sustained in the accident. Ferry pilots flew aircraft from various
depots or assembly and repair facilities to frontline aerodromes in northern France.
Ingalls's flight time for September included 45 hours, 55 minutes of combat missions
and 4 hours, 15 minutes of test hops.

which I realized when my plane landed in the North Sea, I've felt better with a separate gun. And I don't like to be helpless.

Started out with low bombing on Smith's machine as he had taken mine. Well, we came down over Hunland and took an awful while trying to find something worth shooting, and finally did locate a horse transport. We were all good shots by now with our bombs and when we left for home the road was covered for some distance with horses and men but none were moving. It was not a pleasant sight, particularly on an empty stomach, necessary perhaps but nauseating.

A brief respite and off again, this time to take care of some troops reported to be advancing to the front. We were able to get together three flights of four each for this trip, and I led my flight off to the right of Greene's.[51] He was to lead the squadron. He got off and climbed to 4,000 feet, coasted along, and then I saw Greene lead his flight down. "Too soon," thinks I. "We can't be over the new lines yet," I pondered. Very clearly we could all see a long line of troops marching due east on one of the roads through the sort of swamps abounding there. It looked like a column of eight men abreast and extended probably a mile. To my amazement Greene headed for it. "They must be Belgians," I thought, though I didn't know. Down he went and I followed him a while and then decided, "To Hell with it. They must be our men, they see us and don't run, we've not got over the lines." So I swung off and paralleled the road watching Greene and the other two flights. They did a good job of it and the troops scattered, many of them too late. "Probably I'm wrong," thinks I, "but any how!" And I led my boys some miles further east and then down. The ground machine guns assured me of where I was and we picked a village and raised Hell there and came home. Then we had a good row over what Greene had bombed for a while, till suddenly the C.O. came in with a message from headquarters that the Belgians had reported

---

51. Captain Greene was shot down on October 4 but survived. He was shot down again on October 14 and killed. His career and death are detailed in O'Connor, *Airfields and Airmen of the Channel Coast*, 116–17.

an attack by Allied machines, Camels. Then there was some consternation, but no more talk, and our C.O. reported as all other C.O.s, and headquarters advised the Belgians of course the British would not shoot them up and they must be nuts. *Ce la guerre,* but we were more careful thereafter.[52]

Everyone is fed up with this low stuff; Graham is full out for it. 210, 204 [Squadrons] do it from about 5 or 6,000 feet. And if that hadn't been enough, after lunch the C.O. issued orders for the Squadron to go over Lugenboom and bomb and shoot her up. This is the long distance girl who fires into Dunkirk from 15 miles over the lines. Well, we were becoming fewer and fewer just from ordinary strafing. How the others felt I didn't know. How I felt I do, just the same as when a kid I had to go to the dentist. My God, what an aversion I had developed towards this damned strafing. It just didn't appeal. Nothing about it appealed, no competition; either someone was shooting at me and I dodging, or I shooting at somebody and somebody dodging. Really dirty work, both ways, and not my idea of sport. But now to go 15 miles into Hunland in the middle of the day with about eight or ten machines, come down to 100 feet, try to find one camouflaged gun and bomb it. Well, there were no clouds and three strong arguments against us—Archie, the ground machine guns, and the Hun planes flying around. We knew we would be reported as soon as we neared the lines, and the Huns had plenty of time to ensure a hot reception.

It looked to us like pure damn foolishness, nothing to be gained and certain termination for all of us. Greene was to lead and I went to him and says, "This is bunk, we can't get there even if we knew where to go, and can't do any damage to the cannon with our little bombs if we hit the darned thing." And Greene says, "You're right." And we set off. I was just damn sore at the idiocy of it all and led my flight of three behind Greene. I didn't know where Lugenboom was except in a general way.

---

52. In his diary, Ingalls recorded, "The last time Greene leading bombed French troops [friendly fire], I was leading "C" [flight] and bombed some Huns near Gits. But it was a Hell of a mix-up."

We started off as usual and dove down over Hunland and tore along for a while. I realized most of our bunch had dropped out, engine trouble maybe. We were shot at continually, Archie and machine guns, but what kept me twisting and turning in my seat was possible Huns coming down from above. I paid attention to nothing else. And then suddenly I saw Greene dive further and let his bombs go. I could see nothing but a clump of trees, but followed suit as did the rest, and I thought, "I know damn well we couldn't have gotten far enough to be over Lugenboom, but this suits me O.K." I seemed to see more joy in life as we raced homeward. Greene made out a joint report for all, what it was I don't know, but I'm not sure what we bombed and don't give a damn, but I'd give odds we never got near our old friend Lugenboom, and I'm conceited enough to think I generally know where I am over this part of the world.

Dinner was certainly O.K. tonight, sort of unexpected, to be honest. Graham gave a talk after supper and he is sore as the deuce. It's all right to do these low stunts once in a while, but three or four a day every day certainly affect one's nerves. If we keep it up long, the ones left will be too nervous to do anything at all. For example, take the bombing of our own troops. I'm not surprised. It'll probably happen again if we keep on.

———

RAF Flight Report, October 1, 1918: bombing sortie, 1100–1155, Camel D.3378, eight Camels.

———

Official Squadron Summary, October 1, 1918: 3 Low Bomb Raids. (1) Dropped 4 bombs on two trains at Lichtervelde railway station and caused considerable damage by shooting up horse transport in the vicinity. (2) Dropped 4 bombs on barn where about 200 troops had taken shelter. 1 direct hit and fire started. (3) Dropped 4 bombs, 1 on dump SE of Hooglede and others at horse transport; also fired about 200 yards at same;

———

First sortie: Two direct hits on goods train at the station (Lichtervelde railway junction). Shot up and bombed ten wagons (horse transport). Two trains at

Lichtervelde proceeding West. One train (on loop line) stationary without engine. Fifty goods trucks on siding. One train with horses standing alongside also shot up. The bombs all fell in close proximity to objects mentioned;

Second sortie: Camel F.3239, 19 Camels, returned 1410, attack directed at traffic congestion in village northeast of Cortemarck and also convoy at Wynendaele (Wijnendale) crossroads. Dropped about 12 bombs on Cortemarck and branch line near Helle, where considerable machine gun fire was experienced: two machines being hit and badly damaged. Two bombs at, and shot up, huts containing machine gun. No direct hits observed. Nine bombs (including one 112 lb bomb) on motor and horse transport one and a half miles long at cross roads at Wynendaele. Did not shoot up as Camels observed six machines above. Nationality unknown. 111-lb. bomb dropped immediately in front of a chateau and caused considerable damage to transport. Six horse transport in side road under trees were shot up. Ten bombs in farmyard with 12 horse transport in it. Direct hit on barn where about 200 men had taken shelter, and three other bobs within 15 yards. Fire started at cottage containing machine guns. Big fire observed at Roulers (Roeselare). About six bombs were observed to fall in ploughed field;

Third sortie: 1600–1724, 15 Camels, Camel F. 3239, Ingalls dropped bombs from 200 feet. "Nine bombs on dump one mile SE of Hooglede. Two dropped on Hooglede village. Nine on houses containing troops, one on railway and three on horse vehicles stationary in a farmyard. These targets were also shot up.

October 2, 1918. Fairly dud. Lord, but it was dark when we were called today. It was for another strafe, but nobody minds these first trips. If there is any fun in this strafing, it comes on the early morning trip. The Huns are still asleep; one isn't shot at much, and one generally feels that something is accomplished.

Started off leaving 6:30 A.M. We dove across the lines and sped along looking for a target. The C.O. was with us and bombed southeast of Roulers on a farm with two big guns and five ammunition lorries on road under trees.[53] Down we went and I pulled my lever and saw the bomb hit the roof. I was second in the row. As I hoicked about I saw Huns running from the house for the trees and dove firing at them with some success. Then I hoicked again and came down over the gun, pulling my lever and dropping a bomb along side it. Then we circled around to go home. I was off to one side and noticed another farm, took aim, and plunked it. More Huns ran and I circled and dropped another before tearing after the squadron. I got one hit on road near lorries, two on two farmhouses and one next to one big gun. It wasn't bad at all. There is a lot of satisfaction in seeing your bomb hit what you aim at, and these little bombs made a great fuss when they hit. Incidentally, we have never lost a man on one of these early morning strafes, and it's only later that it is not so good for us.

After lunch we had one more trip, but this time we confined our attention to the Hun trenches. Of course, you can't see what damage is done so these trips aren't so certainly successful. Dud afternoon. C.O. and I took side car to "A" mess at Rossendale after tea. Mighty hard luck about Cooper. Cooper, just over a train, hoicked up and then spun right onto train from about 200 feet with bombs still on. Evidently shot, probably in stomach. No hope for him, at all. Nothing was left but a little pile of pieces, and nobody rose from the wreck, not mortally anyhow. Somehow it struck everybody differently than the others we've lost. He was so wrapped up in this damned strafing, seemed to love it. This makes nine men out of 24 in about six days. Also about 25 machines have been used up. This bombing down low is certainly unadulterated hell. Later we went again, but it was all clear, we were supposed to go to the railroad bridge over the canal southwest of Ostend but saw Huns over Ostend so dropped bombs just over lines near Lichtervelde at 4,000 ft. and came back.[54]

---

53. Roulers, a town in Belgian Flanders, was located just behind the front lines, ten miles south of Thourout and about thirteen miles northwest of Courtrai.

54. Lichtervelde is a small Flanders town located a few miles south of Thourout.

When we got back, to my sorrow the C.O. called me in and advised me I was to be relieved and sent to England. Ken MacLeish was to take my place. Of course, I had been expecting something like this for a couple of weeks, as it was then that Capt. Hanrahan, our C.O., had called me up and asked if I had had enough. I had told him, "Hell, no!" but knew that things weren't quite so rosy for my future.

RAF Flight Report, October 2, 1918: First sortie: raid 0530–0650, Camel F.3239, thirteen Camels. Bombed and shot up about six lorries and twelve horse wagons observed on roads which all scattered. Under trees five lorries and wagons, loaded, were bombed and shot up and considerable damage done. Direct hits on two farmhouses and fires started. Transport in yard bombed and shot up. Three direct hits on houses containing troops and one bomb fell in a trench containing troops. Two big guns under trees were bombed and one fell within ten yards and several of crew killed. Big fire observed at Cortemarck and it was noticed that Lichtervelde station and railway had been badly knocked about in recent raids. One train at Lichtervelde station stationary, pointing east with steam up;

Second sortie: 1000–1100, Camel F.3239, Dropped on 12 horse transport at crossroads near St. Pierre Capelle and Zevecote. Target well straddled but no results observed.

Official Squadron Summary, October 2, 1918: Two Low Bomb Raids. (1) Dropped 4 bombs. Set fire to farm (with troops inside) and shot up and bombed two large guns in same locality, killing several of the crew. (2) Dropped 4 bombs at horse transport near St. Pierre Capelle and Zevecote.

October 2, 1918

Dear Dad,

The padre has just arrived for tea. He is a mighty good fellow and just now is laughing like an ordinary man at the C.O.'s repeating an American expression I used the other day—which seems to have become rather popular—when I told some fellow he might "Kiss my royal American Ass." You are probably aware that there is in this God-forsaken country a Push going on. Well, I would push pretty hard to get out of here myself. A Push makes everything different. We are now bombing and shooting up stuff behind the lines. I've never had my fill of flying before. But since they started we've been on the ground only long enough to eat and sleep in any weather. Lots of most amusing things happen even in war. For instance, one raid, the C.O. was chasing a poor beggar down the road on a bicycle shooting at him, when the bloke dodged behind a wall. When the C.O. banked around to see where he had gone, the fellow up and threw a big brick making a tremendous hole in one plane [wing]. Imagine a man stoning an aeroplane. Another time we bombed an artillery column and one fellow saw the Major in charge galloping down the road at full speed. He chased him almost a mile, shooting at him all the time until finally he hit the horse and the gallant Major flew about 20 feet in the air and lit on his bean in a ditch full of water alongside the road, probably soiling his tunic. Honestly Dad you should see men and horses run. We had one chariot race even when two teams of four each, with no drivers, with their guns tore down the road, only to crash furiously. Must now have my tea, Pops, so *au revoir*. Aff. Dave

October 3, 1918. This morning Hanrahan called up and said I was to be detached. Ken [MacLeish] to take my place and I had a slick ride after parking, stunted all around. Left after lunch, very sorry to go. It is certainly tough leaving and my future occupation I suppose will be behind a desk, or preparing more fields for the Marines to fly off of. Saw Joe and Shorty and I went out to squadron for dinner. Well, the C.O. reported the news to one and all and we had a farewell dinner. The C.O. made a darn nice speech to which I replied. There was plenty of liquor, which helped me through the bum speech and we got to bed somehow.

About all I remember is that Di came out and brought some American girl from the hospital.[55]

—

RAF Flight Report, October 3, 1918: test flight, 1110–1140, Camel F.3239.

—

Ingalls Fitness Report 5 July to 30 September 1918

His keenness, courage, and utter disregard of danger are exceptional and are an example to all. He is one of the finest men this squadron ever had.

Major Ronald Graham, Commanding Officer,
No.213 Squadron, Royal Air Force.

—

A most excellent officer and exceptionally good pilot. Good knowledge of aeronautics. Has been attached temporarily to 213 Squad., R.A.F., a British fighting squadron, since Aug. 15th and there has made an enviable record. His work has been spoken mostly highly of by the squadron commander, Major R. Graham.

---

55. His total flight time for October was 5 hours, 50 minutes of combat and 30 minutes of tests/other.

In late May 1918 Ingalls passed through Paris on his way to the U.S. Army bombing school at Clermont-Ferrand. He spent two days socializing, sightseeing, and having his picture taken. The seated figure on the left is his friend John T. "Skinny" Lawrence, serving in the American Field Artillery. Years later Lawrence's son married Ingalls's daughter. The other was "a fellow named Nash who I ran into in Paris." *Courtesy Peter B. Mersky Collection*

In the late spring of 1918 the U.S. Navy created a unit known as the Northern Bombing Group for the purpose of attacking German submarine bases in Belgium. Dave Ingalls volunteered for this duty and was sent to the U.S. Army bombing school at Clermont-Ferrand for instruction. There he learned to fly the Breguet 14B.2, shown here. Never shy about offering an opinion, Ingalls described it as having "no power, clumsy, awkward, rotten." *Courtesy National Archives*

At Clermont, Ingalls was paired with observer/machine gunner Randall R. Browne, a member of the First Aeronautic Detachment that had arrived in France in June 1917. Browne first trained in France and England and then flew at Dunkirk. Ingalls said of his fellow crewman, "He is a great fellow, a little bit of humanity with a good homely face, scared of nothing—not even of having me as a pilot, and a remarkable shot." *Courtesy Naval History and Heritage Command*

After finishing up at Clermont (and enduring a bout with the flu) Ingalls and several other U.S. Navy crews joined No.218 Squadron, RAF, utilizing DH9 day bombers to attack a variety of targets behind the front lines in Belgium. The DH9 was a rather inferior replacement for the DH4 day bomber, with modest speed, an unreliable motor, and a very slow rate of climb. *Courtesy Roger Sheely*

Ingalls and 218 Squadron made several raids against German seaplane and submarine facilities at Ostend, Zeebrugge, and Bruges. Pictured here is an aerial reconnaissance photograph of the dockyards and submarine pens at Bruges. *Courtesy National Archives*

Ingalls's duty with 218 Squadron lasted just a few weeks before he returned to ground duties with the nascent Northern Bombing Group commanded by Capt. David Hanrahan, a veteran destroyer skipper with no aviation experience, pictured here with his officers about the time of the armistice. *Courtesy National Archives*

This chateau at St. Inglevert served as Bob Lovett's headquarters for the night bombing squadrons of the Northern Bombing Group and a frequent point of rendezvous for Ingalls and others of the Yale Unit when they could spare the time. *Courtesy National Archives*

In his rumpled tunic and with his ever-present pipe, Dave Ingalls stands in a field in Flanders, possibly during duty with the Northern Bombing Group in July–August 1918. *Courtesy Ingalls Family Archives*

Ingalls chafed at the inactivity forced on him in late July and begged for a
return to active flight duty. His wishes were granted in early August when
he rejoined 213 Squadron at Bergues. In the next eight weeks he scored
the aerial victories that earned him the distinction of being the Navy's only
"ace" in World War I. He is shown here with two of his 213 Squadron mates.
The jaunty fellow on the left is Capt. John Edmund Greene, a twenty-
four-year-old Canadian who scored fifteen victories but died in combat
in October 1918 on the same mission in which Yale Unit veteran Ken
MacLeish was shot down and killed. *Courtesy Peter B. Mersky Collection*

7

Eastleigh and Home
October–December 1918

In early October, an exhausted David Ingalls departed No.213 Squadron to take up duties as flight officer and head of the Flight Department at Eastleigh, the Northern Bombing Group's massive supply, assembly, and repair facility situated a few miles from Southampton on the southern coast of England. He replaced Ken MacLeish in this job, the latter headed to Flanders to fill Ingalls's old slot with the British. Ingalls spent the next month decompressing from his recent combat tour, testing aircraft assembled at Eastleigh, teaching several enlisted men to fly, and happily pursuing a very active social life. He also met Adm. William Sims and Capt. Noble Irwin, the director of naval aviation, during his extended tour of Europe. Ingalls, who had been rather caustic about Irwin earlier that year, seemed more impressed with the senior officer after their personal encounter.

By this time, the original tiny American naval aviation contingent of April 1917 had morphed into an enormous military force of approximately 40,000 personnel; 2,000 aircraft; and more than 48 patrol stations, training facilities, and supply and repair bases on both sides of the Atlantic. This force compared quite favorably with those of other participants in the conflict. When the guns stopped firing in November 1918, German naval air forces stood at 16,000 men and 1,500 aircraft and airships. France counted 11,000 men and 1,300 flying machines, and Italy tallied 690 aircraft and airships and 4,382 trained personnel. Only Great Britain's RNAS, with approximately 55,000 men and 3,000 aircraft (as of March 1918) exceeded the U.S. effort. Yet even the 40,000 American sailors of the air were dwarfed by the expansion of the U.S. Air Service, which by November counted approximately 20,000 officers and 175,000 enlisted men, 58,000 of them in Europe.[1]

———

October 4, 1918. This morning was the worst ever. Went over to see Di [Gates] in morning, but when patrol returned he was missing. We didn't begin to worry until night.[2]

———

October 4, 1918

Dear Mother:

To start off with, today has been an awful day. I have detached from my squadron and I suppose I'll have a sedentary position or do some rotten job for a change. Needless to state I am very sorry to leave. And

---

1. R. D. Layman, *Naval Aviation in the First World War: Its Impact and Influence* (London: Chatham Publishing, 1996), 206–8. The scope of the American naval aviation campaign was prodigious. Nearly ten thousand officers and bluejackets staffed four principal European supply and repair bases at Pauillac and Brest, France; Eastleigh, England; and Queenstown, Ireland; this was almost as many as the entire French force and twice the size of the Italian effort. For a full discussion of the American effort in Europe, see Geoffrey Rossano, *Stalking the U-Boat: U.S. Naval Aviation in Europe in World War I* (Gainesville: University Press of Florida, 2010). For the even greater growth of the U.S. Air Service, see James Hudson, *Hostile Skies: A Combat History of the American Air Service in World War I* (Syracuse, N.Y.: Syracuse University Press, 1968), and especially Maurer Maurer, ed., *The U.S. Air Service in World War I,* 4 vols. (Washington, D.C.: Office of Air Force History, 1979), the air force's official documentary history of that conflict.

2. Yale Unit charter member Di Gates commanded NAS Dunkirk for several months, but with activity winding down in the autumn of 1918, he received permission to fly temporarily with the French Escadrille St. Pol, piloting SPAD pursuit ships. American aviators George Moseley, Freddy Beach, and William Van Fleet joined him there. In a wild encounter with more than a dozen enemy scouts on October 4, Gates was shot down, but he survived largely unhurt. Captured and imprisoned in Germany, he made several unsuccessful escape attempts and was finally repatriated on November 26, 1918. Gates's great "adventure" is detailed in Ralph D. Paine, *The First Yale Unit: A Story of Naval Aviation, 1916–1919,* 2 vols. (Cambridge, Mass.: Riverside Press, 1925), 2:329–49. See also Marc Wortman, *The Millionaires' Unit: The Aristocratic Flyboys Who Fought the Great War and Invented American Air Power* (New York: Public Affairs, 2006), 245–48, 255–57.

now the really bad news! Good old Di Gates had just started flying a scout with some French squadron and today, about his third patrol, seven of them were attacked by ten or fifteen Huns and Di has been missing since. Honestly I've never felt so terribly in all my life. He was the greatest fellow in the world. The fight occurred about four miles over the lines. All the rest of the patrol dove and got away. But Freddie Beach says he saw Di turn as a Hun fired on him, Di from behind— straight into about six or seven others. That was the last seen of him.

As Di was a very good pilot, tho' he had no experience fighting, he may have gotten away. I'm sure he'll be all right, perhaps crashed on our side of the lines and has been unable to telephone or else, at worst, a prisoner of war. We shall not know for certain for a month, I suppose. He had just been given the Distinguished Flying Cross for flying in a boat to a crashed night bomber and picking them up—off the Hun coast some distance from here. Everybody has been calling for word about him. No one is so popular with every race here, French, English, and American. His father is dead, but he has two brothers and a sister, who, I hope, will console somewhat his mother to whom he was absolutely devoted. Dear old Di, the best fellow God ever made. Well, we'll hope for the best.

⸻

October 5, 1918. No news at all of Di yet. Di is the most wonderful fellow in the world. I just feel he must be all right. Ken and I went to Autingues,[3] saw Hanrahan. Everyone is terribly upset at Di's being missing. I am to leave tomorrow for Eastleigh to be Final Acceptance and Test Officer.

October 6, 1918. Ken [MacLeish], a fellow named Hall, and I took noon leave boat, and after a rather rough trip arrived in London went to [Hotel] Carlton, and to bed.

October 7, 1918. Went to Headquarters, had lunch with Alphi [Ames] and Fearing, did a bit of shopping and bought a slick

3. Autingues was the site of Capt. David Hanrahan's headquarters for the Northern Bombing Group.

>
Dunhill pipe. Had a great dinner with Alphi and saw "Hello
America."[4] Dance at A.O. [American Officers] Inn.

October 8, 1918. Reported at Headquarters, and was introduced to
Admiral Sims who was very nice. Discussed Archie with the old
boy. To my astonishment he knew his oats. Left London at noon
and arrived here [Eastleigh] about 5:00. Saw Frank [Lynch] and
Reggie [Coombe].[5] The station is a wonder on a really large scale.
They expect to turn out 10 machines a day at least. I will be
Chief Pilot when Ken leaves and guess I'll be pretty busy. Wrote
Harry and Alice Davison tonight about Di.[6] Gosh but I certainly
do miss old Di, but think he must be alright.

October 8, 1918

Dear Dad,
I have been detached from 213 Squadron, and after going to
headquarters, passed through London and arrived at a big repair base
of ours. Here I am to relieve Ken MacLeish as acceptance officer,
while he goes out to 213 in my place. This is a tremendous station,
and the work will probably be very interesting, and besides Frank
Lynch and Reggie Coombe, two of my old unit, are here on some kind
of a job. I was certainly embarrassed a few times lately. Trusting to
your discretion, I will state that for some reason, God knows why, I
was taken and introduced to Admiral Sims in London, and the old
buck seemed quite pleased and complimented me on what I'd done
while with 213. As I'd been having the time of my life there, it was
just as good as going on leave, I got fussed as the deuce, but had a
great time telling him about anti-aircraft guns in which he seemed

---

4. *Hello America* played in London in 1918, starring Elsie Janis (Elsie Bierbower),
"the Sweetheart of the AEF."

5. Francis Russell Vincent "Frank" Lynch, NA #88, a member of the First Yale
Unit, served in the United States until May 1918, then at NAS Killingholme, and
finally at Eastleigh, ferrying aircraft to France.

6. Alice Davison was the sister of Trubee and Harry Davison. After the war, she
married Di Gates.

rather interested yet withal rather (deleted). Also Capt. Hanrahan, who is in charge of the Northern Bombing group was very nice. To start everything, Major Graham of 213, gave a farewell dinner at the squadron and made a speech, which I first thought was kidding me. And then darned if your little son didn't have to get up and get revenge by telling them what a slick squadron they were and what a wonderful C.O. they had. There has been no more news of old Di and we are all terribly low about it. Otherwise I've had a pretty good time. We spent two days in London and saw a good show including Elsie Janis, and had a few dances afterwards with some American girls. Lights are going out so cheerio Pops, aff. Dave.

October 10, 1918.

Dear Dad and Mother:

Well, today I took over Ken's job, and so have quite considerable to do. Ken is flying over to France Sunday, if the weather is all right, which same I very much doubt, as it has rained since we touched Dover. In spite of the weather, however, Ken took me up this morning in the observer's seat for a joy ride. It was the first time I'd been up in an American machine and I was certainly agreeably surprised.[7] From the different reports and rumors passing along, I was in doubt as to whether or not an American-built machine could actually fly.

The other two fellows I know here may leave at any time, Frank and Reg, which will be pretty rotten as I know none of the officers here, and besides they are all older men, mostly business men, which of course is natural in this sort of a station, but is too bad. For instance, while at a conference in the Captain's office today I met a Lieut (j.g.) named Haines from Chicago who knows you and seems to be on quite intimate terms with Uncle George and Aunt Catherine.[8]

---

7. This was the much-touted, much-anticipated, American-built, Liberty motor–powered DH-4 day bomber. Up to this point, Ingalls had flown only European aircraft while on active duty.

8. Lt. (jg) J. Allen Haines of Winnetka, Illinois, served previously at Great Lakes U.S. Naval Training Center.

Tonight I got a letter from Dad, the first for some time. It certainly was great to get some mail. The station is very large and very naval. It is just like living on some doggone ship. All the decks are swabbed (floors cleaned perhaps one might say) twice a day, and I can't walk from my office to my room and back at once my arm gets so tired saluting. Maybe it is a good plan to be so military, but it's rough on a civilian like me. However, the C. O. is a perfectly jolly old bird, whose figger sort of reminds me of Santa Claus.[9] And the quarters are wonderful, with running hot and cold water and baths.

Yesterday I boxed with Frank Lynch and got plenty of exercise to last a week, as he is an old Yale end at football and somewhat strong. I was glad to find myself all there as we crawled into a wonderful hot tub afterwards. The mess is mighty good, but even so does not compare to the Ritz dinners we used to get at Dunkerque. There is a great big band here, which beats anything I've ever heard. Especially the drum major, he's a bear cat. And just now a really wonderful quartet of sailors has come in to use the piano in the mess room. Best music I've heard since leaving the states. Also there is a movie with American movies here every night. I ask you, "Is War Hell?"

How long I'll be here is one of the navy mysteries. If I do decently it may be for some time. Also depends on when the navy starts day bombing. Besides, we have just heard that the forces are to be amalgamated.[10] In that case I don't know what will happen to us in the navy flying corps. Perhaps we will not unite in operations— merely in purchasing, etc. I hope so. So Al [Ingalls] has enlisted in the tank service. This is a shock. I thought he was going into the Navy, and rather hoped so too. Nevertheless it is a most interesting service. Can he wrangle a commission out of it? I hope so.

Skinny Lawrence just wrote me. He is in the Artillery and was at Chateau Thierry for the push. Somehow he managed to get into the

---

9. Cdr. Bayard Bulmer assumed command at Eastleigh on September 21, 1918, a position he held until the end of the war. Surviving photographs indicate that he did tend toward stoutness at this point in his life.

10. The question of uniting army and navy aviation services, as the British did by creating the RAF, generated enormous controversy during and after the war. Junior and senior naval officers on both sides of the Atlantic had much to say about the issue. On this subject, see Rossano, *Stalking the U-Boat,* 137–40.

trenches for a push and was the fourth man over the top, and captured a Hun. Darn good for Skinny. Blake is still training here in England, but hopes to get over soon. He wrote that two of my best friends at St. Paul's have been killed, Marshall Bond and Bobby Reath. And also Cord Meyer,[11] the Yale crew captain, who was stationed near us at Dunkerque—a great fellow. Brew[ster] Jennings is likewise over here. He wrote from some destroyer or sub chaser he is on, and says he's been having a pretty exciting time. The war news is certainly great. I hope they don't declare peace till we've knocked Hell out of some or all of Germany. Must stop, With love, Dave.

October 11, 1918. Received official notification of award of D.F.C. Pretty nice. But haven't heard anything of Di yet, which is not so good.[12]

October 11, 1918

Dear Mother and Dad,

I just received this message from Capt. Hanrahan last night after I had mailed a letter to you so I thought I'd try again. Pretty nice of the British to slip me this, not so? With a little luck I ought to write you pretty often from this place, as we dine at 5:30 P.M. and there is nothing one has to do afterwards. Do you remember all the attractive attractions I mentioned in my last letter? Well, when I returned to my room, what should be going on but a big party in the Captain's room with a wonderful sailor orchestra and quartet playing and singing for them. The weather was awful today so we flew *pas de tout*. We

---

11. Cord Meyer trained at Issoudun, France, and served in the 103rd Aero Squadron. He was injured but not killed when his aircraft hit a telegraph wire and crashed.

12. Ingalls received the British Distinguished Flying Cross for his service with No.213 Squadron, the first U.S. naval aviator so honored. After making this entry, Ingalls set aside his diary and failed to make additional remarks for nearly a month—and only a few thereafter. Instead, his activities during the closing weeks of the war can be traced in a series of detailed letters he dispatched to his mother and father. Social activities seemed to occupy an increasing percentage of his time. Life was far better in Southampton than at the front.

are going to see Billie Burke in the movies tonight,[13] perhaps and tomorrow night are going to a dance nearby where Ken says there are some English girls who can really dance, maybe so. Aff. Dave

P.S. Almost forgot to tell you that I ran into Pete Newell, who is a Chief Petty Officer in the engine shop[s] here. I was certainly surprised to see him. He looks well and in better form than I have ever seen him. D.S.I.

October 13, 1918

My Dear Mother,

At the present moment the war news certainly looks good for our side. But I hope that peace is not declared, nor an armistice granted until Germany is put in a position from which she can never recover. This is the time to finish her up for good. Of course just now the main topic of conversation is if peace is actually declared when will we be able to get home? Probably not for ages at any rate. The weather the last two days, for some unaccountable reason, has been fairly good. So I have been aloft a bit. This morning Ken and Frank flew over-seas, as they call it—Ken to go out with 213 Squadron. Imagine a fellow engaged to a wonderful girl, as Ken is, wanting to go looking for trouble. Engaged people must be bored to death, for all the ones I know over here are absolutely crazy. Gosh, I wish I could go along with Ken. We would have some time together there as the C.O. would let us run around to suit ourselves. Also I might be able to give him some good dope, good pilot as he is. It's the first scraps that are a bit dangerous and maybe I could ease him over a few bad points.[14] Last

---

13. Mary William Ethelbert Appleton "Billie" Burke (1884–1970), an American stage and screen actress and wife of showman Florenz Ziegfeld, was best known for her role as the Good Witch Glinda in the 1939 movie *The Wizard of Oz*.

14. This comment was almost prophetic. The very next day, the talented but relatively inexperienced MacLeish was shot down and killed over Belgium. Ingalls returned to these thoughts when he spoke at a Yale Unit reunion in 1924. See pp. 117–19 of the speech transcript in Davison Papers, Yale University Archives. The army's first ace, Douglas Campbell, later remarked that many fliers "were shot down in the early part of their career before they really learned how to see [the approaching enemy]." Quoted in Edward M. Coffman, *The War to End All Wars: The American Military Experience in World War I* (Madison: University of Wisconsin Press, 1986), 200.

night several of us went to a dance at a wonderful English place near by. It was pretty good fun, though only one or two of the girls could dance. George Laughlin,[15] a fellow from St. Paul's, came on today to get a machine, but will pull out tomorrow, I suppose. Well, good night Muzzy. Aff. Dave

October 16, 1918.

My Dear Mother:

You really should see where I live now. I have the cutest little room in the world with a bed, stove, table, and bureau. The window has beautiful curtains, and when I have purchased, or requisitioned, a nice big Morris chair, I will be as comfortable as possible. You know I am beginning to like this British system of no steam heat or radiators, because a little stove is just as hot and a lot more pleasant.

Ken and Frank have gone to France and yesterday Reggie left for 10 days leave in Scotland. If I had been stationed here a little longer and had someone to take my place, I would have liked to have gone along—not having had any leave now for about 15 months I sort of rate it. On the night before he left, Reg Coombe and I went into Southampton on a party. We had a great time; having decided to see an awfully good show running there we had to slip dinner, so went in for tea—high tea. The only way we could get enough to eat was to tour around the tea-shops—reminded me of dancing between courses.

Yesterday Capt. Irwin, in charge of naval aviation at Washington, visited the camp with our old C.O. Chevalier.[16] As one of the heads of the department I had to go around with him and make clear any little matters. Well, I hand it to him for asking the doggondest questions imaginable; he must have been an examination instructor at some school or college.

15. George Laughlin, NA #165, trained with the navy, transferred to the Marine Corps, and flew with the First Marine Aviation Force/Northern Bombing Group.

16. Lt. Godfrey Chevalier served as the first commanding officer at Eastleigh in the summer of 1918. Chevalier had earlier commanded NAS Dunkirk. Capt. Noble Irwin, the director of naval aviation, made his first trip to the war zone in the early fall of 1918.

There is a young English lord here, more as a guest than anything else, though officially he is instructing us in guns and shooting. Well, the youngster took me out to dinner last night at the place where the dance came off the other night. It sort of worried me to find that he and I were the only guests, and in addition the poor nut got us there an hour too early by mistake, so we sat around waiting for Mr. and Mrs. [Moreton] and the daughter.[17] But they are very nice and I had the time of my life. The old man was a quiet and respectable sort of bird. Mrs. Moreton was very amusing, and the daughter is the only English girl I have seen (or heard of) who can really dance.

Mrs. Moreton kidded me quite clubbily about my accent, and I sympathized with the daughter who had never had a chance to go to school but had always had a governess. And after dinner at least three wines, and little odds and ends like whiskey and soda, port, sherry, etc., were served, the old boy and I agreed famously that alcoholic drinks were an abominable sin.

Well, mother, I have been writing letters for two hours since dinner, but it is only 8 P.M. It's a wonderful idea, this early dinner. Reminds me of the time when Al and I were kids and ate in the nursery at 5:30. Three weeks mail has been lost, so everyone agrees. From August 21 or so until Sept. 15, so anything you said then has missed me. The war news looking pretty *bon,* mother. It doesn't seem possible that Peace could actually come does it? But it may, one never knows, does one? Aff. Dave

October 19, 1918

Dear Dad,

Some day someone who has something to do with the mail service between USA and here is going to run into to me, awfully hard, and

---

17. The Moretons were a prominent local family that extended great hospitality to American troops in the area. They hosted weekly dances at their country home and always drew a large delegation of officers. The Americans supplied the jazz band, white bread, ham, and other meats. "To attend once was to become a regular guest," according to Lt. (j.g.) J. Allen Haines. See T. Francis Bludworth, *The Battle of Eastleigh, England: U.S.N.A.F., 1918* (New York: Thompson, 1919), 130.

will have slightly more interest in said mail service thereafter. In short, Dad, either four or five weeks have passed with one letter from you and mother ensemble, as far as I can remember. Well, I dined with the Royalty [Moretons] again last night, and had a fine time. Shorty Smith, who is visiting various British schools to procure some dope before going home to get married (and, a minor detail, to start a school on advanced principles) came here to see me for a bit, and "Monty," I get clubby as hell with the Royalty, and I took Shorty along to dinner. He said he had the time of his life. The young scion (can the daughter of a noble race be a scion, anyway it sounds well) sang most beautifully for us. Also they had my pre-war ideal Englishman there, a major of a nearby remount station. Shorty and I couldn't help laughing every time he opened his face, but he thought he was humorous as the deuce so didn't mind in the least. Lordy, Dad, what terrible thing do you think has happened now. Ken MacLeish in his first scrap was shot down. Of course there is a chance he is a prisoner, but believe me it is awful. We've been together ever since leaving college, and I miss him like the devil.[18] I'm leaving now for the movies, Aff. Dave

October 22, 1918

Dear Dad,

When this station has been running for a while, I suppose it will be sort of monotonous here, but for now I have never been more

---

18. Ken MacLeish flew from Eastleigh to Dunkirk on October 13 and the following morning set out on patrol with No.213 Squadron. During that action, he downed a German aircraft. On a second mission later that day, he was shot down, but no word of his fate could be obtained. A Belgian landowner returning to his ruined farmstead at Schoore near Ostend on December 26 found MacLeish's body. His final mission is recounted in Paine, *First Yale Unit,* 359–73, and in Geoffrey Rossano, ed., *The Price of Honor: The World War One Letters of Naval Aviator Kenneth MacLeish* (Annapolis, Md.: Naval Institute Press, 1991), 221–36. MacLeish left behind a fiancée, Priscilla Murdock, and a cache of letters. A similar fate befell Quentin Roosevelt and his fiancée, Flora Payne Whitney. Quentin, the youngest son of former president Theodore Roosevelt, was killed in July 1918. His letters to Flora survive to this day. See Thomas Fleming, "Their Golden Glory," in *The Great War: Perspectives on the First World War,* ed. Robert Cowley (New York: Random House, 2001), 286–303.

interested in any sort of work before. As everything is new, all kinds of little troubles are occasionally cropping up, and it is great fun experimenting with one thing and another. Besides, it is a pleasure to work with the men here. They are certainly a picked crowd. Socially, too, I have been quite active. Attended a good show here the other night with sailor talent. The next night Haines and I went dining with the Royalty again [Moretons] and had a slick time. And last night I saw a good show in town. Also tomorrow there is another dance. Haines evolved the great idea of our supplying the jazz band, food, and liquor, and Mrs. Moreton would supply the house and girls once every week or two weeks, I forgot which. All of these little things help you know. I hope that several of the girls can dance. Enclosed are a few photos some fellows took and gave me. They aren't half bad. Pete Newell is doing darn well here. I think I told you he was a chief in the engine shops. The head of his department tells me he is the best man he has and that he just recommended him for a commission. I received a box of gum yesterday, but no mail yet. Aff. Dave

October 24, 1918

Dear Dad,

A few letters arrive for me yesterday—one from you of Sept. 29—through C.P.S. I'm glad you are using that address, though if I expected to be here long, it would be better to use a British one. However, I have never been more than six weeks at the most in any one place, so better stick to C.P.S. The best news in the world came in last night about Ken and Di. When Ken was shot down five other Britishers were too; well, Frank Lynch was over there and saw one Belgian woman who saw an American naval officer and a Canadian taken prisoner the day Ken was missing. So he must be O.K. Then Di's machine has been found on what was Hun land but is now captured territory. As it is in good shape except that it was burnt up, it is thought that Di got down alright and then he or the Huns set fire to the aeroplane. It has been identified, so I understand by the motor number. I can't tell you how glad I am. Wouldn't be surprised if they escaped and turned up some fine day. Last night there was a slick dance here. Our station supplied a jazz band, and it was some success. I am enclosing a story of a low bombing raid I went on. As the Allies now have the coast it could in no way help the Huns to read it. But please don't stick it in the paper or anything like that will you. I thought it might be interesting to you and mother. Aff. Dave

October 29, 1918, Eastleigh.

Dear Dad:

Just a moment ago this picture, enclosed, of the three naval officers was given me, and I certainly had to laugh. Never thought I looked so doggone fruity. I think I'll never have another camera pointed my way. It's too discouraging.

Well, there's been lots to do lately, but yesterday afternoon I slipped off to Southampton to get some clothes and afterwards Frank, Reg and I had some dinner and saw a good show. It is great having Frank and Reg back again. Also I had a couple of dinners with the Royalty since last writing. This afternoon Alphi Ames called up from Headquarters and said that it is practically certain that Ken and Di are O.K. tho' prisoners. It is certainly fine news.

Yesterday we sent off some machines for France and several, owing to dud weather, landed at different aerodromes. So this morning I took a machine and, accompanied by an old navy man, a machinist, the funniest pirate I ever saw,[19] flew over and stopped at two aerodromes and saw that they were alright. One place was Shoreham, and I found the Major in charge was Cloete, the fellow who was my instructor at Gosport. It was darn nice to see him again. Besides him there were two or three other Gosport instructors.

There was one of the new British scout machines just arrived there, and Cloete let me take a ride in it, and I had the time of my

19. Born in Norway in 1880, Einar "Dep" Boydler enlisted in the navy in 1903 and was assigned to Alfred Cunningham, NA #5, as head mechanic for the Wright B-1 aircraft in September 1912. He flew with Victor Herbster, NA #4, in the Wright B-2 in November 1912. Boydler became a student naval aviator at Hampton Roads in January 1918. His overseas postings included Pauillac, Northern Bombing Group, and Eastleigh. He was designated NA #1736 in November 1918.

life. It beat anything I'd ever been in by a million miles. It was only about 50 miles or so from here, going along the coast, so we got back in time for 12 luncheon, though we didn't start till 9:30, made altogether seven flights and spent quite a time at each aerodrome. One can do a lot of traveling by aeroplane. I'm planning to go to Shoreham for a dance in a week or so, leaving the plane in a hangar there over night. Great idea, isn't it? I'm also enclosing some photos of my flight commander and me in our machines. I called mine "Norma." Well, night is drawing nigh. Aff. Dave.

November 1, 1918. I certainly get enough flying now. The machines are sent over from the States already to set up, and take only a short time to put together. The assembly department is enormous and is organized under Lieut. Howard most efficiently.[20] The great hangars look like the machine shops of an automobile industry, rows of planes in various stages of assembly, and rows of motors similarly. We overhaul every motor on receipt, as they arrive in terrible condition. It's a crime. The best ones are those from the Ford Company, the worst the Packard, but all are bad and always filings and junk are taken from the crankcases, the bearings are seldom O.K. And the oiling system is so bad we've had to run a new line into the head of the motor. God knows why they couldn't have done better at home.

When the planes are assembled they are turned over to my department. I have about 30 men under two very good chief petty officers. My crew look over the machines, test the motors, make certain the controls are O.K., etc. Then I take a look over the whole plane when it's wheeled out on the field, and then I take the ship up for a short flight. About five minutes and I come down and have the boys change the ailerons, the tail plane, or any one of half a dozen things. Sometimes the ship is so badly lined up it's really difficult to get up and down O.K. The boys fiddle around for a while and up I go again. Sometimes a couple of trips are enough; sometimes we just can't seem to get the ship perfect

20. Lt. O. W. Howard was head of the Assembly and Repair Department at Eastleigh.

and it takes half a dozen trips and changes. When it seems right
I stunt it for a while to get the kinks out and see nothing is weak.
Then one final hop and the ship is ready for the front.

I have four or five ferry pilots, Marines, to take the ships
across, and have a lot of trouble with them, they won't take any
advice and as a result smash up or ruin a motor every few times.
How the Marines will ever keep any of these planes going at the
front mystifies me. But these planes are wonderful, both the D.H.
9s and the D.H. 4s. I have had sham battles with every kind of
British ship from different schools around here and never failed
to just make monkeys of them. What wouldn't I give to get loose
on the front with a good shot for observer in one of these things. A
fellow could just slaughter Huns. They out-climb and out-speed
and out-dive anything at the front with ease and simplicity.

November 1, 1918

Dear Mother,

Cheerio, yesterday some mail came in, and I received two letters
from you written September 12 and October 1. Also one from Dad
enclosing a letter to undergraduates. My mail has certainly been
well mixed up, and it is rotten not to get it regularly. It is practically
certain now that Ken and Di are prisoners and all O.K. Thank
goodness for that. The weekly dance came off Wednesday, and the
girls having improved slightly, due to much laborious practice, it was
quite good fun. At last an assistant has been sent to me, though not
the one I asked for. However, he's a pretty cautious and conservative
flyer, due most likely to his age, so he'll probably be pretty good.
Also I've been taking a half hour off for a cross-country run every
afternoon, so I feel much better. After all, health is the greatest thing,
isn't t? Our padre has been ill lately, and it is a shame. He is a peach,
most popular with the men, and I hate to see him laid up.[21] He's the

21. The station "souvenir" volume prepared at the end of war, *The Battle of Eastleigh, England* (New York: Thompson, 1919), 16, spoke very highly of chaplain Lt. (jg)
Norris Tibbets, calling him "a good scout . . . heart, soul, and mind with his boys. . . .
He doesn't preach too much church, but just enough to make you like it. If I had his
personality I'd charge admission."

first U.S. Navy padre I've run into and I think he's a great addition to the place. Well, Mother, I've got to stop. With love, Dave

———

November 2, 1918

Dear Pater:

As such, I have been informed by the royalty, I should address you. How do you like it, Dad? To me it sounds too religious, very much like calling on some Latin Saint. You see, last night Push Coombe and I dined with the royalty, and I taught the daughter some American and she pulled off a few British methods. Tonight we are going over again. While Push is awfully fond of music and art, so he gave Mrs. Royalty a good time.

The weather has been about as bad as possible. Too bad to fly any machines to France, or even instruct these confounded ferry pilots. I tried letting one of them fly me the other day, me sitting in the observer's seat with a most inefficient stick and rudder. Well, he almost smashed us all up. It's a nice soft job they've slipped me alright. Last night it cleared up beautifully and I thought everything would be better, but this morning it has been raining hard continuously. Believe me, I will be glad to get back where the sun shines in the day time and the moon at night.

Well, we got one of the training machines [DH.6] set up yesterday and we had a time; it is an awful old tub but fine for instruction.[22] It makes about 40 or 50 miles per hour, I guess. Also there was about a 40 or 50 miles wind yesterday, so at about 1,000 feet the darned machine stood still in relation to the ground. I was afraid to turn with the wind for fear I'd never get home. It is the funniest machine I ever saw—everyone collected around to see it fly and cheered when it took off. I almost died laughing when I flew it. Some machine! Lunch is due, so I'll knock off and eat. With love, Dave.

———

22. Known as "the Old Bus," this obsolete DH6 was used as a training machine; thousands were produced during the war.

November 5, 1918. I've been having a lot of fun with the D.H. 6 training machine and instructing some of my men (*see below*). The instructor sits behind, the pupil in front in the sort of bathtub cockpit. There are dual sets of controls and in the instructor's place a lever so he can cut off the front pilot's controls. Well, I took Reg up one day and flew the thing for a while and then I shoved the lever over and watched. The thing flew O.K. for a few seconds, then began to tip sideways. I saw Reg move his stick to counteract the tip; he pushed it over further and further, sat up straighter in his seat. All the time we were getting further up on one wing. Finally he turned his head around and motioned at his stick, which he pushed back and forth to no avail. I held my hands up and pretended I didn't understand and motioned to him to go on and fly it, meanwhile pushing my knee up against my stick so our damned old plane got more and more on an angle. Well, Reg yelled at me, cussed, I sort of thought, and waved violently, letting go of the stick. So I shoved the lever back in place so his control would work again and paid no attention to him. He happened to try his stick again and found it worked. I may say he certainly takes things easy. If I'd been he I would have been sort of worried, but I honestly don't believe he was scared at all. When we got down I told him about the control lever and showed it to him. All he said was, "Huh! I thought it was a bit queer."

The darn machine is useful, though. I've been taking it over to the Moretons and taking young Iris, the scioness, up for hops. She loves it. But the old lady caught her once, and, by George, insisted I take her up. Well, I consented, got her in the cockpit, and we were off. The old lady (about 80, I guess) seemed to sink down and down and only looked down into the cockpit floor. I tapped her on the shoulder and laughed and yelled, "It's all right," but got nothing outside of one quick glance around out of her. I thought she was going to die on my hands and headed down immediately. I don't suppose we were up two minutes. She was O.K. when we stopped safe on land and has talked about her flight ever since. But, no more old ladies for me. I like 'em younger, anyway.

Iris is a darned good scout, pretty, and does everything well, that is, everything that I've done with her. But, My God, she is spoiled. I'd hate to marry a girl that's spoiled. She only sings for instance when she wants no matter what her mother says.

———

U.S. Naval Aviation Repair Base
Eastleigh, England

October 24, 1918

From: Chief Pilot (Ingalls)
To: Commanding Officer, N.B.G. (Hanrahan)
Via: Commanding Officer (Bulmer)
Subject: Recommendation for Commission for Observers[23]

1. When Lieut. MacLeish left the Eastleigh Air Station for France he had the intention of taking up with you the matter of making the following observers commissioned officers:

Meyers, C. J. CQM
Fallows, L. F. CMM

---

23. The question of training enlisted observers to fly and giving them commissions was much discussed when navy crews took bombing instruction at the AEF school at Clermont-Ferrand. George Moseley strongly advocated the idea as a way for the men to interact more freely concerning their duties and to increase the chances of a plane getting down safely if the officer-pilot was wounded or killed. Both Ken MacLeish and Dave Ingalls agreed and took steps to implement the proposal. On October 10, MacLeish wrote, "I got hold of several of our observers today for the first time in months, and they are surely in rotten spirits. They have been treated like dogs, and it's about time something was done about it. I don't know whether they can be taught to fly or not, but I think they can. If so, they will be able to get commissions. I feel guilty about them as I once had the power to get them commissions, but it fell through." Quoted in Rossano, *Price of Honor,* 225. Ingalls's October 24 letter was forwarded, approved by Commander Bulmer, to Captain Hanrahan. After Ingalls returned to the United States at the end of November, Lt. Ralph Loomis pursued the matter, recommending on December 19 that Chief Machinist Mate Browne, Ingalls's observer in the spring and summer, be designated a naval aviator, based on his length of service—150 hours in the air over land and sea and 26 hours of solo flying time, "proving himself an excellent pilot." Commander Bulmer approved this recommendation as well. Nothing came of it, however, and Browne's discharge papers, dated April 26, 1919, show his final rank as Chief Machinist Mate (A).

Bowry, C. J. CQM
Stevens, V. A. CMM
Browne, R. R. CMM
Sylvester, C. L. CGM
Sheely, I. E. CMM

2. At the time Lieut. MacLeish had gone into the subject in detail, and had letters of recommendation from Major Wemp of 218 Squadron, and also from the major in charge of the Army Bombing school at Clermont-Ferrand.

3. As Lieut. MacLeish was missing shortly after leaving here perhaps he did not have the time to see you about this.

4. I am very much interested in these men obtaining a commission, and would be greatly obliged if you would let me know whether or not the matter has been placed in your hands, and if so, with what result.

D. S. Ingalls, Lieut. (jg).

November 5, 1918

Dear Mother,

Today I received a letter from you Sept. 16, and one from Adele C. Sept. 27. About time for them to arrive, isn't it? However, Thursday is usually the big day, so I am looking forward to it. H. P. Davison was here yesterday. It was certainly great to see him again, and we had quite a talk with him. He had most encouraging news of Di and Ken, it is practically certain that they are alright. Also he seems to think this war news is *Hors tres bon*. I hope he is right in his prediction, he usually is. He says that Harry is expected to go home soon now with a couple of instructors. Poor old Harry will be sore, though just now he is doing nothing, in fact very few of the naval aviation men are. Talk about plenty to do, I've been certainly busy here. I'm tired as the deuce every night, and pretty glad that my assistant seems to me a pretty good flyer. I am enclosing a note from one of my yeomen who has just left to become an ensign for liaison work, being adept at French. Thought it would make you and Pops laugh at your young son's dignified position. With Love, Dave

———

Lt. Ingalls: Dear Sir: I was in to say goodbye before I left, but you were out. I enjoyed very much working for you; my only hope is that my next boss will be as agreeable as you were. I hope I'll see you in Paris some day. Respectfully, "Frenchy," Rod. J. Chandonnet

———

And then the Armistice!!

———

Nov. 12, 1918.

Dear Dad:

Peace at last! It is certainly the greatest news ever, and everyone is crazy with delight over here, and all one thinks about is—when will we get home. Yesterday the Capt. went to London to discover the future of the station, so we ought to learn something definite soon. It does not seem to me that we will be kept here more than a month, but then one never knows, and it's quite possible that Christmas and a few more months will see me still in England and France. My Lord, I hope not.

A lot of mail has arrived from you, the latest Oct. 15 from C.P.S. and I was awfully glad to get them, they were most interesting. Saturday, Mr. Howard, the lieut. in charge of A & R [assembly and repair] and I went to France in a DH-9. We covered all of Belgium, and it was quite a wonderful trip, seeing Ostend, Bruges, etc. It seemed quite strange flying over once Hun land and not being shot at, I couldn't get used to it, and seemed to imagine I heard a machine gun every now and them. We went to all the aerodromes I once bombed and shot up, and flew along the road where we once shot Hun transports. Gosh, it was great. Ostend is certainly a wreck, Pops, but Bruges is not greatly damaged.

We spent the night at Lovett's aerodrome and saw Harry and the rest. Harry and I talked over after-war plans and it was pretty nice. We both want to go to Yale again and room together, next fall. What do you think about it dad? Has this war business lowered our finances too much to do that? Sunday morning we flew back again and this afternoon I rode with Miss Morton and had dinner and danced there. Quite a two days work, wasn't it? By the way, there is no harm now in saying that we went from here to Calais in just 1 hour. Pretty swift going, eh? And we figure we covered altogether about 450 miles in 4 ½ hours, without doing more than putting in a little gas, so as to make sure of not running short. A pretty good record for the Liberty motor, isn't it?

Old Howard will never know what a close escape he had from perdition. The flight home was so darned monotonous and I was sort of woozy, I guess. When we got back to our aerodrome there were a lot of people around and I decided to spin down. Well, the barometer read 4,000 feet and I put her in a spin. We spun and spun and I watched the barometer. When it showed we were about 500 feet up the ground seemed awfully close to me for some reason. Anyway, I decided to pull out and did so. As we came out of the spin I realized we were almost on land and yanked the stick back. We leveled off so close the wheels were only a foot or two off the earth. If I'd waited one second more, we'd have dived head on into the ground. By golly, I got a chill when I realized how close it had been. Queer one should lose his senses like that. No more spins for me after a long flight.

There was quite a bit of excitement around here yesterday.[24] Everyone was quite crazy and I could find no one with a grouch. Well, Dad, I'd give anything to be home for Xmas, but such luck I suppose couldn't be. With love, Dave.

—

Nov. 14, 1918

Dear Mother:

Things seem to be over now, don't they? But the last few weeks are always the slowest. It's funny, I've been here almost fourteen months and never worried much about going home till a couple of

---

24. The base erupted in celebration with the news of the armistice. The band played, and Commander Bulmer led the station contingent in a giant snake dance across the airfield. Similar celebrations broke out at facilities all across Ireland, England, France, and Italy.

weeks ago. And it gets worse every day. This morning Frank and Reg left, to sail at the end of the week with Mr. Davison and Harry. They are certainly lucky. Frank and Harry have been over only two or three months, I think, and they are the first to get home again. I almost slipped off with them, but I guess the Captain here thought he might have something for me to do, so he put his foot down. However a couple of weeks more ought to do business up. But one never knows.

This morning I flew over to France and back between breakfast and lunch; it was a pleasant trip and enabled me to get the rest of my baggage, so I've just finished packing and am all set. I took my touring car again. It's a peach and we certainly did travel. Just one hour and eight minutes from Dunkirk to here. 'Tis a mystery to me why I am not tired tonight, as we had a great dance last night, sort of a peace party at the Moretons'. I got to bed about 3 A.M., in addition to which Frank and Reg pulled me out of bed at 7 A.M., being such jovial spirits at leaving. Likewise I flew most of the afternoon. Don't expect to have too much more flying now, as there is no use wasting petrol.

What do you think I did yesterday afternoon? Well, I am certainly ashamed. I crashed a D.H.-4 landing in a fancy way. Although we stuck where we hit, only radiator and wheels and prop were broken. The entire absence of any real shock surprised me very much. I thought when one changed speed from fifty-five to zero miles per hour one might suffer at least a jar.

Two letters today from Dad through C.P.S. and a note from Miss Guthrie.[25] I'm certainly sorry to learn that nothing has yet been heard from Ken. It looks mighty bad for him. Di will, I imagine, be with us in about a week now, as prisoners are given up immediately. Well, Muzzy, I am praying and hoping to be with you all by Xmas.

November 19, 1918. I counted up my flights while here at Eastleigh. I have made just 116 flights since October 12th. In 38 days

---

25. Emma Guthrie worked at the Paris offices of Carson, Pirie, Scott and Co., Ken MacLeish's father's firm, and she played a key role in expediting mail and packages to MacLeish and Ingalls. MacLeish referred to her as "a sort of a Paris aunt to me." See Rossano, *Price of Honor*, 176.

that is an average of 3.05 per day. When you think of the awful weather we've had during this five weeks, I figure that's a pretty good record, at least enough to earn my additional flying pay. Yesterday morning I flew up to London to see if I could help myself get orders for home. Funny how much I'd like to get back all of a sudden. Well, I think I did myself some good, at least they promised some action. It was a pleasant flight, and I saw a lot of people around headquarters I knew, including Alice [Bowler]. Then today I flew back again.

November 1918. Well, my orders to report for home finally arrived, dated November 19th. My trip to London was productive and I beat it for Liverpool and got aboard the **Mauretania**.[26]

November 27, 1918. Being in a most happy and contented state, for why? Because I am aboard H.M.S. **Mauretania** bound for home. Alphi Ames, Roger Poor, and Russell Lord are along. It is rather rough, but we should worry; we hope to get in on Sunday at the latest, thus arriving only a day or two after Harry [Davison]. I was at Eastleigh Repair house for six weeks roughly, and have never more thoroughly enjoyed any work. It was much more interesting than anything I have ever done. A wonderful bunch of men full of ideas, a good C.O., and we were accomplishing things. The board investigating things over here [Westervelt Board] said that it would have been the best station in the world in another six months.[27] It was very military and yet business-like. Good discipline, but no militarism interfered with the getting out of planes. Any new idea was taken up, every trouble met with promptly, and the cooperation between

26. The *Mauretania,* sister ship of the ill-fated *Lusitania* and the fastest vessel on the Atlantic run from 1906 until 1929, carried a wide assortment of passengers home to the United States, including thousands of doughboys.

27. The navy created the Westervelt Board near the end of the war to examine issues relating to the transport, distribution, and quality problems plaguing aircraft and equipment shipped to Europe in 1918. For the work and recommendations of this board, see Archibald D. Turnbull and Clifford L. Lord, *History of United States Naval Aviation* (New Haven, Conn.: Yale University Press, 1949), 142–46.

departments was remarkable. The only ill feeling was concerned with the executive who was an inefficient damn fool, but who had practically no authority, and was about to be fired.[28] Almost everyone was contented, and happy, and work, the men were so easy to work you couldn't knock them off. I managed to teach Dep Boydler, Bill Miller,[29] and seven of the observers to fly in the rotten old D.H. 6 aer[oplane] we got. That certainly tickled them. And when I came to leave the men gave me a peach of a merschaum pipe, watchcase, and tobacco pouch. Darn nice of them. Also one of the observers gave me a Hun gun he picked up at Varssenaere aer[odrome]. I had two trips to France which were very nice, and one to London via aeroplane. And now for home on the fastest ship of the ocean.

December 1918. The trip back was uneventful, very rough, terrible wind. We stood practically still one day. There was a lot of bridge, a lot of bull over the war, and a lot of rejoicing parties, and then New York. We were towed to the docks by tugs and I saw Mother and Dad and the Davisons. *C'est la Guerre!*

28. The executive officer at Eastleigh was Lt. Joseph Dunn.

29. Born in North Dakota, William "Bill" Miller enlisted in the navy in 1907; received ground and flight training at various intervals in 1917 and 1918 in the United States, France, Italy, and England; and was designated NA #1735 at Eastleigh in November 1918. He had worked with the Yale Unit in the summer of 1917 and was a member of a crew that flew a Caproni bomber six hundred miles from Milan to France to Eastleigh on October 1, 1918. Both Miller and Boydler were instructors in the Flight Department.

After eight weeks of continuous action a victorious but exhausted Ingalls departed 213 Squadron and assumed the role as head of the Flight Department at Eastleigh, the U.S. Navy's sprawling assembly and repair base in southern England. *Courtesy National Archives*

As Chief Flight Officer at Eastleigh, Ingalls relied heavily on the efforts of veteran Warrant Officers Einar "Dep" Boydler (*left*) and William "Bill" Miller (*right*). Both earned the golden wings of naval aviators. *Courtesy Roger Sheely*

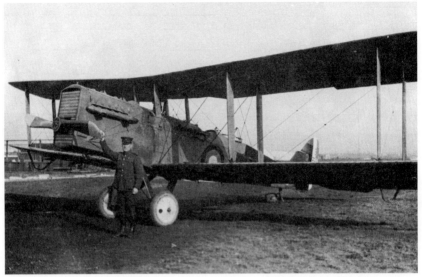

Ingalls's department tuned and tested aircraft assembled for duty with Marine Corps day bombing squadrons of the Northern Bombing Group. Here a Liberty motor–powered DH-9a day bomber is ready for shipment to France. Standing with his hand on the propeller is Warrant Officer William "Bill" Miller, one of Ingalls's trusted aides. *Courtesy Roger Sheely*

At Eastleigh Ingalls worked with an experienced crew of enlisted ratings, several of them members of the original First Aeronautic Detachment and combat verterans many times over. These included Ingalls's observer from his bombing days, Randall Browne. *Courtesy Naval History and Heritage Command*

With the end of the war quickly approaching, the mood at Eastleigh lifted, and Ingalls could assume a relaxed pose with one of his fellow officers.
Courtesy National Archives

The armistice brought celebration, relief, and numerous group photos meant to commemorate the base's activities and personnel before demobilization scattered them all to the four winds. A portion of the senior officer corps is pictured here, with Ingalls seated second from the right, puffing contemplatively on his pipe. *Courtesy National Archives*

(*above*) David Ingalls enjoyed enormous popularity with the enlisted personnel of the Flight Department of Eastleigh. In this photograph taken at the end of the war he is seated front and center with a teenager's grin on his face. *Courtesy National Archives*

(*left*) Ingalls returned to the United States in early December aboard RMS *Mauretania*, what he called "the fastest ship on the Ocean." His parents met him in New York harbor the moment he stepped ashore. *Author's collection*

8

A Glance Back
June 1924

During the 1920s and 1930s, surviving members of the First Yale Unit and their friends gathered for a series of reunion dinners—opportunities to renew friendships, toast lost comrades, cement social and business relationships, and reminisce about events that now seemed to reside in a surprisingly distant past. At each dinner, a number of the young veterans marched to the podium and recounted various aspects of their military experiences, whether in the air, in Washington or Hampton Roads, in Key West, or "over there." For their June 14, 1924, gathering, held at the Brook Club in New York City, the group hired a stenographer to transcribe the after dinner remarks. The lengthy manuscript from that night constitutes the largest single oral history archive of the unit's exploits. Excerpts from the informal comments delivered by Di Gates and David Ingalls are reprinted here.

Di Gates Speaking about David Ingalls

. . . The next people of the Unit to officially report to Dunkirk were Freddie Beach and Chip [McIlwaine]. Dave Ingalls went back to train on bombing machines [at Clermont-Ferrand] with Chip, and then they came back with Freddie Beach, so there were four of us there [NAS Dunkirk]. We came back and were assigned to the British Squadrons in that area, to get experience in bombing machines. Chip, I believe, got one Hun while flying a bombing machine and was officially credited with it.

Then later on they were taken off that and just waiting around for the Northern Bombing squadrons to be started. They were more or less marking time when they were up there. Dave Ingalls was hanging around begging daily for something to do, and finally he conceived the idea he could go back and spend some time with his 213 Squadron, and we fixed that up, and he went back and everyone knows how he went back and did his work there.

. . . I remember one night there were several American nurses there, and they conceived the idea of giving a party up the coast from Dunkirk five or six miles, picking out that place because it was away from the city and any bombing to be done would not be done on that hotel. We had a very nice party. Dave came in very late. We could not understand it, as he was one of the competitors for one . . . nurse's hand, and we were all very curious to find out what happened. He told us before rushing off to the dance with this young lady which I spoke about that he had his control wire shot off, he had been in a fight just before that and had come back controlling his machine by his motor, and therefore was late getting there. That is the night that I think I have spoken about before. . . .

. . . Another incident happened at Dunkirk. A machine crashed during the day about 20 miles from Dunkirk. It was very misty and low clouds, so we sent a couple of machine out to find it, Dave Ingalls going out in a single-seater to find the spot where the machine had crashed and come back and get a motor boat and try to lead the motor boat to the place. It was in the morning. Dave went out and nothing more was heard of him. Another machine went out to find Dave's machine and bring it back, and still Dave was missing. So we had to get more machines out to find Dave. Finally, at 7:30 we sent out our last patrol. It was getting dark. Just after it was dark we got word that Dave had arrived safely, that place being miles away down the coast, and miles from where the patrol was. He had apparently run out of gas and come down and found a nice French summer resort and decided to stay. . . .

. . . I think someone ought to touch on Dave Ingalls' work from Dunkirk, because that was important work, also McIlwaine's work with 217 Squadron, and Freddie Beach, in addition to being with the French SPAD squadron [Escadrille St. Pol], had a lot of experiences with the day bombing squadron. . . .

MR. DAVISON: I don't know anybody who is better equipped to picture David Ingalls' work and to give him really the credit he deserves for work that was wonderful than Dave Ingalls.

MR. INGALLS: I thought I might tell you a little about Di [Gates]. The first impression that I got of him when I came back from training at the Army camp [Clermont-Ferrand], I walked into the station and saw one of the Filipino mess boys walking up and down about ten steps and coming back with two big bricks under each arm. I says, "What is he doing?" He says, "That is all right, I am punishing him." He had to do that for two or three days.

There were a couple of other things I happened to think about Di while he was talking, that I remember, and I thought I might say something about them. One was I remember going out in a patrol when I was flying single-seaters one morning, and he was flying the DD's and I was flying the single-seater, and it happened that none of the others could get machines, and we were flying a few miles out of Ostend and Zeebrugge and I saw Di go down and get into the water. I thought I had better not leave him alone, so I went down to take a look at him, and he was waving his arms and I didn't know what was the matter with him, and I kept on flying. Pretty soon he began to shoot at me with a Very pistol, and I pulled out my pistol and started shooting at him, and I shot up all my cartridges and thought I had better go back and tell the motor boat crew about him, and it went out after him. Nothing seemed to worry him very much.

The other incident was when one of the [British] DH's was shot down off Ostend some place along the coast. They send in a report to our station to go out and rescue the men, and of course Di was the first fellow that went out to rescue the men. I was flying with the Camel squadron [No.213 Squadron, RAF] at the time, and we went out to escort him, and we went out and flew over him and he went down and landed and had to shut off his motor to land. It was not a very nice place. As I remember there were some Hun machines flying around pretty near and it was pretty near the coast and was along the coast up in German territory, and I know I would certainly have hated to land there and shut off my motors. But that was another thing that did not seem to worry Di. He shut off his motor and landed on one wing and picked up one man and started off again and dropped down with the other wing and picked up the other man, and flew back with them.

The first thing I remember about flying with the British was when Ken [MacLeish] and I were down at Brighton [Gosport], where Bob [Lovett] had placed us in December. We had a pretty good time there. Bob came up to me and said he had a darned good job for me. He said he and Di and I were to fly scout machines, and were to fly ships for training. I was tickled to death. I waited around and about three weeks later we were finally sent up. By that time Di had been sent to Dunkirk and Bob had been taken in to use his brains in Paris, and I was the only one left of the original three to fly the machines, and they picked up Shorty Smith and Ken MacLeish, and we three were to go through the English course in training on land machines. We played around in Paris for about three weeks. That was the first time I got very well acquainted with Ken, and we were together all the time, and I remember being very much impressed by him throughout. He always ran the three of us, and nothing would do but the best, and I always admired him for his ability to get on with almost everybody that he ran into. He always seemed to get along well with the French and the English. He even got along with the French girls pretty well. Finally we went over and he was sent first to this British station at Gosport. That station is a station for instructors, and therefore is just the same as the various all over England, for the young men, except perhaps that it is a little better, the system being to take up the new man in the two-place machines and teach them how to fly correctly. I decided that I had never known anything about flying at all when I went up there with this instructor, who was a South African named [Dirk] Cloete. He said to make a turn and I did, and he said it was terrible. We had these little ear phones and could talk back and forth. He made a turn then and I didn't see that it was much different than mine, but he told me no-one really knew how to make a turn in the air until he had gone through this experience, and it may have been true, because it was a regular art the way they worked there.

We were there a month and there was nothing very exciting except when Shorty went up once and tried to loop. They have a stick in those machines in both seats and a strap to hold you in the seat, and the strap in the front seat when Shorty was going over the loop went over his stick and the machine went up and down like this [indicating], and he went pretty close to the ground when he happened to think about side slipping, and his brain was working pretty well just then, so he side slipped and landed safely and actually did not break anything at all. I remember he laughed pretty near continuously for six hours after that, he was so hysterical.

While we were there I remember about Ken, that several of the instructors said they had never seen as good a flyer as Ken was. They all admired him very much. Shorty and he and I used to fly a good deal together in these Camels, and Ken was always able to sit on our tails—an enviable position; these machines all shooting straight ahead, the idea is to get behind them.

We were there about a month and then went to a place called Turnberry, a famous summer resort. There we went through a course in gunnery, which was very tedious. It was mostly sitting on hard benches and listening to lectures. But we learned a good deal about machine guns, taking them apart and putting them together. We met a good many American Army pilots there, and we met a lot of South Africans and had a pretty good time in spite of the hard work, which took seven or eight hours every day.

After that we went to a place called Ayr, which is a school of aerial fighting. This is where they go after Turnberry, and theoretically learn how to fight. They go up with an instructor who plays around with them in the air, and they try to shoot him down theoretically, using cameras instead of guns. I thought it was a good deal of fizzle, because they did not have enough machines. I think all of us flew about an hour and a half there, and we did not learn a good deal, but we had a fairly good time. While we were there the Navy [First Aeronautic Detachment] men who were sent over, who were supposed to be our flights [at Dunkirk]—I think the idea originally was that we were to have three flights, and a number of gobs were sent over to learn how to be our flights. They came over and were an awful crowd, we decided. They turned out pretty well, some of them, but the first few days they flew Camels at Ayr, I think either two or three were killed, and they really did not know anything about flying, and they ought not to have been allowed to go up there.

After that I think we went to Dunkirk and joined Di and waited for these scout machines to be fixed up. Then from there we went and trained in an Army school where we had a pretty unfortunate experience. We did not like them and they did not seem to be very fond of us. And after that, I guess around the time Ken and Shorty and some lieutenant who was at Dunkirk—what was his name, that big Navy man?

A VOICE: [Willis] Haviland

MR. INGALLS: Yes, they were sent out to this big 213 Squadron and were there two months. It was then a navy station, and did nothing but patrolling the seas. The only interesting thing that happened all the time we were there was that we made a raid on the mole at Zeebrugge, the raid being to carry three or four bombs weighing 20 pounds apiece, and diving out of this cloud and letting the bombs go, and getting back up to the clouds as soon as we could. I remember Shorty was lost and went down and bombed Ostend all by himself, and had a pretty good time. That was really the only interesting thing that happened to us while we were with this squadron for a whole month. Flying around the sea in a land machine was not very interesting, and we did not like it, because any time a motor would stop we would stop too.

The second time I went out with the British squadron was, as Di says, after I had been hanging around visiting him for a week or so. After we had got the station nicely fixed up for the Marines, Di managed to get orders for me to go out and join this 213 Squadron. The squadron had about 15 men, and there were 15 or 18 Camels there and a large number of mechanics, and it was on the same field as a bombing squadron, 218, where Di was for some time. The men at that squadron had already been changed into the RAF, so it had five duties to perform: a high offensive patrol, which was going out and flying over the lines, and if possible getting into any fights that there were, and they occasionally went out and helped patrol the fleet. Then there were the low bombing raids. We did two or three of those on various aerodromes behind the lines, which consisted in the squadron going over and coming down and dropping the little bombs on the aerodromes and shooting the place up. And also when the push began in October we were sent out with bombs and told to go over and destroy anything we could find. And we usually would fly over the lines and drop the bombs on any artillery or ammunition trains we could see and shoot them up and come back.

MR. DAVISON: Tell about the night you played for the dance and also tell us about Ken, when he was shot down.

MR. INGALLS: Well, about Ken. I think Hanrahan called me up some time about the fourth or fifth of October and Ken MacLeish was to

take my place and I was to go to England and be the acceptance pilot
at Eastleigh, and very soon after that Ken came over to Dunkirk to Di's
station, and we went in and talked things over, and we went back to
Eastleigh, and he sort of broke me in to testing machines, to see how
they flew and what stuff there was, and then he was there about two days
getting me fixed up in that job, and then he took a DH and flew it over
to where the boys were flying on the front with DH's, and left for the
position that I had with 213 Squadron. The only thing I know about him
is what I heard. I saw a few of the 213 men afterwards. They said, I think,
it was the second flight he went out on, or the first . . .

A VOICE: He went out on one in the morning and then in the
afternoon.

MR. INGALLS: He went out on this flight in the afternoon and got
into a fight and left his flight and went over and attacked a number of
Huns, and when he went out there a Canadian by the name of George
[J. E.] Greene went over to join him, and I think Ken shot down one
German, and then he was shot down in flames, and Greene was shot
down and jumped out, as I understand.

DI GATES: Greene came down on our side of the lines, but was
killed. No one was left of Ken's flight. They don't know the exact story.

MR. PAINE: How many of them?

A VOICE: One fellow got back, Di.

DI GATES: I understand there were three. One came back on our
side and Greene came down on our lines and was killed, and Ken. They
never knew what happened to him.

A VOICE: There were three Huns who came down and they don't
know whether Ken was credited with two of them or three.

MR. INGALLS: I remember telling Ken that I thought he ought to
be careful as he possibly could, particularly at the first, as there was not
much point in going ahead very fast for the reason that in my opinion
the first two or three fights he would be going into were entirely a
matter of luck, and the more careful he was the more chances he had of
getting through them, and really accomplishing something in the end.
And I told him about the first experience I had, which was in sort of a
fight when I had been there about a week or so, and I had flown out on
these patrols, and the first time I saw a Hun he dove on this two-seater,
and I had always heard about getting up close to them before starting to

shoot, so I had the motor wide open tearing after this Hun. There were three of us in the formation and my commander was a little ahead and I was about to shoot when this Hun burst into flames at what appeared to me to be an incredible distance. But apparently the commander had started to shoot when we were abreast, so it sort of changed my idea.

The second time I struck at Huns was about a week after that. We had been on several patrols and I had not seen anything, so I went out by myself and thought I might see something. I went up to about 20,000 feet and cruised around until I got cold and groggy from the high altitude, and I thought there was nothing around and came down. I came down to about 14,000 feet and happened to look to one side and saw three monoplanes about 300 feet away. As I saw them they started to dive and turned and dived at me. I was about three or four miles over the lines. I thought I had got into trouble. I remember cursing myself for not watching what I was doing. From there I would go up and down to the right and left and these three Huns would dive one at a time, shoot and then pull up and get up high and come down again shooting. At first they did that from quite a little distance and the tracers did not come very close, so I didn't worry particularly. But as we got nearer the lines they began getting closer and closer, so finally I thought I might as well have a little fun, and so when they would dive and start up again I would start after one particular Hun. And I did that two or three times and would take a crack at him, and then beat it for our lines again. And each time I would lose sight of the other two Germans, and the result would be that I would hear shooting and I would not know where it was coming from, and I could not dodge, and it did not work out too well. And after I had done that twice the Hun I went after the last time disappeared, at least I never saw him again. I don't know what happened to him. I suppose he dove down, and the other two fellows followed me and finally the last one shot at me all by himself and he turned and started for home, and I took a last shot at him and he dove down and disappeared, and I went home, sitting in my seat and jumping around. When I got back there were four or five bullet holes in the machine, and the British fellows had got back and they were all looking at a hole in their machine, and I thought this is slick. I have more than they have, and told them all about it, and the commander gave me the dickens for going out by myself.

I think I told you about the Varssenaere aerodrome air raid last
year didn't I? I was between Zeebrugge and Bruges. It was a very big
aerodrome. On the east side it had night bombers and on the other side
Fokker machines. The British thought it was a good idea to go over and
shoot it up. They had four or five squadrons of Camels, including an
American Army squadron which had got Camels from the British, and
I think some DH's went up to bomb also. We were awakened very early
in the morning and went over to the mess hall and had breakfast in the
dark and got out and started in flights while it was still pitch dark. It
was kind of hard work to fly, I mean you could really not see much of
anything, and you couldn't see straight up. They said just take off and go
around and around and circle and climb and we will meet over Dunkirk
at about 4,000 feet. I was one of the first ones to start up and had gone
around the field about once when I heard a most awful clatter in my
machine, apparently one of the connecting rods had broken, so I had to
come down. And I had four bombs in the bottom and I thought here
is where I blow myself up for sure. But I came down and it was pretty
dark, but I could make out the canal and the trees and I landed and just
missed coming down on one of our DH's, and then I ran over and got
another machine, and by that time I was the last one to get up, and as
I rose up over Dunkirk I had a view of the whole squadron up there,
and it was the prettiest thing I ever saw, because the sun was just coming
up and there were all these different flights, and each commander had
a different colored Very pistol, and they would shoot them off trying
to get their flights congregated after going up in the dark. After we got
together we started off one flight after another. I think there were about
75 machines, and we went straight out from Dunkirk about two or three
miles, and then flew along the coast and beyond Ostend, and then came
in diving down so as to cross the coast at about a thousand feet, and
then came down right close to the ground where nobody could shoot
us with Archie, and we thought we would get down before the Huns
knew anything about it. It worked to perfection. We came down to
about a few hundred feet over the ground and skimmed along in a row
towards the aerodrome. We flew around I suppose five minutes trying
to find this aerodrome, and finally we had to split into two crowds, in
two long rows parallel. Finally I saw the aerodrome ahead, and the men
ahead going over and diving down and dropping their bombs and going

up and around. I got so excited that I saw—there were six Fokkers lined up besides the sheds on the right hand side and men cranking them, and some of the motors were running and some men were running from the Fokkers to the sheds trying to get away, and I saw the men running and I started to shoot when I happened to notice I was shooting through the wings of the fellow straight ahead of me. I thought it was worrying him so I stopped. And then I started to bomb and watched mybombs landing about 200 yards away from the place I wanted to hit. But we did start several good fires.

We were there several minutes, just zooming up and down. It was an awful mess. I don't know why no-one was injured. Finally they shot off a lot of white Very pistol lights to send us home and everybody started to leave, and we tore across and some way or other got pretty well parallel across from the coast. I suppose we started a mile from the coast and had machines extending for about five miles south in a wide straggling course, and we went back towards our hangars. By that time the Huns were all awake and there were a few machine guns shooting and the Archie battery began waking up, and anytime one would wake up, the nearest machine would dive down to it and shoot and that silenced every one of them. And we tore across the lines and landed and found that no-one was hurt in any way out of the whole crowd, and I guess we all did some execution. It was supposed to be a pretty effective raid.

Another incident was one time a young Canadian named [George] MacKay, who had not been in command of any flights, took a flight over on a high patrol. I think there were five or six of us together, and we started off and got up pretty high and got over the lines and saw six Fokkers looping and zooming and having a fine time across the lines. I happened to look over and saw a lot of machines back of our lines, but paid no special attention to them. MacKay saw them too and thought they were Camels, and MacKay started to dive down. We were up about 10,000 feet, and we got about half way down and I saw all these machines coming at us like the dickens from behind. There were about 30 of them, and they came between us and our lines, and we were cut off, and to get back to our lines we had to go around in a big circle then west to get back to our lines. Of course, the fellows back of the V formation we always fly in, were in the fortunate position of being nearest the lines, and they dove back behind MacKay and myself. The fellow behind me disappeared and we heard nothing of him for two months, and then we found out he had landed in Holland. I suppose he dove after the Fokkers, and I don't know what happened to him, but I know he was interned and I suppose that is what he did. We went around in a circle, MacKay and these two fellows dove down so as not to be too near us, and they were about 1,000 feet below us. The Huns followed us I suppose for ten minutes while we made this big circle, and never dared to get within less than 300 yards of us, although they could do so easily enough because they always had faster machines than we did. When we got back we decided they were decidedly yellow. There were 30 and another squadron of 12 came up. They just shot from around 300 yards, which was a little too much for them to hit us. They were apparently hoping for a long shot to take effect. Of course, if they had got close enough we would have had to turn and fight, but with the two of us up high and the two below we would have been in a tight place if they wanted to fight, but they never came close enough to worry us. The tracers would go by but they never came very close. We all came back except for this poor fellow who landed in Holland.

A VOICE: Why not tell us about some of the ones you did hit.

MR. INGALLS: Well, I remember one time we were doing patrol work or we were escorting 218 [Squadron] which was the bombing squadron, and they had 12 DH's, and we had three flights of Camels, five each. We would fly along, one flight each side of these 12 and about a thousand feet above them, and we would go out along the coast and then come in across between Ostend and Zeebrugge, and go straight towards Bruges. I was at this time leading the flight on the right hand side with five Camels back, and four Huns came up from Ostend for us. That was the only time I saw a small bunch of Huns attack any number of British machines. These four Huns came up and I thought that was slick, and my flight naturally turned and came up behind me. I remember pointing at one and I shot at him and he turned first and I turned after him and then for several minutes we were flying around there, and I would get a shot at some German and then climb up as fast as I could and turn around and look at another German and fire at him, and climb up. I always tried to climb above. No one could shoot you if you were above him. I was impressed right away by the fact I did not see but four Huns and did not see any of my own machines at all. It turned out that the two fellows behind me had their gasoline tanks perforated and had to go back and the other two men in the rear had beat it for home as soon as we started for the Germans, which as a matter of fact was a perfectly natural things to do. They were young kids just out from England, and the young fellows nearly always did the same thing the first ten or fifteen times. As soon as they saw a Hun they would beat it for home as fast as they could. But I played around with these four Huns for quite a while, and meanwhile the DH's had gone over Bruges and bombed Bruges and come back, and while I was still there one of the DH's came along and had a bad motor, and was below the eleven others and also somewhat behind, and I noticed as it came along, I happened to see it and two Huns, one right in front and one directly behind it. So I thought what I should do was go over and protect that DH, and I went as fast as I could and went broadside and I came roaring along and took a shot at the fellow in the back of the DH. I just took one quick burst, and then I hoiked around and started to shoot at the fellow a little bit in front of the DH. I got up within half the width of this room, almost on top of him practically, and I could see the tracers going straight in, and he sort of slopped over and went down. I thought it was great, that I had shot him, and I went in and reported that I had shot a Hun in front of the DH, and just then the pilot of the DH came in, and he said, "I saw that Hun and he straightened out just before he hit the ground." So I was discouraged. But just then the phone range and the DH station had called up and reported that this Hun that was behind, which I did not think I got at all had burst into flames and gone down, and that certainly astonished me. I had not thought I had hit him at all and the fellow I thought I had hit got away.

Now I guess it's time for me to stop.

(Cries of "Go On.")

MR. INGALLS: This time Di was talking about was sometime later, when we had spent a whole day or two on long patrols and had not seen any Huns at all. Now, I know what happened now. We had gone out in the morning and run into twelve or fifteen Huns. There were five of us. This fellow [Colin Peter] Brown was leading us.[1] I think he is the fellow

---

1. Colin Peter Brown (1898–1965) flew with Ingalls in No.213 Squadron, served in the RAF until 1954, and retired as an air vice marshal.

who shot down [Baron Manfred Von] Richthofen. In the morning we had had a fight with quite a number of Huns, and a little fellow named Smith, I don't know whether he had been hit, but anyhow one of the Huns had got on his tail and was following him, so I left the flight and went after this bird behind Smith, and was trying to fix this German behind him. They were too far below and I did not get him, and I lost my chance of getting one of them because I had left the main part of the fight. So just before supper I went out again with a fellow named [George Stacey] Hodson and flew up and down looking for two-seaters. They usually had two-seaters with observers. And we flew around and around, and we turned around and I happened to see an Archie near our lines, and I shot my guns off as a signal to Hodson to attract his attention so he would follow. So I went over towards Nieuport, and when I got pretty near I saw this big two-seater down very low, it was one of the German Rumplers. And I remembered having heard about shooting down a two-seater by going down underneath the tail and coming up underneath and shooting the pilot down and watching him disappear. So I went carefully up and down around and behind and climbed up under him, and I found I was away ahead of him, because the Camel has more speed; the Rumpler went about 40 miles an hour and I was going about 120 miles, and he was away behind me. And I went and turned and was after him again. He went so slow and I went so fast that we circled four or five times, and about that time I was almost to Ostend. Finally I came up I remember one time, and I did not come up quite right and I came up behind him but a little to the right, and I could see this Hun. He had a black leather helmet and his hand was one his machine gun and he was trying to point it, but his rudder was in the way and all the tracers were going to the right hand side. Finally I got mad and so I went down behind him in a straight line and shot at him as fast as I could, and I saw a puff of smoke and I dove to the ground and I got down to the ground. We always used to go home, when we got over across the lines, down very near the land, because there was less danger of being shot down by Archie and Onions, and also no Huns could pick you up. The only danger was the machine guns, and I had gone down around that land a good deal and I thought I knew where the machine gun nests were, and I would miss them. And I went along quite a while, and then I heard a machine gun shooting from one side and a cloud of vapor came up around the engine and it stopped and the machine tilted. I was only about 200 feet up and there was a little clump of trees, and I was trying to figure whether I would get over the trees and land on the ground beyond or land in the trees, and in the meantime I was fiddling with the controls. Just as I got up to the trees the motor started again and it hit on about five or six cylinders out of the nine. And the machine is built so that when the motor is going full it draws the front up and it will climb. So when the motor began to run again it pulled up and I skimmed along and then I began to experiment and I found that my controls to go down were working but the ones to come up were very stiff, and I knew something had happened and I did not dare move any of the controls except to go ahead. And I went over the machine gun posts, and every one was having a slick time and shooting at me, but anyhow nobody did hit me and I got across and I had an awful time landing. I could go down all right, but I could not stop going down when I started unless I turned on the motor and if I turned on the motor I would go up again. Finally I did skim in just over an aerodrome and managed to land. (Applause)

Afterword

David Ingalls reached New York in early December 1918 after nearly fifteen months overseas and twenty-one tumultuous months since he and the rest of the Yale gang traveled to New London to enlist in the navy. The voyage home proceeded more joyously than the one heading into the war zone in October 1917. And Ingalls was still two months short of his twentieth birthday. He went back to Yale, where he roomed with Harry Davison and captained the varsity hockey team. On a postwar visit to the United States, the Prince of Wales presented Ingalls with the Distinguished Flying Cross he earned for his exploits with No.213 Squadron. Like many other veteran-undergraduates, Ingalls received college credit for work performed while in the service, and he graduated with his class in the spring of 1920, entering Harvard Law School that fall. He received his discharge from the navy on March 25, 1921, and the following year married Louise Harkness, a Standard Oil heiress. The wedding party included Trubee and Harry Davison, Brewster Jennings, and Di Gates.

After Ingalls's graduation from Harvard in 1923, the couple settled in the Cleveland area and eventually raised five children: Edith, Jane, Louise, Anna, and David Jr. The young veteran began his civilian career with the Cleveland legal firm of Squire, Sanders & Dempsey. He continued to be strongly interested in aviation, however, and in 1925, while on the aviation committee of the Cleveland Chamber of Commerce, he helped develop plans for the new Cleveland airport. The following year, still in his midtwenties and just three years out of Harvard Law School, the well-connected Ingalls entered the world of politics when he was elected to the Ohio House of Representatives. While there, he cosponsored the Ohio Aviation Code, a model for codes in other states. Ingalls's frequent trips from Cleveland to Columbus in his own airplane earned him a nickname as "the flying legislator." During this era and for decades after, he maintained a grass airstrip at his estate in Hunting Valley, Ohio, and he helped develop a new airport at neighboring Chagrin Falls, dedicated in 1932. Attendees at the dedication included flight luminaries such as Buckeye native Eddie Rickenbacker, Jimmy Doolittle, and Alexander de Seversky. Ingalls's business interests at the time included a stint as an officer of Continental Shares, Ltd., an investment trust created by financier Cyrus S. Eaton that had substantial holdings in the Midwest and was listed on the New York Stock Exchange.

Thanks to the recommendations of friends such as Cdr. John Towers, wartime patron of the First Yale Unit and now assistant chief of the Bureau of Aeronautics, and Newton Baker, a fellow Ohioan who was mayor of Cleveland during Ingalls's childhood and a former secretary of war, the thirty-year-old aviator became the nation's second assistant secretary of the navy for aeronautics in March 1929, replacing Edward Warner.[1] In filling the post, the recently elected president, Herbert Hoover, had sought a man thoroughly familiar with aeronautical issues, preferably a flier who possessed administrative ability and understood the viewpoint of pilots, legislators, and navy officers alike. Ingalls fit the bill.

The president and the junior cabinet member formed an immediate bond, and in an interview conducted many years later, Ingalls recalled the chief executive's friendliness, intelligence, and great mental attainment and ability, as well as his interest in aviation. Hoover frequently invited Ingalls and his Yale Unit companion Trubee Davison, then serving as assistant secretary of war for aviation, to visit the White House for tea or to spend a weekend at the president's rustic fishing camp at the headwaters of the Rapidan River in the foothills of the Shenandoah Mountains. There, the men often shared a very early breakfast. On one of these trips, Ingalls arrived at the controls of a Navy Department autogiro and proceeded to take Herbert Hoover Jr. up for an hour-long ride.[2]

Once installed in his new office, Ingalls began taking trips around the country to carry out his varied duties.[3] His perks of office encompassed

---

1. Ingalls had been reelected to the Ohio legislature but resigned his seat when he went to Washington.

2. Oral History Interview, November 5, 1969, for the Herbert Hoover Presidential Library and the Hoover Institution on War, Revolution, and Peace. Ingalls also developed a fondness for Mrs. Hoover, whom he called "a wonderful person."

3. He took one extended trip in the fall of 1929 along both the Atlantic and Pacific coasts, inspecting naval aviation facilities in a large Ford trimotor aircraft.

personal use of a Boeing F4B fighter or a Curtiss F8C Helldiver with a large greenhouse canopy, painted a deep navy blue. His passengers included, among others, Secretary of the Navy Charles Francis Adams III. Some assignments were purely formal, such as greeting famed aviatrix Ruth Nichols, the "Flying Debutante," on her visit to Washington; meeting with Charles Lindbergh; speaking at the christening of *Akron,* one of the navy's newest airships; attending the annual air races; or presiding at ceremonies at naval air stations or aboard the fleet's aircraft carriers. His high-profile appearances in Washington and elsewhere earned him a photograph on the cover of *Time* magazine on March 2, 1931. Later that year, he received a commission as a lieutenant commander in the Naval Reserve.

Ingalls's most substantive accomplishments resulted from his close partnership with Adm. William Moffett, the first and long-serving chief of the Bureau of Aeronautics. The admiral's recent biographer, William Trimble, noted that though the officer's relationship with the "cerebral and egocentric" former assistant secretary, Edward Warner, had been cool and formal, Moffett "found Ingalls far more congenial and the two developed a cordial working relationship." The young man's vigorous advocacy for aviation in the navy, his celebrity, and his winning personality were all assets the chief could deploy in ongoing battles to secure necessary appropriations from Congress or increased influence within the Department of the Navy. The two also maintained their relationship after Ingalls departed Washington, corresponding on a host of issues, including departmental policy and relations with Congress. In the depths of the Depression, Moffett lamented to his former associate, "Things could not be worse as far as the Navy is concerned ... the situation is more outrageous than it has ever been before, and you ought to be thankful you are not here."[4]

During Ingalls's Washington years, a long and varied list of important matters came across his desk. In a difficult fiscal environment, he pushed to implement the navy's five-year aircraft procurement plan, approved back in 1926. During his tenure, the fleet tripled its roster of aircraft, and he test-flew all new machines. He strenuously advocated a fully deployable carrier task force and backed construction of additional vessels. Vigorous discussions revolved around proposed flying-deck cruisers, various aircraft

4. William F. Trimble, *Admiral William A. Moffett: Architect of Naval Aviation* (Annapolis, Md.: Naval Institute Press, 1994), 228, 251.

Hero of the Angry Sky

330

contracts, the role of rigid airships in fleet operations, and the 1930 London Naval Conference. Ingalls also played a significant role in the crucial and bruising budgeting process and testified frequently before congressional committees.

After three years of service, the young assistant secretary resigned his post in 1932 to mount a campaign for the office of governor of Ohio, but he failed to secure the Republican Party's nomination. He later served as Cleveland's director of public health and welfare in the return administration of Harry L. Davis,[5] but he resigned in 1935 when the mayor refused to install X-ray equipment in City Hospital. It was during this period that Ingalls became a fierce critic of Franklin Delano Roosevelt (FDR) and the New Deal.

Whatever his duties, the aviator turned politician turned businessman retained the energetic, outgoing personality of his youth. Relatives remember him as being social and congenial and loving a good time. One gandson described Ingalls as a ton of energy, a man who took you along with him whenever you were around him. He possessed a great sense of humor and a devil-may-care approach to life. He loved to dance and to laugh his high-pitched laugh.[6] The pipe so evident in his World War I photographs and letters remained with him throughout his life. "Ya gotta live life," Ingalls told his kids: "Don't ever look back, move ahead." In some ways, he raised his daughters like sons. They would canoe, camp, fish, milk the cow, and clear trails on family property; he taught Jane to drive at the age of eleven. Ingalls also insisted his children pick up after themselves: "Don't have others do for you what you can do youself." He would often ask in his conspiratorial way, "Hey kids, what do you want to do? Don't tell your mother." And despite his achievements and prominence, Ingalls remained modest and unassuming. He never talked of his war experiences with his family, and his daughters did not know of his exploits until a 1965 Yale Unit reunion.

In the late 1930s, after a few years of relative inactivity, Ingalls turned his considerable energy toward promoting the Senate candidacy of his cousin

---

5. Harry L. Davis (1878–1950), a Republican, was elected mayor of Cleveland in 1915 and served until 1920, when he resigned to campaign, successfully, for the governorship (1921–23). He served as mayor of Cleveland again from 1934 to 1935.

6. During the war, Ken MacLeish had written, "Crock is the most amusing man I've ever met in my life. . . . He's getting quite touchy now because we've kidded him too much about that passionate laugh of his." Quoted in Geoffrey Rossano, ed., *The Price of Honor: The World War One Letters of Naval Aviator Kenneth MacLeish* (Annapolis, Md.: Naval Institute Press, 1991), 64.

and friend Robert A.Taft. He would play a major role in the successful 1938 campaign, defeating incumbent Democrat Robert Bulkley. According to Taft's biographer, Ingalls served as a "faithful lieutenant" and possessed several key assets:"He was handsome and genial, had the special advantage of being a millionaire, and proved a useful fundraiser." Ohio historian Andrew Cayton described Taft's victory as a "repudiation of years of Democratic rule at both the state and federal levels, a populist uprising by Ohioans in small towns, rural areas, and cities such as Columbus against the growing assertiveness of labor and the celebration of government as the solution to Ohio's woes." He noted that "suspicion of big government, big labor radicalism, and radicalism" remained at the center of Taft's career to the end. In this regard, both Robert Taft and his cousin David Ingalls saw the world in much the same terms, and the political relationship the two forged in the 1930s lasted unbroken until the senator's untimely death in 1953. Ingalls undertook fund-raising missions from 1938 to 1940 and served as an Ohio delegate to the 1940 Republican National Convention, where he saw his cousin's bid for the presidential nomination derailed by Wendell Wilkie.[7]

With fighting raging in Europe and war clouds rapidly darkening over the United States, Ingalls and many of his Yale Unit compatriots hastened to join the nation's accelerating preparedness efforts. Erl Gould returned to active duty at the Bureau of Aeronautics in January 1941. Robert Lovett became assistant secretary of the army for air in April, and Di Gates assumed the newly created post of assistant secretary of the avy (AIR) the following September.[8] Known as a "zealous advocate of a strong air force," Ingalls began his efforts in 1940 when he became vice president and general manager of Pan American Ferries overseas operations.[9] Pan American's president, Juan Trippe, had contracted with the federal government to ferry combat and military aircraft to England and build way stations in

7. The Ingalls-Taft relationship is detailed in James Patterson, *Mr. Republican: A Biography of Robert A. Taft* (Boston: Houghton Mifflin, 1972), 161, 208, 212–18. Concerning the political landscape in Ohio during the 1930s, see Andrew R. L. Cayton, *Ohio: The History of a People* (Columbus: Ohio State University Press, 2002), esp. 312–27. At least one newspaper identified Ingalls as the manager of Taft's presidential effort.

8. Lovett's World War II years in the Pentagon and his tremendous impact on the nation's aircraft program are summarized in Walter Isaacson and Evan Thomas, *The Wise Men: Six Friends and the World They Made* (New York: Simon and Schuster, 1986), 190–96, 202–9.

9. Patterson, *Mr. Republican*, 198. Pan American Ferries was a subsidiary of Pan American Airways.

South America for military equipment being flown to Africa, the Middle East, and Russia. Ingalls directed these far-flung operations from offices in Miami. He continued that work after Pearl Harbor plunged the nation back into war, but in November 1942, he rejoined the navy.[10]

Back on active duty, the still youthful Ingalls filled several important staff and administrative positions in the Pacific theater during the next three years. He first served as assistant operations officer on the staff of the commander of Air Forces Pacific, where he helped develop NAS Honolulu as a base for the new Naval Air Transport Service (NATS), and then as chief of staff for the Forward Area and Air Center Command at Guadalcanal, directing the transport of supplies and matériel. Throughout this period, he inspected and surveyed various Pacific islands for NATS bases and routes. In 1944, he became plans officer/South Pacific Forces and finally commanding officer at NAS Pearl Harbor. Ingalls's picture appeared often in the pages of *Life* magazine. He retired from active duty on November 8, 1945, and transferred to the retired list on February 1, 1959, as a rear admiral. Despite his demanding wartime duties, he found time to maintain his personal and political correspondence with Senator Taft back in Washington.[11]

Following the war, Ingalls renewed his association with Pan American Airways, and between 1945 and 1949 he served on its board of directors. As an airline executive, he participated in the company's first around-the-world passenger flight, stopping for tea at 10 Downing Street. Ingalls also resumed his strenuous political activities, laboring to reelect cousin Bob Taft to the Senate and advising or directing the Ohio senator's presidential bids in 1948 and 1952. Ingalls acted as a delegate to the party's 1948, 1952, and 1956 conventions and served as a member of the GOP's national committee. In 1952, during Taft's final, unsuccessful effort to secure the Republican presidential nomination, Ingalls acted as campaign director; in that capacity, he was "loyal, genial, almost boyishly enthusiastic about his cousin's prospects," but he also offered some sharp criticism of rival Dwight Eisenhower, earning a mild reproach from his candidate. In his private plane,

---

10. Trippe's work ferrying aircraft to the war zone and Lovett's efforts to convince the fellow Skull and Bones man to carry out the activities are recounted in Isaacson and Thomas, *Wise Men,* 202–3.

11. Ibid., 269, 303. For his wartime service, Ingalls received the Bronze Star and the Legion of Merit.

Ingalls flew tens of thousands of miles around the country soliciting funds, shoring up support, and aggressively buttonholing delegates.[12]

In addition to politics and aviation, Ingalls pursued several new interests in the postwar era. He spent four years (1954 to 1958) as president and publisher of the *Cincinnati Times-Star,* as well as vice chairman of the Taft Broadcasting Company, before returning to the practice of law. Other business activities included serving as a director of the Cleveland Trust Company, director of South Eleuthera Properties, and vice president of Virginia Hot Springs, Inc.[13] Following long family tradition, he and his wife, Louise, became active philanthropists, in 1953 creating the Louise Harkness Ingalls and David Sinton Ingalls Foundation, dedicated to supporting educational, medical, and cultural initiatives. Ingalls also served as president of the Central Eyebank for Sight Restoration, trustee of Laurel School, and honorary trustee of the Young Men's Christian Association.[14]

Throughout his life, David Ingalls pursued a busy schedule as a sportsman—hunting fox and other animal; camping; and playing polo, tennis, and golf. In 1928, he placed second in the citywide squash tournament, and an account of his near heroics also described him as a "crack polo player." During his 1929–32 stint in Washington, he played polo with the U.S. Army's renowned White team. Ingalls co-owned two shooting properties in Florida with childhood friend and fellow Yale aviator Robert Livingston Ireland—the Ring Oak and Forshalee plantations. When Trubee Davison traveled south on a hunting visit, Ingalls prepared a special wagon for the disabled founder of the First Yale Unit. The navy's first ace also maintained his lifelong passion for flying. He enthusiastically supported the Cleveland Air Races for two decades (1929–49),[15] and he continued

---

12. Patterson noted that Ingalls was a devoted admirer without political ambitions of his own. For Ingalls's political activities from 1948 to 1952, see Patterson, *Mr. Republican,* 399, 409–12, 505, 511, 513, 515, 519, 539, 541, and 553–73.

13. This resort had been developed many years before by David Ingalls's grandfather, railroad magnate Melville Ingalls. David and Louise Ingalls honeymooned there.

14. Louise Harkness Ingalls died in 1978. David Ingalls later married Frances Wragg.

15. Cleveland first hosted the National Air Races in 1929, the same year that witnessed the initial women's Air Derby, later known as the Powder Puff Derby. Cleveland put on quite a show for the event. A country club ball was held for six hundred attendees, among them aviatrixes Amelia Earhart and Ruth Nichols. Ingalls hosted several events, including one where he showed movies of naval aviation, with Charles Lindbergh among his guests. See the account in the *Clevelend Plain Dealer,* September 1, 1929.

piloting a series of Beechcraft models into his eighties, amassing fourteen thousand hours aloft in an aviation career spanning more than sixty years. For a lifetime of achievement in aeronautics, he was enshrined at the National Aviation Hall of Fame in 1983 and the Naval Aviation Museum Hall of Honor three years later.

In his eight-five years, David Ingalls lived many lives, moving seamlessly from law to politics, government, publishing, military service, business and finance, aviation, and philanthropy. He served one president and almost elected another. He was a sportsman, family man, devoted friend, and gregarious host. Those who knew or observed Ingalls remarked on his zest, contagious enthusiasm, humor, courage, eagerness to accept a challenge, and strong opinions, as well as his ability to lead others and sweep them along with him, always moving ahead to the next big phase of his energetic march through life.

Most of those personal attributes first became manifest in the bloody campaign waged in the angry skies over Europe during World War I, the vast and tragic conflict that shaped the twentieth century. As a teenaged member of the navy's infant aviation arm, Ingalls took to the air in the flimsiest of machines, dependable only in their capacity to kill. His personal abilities and a healthy measure of luck allowed him to survive and flourish. Along the way, he participated in the birth of modern naval aviation, ultimately one of the most powerful military forces ever unleashed. Though Ingalls went on to achieve prominence in many areas, he always carried with him the title of the navy's first ace. David S. Ingalls died in April 1985, one of the last survivors of the First Yale Unit with which he had gained such fame.

David Ingalls came home a hero. He was still only nineteen years old and a full life awaited him. He performed some his most important work as Assistant Secretary of the Navy for Aeronautics in the Herbert Hoover administration. Always on the go, he toured bases and met with officers and personnel across the continent. He is shown here in 1929, still impossibly boyish, meeting in San Diego with Admiral H.V. Butler, newly appointed Commander, Aircraft Squadrons, Battle Fleet. *Courtesy National Archives*

Appendix 1

David Ingalls's Victories with No.213 Squadron, RAF

Date	Time	Unit	Aircraft	Opponent	Location
1. 8/11/18	0955	213	Camel C73	Albatross C	NE of Dixmude
2. 8/21/18	1850	213	Camel N6376	LVG C	S of Zevecote
3. 9/15/18	1400	213	Camel D9649	Rumpler C	Ostend
4. 9/18/18	1050	213	Camel D9649	Balloon	Le Barriere
5. 9/20/18	1045	213	Camel D8177	Fokker D.VII	Vlisseghem
6. 9/24/18	1730	213	Camel D9649	Rumpler C	St. Pierre Capelle

1. Shared w/ Lt. Colin Brown

2. Shared w/ Capt. Colin Brown and Lt. Harry Smith

3. Shared w/ Lt. Harry Smith

4. Shared w/ Lt. Harry Smith and Lt. George Hodson

6. Shared w/ Lt. George Hodson

Appendix 2

David Ingalls's Technical Notes, Turnberry, Scotland

While at the Turnberry gunnery school, David Ingalls compiled a collection of technical notes gathered from lectures and instruction pamphlets covering the use and maintenance of machine guns, synchronization gears, and gun sights. The importance of this information could not be overstressed. A pilot's life depended on it. Each student assembled such a collection, but very few of these compilations have survived to this day. Though seemingly tedious and arcane, Ingalls's extensive notes reveal how complicated and technologically sophisticated such equipment had become by 1918; they also indicate the degree of knowledge and skill necessary to understand, maintain, and use that weaponry. His writings are reproduced here in the order that he entered them into his notebooks.

Training/Technical Notebook Compiled at Turnberry, February 1918

SOPWITH-KAUPER GUN GEAR, TYPE NO. 3

A cam is attached to some suitable part of the engine such as the distributor and has two depressions or firing points in its contour, this providing two firing positions per revolution. Tappets and guides (one for each gun) are fixed to the back plate of the engine so that their roller can run in contact with the cam, and so that the angle between them is the same as the angle between the gun and the center line of the propeller.

A light spring acts on the bell crank and serves to lift the roller out of contact with the cam while the gear is out of action.

A three-pin lever is connected to a short pull rod, which acts on the actuating lever of the trigger shaft. This rocks in a bracket fastened to the rear cover of the gun, so that its end can operate the trigger of the gun through a hole cut in the rear cover. The ordinary firing mechanism of the gun and the trigger bore(?) are removed.

The gear is arranged so that the gun is fired when the roller of the tappet runs down to the lowest part of the cam and allows the main spring of the gear to pull the long pull rod to the rear, and so operate the trigger lever.

The action of the gun can now be understood if it is assumed that the main spring can be pulled by some means when it is desired to fire the gun.

When the spring is pulled it tries to pull the three-pin lever to the rear, and by so doing to pull the trigger shaft, actuating lever by means of the short pull and so to fire the gun.

The movement of the three-pin lever, however, is controlled by the cam by means of the roller, tappet push rod, bell crank lever, and pull rod, it only being able to move to the rear and allow the gun to be fired when the roller runs down into one of the depressions in the cam.

The tendency of the light spring to keep the roller out of contact with the cam is of course overcome by the action of the main spring, which is of sufficient strength to make the roller follow the cam all the time it is desired to fire the gun.

In the non-firing position the feathers on the guide rod are caught up on the edges of the front spring anchorage, and are unable to move down the slots provided for them. The main spring is thus held extended and so unable to pull the front and rear anchorages together and the whole unit may be moved to the extent permitted by the end pillar without any influence from the main spring.

The light spring therefore serves to draw the pull rod and main spring unit forward and so lifts the push rod and raises the roller clear of the cam.

When the Bowden control is operated the end lever is rotated and the projections provided on its forward face wedge their way out of the grooves cut in the rear face of the end pillar, and pull the whole spring unit back a distance equal to the depth of the stop. If the end lever is rotated only sufficiently just to draw its projections out of the grooves and no more, the guide rod feathers will still be caught on the steps of the front spring anchorage, and the main spring will still be inoperative, but the main unit will have been drawn back against the action of the light spring and the roller will have been brought into contact with the cam at its highest point.

Contact of the roller with the cam at these high points will serve to draw the front spring anchorage forward and will lift the guide rod feathers clear of their steps each time, only to be caught up again each time the high points have passed.

Any further rotation of the end lever by means of the Bowden control will turn the guide rod feathers clear of their steps opposite their slots and will allow the spring to draw the front spring anchorage to the rear and so keep the roller in contact with the cam during the whole of its revolution, thus pulling the trigger shaft into the firing position at each low point of the cam.

When the Bowden control is slightly released the torsion of the spring tends to turn the end lever back and allows the feathers to twist out of their slots and catch on the steps, thus stopping the firing of the gun. The roller will still, however, be touching the high points of the cam, and the gear be still slightly in action. A further release of the Bowden control allows the end lever to rotate further and allows the light spring to draw the gear completely out of action, as the end lever projections find their way into the grooves on the end pillar.

Fitting and adjustment of gear:

1. The main spring should be assembled on the front and rear spring anchorages, so that when in the non-firing position there is about a quarter of a turn of torsion on the spring, tending to keep the guide rod feathers firmly on the steps of the front spring anchorage when the spring is held extended or hung up. The front spring anchorage should then be pinned to the three-pin lever and the rear spring anchorage put in position on the end pillar. The end lever should be securely fixed into position so that its projections are in the grooves provided for them when the rear spring anchorage is very slightly rotated against the torsion of the spring. This makes it certain that the feathers coming up hard against their steps will not prevent the projections registering correctly with their grooves. The lift of the rear spring anchorage in the end pillar should be such that the light spring is able to draw it freely forward.

2. The long pull rod should now be adjusted so that the roller is 1/16th inch clear of the cam. This clearance is readily determined by turning the engine so that the highest part of the cam is opposite the roller and then pulling the end lever away from the end pillar. The amount by which this

can be done gives the amount of clearance between the roller and cam when it is allowed to go forward. The Bowden lever should then be pulled sufficiently just to draw the projections of the end lever out of their grooves. The engine should be turned so that the highest part of the cam passes backwards and forwards past the roller. The front spring anchorage should have appreciable movement each time this happens. Such movement is essential to make certain that when the gear is in a firing position and the Bowden is released, the feathers will be drawn clear of their slots and will readily engage upon the steps of the front spring anchorage. It is desirable to set the long pull rod so there is more movement in this position than clearance between the roller and the cam when the two projections of the end lever are in their grooves, because any wear on that gear will tend to increase the roller clearance and diminish the other movement.

3. The short pull rod should now be adjusted so that the trigger of the gun is just tripped when the engine is turned slowly, and the roller runs down to the lowest point of the cam. The adjustment must be set very fine or the grouping will be wide.

4. If a two-bladed propeller is used it should be set so that the trigger of the gun is tripped when the trailing edge of the propeller has just passed the line of fire. The propeller can be accurately set by the Vernier adjustment provided by the number of bolts in the propeller boss, and the number in the nosepiece of the engine. Better to set the gear early than late. For two guns both must be timed independently. The actual line of aim should be checked when propeller is turned forward and back. If the timing has been correctly done, these points should be quite near together.

Maintenance:

All lock nuts and bolts should be kept tight, and all pins securely split-pinned. All joints and the tappet and roller should be freely lubricated. Timing and adjustments should be checked each morning as follows:

1. Unload gun

2. Press the thumb piece so as to fully operate Bowden control.

3. Turn propeller slowly till lock trips, and then keeping propeller in that place examine by mirror reflector to see that propeller is in correct position relative to barrel.

4. Give propeller half a turn and repeat action for (3); this is to ensure that the other cam depression also operates trigger at correct time

Any wear on joints of gear will tend to make point of aim earlier and should be adjusted as necessary.

Owing to the distance between supporting points of gear any undue strain on fuselage may cause sufficient movement on any one part of gear so as to necessitate re-adjustment to length of pull rods. Adjustment will be necessary until gear is run in, but should be required only rarely afterwards if joints, etc., are kept carefully lubricated.

The clearance between the roller and cam putting the gear in and out of action should be frequently checked and adjusted as necessary by means of the long pull rod and the torsion of the main spring. Too much torsion makes Bowden stiff and too little makes stopping of firing uncertain.

If it is found that the guns fire at slightly different points at each half revolution of engine, it is due to cam being mounted eccentrically on the distributor of the engine. If it is serious the cam must be correctly centered.

Care must be taken that the short pull rod, etc., take up their correct positions when the rear cover of the gun is closed. No force is necessary to shut cover, and none must be used.

Note—Make certain that the lock cannot be tripped either before the cam depression is touching the tappet roller or after. When firing do not press too hard on the thumb pieces operating the Bowden control as too great pressure may cause the feathers on the guide rod to bind against the walls of the slots on the front anchorage and so prevent the gun from firing.

Caution—Always unload gun before leaving machine.

NOTES ON SYNCHRONIZED C.C. FIRE CONTROL

1. A S.F.C. [Synchronized Firing Control] so controls the mechanism of the gun to which it is attached as to make its fire semi-automatic instead of automatic; that is, the trigger is tripped by the gear for each individual shot fired, the tripping of the trigger being so timed relative to the speed of the propeller as to ensure that no blade of the propeller is in the line of fire at the moment the bullet passes through the plane in which the propeller revolves.

2. Fitting the gear. The generator is usually fitted to a bracket, which is in turn fastened to the crankcase. The generator usually runs at twice

propeller speed. Generator gear wheel usually is fitted to generator cam shaft by means of a split ring and a coupling or by means of the coupling and taper pins driven through the cam shaft and coupling spindle, these pins then to be riveted over. Generator to be fitted to the pipeline connection to the bottom if possible. See that generator gland nut has some blocking device.

3. Preparing of gun. Take off firing lever, firing lever bowl, safety catch, safety catch spring with piston and trigger bar lever. Open out pawl way. File away bridge piece above the safety catch spring.

4. Fit trigger motor without spring and see that the Banjo piece is firm and that the plunger works freely. Fit C.C. type trigger bar lever. See that it has a little play in every direction, and again see that the plunger is quite free through the length of its stroke. Take trigger bar out, hang the lock with its lug in the slot of the trigger bar lever, move the plunger through its full stroke, and see that the trigger bar does not lift. If it does then open out with a file the jaw of the trigger bar lever.

5. Set the trigger bar lever at the rear end of its stroke and with the trigger bar in its guide way, hang its projection beyond the rear cross piece. Then see that the trigger bar cannot be pushed past the rear lip of the trigger bar lever

6. Replace trigger motor spring and with trigger bar in its guide way and having its projection engaged in the fork of the trigger bar lever, see if when trigger motor plunger is pushed fully forward the lock will trip and allow approximately one m/m movement of the trigger bar beyond. (Correction—Turn down the seating of the Banjo piece of A.L. type trigger motor, or if A type trigger motor shorten trigger motor spring by grinding it.) Assemble Tee piece to trigger motor body and see that the top of the trigger bar lever moves backwards slightly as the union is finally tightened up. Check to see that trigger bar is drawn back slightly on closing rear cover, using the rear cover lock axis pin as a feeler. Check clearance between trigger and end of slot in trigger bar. This should be approximately one m/m.

7. Fit so that the handle clears all controls in all possible positions of both handles and controls. Set as nearly vertical as possible, provided it is handy for pilot to reach and pull up handle. If possible it should be fitted

not more than 45 degrees from the vertical when tail of machine is on ground. See that the Bowden cable can be led away as straight as possible and that the filler cap is accessible with a petrol syringe. Bowden cable should be well greased before being put in casing. The reservoir should be very firmly fastened to the machine.

8. Pipe lines (main line). Lead away with as easy bends as possible and with a steady rise so that no air pockets can be formed. Clip securely whenever possible, placing rubber between clip and pipe. (Secondary Line) Bind with whipcord to main line as far down pipe as possible. Lead to reservoir as gently as possible. Take great care not to strain soldered joints.

9. Filling. Mixture to consist of 90 percent of paraffin to 10 percent of B.B. Mobiloil. In extreme cold weather perhaps advisable to use P.924 instead of B.B., mixing oils so as to give approximately same density as when using B.B. Note—It is very important that mixture be well strained before pouring into reservoir as least particle of grit is likely to prevent H.P. valve closing. In order to expel air from pipe lines, etc., after filling whole system with oil, slightly loosen the generator and T.M. union nuts, and air release needle valve, and nip these up again in order given when oil flows out free of air bubbles. Important to tighten these while oil still flows. Ease down handle of reservoir with Bowden lever pressed.

10. Timing the Gear. Raise reservoir H. [Handle?] to top of stroke and press B.L. [Bowden lever?] Turn generator shaft gently till peak of cam passes the piston in cylinder, and then turn back until you can just feel the peak of the cam brush past the piston. Mesh the gear wheels with blade in correct position relative to axis of gun barrel.

11. Faults. Possible faults which will cause slowing down of firing: A. Thick rim cartridges; B. Protruding caps; C. Fault in feed preventing recoiling portions going home and extractor horns therefore catch against underside of solid cams; D. Fusee spring too light; E. Recoiling parts too heavy; F. Faulty fitting of empty dip chute; G. Weak lock spring. Note—At 1200 revolutions/minute of propeller a one second delay causes shot to be 7.2 degrees late.

DAILY CARE OF C.C. GEAR AND VICKERS GUNS

Carry out following daily before starting motor. Numbers and letters referred to are those given in C.C. gear handbook.

1. Fill up reservoir through the filler tube at 37 each morning with special mixture 90 percent paraffin and 10 percent B.B. oil carefully mixed and well strained. Usually very little if any oil is needed. A large amount required denotes leak at needle (42) and gland (41), or in one of the joints of the system. Find fault at once.

2. Fill up the union (8) at the oil chamber on generator with Mobil A.

3. Pull Bowden control (49). After a short fall of about ¼ inch reservoir handle should remain steady, as if it had hit something solid. Deal with any failure of handle to behave as stated in three or four according to fault table.

    1. Inspect trigger bar and trigger bar lever to see if bent or broken.

    2. Dry clean barrel each morning.

    3. Replace lock of gun oil with P.924 non-freezing oil only.

    4. Check timing daily by pulling up reservoir handle, pressing Bowden control and watching movement of reservoir handle while propeller blade is moved past point of aim. The handle should be at the top of its movement when blade is in correct position. This position will vary slightly in different type machines, but usually is blade opposite gun.

    5. Take out lock at night and store it in armory. Trip slide and trigger to release tension on lock spring.

    6. Clean barrel as soon after firing as possible and leave it oily. (Barrel will always be left oily overnight whether gun has been fired or not.)

    7. Let down reservoir handle each night, to release the tension of its spring by repeated operation of the Bowden control. Move propeller blade past the point of aim after each movement of the Bowden control if there is any difficulty.

8. Remove, clean, and oil with P.924 the recoiling portions every time the gun has been used if the position of the gun in the aeroplane allows of it, and in any case as often as possible.

Remarks. Stray shots are more likely to be caused by lack of attention to gun than by faults in the gear. The weight of the recoiling parts should be made as low as possible, certainly not more than two pounds by packing barrel with 6" to 8" of packing in the front gland and two turns in the cannelure. The fusee spring will vary with different guns but about nine pounds should be used. With the screwed nozzle cup and the heavy recoil washer the tension may be raised slightly higher without causing No. 1 stoppages at a height. Only P.924 oil should be used.

C.C. GEAR FAULT TABLE

Failure in the gear is always shown by the behavior of reservoir handle and can easily be localized.

I. Note—After pulling reservoir handle to top of stroke it sinks at once to bottom without operation of Bowden control.

Action—Unscrew filler cap, fill up reservoir, and expel air from system. Fault—Not enough liquid in reservoir.

II. Note—After pulling up reservoir handle it sinks slowly without operation of Bowden control.

Action—Press Bowden control lever half way, if this stops fall.

A. Fault—High pressure valve leaking due to 1) grit under ball valve, 2) damaged valve seating. Repairs 1) Clean valve seating, 2) Tap the steel ball with a copper drift to bed it on to the seating.

B. If it does not stop the fall press Bowden lever fully home. Reservoir handle will drop quickly about one inch. If handle then falls as same rate as was noticed before pressing Bowden lever—Fault—High pressure cup packing (30) at foot of high pressure piston road. Repair—Fit new cup packing.

C. Action—If handle falls quicker than before Bowden lever was pressed. Fault—Leak in line in addition to high pressure valve leaking. Repair—Go around all unions and screw up. If leak is found in copper pipe lines or joints, change pipe lines.

Note—If after standing overnight the reservoir is found to have emptied itself, the leak is probably in the union of the small bore pipe to the reservoir or at the leather through which the control needle passes. If the latter, the leather must be replaced.

Re: Action gives no notification (4) be careful to close small valve (23) while liquid is still being pressed through. If any difficulty is experienced in expelling all the air from the system, run the engine with all the unions and needle valve tightened up. Pull the handle (34) and operate Bowden control about 30 times. Stop engine and repeat action as given.

I. Notification: After pulling reservoir handle up, it remains steady, but on pressing Bowden Control it sinks slowly to the bottom. Action: Fill up reservoir until oil is level with top of filler tube at (37). Press Bowden lever fully home. Fault: If oil overflows at point (37) low pressure valve leaking due to either damaged needle or worn low pressure port. Repairs: Fit new needle (42) or new valve box to bottom of reservoir.

II. Notification: When Bowden control is pressed reservoir handle drops too far and does not come to a definite stop. Actions: Open needle valve (23), hold reservoir handle, press Bowden control till liquid flows through needle valve free of any air bubbles. Fault: Air in system.

TIMING

The position of the propeller blade relative to the axis of the barrel at the moment the lock trips varies according to the minimum and maximum propeller speeds between which it is desired to fire the gun. The following helps to explain:

Speed of propeller in revolutions/minute	Propeller movement in degrees during the interval of time between actually tripping lock and when the bullet passes through the plane in which the propeller is revolving. This period of time is known as A
300	12 degrees
500	20 degrees
900	36 degrees
1000	40 degrees

From this table it will be seen that during the period of time A, the angular movement of the propeller increases 6 degrees for every 100 rpm increase in propeller speed.

Owing to the fact that the period of time A varies slightly with the different types of machines, the figure and degrees can only be taken as approximately correct, but it is accurate enough to allow of its being used to assist in deciding where to time the propeller relative to the axis of the barrel on any type of machine. For instance, if you time a four bladed propeller so that at the moment the lock trips the center of the blade is opposite the axis of the barrel, you then know that when the blade is moving at 100 rpm the center of the blade will have moved 6 degrees past the axis of the barrel at the moment the bullet passes the blade, or 16 degrees past at 400 rpm, or 24 degrees past at 600 rpm (propeller speed). Note—Be careful that all speeds referred to are propeller speeds, not engine revolutions.

GENERAL AIMING

When aiming from a stationary position at a moving object allowance must be made for the speed of the moving object. If the firer is also moving and his gun can be deflected so as to fire at an angle to his line of flight, allowance must then be made for his speed as well.

A Vickers gun for the use of a pilot is always fixed so as to fire parallel or approximately parallel to the line of flight of the machine. It is unnecessary, therefore, for the gunner to make any allowance for his own speed.

The allowance for speed of the enemy machine is made by means of the ring or Aldis sight, or rather by the gunner with their own assistance.

The Vickers 100 mph ring sight consists of a foresight composed of two concentric rings connected by cross wires (the outer or deflection ring of 5" diameter; the inner ring about 1" diameter is used merely as a means of centering the back sight) and a bead back sight.

The ring foresight must be placed 40" from firer's eye in order to give the correct deflection allowance for an enemy machine of 100 mph speed. The bend back sight is fixed about 18" behind the foresight.

In some machines it may be found impossible to fit the foresight 40" from the firer's eye; a sight of smaller diameter would therefore be fitted, placed proportionately closer to the firer's eye in order to give correct deflection.

Rules for aiming with ring sight:

1. Place bead back sight in the center of the ring foresight.

2. Firer's eye must be kept the correct distance from the foresight.

3. Maneuver so as to place enemy machine correctly in ring according to his appearance.

   (a) Maximum Deflection—If enemy machine is flying across firer's front at right angles, place pilot's sight on outer edge of ring.

   (b) No Deflection—If enemy machine is flying directly towards or away from firer place propeller boss or pilot's seat in center of ring, (i.e. cover by bead which must always be in center of ring—See Rule 1)

   (c) Varying Deflection—If enemy machine is flying towards or away from firer at any angle place pilot's seat within the ring at a distance from the center varying with its appearance, i.e. the more the body of the enemy machine appears foreshortened, the nearer to the center should be placed the pilot's seat.

4. It is necessary invariably to have the enemy machine flying into the center of the ring, that is to say, an imaginary line drawn through the tail plane and propeller boss would also pass through the center of ring. The above rules assume the enemy's speed is correct for the size ring sight being used (i.e., 100 mph fast).

If it is known that enemy's speed is greater or less than the sight is designed for, or that his speed is temporarily increased or decreased due to diving or climbing, allowance can be made by placing him further from or closer to the center than normally.

It is unnecessary to make this allowance unless the difference is large. *A variation of 10 mph is negligible.*

Ring sight as range finder—The ring sight may be used for roughly estimating range as follows: a machine of ordinary span (a machine of 30 yard span at 100 yards covers 5/8 of ring, at 200 yards ½—an ordinary machine.)

ALDIS SIGHT—FIXED GUN

Description—Aldis sight is virtually a telescope which does not magnify or diminish and which unlike an ordinary telescope can be used with the eye several inches from the end of the tube. The most convenient distance is 4" to 8". When looking through this tube at a distant object, the effect is exactly as though one were looking through a napkin ring; the object appears the same whether seen through or outside the tube. Within the tube is a glass screen carrying the sighting circle, which is so placed between lenses that on looking through the tube at a distant object the ring is seen with its center on the spot at which the tube is pointing, no matter where the eye is placed. If the eye is moved sidewise, the ring appears to move with it and the direction in which the tube points is always the center of the ring. The tube, which is 1.8" in diameter, when fixed rigidly to a gun, therefore, constitutes a sight which offers practically no obstruction to the view, and which shows instantly the spot on which the gun is trained, without the necessity of aligning the eye upon a front and back sight. The sight can with advantage be used with both eyes open, one eye sees the object and the circle through the tube, and one sees the object directly. The effect after a little practice is that the object is as clearly seen as though there were no sight at all, but that a circle appears in the sky, the center of which is the point where the tube is aiming.

USE OF THE ALDIS SIGHT

For use with the fixed gun, firing directly forward from the machine, the sight must be fixed parallel to the axis of the gun. The center of the circle will then always fall on the point that the gun will hit, if that point is not moving through the air; and in this case no allowance for the speed of the gunner's aeroplane is necessary. The ring seen in the sight forms a guide as to how much to aim off for the speed of the enemy, the enemy being placed in the ring in such a way that it will fly into the center of the ring when the bullet has arrived. For this are the same instructions as for ring and bead sight. The telescope, in fact, when fixed exactly replaces the ring and bead sight used with fixed gun, except that with the telescope the gunner is released from the necessity of holding his eye aligned on two sights or of keeping his eye at a fixed distance from the ring. The training with the ring sights is exactly applicable to the Aldis, except that those parts of the training relating to aligning of the eye and fixing the bead are not necessary.

FIXING OF ALDIS SIGHT

For fixed guns firing straight ahead, the telescope is held in a pair of brackets which are adjusted for line, so far as possible the fixing of the telescope is so arranged that once adjusted it remains correct. But it is necessary to check it from time to time. This can be done in the usual way by looking through the barrel of the gun at a distant mark with the aid of a mirror and seeing that the mark falls in the center of the ring. The sight should be removed when not in use by loosening the wing nuts on the clips attaching it to the brackets.

SPAD GEAR

1. The Spad gear is used only on Spads and it is advantageous to put propeller on propeller boss so that the blades are in the same vertical plane as the [Keyway?], so, if this is done, one gear is correctly timed it is not necessary to re-time it when new propeller is fitted. But timing should be checked to see that propeller has been so put on.

2. No trigger bar must be used in Spad gear.

3. Timing of Spad gear

   (a) With propeller on shaft turn engine till the trailing edge of one of the blades is 1" past axis of gun barrel.

   (b) Take off starboard overhead cam shaft cover, and then laying it with its base flat on table measure vertical distance from table to the center of the tappet (Assume this to be 1")

   (c) Withdraw the four-peaked cam ring from the engine cam shaft and place it on again in a position that one of the peaks on the port side of cam shaft is x" in a vertical measurement from an imaginary line drawn across the base on which the cam shaft cover will rest when replaced across top of water jacket.

   (d) Lock the four-peaked cam ring in that position by means of the eccentric pin castle nut and split pins, taking care to wrap the ends of the split pin close to sides of the nut.

   (e) Adjust trigger push rod by means of fine adjustment head until trigger just trips, where a peak of the cam ring passes the tappet with the Bowden lever pressed.

If enough adjustment cannot be obtained, then the ball socket must be screwed either further in or out of the cam shaft cover as may be required.

4. To Check firing

    (a) Unload gun

    (b) Have propeller turned with Bowden control pressed

    (c) When the lock trips stop turning propeller and see if the blade is in the correct position relative to the axis of gun barrel

5. To Take out recoiling parts of gun

    (a) Take off nuts holding down the bearing cap to front cover bracket

    (b) Lift up transmission rod

    (c) Hang lock, lift up front cover, take out the feed block and carry on in usual manner

6. Faults of Spad gear

    (a) Broken tappet—Gun will cease to fire

    (b) Tappet guide badly worn—Tappet is liable to stick in firing position and cause automatic firing. Examine these parts frequently.

    (c) Wear in the ball socket—Likely to cause intermittent fire; any wear should be taken up by readjusting ball socket plug, but this plug must not be screwed up hard on the transmission rod.

    (d) If the Bowden control works stiffly it may be due to the ball socket being too far in the cam shaft cover, so bringing the lever to wear the tappet. To correct— Unscrew ball socket a complete turn out of the cam shaft cover and lock it in that position by means of the locking nut. Then if necessary readjust the length of the trigger push rod by means of the fine adjustment head. Note—The transmission rod should be a sliding fit in the steel bush[ing] which functions as a universal bearing near the top lever.

Lecture of February 9, 1918

POINTS BEFORE, DURING, AND AFTER FLIGHT

A. Before

1. See that barrel is perfectly clean and has slight film of oil

2. Frictional parts are lightly oiled with P924 in winter, mixture of oil lubricating GS and P924 in summer

3. Weigh recoiling portions—should not exceed two pounds

4. Weigh fusee spring—with mark 1 muzzle cap 9–11 pounds, with Mark 2 muzzle cap and .05 heavy recoil washer 10–12 pounds

5. Inspect muzzle attachment, the steel dish and muzzle cap should be cleaned and bright. With Mark 2 muzzle cap the .05 washer must be in position.

6. Gun accurately and securely fixed on mountings

7. Loading handle correctly fitted and does not interfere with movement of crank handle

8. See [Ferodo] springs and rear cover catch are correctly fixed

9. See spare lock and [Ferodo] jam clearer are in machine

10. Examine ammunition box and chutes to see they are correctly fitted

11. See link belts are correctly fitted and placed in the ammunition box

12. See first round of the belt is engaged in front of bottom pawls

13. Test gear fitting and timing

14. Check harmonization of sights. Range at which sights are harmonized varies at different speeds. This harmonization must be tested by firing short bursts on range.

B. During Flight

1. Fire occasional short bursts to prevent working part from becoming clogged by congealed oil

2. Unload gun before landing

C. After Flight (Under supervision of Armory Officer)

1. Unload

2. If possible remove recoiling portions, take to armory, see they are cleaned and re-oiled

3. Clean non-recoiling portions with petrol or spirits of turpentine to remove clogged oil. Thoroughly dry and re-oil.

4. Have *all unused ammunition* retested

5. Examine chutes for damage or misplacing

6. Examine sights for damage

7. Any stoppages or apparent defect in working of gun, immediately report to Armory officer. Should it be necessary to remove gun from machine, for testing on range, pilot must be present during tests.

8. Fill up history sheet

REPAIRS AND ADJUSTMENTS

1. Weighing and adjusting fusee spring—Remove lock and place loops of spring bal[ance?] over knob of crank handle, press down check lever with right hand. Pull spring balance vertically up resting left wrist on breech. First movement of crank handle gives weight. Mark I = 9.1 pounds, Mark II = 10–12 pounds. Weight may be adjusted by vice pin. Six clicks, three revolutions equals one pound out or—in lighten.

2. Weighing recoiling [?] Put machine in flying position, remove fusee spring, place crank handle vertical, place loop of spring balance over crankshaft, pull slowly, horizontally. First movement of shaft give weight, not exceeding two pounds. Lighten oil clear, take look at packing.

3. Testing and adjusting length of connecting rod. This should be done once a week, with both locks. Remove fusee spring, raise rear cover, pull crank handle onto roller, insert armorer's dummy on face of extractor opposite firing pin hole. Lift extractor to top of its stroke, see barrel is fully home. Turn crank handle towards check lever, guiding dummy into chamber, push check lever back just clear of crank handle; force crank handle down gently to check lever. If connecting rod is correct length a slight check will be felt just before crank handle reaches check lever. If no check is felt, connecting rod

is not long enough, namely lock not fully home. For purposes of adjustment washers no. 1 and 2 are used. To adjust length remove lock, determine number of washers required by first placing a no. 1 on outer face of adjusting nut. Retest adding washers if necessary. Place obtained number of washers on connecting rod, screwing down adjusting nut tight. From point of view of glass following should be frequently tested:

1. Weight of lock spring—Remove lock and fully cock it. Place bottom of lock on flat surface. Place spring balance against shoulder on side lever head. Draw side lever head vertically up by spring balance, first movement of lever give weight, correct 12–14 pounds, not under 12 (to change muzzle cup disk pry loose till you grab with pliers, put new one on, tap lightly on tight).

2. Bent of sear and firing pin: Remove lock, fully cock it, place bottom of lock on flat surface, raise extractor to top of stroke, force tail of trigger to rear; if bent of firing pin has become engaged with bent of sear firing pin will not be drawn forward by lock spring.

3. Nose of trigger and bent of tumbler—remove and cock lock, release sear-firing pin should be held back.

4. Side and extractor levers—Remove and cock lock, press down side lever head slowly. Extractor should have risen evidently to top of stroke before bent of firing pin becomes disengaged from bent of sear. These tests should be for spare lock also.

AMMUNITION DEFECTS

1. Cracks around indentations joining cartridge case to cannelure of bullet

2. Bullet round

3. Length of cartridge

4. Thick rim

5. High or deep set cap

6. Loose bullet

7. Other defects

Ammunition should be tested on test bench; new Vickers barrel sunk in bench, kept clean—a good Vickers extractor from which gib and spring are removed is screwed to the bench. Above this is placed arch with fine adjustable set screw locking nut with height and length of standard cartridge. After cartridge has been cleaned and inspected, drop into barrel to test diameter. Each should go fully home into chamber without force, and be easily removed. Cartridge should be then passed along grooves of extractor to test for thick rim by rotary motion, also length is tested by arch above simultaneously. Careful testing makes only gun stoppages due to defective as those due to a badly drawn cartridge case or weak charge, both of which are only detected when cartridge is primed. All unused rounds must be re-tested.

———

I.A. is defined as instant application of a probable remedy for a stoppage based on position of crank handle.

IMMEDIATE ACTION

The position of the crank handle gives indication of IA necessary to remedy any particular stoppage. For instructional purposes the stoppages are known as 1, 2, 3, 4 stoppages. The following table of temporary stoppages set in columns shows in Column 1 the four positions of crank handle when gun stops firing. The second and third positions may vary slightly. The position of the crank handle forms ready indication of the IA to be applied. Column 2 gives detailed description of IA to be performed by pilot. Column 3 gives probable causes of stoppages. Column 4 gives method of preventing the occurrence of certain stoppages. They can generally be prevented by careful examination of preparation of the gun, link belts, and ammunition before flight.

Stoppage No. 1

Position of crank handle—vertical

A. Pull crank handle into roller, let go, fire. Probable Cause—1. Defective ammunition, weak charge, deteriorated ammunition, 2. Tight packing in links. Prevention of occurrence—1. Cannot be provided against, 2.

Correct gauging of ammunition and filling of belts.

B. If failure recurs repeat A till gun is warm. Probable Cause—Excessive friction due to congealed oil. Prevention of Occurrence—Fire occasional short bursts.

C. Stoppages arising from causes given in this group cannot be remedied in the air. Probable Cause—Weight of fusee spring excessive, worn barrel, friction on working parts, packing of cannelures too tight. Prevention of Occurrence—A high standard of training of armorers and pilots should prevent these occurrences, particularly if points before flight have been carried out.

Stoppage No. 3

Position of Crank Handle—may stop in any position from top of check lever to practically on but clear of check lever

A. Strike down check lever and continue firing. Should stoppage occur again repeat until gun is warm. Probable Cause—Excessive friction due to congealed oil; friction on lock obstructing upward movement of extractor. Prevention—Fire occasional short bursts during flight; good armorer's inspection of lock.

B. If A fails look at pawls, pawls not protruding, engage [Ferodo] spring on check handle and lightly raise check handle, push belt into correct position in feed block, disengage [Ferodo] spring, strike down check handle, fire. Probable Cause—Slight cross feed; slightly misshapen links. Prevention—Correct loading action; inspection of links while filling belts.

C. If pawls are protruding engage [Ferodo] spring on check handle, draw back check handle, raise rear cover, remove first round in feed block by jam clearer, remove [Ferodo] spring from check handle, close rear cover, half load, fire. Probably Cause—Double Feed due to bad loading. Prevention—Good training and good loading of gun.

Stoppage No. 4

Crank Handle Position—Crank Handle on the Check Lever

IA—With CC gear pull up reservoir handle. Probable Cause—Lack of pressure in HPR. Prevention—No means of detection

IA—If reservoir handle is up, half load, fire. Probable Cause—Miss fire, defective ammunition. Prevention—No means of detection

IA—If A fails unload, change lock, change lock, reload, fire. Probable Cause—Damaged or broken firing min; broken lock spring. Prevention—No means of detection

The following would cause prolonged stoppages.

1. Loose or broken muzzle cup

2. Broken gib or gib spring

3. Broken fusee or fusee spring. In the event of one of these breakages taking place pilot necessarily stops firing and goes home

The Following Cause Runaway Gun

1. Broken nose of trigger

2. Broken bent of tumbler

3. Breakage of short arm of lock spring about quarter of inch from end. To stop firing then, use loading handle to prevent C.H. going fully home. This brings front portion of loading handle into contact with C.H. giving a no. 3 stoppage

CARE AND CLEANING

1. Guns must be examined daily after cleaning

2. Avoid damage to gun through careless handling

3. Never play with CH unless lock is on gun

4. Never keep lock spring compressed unnecessarily

Oil to be used

P. 924 does not clog at 11 F in winter

P. 924 and lubricating GS in equal parts summer. For high altitudes not too much oil

Fouling

Superficial—from solid products of production being deposited on the bore of the barrel. To remove use cleaning rod and flannelette (4 x 2) when barrel is warm. If left it cakes, so immediately run oily 4 x 2 through barrel.

Internal—From harmful gasses resulting from chemical combustion of cordite, penetrating the [] of bore of barrel while hot. Remove by pouring through barrel boiling water.

Metallic—Caused by minute portions of the cupro-nickel envelope being left on the bore. It appears as a whitish streak on the lands?? or as a roughness on edge of grooves. Remove by use of double pull through or by [Rynox?] nickel solvent

Daily Cleaning

(After firing less than 600 rounds) Remove recoiling portions, clean barrel with rod and rag 4 x 2 and oil, clean outside of gun and all parts of mechanism with oily rag. After careful cleaning of parts wipe them dry, re-oil and re-assemble. To clean mechanism use mixture of equal parts paraffin and lubricating GS. Should any part be clogged with dry oil use spirits of turpentine to remove it. After each part is cleaned it should be thoroughly dried and re-oiled. Hanging the lock and working the recoiling portions affords a ready means of working same and the bearing part of the barrel, i.e., just in front of barrel block, which can only be got at by removing feed block.

After firing more than 600 rounds the method to be adopted in cleaning gun in this case is exactly the same as that followed after firing less than 600 rounds with addition that internal fouling should be carefully removed in manner previously detailed.

Weekly Cleaning

The gun should be thoroughly overhauled and cleaned and examined by squadron gunnery officer.

Ammunition boxes and chutes

See to following for ammunition boxes.

1. Boxes must be tightly fixed
2. They must be in perfect alignment with feed block and lead straight into it
3. See that upper pawls are not fouled by top edge of box
4. See that the roller is working freely
5. Boxes must be examined before and after flight to see they are not damaged or displaced
6. When filling boxes see that the belt is properly arranged in layers and not in a coil

Concerning Chutes

1. Chutes must be tightly fixed

2. They must be placed exactly opposite the ejector openings for which they were intended

3. They must not contain any sharp angles or the gun will be jammed by an accumulation of empties or links

4. They must be examined before and after flight for damage or misplacement

5. They must be clear of pilot's feet and all controls

6. When special brackets are fitted on front cover of the gun care should be taken to see that the rivet do not file the upper lever of feed block

Lecture by Capt. [Not Identified], Sighting

For gun firing through propeller take no heed of own speed, but of enemy. Velocity of bullet 2440 ft/sec, or 600 ft in ¼ second. Machine at 100 mph goes 36 ⅔ feet at 200 yards, 18 ⅔ at 100 yards. Ring 40 inches from eye, diameter 4 ⁸⁄₉ approximately 5. Owing to triangle formed by machine's flight and your sight, the sight holds good for any distance of firing. But the more foreshortened the further within ring, but a machine flying at 40 degrees comes just ⅓ within ring, as you are dealing with circles and arcs. Ring sight also range finder. At 100 yards an aeroplane, 30' span, about ⅝ of ring, at 200 yards ½. Aldis sight length 20 inches, rings in one end, five lenses, more compact, no bead, makes no difference where your eye is as long as you can see through. Often covered by oil, dust, or damp.

Lecture on Kauper Gear

Great care must be used. Always check timing after landing so that parts worn at all are replaced. When tappet is over low part of cam it trips lock. Just reverse from other. Cam prevents lock from tripping instead of tripping. Peak of cam, by levers, draws forward long pull lever extending spring and stopping firing. Pushing Bowden control straightens leaves and allows spring to fire lock if tappet is not on peak of cam. Loosening Bowden control allows spring to [stretch?], is also twisted. Turn leave to catch in step. Faults—differences of depth of cam of ¼". There are six rods connected, so little jolt landing, as one part of gear is fixed to longerons and other part to gun, likely moves one part on gun forward and puts timing out, causes early or late shot. There are a number of pins, if these are not well oiled they wear and cause same trouble. As Bowden control sticks forward, accidentally gun may fire when it is loaded, so always take care.

Lecture on C.C. Gear

Necessary velocity 600, propeller varies.

Two types, mechanical and CC.

Advantage, one bad landing tends to throw gun toward engine thus bad for mechanical = CC is not disturbed.

Do away inertia.

Generator—Mobil A keep full.

Separated from reservoir oil by washer.

Holes in cylinder to leak.

Washer on high-pressure piston always goes dud on new one, has rotted, change it.

Two-gun generator cam ring must be perfectly central and angle between guns equal to angle at which generators approach cam ring.

Be sure to cross pipelines from generator to guns so that left fires first.

Fit reservoir at steeper than 45 degrees, steep as possible permitting also good pull.

Be sure handle can't catch.

Bibliography

Primary Sources

LOUISE H. AND DAVID S. INGALLS FOUNDATION, SHAKER HEIGHTS, OHIO

David Ingalls Papers

NATIONAL ARCHIVES OF THE UNITED STATES (NA). WASHINGTON, D.C.

RG 45 Sub File 1911–1927, Naval Records Collection of the Office of Naval
Records and Library

NATIONAL ARCHIVES OF THE UNITED KINGDOM, KEW, ENGLAND (NAUK)

Record Group AIR 1 Air Historical Branch: Papers (Series 1)
Record Group AIR 27 Air Ministry and Successors: Operations Record Books,
Squadrons, or inherited by the Air Ministry, the Royal Air Force, and related bodies

NAVAL HISTORY AND HERITAGE COMMAND (NHHC), WASHINGTON, D.C.

Navy Department Library, Archives, Photographic Section
Randall Browne Papers

YALE UNIVERSITY LIBRARY AND ARCHIVES, NEW HAVEN, CONNECTICUT

F. Trubee Davison Papers

Secondary Sources

Abbatiello, John. *Anti-Submarine Warfare in World War I: British Naval Aviation and
the Defeat of the U-Boats.* London: Routledge, 2006.
Adams, Briggs. *The American Spirit: The Letters of Briggs Kilburn Adams.* Boston:
Atlantic Monthly Press, 1918.
Arthur, Reginald Wright. *Contact! Careers of Naval Aviators Assigned Numbers
1–2000.* Washington, D.C.: Naval Aviation Register, 1967.

Berry, Henry. *Make the Kaiser Dance: Living Memories of a Forgotten War—The American Experience in World War I.* Garden City, N.Y.: Doubleday, 1978.

Bludworth, T. Francis. *The Battle of Eastleigh, England: USNAF, 1918.* New York: Thompson, 1919.

Bowyer, Chaz, ed. *Royal Flying Corps Communiqués, 1917–1918.* London: Grub Street, 1998.

Bruce, J. M. *War Planes of the First World War.* Garden City, N.Y.: Doubleday, 1969.

Cayton, Andrew R. L. *Ohio: The History of a People.* Columbus: Ohio State University Press, 2002.

Chambers, John Whiteclay, II. *The Tyranny of Change: America in the Progressive Era, 1900–1917.* New York: St. Martin's Press, 1980.

———. *To Raise an Army: The Draft Comes to Modern America.* New York: Free Press, 1987.

Christiansen, Friedrich. "Battle Flights over the Channel." *Over the Front Journal* 15, no. 3 (Autumn 2000): 230–32.

Coffman, Edward M. *The War to End All Wars: The American Military Experience in World War I.* Madison: University of Wisconsin Press, 1986.

Cole, Christopher, ed. *Royal Air Force Communiqués, 1918.* London: Tom Donovan, 1990.

Cowley, Robert, ed. *The Great War: Perspectives on the First World War.* New York: Random House, 2001.

Davison, Daniel. "The First Yale Unit." *Over the Front Journal* 12, no. 3 (Autumn 1997): 265–69.

DeWeerd, Harvey. *President Wilson Fights His War: World War I and the American Intervention.* New York: Macmillan, 1968.

Duffy, Herbert S. *William Howard Taft.* New York: Minton, Balch & Co., 1930.

Edwards, W. Atlee. "The US Naval Air Force in Action, 1917–1918." *United States Naval Institute Proceedings* 48, no. 11 (November 1922): 1863–82.

Eisenhower, John S. D. *Yanks: The Epic Story of the American Army in World War I.* New York: Free Press, 2001.

Farwell, Bryan. *Over There: The United States in the Great War, 1917–1918.* New York: Norton, 1999.

Fleming, Thomas. *The Illusion of Victory: America in World War I.* New York: Basic Books, 2003.

Fredette, R. H. *The First Battle of Britain.* London: Cassell, 1966.

Fussell, Paul. *The Great War and Modern Memory.* Toronto: Sterling Publishing, 2009.

Gilbert, Martin. *The First World War: A Complete History.* New York: Henry Holt, 1994.

Hagedorn, Hermann. *Leonard Wood: A Biography.* 2 vols. New York: Harper and Brothers, 1931.

Hallam, Squadron Leader T. D. *The Spider Web: The Romance of a Flying-Boat War Flight.* Edinburgh: William Blackwood and Sons, 1919.

Harries, Meirion, and Susie Harries. *The Last Days of Innocence: America at War, 1917–1918.* New York: Random House, 1997.

Heckscher, August. *St. Paul's: The Life of a New England School*. New York: Charles Scribner's Sons, 1980.

Hess, Stephen. *America's Political Dynasties from Adams to Kennedy*. Garden City, N.Y.: Doubleday, 1966.

Hildreth, Alonzo. "Over There—World War I." *All Hands,* Bureau of Naval Personnel Information (June 1962): 56–63.

Hudson, James. *Hostile Skies: A Combat History of the American Air Service in World War I*. Syracuse, N.Y.: Syracuse University Press, 1968.

Imrie, Alex. *German Naval Air Service*. London: Arms and Armour Press, n.d.

Isaacson, Walter, and Evan Thomas. *The Wise Men: Six Friends and the World They Made*. New York: Simon and Schuster, 1986.

Jane's Fighting Aircraft of World War I. New York: Military Press, 1990.

Keegan, John. *The First World War*. New York: Knopf, 1999.

Keene, Jennifer D. *The United States and the First World War*. Harlow, U.K.: Pearson Education, 2000.

Kelley, Brooks Mather. *Yale—A History*. New Haven, Conn.: Yale University Press, 1974.

Kennedy, David M. *Over Here: The First World War and American Society*. New York: Oxford University Press, 1980.

Kennett, Lee. *The First Air War, 1914–1918*. New York: Free Press, 1991.

Knepper, George W. *Ohio and Its People*. Kent, Ohio: Kent State University Press, 1997.

Lane, Jack. *Armed Progressive: General Leonard Wood*. Lincoln, Neb.: Bison Books, 2009.

Layman, R. D. *Naval Aviation in the First World War: Its Impact and Influence*. London: Chatham Publishing, 1996.

Layman, R. D., and E. J. L. Halpern. "Allied Aircraft vs. German Submarines." *Cross and Cockade* 11, no. 4 (Winter 1970): 289–304.

Leeson, Frank M. *The Hornet Strikes: The Story of No.213 Squadron, Royal Air Force*. Tunbridge Wells, U.K.: Air-Britain (Historians), 1998.

Lord, Clifford L. "The History of Naval Aviation, 1898–1939." Unpublished typescript report. Washington, D.C.: Office of the Deputy Chief of Naval Operations (Air), Naval Aviation History Unit Office, 1946.

MacLeish, Kenneth. *Kenneth: A Collection of Letters Written by Lt. Kenneth MacLeish*. Edited by Martha MacLeish. Chicago: privately printed, 1919.

Maurer, Maurer, ed. *The U.S. Air Service in World War I*. 4 vols. Washington, D.C.: Office of Air Force History, Headquarters USAF, 1978–79.

McCallum, Jack. *Leonard Wood: Rough Rider, Surgeon, Architect of American Imperialism*. New York: New York University Press, 2006.

Mersky, Peter. "David S. Ingalls: Naval Air Reservist, First Navy Ace." *Foundation* 12 (Spring 1991): 81–91.

Messimer, Dwight R. *Find and Destroy: Antisubmarine Warfare in World War I*. Annapolis, Md.: Naval Institute Press, 2001.

Morrow, John H., Jr. *The Great War in the Air: Military Aviation from 1909 to 1921*. Washington, D.C.: Smithsonian Institution Press, 1993.

Moseley, George. *Extracts from the War Letters of George Clark Moseley During the Period of the Great War.* Privately printed, 1923.

Munson, Kenneth. *Fighters: Attack and Training Aircraft, 1914–1919.* London: Blandford Press, 1968.

O'Connor, Mike. *Airfields and Airmen of the Channel Coast.* Barnsley, South Yorkshire, U.K.: Pen and Sword Books, 2005.

Paine, Ralph D. *The First Yale Unit: A Story of Naval Aviation, 1916–1919.* 2 vols. Cambridge, Mass.: Riverside Press, 1925.

Patterson, James T. *Mr. Republican: A Biography of Robert A. Taft.* Boston: Houghton Mifflin, 1972.

Pierson, George Wilson. *Yale College: An Educational History, 1871–1921.* New Haven, Conn.: Yale University Press, 1952.

Pringle, Henry F. *The Life and Times of William Howard Taft.* 2 vols. New York: Farrar and Rhinehart, 1939.

Reynolds, Clark. *Admiral John Towers: The Struggle for Naval Air Supremacy.* Annapolis, Md.: Naval Institute Press, 1991.

Rossano, Geoffrey. "The Apprenticeship (How the Allies Trained the American Air Service)." *American Aviation Historical Society Journal* 28, no. 1 (Spring 1983): 22–31.

———, ed. *The Price of Honor: The World War One Letters of Naval Aviator Kenneth MacLeish.* Annapolis, Md.: Naval Institute Press, 1991.

———. *Stalking the U-Boat: U.S. Naval Aviation in Europe in World War I.* Gainesville: University Press of Florida, 2010.

Sheely, Lawrence. "Irving Edward Sheely—Naval Observer." *Over the Front* 3, no. 2 (Summer 1988): 99–133.

———, ed. *Sailor of the Air: The 1917–1919 Letters and Diary of USN CMM/A Irving Edward Sheely.* Tuscaloosa: University of Alabama Press, 1993.

Shirley, Noel. *United States Naval Aviation, 1910–1918.* Atglen, Pa.: Schiffer Military History, 2000.

Shores, Christopher, Norman Franks, and Russell Guest. *Above the Trenches: A Complete Record of the Fighter Aces and Units of the British Empire Air Forces, 1915–1920.* London: Grub Street, 1990.

Sims, William. *The Victory at Sea.* New York: Doubleday, 1920.

Springs, Elliot White. *War Birds: Diary of an Unknown Aviator.* New York: Grosset and Dunlap, 1926.

Still, William N., Jr. *Crisis at Sea: The United States Navy in European Waters in World War I.* Gainesville: University Press of Florida, 2006.

Stratham, D. G. *The Gosport Diaries.* Privately published, 1981.

Swanborough, Gordon, and Peter Bowers. *United States Naval Aircraft since 1911.* New York: Putnam, 1968.

Toland, John. *No Man's Land: 1918—The Last Year of the Great War.* New York: Konecky and Konecky, 1980.

Treadwell, Terry. *America's First Air War: The United States Army, Naval, and Marine Air Services in the First World War.* Osceola, Wis.: MBI Publishing, 2000.

————. *The First Naval Air War.* Stroud, U.K.: Tempus Publishing, 2002.

Tredrey, Frank. *Pioneer Pilot: The Great Smith Barry Who Taught the World to Fly.* London: P. Davies, 1976.

Trimble, William F. *Admiral William A. Moffett: Architect of Naval Aviation.* Annapolis, Md.: Naval Institute Press, 1994.

————. *Hero of the Air: Glenn Curtiss and the Birth of Naval Aviation.* Annapolis, Md.: Naval Institute Press, 2010.

Turnbull, Archibald D., and Clifford L. Lord. *History of United States Naval Aviation.* New Haven, Conn.: Yale University Press, 1949.

Whistler, Richard T. "The Making of a Dunkirk Aviator: The War Experiences of Ensign James Henry O'Brien, USNRF," pts. 1 and 2. *Over the Front* 14, no. 4 (Winter 2001): 347–61, and 17, no. 1 (Spring 2002): 4–25.

Whitaker, Herman. "Flying Sailors." *Land and Water* 2 (May 2, June 27, October 17, 1918).

Wickes, Lt. Z. W. "Destruction of the Flanders Triangle." *United States Naval Institute Proceedings* 45, no. 7 (July 1919): 1093–1116.

Wortman, Marc. *The Millionaires' Unit: The Aristocratic Flyboys Who Fought the Great War and Invented American Air Power.* New York: Public Affairs, 2006.

Wright, Peter. "Dunkerque Days and Nights." *Cross and Cockade International* 23, no. 2 (Summer 1992): 131–44.

Index